lonely planet

Greek

Phrasebook & Dictionary

Acknowledgments
Product Editor Kate Mathews
Book Designer Fergal Condon
Language Writer Thanasis Spilias
Cover Image Researcher Gwen Cotter

Published by Lonely Planet Global Limited
CRN 554153

8th Edition – June 2023
ISBN 978 1 78868 830 7

Cover Image View over Fira, Santorini, Greece. vitmark / Shutterstock ©

Printed in Malaysia 10 9 8 7 6 5 4 3 2

Contact lonelyplanet.com/contact

make the most of this phrasebook...

Anyone can speak another language! It's all about confidence. Don't worry if you can't remember your school language lessons or if you've never learnt a language before. Even if you learn the very basics (on the inside covers of this book), your travel experience will be the better for it. You have nothing to lose and everything to gain when the locals hear you making an effort.

finding things in this book

For easy navigation, this book is in sections. The Basics chapters are the ones you'll thumb through time and again. The Practical section covers basic travel situations like catching transport and finding a bed. The Social section gives you conversational phrases, pick-up lines, the ability to express opinions – so you can get to know people. Food has a section all of its own: gourmets and vegetarians are covered and local dishes feature. Safe Travel equips you with health and police phrases, just in case. Remember the colours of each section and you'll find everything easily; or use the comprehensive Index. Otherwise, check the two-way traveller's Dictionary for the word you need.

being understood

Throughout this book you'll see coloured phrases on each page. They're phonetic guides to help you pronounce the language. You don't even need to look at the language itself, but you'll get used to the way we've represented particular sounds. The pronunciation chapter in Basics will explain more, but you can feel confident that if you read the coloured phrase slowly, you'll be understood.

communication tips

Body language, ways of doing things, sense of humour – all have a role to play in every culture. 'Local talk' boxes show you common ways of saying things, or everyday language to drop into conversation. 'Listen for …' boxes supply the phrases you may hear. They start with the language (so local people can point out what they want to say to you) and then lead in to the pronunciation guide and the English translation.

CONTENTS

Greek

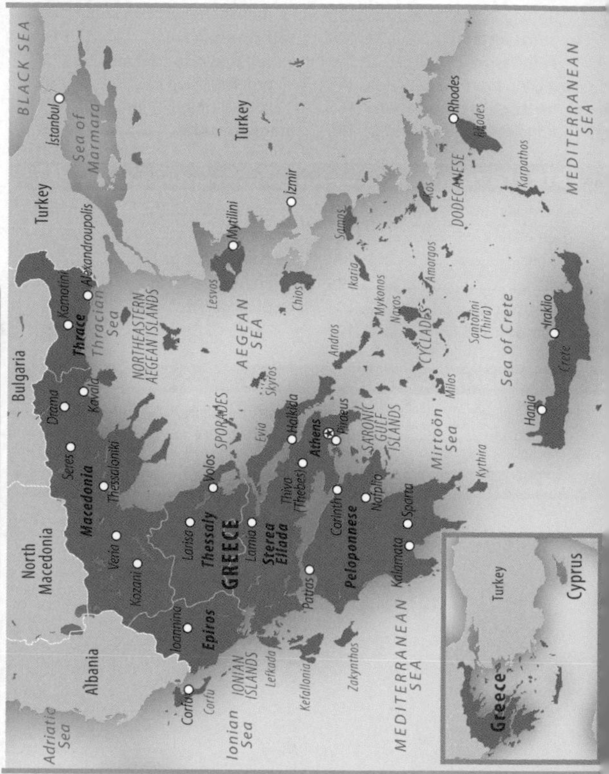

■ official language

For more details, see the **introduction**.

ABOUT GREEK
Εισαγωγή

Aristotle, Homer, Plato, Sappho, Herodotus and Alexander the Great can't all be wrong in their choice of language – if you've ever come across arcane concepts such as 'democracy', exotic disciplines like 'trigonometry' or a little-known neurosis termed 'the Oedipus complex', then you'll have some inkling of the widespread influence of Greek language and culture. With just a little Modern Greek under your belt, you'll have a richer understanding of this language's impact on contemporary Western culture.

Greek is the official language of Greece and a co-official language of Cyprus, in addition to being spoken by emigrant communities in Turkey, Australia, Canada, Germany and the United States. In total, there are over 13 million Greek speakers worldwide.

Modern Greek constitutes a separate branch of the Indo-European language family, with Ancient Greek its only (extinct) relative. The first records of written Ancient Greek were found in the fragmentary Linear B tablets, dating from the 14th to the 12th centuries BC. By the 9th century BC, the Greeks had adapted the Phoenician alphabet to include vowels – the first alphabet to do so – and the script in use today came to its final form some time in the 5th century BC. The Greek script was the foundation for the Cyrillic script (used in Slavic languages) and the Latin alphabet (used in English and other European languages).

Although written Greek may have been remarkably stable

at a glance ...

language name: Greek

name in language:
Ελληνικά e·li·ni·*ka*,
Νέα Ελληνικα *ne*·a e·li·ni·*ka*
(Greek, Modern Greek)

language family:
Indo-European
(Hellenic branch)

key countries:
Greece, Cyprus

approximate number of speakers:
13 million worldwide

close relatives:
Ancient Greek

donations to English:
anarchy, astronomy, cosmos, democracy, drama, logic, politics ...

over the millennia, the spoken language has evolved considerably. In the 5th century, the dialect spoken around Athens (known as 'Attic') became the dominant speech as a result of the city-state's cultural and political prestige. Attic gained even greater influence as the medium of administration for the vast empire of Alexander the Great, and remained the official language of the Eastern Roman Empire and the Orthodox Church after the demise of the Hellenistic world. Once the Ottoman Turks took Constantinople in 1453, the Attic dialect lost its official function. In the meantime, the common language – known as *Koine* (Κοινή ki·*ni*) – continued to evolve. It developed a rich history of popular songs (δημοτικό τραγούδια ţhi·mo·ti·*ka* tra·*ghu*·ţhia) and absorbed vocabulary from Turkish, Italian, Albanian and other Balkan languages.

When an independent Greece returned to the world stage in 1832, it needed to choose a national language. Purists advocated a slightly modernised version of Attic known as *Καθαρεύουσα* ka·tha·*re*·vu·sa (from the Greek word for 'clean'), which no longer resembled the spoken language. *Koine*, or *laiki* as it was also known (λαϊκή la·*i*·ki means 'popular'), had strong support as it was spoken and understood by the majority of Greeks – in the end, this was the language which gained official recognition. By the mid-20th century, *Koine/laiki* was known as 'demotic' and continued in daily use. It was banned during Greece's military dictatorship (1967-74) but then reinstated as the official language of the Hellenic Republic.

This book gives you the practical phrases you need to get by in Greek, as well as all the fun, spontaneous phrases that can lead to a better understanding of Greeks and their culture. Once you've got the hang of how to pronounce Greek words, the rest is just a matter of confidence. Local knowledge, new relationships and a sense of satisfaction are on the tip of your tongue. So don't just stand there, say something!

abbreviations used in this book

a	adjective	n	neuter (after Greek)
acc	accusative	n	noun (after English)
f	feminine	nom	nominative
gen	genitive	pl	plural
inf	informal	pol	polite
lit	literal	sg	singular
m	masculine	v	verb

The pronunciation of Greek is easy to master, as most of the sounds correspond to those found in English. Use the coloured pronunciation guides to become familiar with them, and then read directly from the Greek when you feel more confident.

vowel sounds

Greek vowels are pronounced separately even when they're written in sequence, eg ζώο *zo*·o (animal). You'll see though in the table below that some letter combinations correspond to a single sound – ουρά (queue) is pronounced u·*ra*.

When a word ending in a vowel is followed by another word that starts with the same or a similar vowel sound, one vowel is usually omitted and the two words are pronounced as if they were one – Σε ευχαριστώ se ef·kha·ris·*to* becomes Σ' ευχαριστώ sef·kha·ris·*to* (Thank you). Note that the apostrophe (') is used to show that two words have been joined together.

symbol	english equivalent	greek example	transliteration
a	car	αλλά	a·*la*
e	bet	πλένομαι	*ple*·no·me
i	lid	πίσω, πόλη, υποφέρω, είδος, οικογένεια, υιός	*pi*·so, *po*·li, i·po·*fe*·ro, *i*·ţhos, i·ko·*ye*·ni·a, i·*os*
o	lot	πόνος, πίσω	*po*·nos, *pi*·so
u	put	ουρά	u·*ra*
ia	nostalgia	ζητιάνος	zi·*tia*·nos
io	ratio	πιο	pio

consonant sounds

Most Greek consonant sounds are also found in English – only the guttural gh and kh might need a bit of practice. Double consonants are only pronounced once – άλλος *a*·los (other).

symbol	english equivalent	greek example	trans-literation
b	bed	μπαρ	bar
d	dog	ντομάτα	do·*ma*·ta
dz	adds	τζαμί	dza·*mi*
f	fit	φως, αυτή	fos, af·*ti*
g	gap	γκαρσόν	gar·*son*
gh	guttural sound, between goat and loch	γάτα	*gha*·ta
h	heat	χέρι	*he*·ri
k	kit	καλά	ka·*la*
kh	loch (guttural sound)	χαλί	kha·*li*
l	let	λάδι	*la*·ţhi
m	mat	μαζί	ma·*zi*
n	not	ναός	na·*os*
ng	singer	ελέγχω	e·*leng*·kho
p	pin	πάνω	*pa*·no
ps	lapse	ψάρι	*psa*·ri
r	red (trilled)	ράβω	*ra*·vo
s	sad	στυλό	sti·*lo*
t	top	τι	ti
th	theatre	θέα	*the*·a
ţh	the	δεν	ţhen
ts	hats	τσέπη	*tse*·pi
v	vase	βίζα, αύριο	*vi*·za, *av*·ri·o
y	yes	γέρος	*ye*·ros
z	zoo	ζέστη	*ze*·sti

word stress

Most Greek words have only one stressed syllable, but some have two. Stress can fall on any of the last three syllables. In our pronunciation guides, the stressed syllable is always in italics, but in written Greek, the stressed syllable is always indicated by an accent over the vowel, eg καλά ka·*la*.

If a vowel is represented by two letters, it's written on the second letter, eg ζητιάνος zi·*tia*·nos (beggar). If the accent is marked on the first of these two letters, they should be read separately, like in Μάιος *ma*·i·os (May). Where two vowels occur together but are not stressed, a diaeresis (¨) is used to indicate that they should be pronounced separately, eg λαϊκός la·i·*kos* (popular). When stress falls on a capitalised vowel (like in Έχασα *e*·ha·sa (I lost)), the accent is written to the left of the letter.

intonation

Intonation in mainland Greece is rather flat, except in questions, when the voice is raised at the end of the sentence. Many island dialects have a more 'singing' intonation.

spellbound

You may have noticed that sometimes two Greek letters in combination form one single consonant sound – the combination of the letters μ and π makes the sound b, and the combination of the letters ν and τ makes the sound d. This is particularly the case when each combination appears at the start of a word – in the middle of a word they sound more like the 'mb' in 'amber' and the 'nd' in 'indigo' respectively. In this book, we've used the same symbols regardless of the position of these letters within a word – you'll be understood just fine if you follow our pronunciation guides.

reading & writing

The Greek writing system was simplified in 1982, when the old stress symbols and aspiration marks (ie an accent indicating that a sound is pronounced with a puff of air before it) were abolished, although they may still be found in old books.

The modern Greek alphabet consists of 24 letters. Their pronunciation is shown in the box below for spelling purposes, eg when you need to spell your name to book into a hotel. Many of the letters of the Greek alphabet are also used in the Roman alphabet. Some letters, however, are a little misleading – they look like English letters but are pronounced very differently. For more information, see the consonant table on page 12 and the box on page 34.

Greek punctuation uses the same symbols as in English, except for the question mark – this is written as a semicolon (;).

greek alphabet

Α α *al*·pha	Β β *vi*·ta	Γ γ *gha*·ma	Δ δ *ţhel*·ta
Ε ε *ep*·si·lon	Ζ ζ *zi*·ta	Η η *i*·ta	Θ θ *thi*·ta
Ι ι *yio*·ta	Κ κ *ka*·pa	Λ λ *lam*·ţha	Μ μ mi
Ν ν ni	Ξ ξ ksi	Ο ο o·*mi*·kron	Π π pi
Ρ ρ ro	Σ σ/ς* *sigh*·ma	Τ τ taf	Υ υ *ip*·si·lon
Φ φ fi	Χ χ hi	Ψ ψ psi	Ω ω o·*me*·gha

* The letter Σ has two forms for the lower case – σ and ς. The second one is used at the end of words.

a–z phrasebuilder

κατασκευή φράσεων

contents

The index below shows the grammatical structures you can use to say what you want. Look under each function – in alphabetical order – for information on how to build your own phrases. For example, to tell the taxi driver where your hotel is, look for **giving instructions** and you'll be directed to information on **negatives, prepositions** and **requests**. A glossary of grammatical terms is included at the end of this chapter to help you.

Abbreviations like nom and acc in the literal translations for each example refer the case of the noun or pronoun – this is explained in the glossary and in **case**.

making statements

naming people/things

negating

pointing things out

possessing

adjectives & adverbs

describing people/things

Adjectives in Greek normally come before the noun, just like in English. They take different endings to agree with the noun they qualify (see **case**, **gender** and **plurals**) – we've given their standard forms below. Adjectives are shown in the nominative form in lists throughout this book and in the **dictionary** – these forms won't always be strictly correct within a sentence, but you'll still be understood. To find out more, see **case**.

	masculine	feminine	neuter
singular	καλ**ός** δρόμος ka·*los* *ţhro*·mos good road	καλ**ή** τύχη ka·*li* *ti*·hi good fortune	καλ**ό** ποτό ka·*lo* po·*to* good drink
plural	καλ**οί** δρόμοι ka·*li* *ţhro*·mi good roads	καλ**ές** τύχες ka·*les* *ti*·hes good fortunes	καλ**ά** ποτά ka·*la* po·*ta* good drinks

Adverbs normally end with the sound a (eg καλά ka·*la* 'well').

He filled in the form quickly.
Συμπλήρωσε το έντυπο γρήγορα. — si·*bli*·ro·se to *e*·di·po *ghri*·gho·ra
(lit: filled-in the-acc form-acc quickly)

articles

naming people/things

The Greek words for 'a' and 'an' change form to agree in gender and case with the noun they refer to.

		masculine	feminine	neuter
indefinite article (a/an)	nom	ένας e·*nas*	μια mia	ένα *e*·na
	acc	ένα(ν) e·*na(n)*	μια mia	ένα *e*·na
	gen	ενός e·*nos*	μιας *mi*·as	ενός *e*·nos

The Greek equivalents of 'the' also change form according to the noun – see also **case, gender** and **plurals.**

			masculine		feminine		neuter	
definite article (the)	nom	sg	ο	o	η	i	το	to
		pl	οι	i	οι	i	τα	ta
	acc	sg	το(ν)	to(n)	τη(ν)	ti(n)	το	to
		pl	τους	tus	τις	tis	τα	ta
	gen	sg	του	tu	της	tis	του	tu
		pl	των	ton	των	ton	των	ton

Articles alway come before the noun:

a road	**ένας** δρόμος	*e*·nas *ţhro*·mos
the road	**ο** δρόμος	o *ţhro*·mos

be

making statements

The verb είμαι *i*·me (be) changes depending on who or what is the subject (doer) of the sentence. These are the forms for the present and past tenses.

present			**past**		
I am	είμαι	*i*·me	**I was**	ήμουν	*i*·mun
you are sg inf	είσαι	*i*·se	**you were** sg inf	ήσουν	*i*·sun
you are sg pol	είστε	*i*·ste	**you were** sg pol	ήσαστε	*i*·sa·ste
he/she/it is	είναι	*i*·ne	**he/she/it was**	ήταν	*i*·tan
we are	είμαστε	*i*·ma·ste	**we were**	ήμαστε	*i*·ma·ste
you are pl	είστε	*i*·ste	**you were** pl	ήσαστε	*i*·sa·ste
they are	είναι	*i*·ne	**they were**	ήταν	*i*·tan

The future tense is formed by placing the word θα tha (will) in front of the present tense forms.

I'll be there tomorrow.
Θα είμαι εκεί αύριο. tha *i*·me e·*ki* *av*·ri·o
(lit: will be there tomorrow)

case

doing things • indicating location • naming people/things • possessing

Greek uses four different cases, usually shown by word endings, to indicate a noun's role and its relationship to other words in the sentence. Adjectives, articles, demonstratives and pronouns also change their form to agree with the noun they go with.

nominative nom – shows the subject of a sentence

The car won't start.
Το αυτοκίνητο δεν αρχίζει. to af·to·*ki*·ni·to ţhen ar·*hi*·zi
(lit: the-nom car-nom not starts)

accusative acc – shows the direct object of a sentence

Please bring the menu.
Παρακαλώ φέρε το μενού. pa·ra·ka·*lo* *fe*·re to me·*nu*
(lit: please bring the-acc menu-acc)

genitive gen – shows possession or the indirect object of a sentence

What's the address of the hotel?
Ποια είναι η διεύθυνση του ξενοδοχείου; pia *i*·ne i ţ*hi*·ef·thin·si tu kse·no·ţho·*hi*·u
(lit: which is the-nom address-nom the-gen hotel-gen)

vocative voc – to address someone directly

Officer, I think there's been a mistake.
Κύριε, νομίζω ότι έχει γίνει κάποιο λάθος *ki*·ri·e ni·*mi*·zo o·ti *e*·xi *yi*·ni *ka*·pio *la*·thos
(lit: sir-voc I-think that has been some-nom mistake-nom)

Greek nouns in the **dictionaries**, the **menu decoder** and word lists in this book are given in the nominative case. You can use this form as a default and, although this won't always be grammatically correct within sentences, you'll still be understood.

demonstratives

indicating location • naming people/things • pointing things out

The words for 'this' and 'that' in Greek change their endings depending on the form of the noun they determine (see **case**, **gender** and **plurals**). We've only given the nominative forms here – in most cases you'll be understood just fine.

		masculine		feminine		neuter	
this	sg	αυτ**ός**	af·*tos*	αυτ**ή**	af·*ti*	αυτ**ό**	af·*to*
	pl	αυτ**οί**	af·*ti*	αυτ**ές**	af·*tes*	αυτ**ά**	af·*ta*
that	sg	εκείν**ος**	e·*ki*·nos	εκείν**η**	e·*ki*·ni	εκείν**ο**	e·*ki*·no
	pl	εκείν**οι**	e·*ki*·ni	εκείν**ες**	e·*ki*·nes	εκείν**α**	e·*ki*·na

Does this train go to Lamia?
Πηγαίνει αυτό το τρένο στη Λαμία; pi·*ye*·ni af·*to* to *tre*·no sti la·*mi*·a
(lit: goes this-**nom** the-**nom** train-**nom** to Lamia-**acc**)

That bag is mine.
Εκείνη η τσάντα είναι δική μου. e·*ki*·ni i *tsa*·da *i*·ne ţhi·*ki* mu
(lit: that-**nom** the-**nom** bag-**nom** is mine)

This is my bag.
Αυτή η σάκα είναι δική μου. af·*ti* i *sa*·ka *i*·ne ţhi·*ki* mu
(lit: this-**nom** the-**nom** bag-**nom** is mine)

gender

naming people/things

Greek nouns have gender – masculine **m**, feminine **f** or neuter **n**. You need to learn the grammatical gender for each noun as you go, but you can often identify it by the noun's ending as shown in the table below. Adjectives, articles and pronouns take the same gender to agree with the noun they qualify.

common noun endings				
masculine	sg	**-ας** πατέρας pa·*te*·ras father	**-ης** ναύτης *naf*·tis sailor	**-ος** δρόμος *thro*·mos road
	pl	**-ες** πατέρες pa·*te*·res fathers	**-ες** ναύτες *naf*·tes sailors	**-οι** δρόμοι *thro*·mi roads
feminine	sg	**-α** πόρτα *por*·ta door	**-η** τύχη *ti*·hi fortune	
	pl	**-ες** πόρτες *por*·tes doors	**-ες** τύχες *ti*·hes fortunes	
neuter	sg	**-μα** όνομα *o*·no·ma name	**-ι** αγόρι a·*gho*·ri boy	**-ο** ποτό po·*to* drink
	pl	**-τα** ονόματα o·*no*·ma·ta names	**-α** αγόρια a·*gho*·ria boys	**-α** ποτά po·*ta* drinks

have

possessing

The verb έχω *e*·kho (have) only changes form according to who or what is the subject (doer) of the sentence. To form the future tense (as in the example on page 22), just place the word θα tha (will) in front of the present tense forms.

present			past		
I have	έχω	*e*·kho	I had	είχα	*i*·kha
you have sg inf	έχεις	*e*·his	you had sg inf	είχες	*i*·hes
you have sg pol	έχετε	*e*·he·te	you had sg pol	είχατε	*i*·kha·te
he/she/it has	έχει	*e*·hi	he/she/it had	είχε	*i*·he
we have	έχουμε	*e*·khu·me	we had	είχαμε	*i*·kha·me
you have pl	έχετε	*e*·he·te	you had pl	είχατε	*i*·kha·te
they have	έχουν	*e*·khun	they had	είχαν	*i*·khan

I'll have no money by the end of my trip!
Δεν θα έχω χρήματα με το τέλος του ταξιδιού! — ţhen tha *e*·kho *khri*·ma·ta me to *te*·los tu tak·si·*ţhiu*
(lit: not will I-have money-acc with the-acc end-acc the-gen trip-gen)

negatives

giving instructions • negating

To make a statement negative, add the word δεν ţhen (not) before the verb:

I speak Greek.
Μιλώ Ελληνικά. — mi·*lo* e·li·ni·*ka*
(lit: speak Greek)

I don't speak Greek.
Δεν μιλώ Ελληνικά. — ţhen mi·*lo* e·li·ni·*ka*
(lit: not speak Greek)

In commands, use the word μην min (not) instead:

Don't swim here.
Μην κολυμπάς εδώ. — min ko·li·*bas* e·*ţho*
(lit: not swim here)

Note that, unlike English, Greek has double negatives:

I don't want anything.
Δεν θέλω τίποτε. ţhen *the*·lo *ti*·po·te
(lit: not want nothing)

personal pronouns

doing things • making statements

In Greek, there are two words for 'you' – an informal one, εσύ e·*si* (used with friends, younger people or family members), and a formal one, εσείς e·*sis* (used when addressing strangers, authority figures or older people). In this phrasebook we've used the form of 'you' (and the verb form) appropriate for each situation.

	subject nom			
I	εγώ		e·*gho*	
you sg inf	εσύ		e·*si*	
you sg pol	εσείς		e·*sis*	
he/she/it	αυτός/αυτή/αυτό		af·*tos*/af·*ti*/af·*to*	
we	εμείς		e·*mis*	
you pl	εσείς		e·*sis*	
they m/f/n	αυτοί/αυτές/αυτά		af·*ti*/af·*tes*/af·*ta*	
	direct object acc		**indirect object** gen	
me	με	me	μου	mu
you sg inf	σε	se	σου	su
you sg pol	σας	sas	σας	sas
him/her/it	τον/την/το	ton/tin/to	του/της/του	tu/tis/tu
us	μας	mas	μας	mas
you pl	σας	sas	σας	sas
them m/f/n	τους/τις/τα	tus/tis/ta	τους	tus

Greek pronouns vary according to case – the subject or doer of an action is in the nominative case while the object is in the accusative or genitive case.

Both direct and indirect object pronouns are placed before the verb. If you have both in a sentence, the indirect pronoun comes first. In commands, they come after the verb.

I gave my passport to him.

Του έδωσα το διαβατήριό μου. — tu *e*·ţho·sa to ţhia·va·*ti*·ri·*o* mu

(lit: him-**gen** I-gave the-**acc** passport-**acc** my)

I gave it to him.

Του το έδωσα. — tu to *e*·ţho·sa

(lit: him-**gen** it-**acc** I-gave)

It's not necessary to use a subject pronoun in Greek, as verb endings show who the subject is. A subject pronoun can be used for emphasis or when there's no verb in the sentence.

I go to school everyday.

Πηγαίνω στο σχολείο κάθε μέρα. — pi·*ye*·no sto skho·*li*·o *ka*·the *me*·ra

(lit: go-I to school-**acc** every day)

***I* did it.**

Εγώ το έκανα. — e·*gho* to *e*·ka·na

(lit: I-**nom** it-**acc** did)

plurals

naming people/things

Plural nouns take different endings depending on gender – see the table under **gender** for the most common ones. Adjectives, articles, demonstratives and pronouns also have plural forms to agree with the plural noun.

possessives

possessing

Possession can be expressed not only with the verb 'have' but with possessive pronouns and adjectives as well.

The possessive adjectives (my, your, his etc) are placed after the noun, with the definite article before the noun (also see **articles**). They don't change for case, gender or number.

possessive adjectives		
my	μου	mu
your sg inf	σου	su
your sg pol	σας	sas
his/her/its	του/της/του	tu/tis/tu
our	μας	mas
your pl	σας	sas
their	τους	tus

I've lost my car keys.

Έχασα τα κλειδιά του αυτοκινήτου μου. — e·kha·sa ta kli·*ţhia* tu af·to·ki·*ni*·tu mu

(lit: lost the-acc keys-acc the-gen car-gen my)

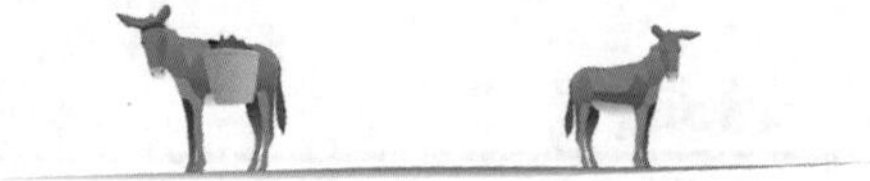

Possessive pronouns (mine, yours etc) are formed by adding the word δικός/δική/δικό thi·*kos*/thi·*ki*/thi·*ko* m/f/n in front of the possessive adjective. This word agrees in gender and case with the noun it refers to – endings are the same as those the adjectives take (see **adjectives & adverbs**). To keep things simple we've only given the nominative case in the next table.

possessive pronouns			
	masculine	**feminine**	**neuter**
mine	δικός μου ţhi·*kos* mu	δική μου ţhi·*ki* mu	δικό μου ţhi·*ko* mu
yours sg inf	δικός σου ţhi·*kos* su	δική σου ţhi·*ki* su	δικό σου ţhi·*ko* su
yours sg pol	δικός σας ţhi·*kos* sas	δική σας ţhi·*ki* sas	δικό σας ţhi·*ko* sas
his/hers/its	δικός του/της/του ţhi·*kos* tu/tis/tu	δική του/της/του ţhi·*ki* tu/tis/tu	δικό του/της/του ţhi·*ko* tu/tis/tu
ours	δικός μας ţhi·*kos* mas	δική μας ţhi·*ki* mas	δικό μας ţhi·*ko* mas
yours pl	δικός σας ţhi·*kos* sas	δική σας ţhi·*ki* sas	δικό σας ţhi·*ko* sas
theirs	δικός τους ţhi·*kos* tus	δική τους ţhi·*ki* tus	δικό τους ţhi·*ko* tus

Those bags are ours.

Εκείνες οι τσάντες είναι δικές μας. — e·*ki*·nes i *tsa*·des *i*·ne ţhi·*kes* mas

(lit: those-nom the-nom bags-nom are ours)

prepositions

giving instructions • indicating location • pointing things out

Many prepositions require the noun used after them to be in a particular case (see **case**) – σε se (to/at/in), από a·*po* (from), με me (with), για yia (for), προς pros (towards), κάτω από *ka*·to a·*po* (under), πάνω σε *pa*·no se (on) are all followed by the accusative. The genitive is used after μεταξύ me·tak·*si* (between).

I'd like to book a seat to Athens.

Θα ήθελα να κρατήσω μια θέση για την Αθήνα.	tha *i*·the·la na kra·*ti*·so mia *the*·si yia tin a·*thi*·na

(lit: I-would like to book a seat-acc for the-acc Athens-acc)

What's the difference between 1st and 2nd class?

Ποια είναι η διαφορά μεταξύ πρώτης και δεύτερης θέσης;	pia *i*·ne i ţhia·fo·*ra* me·tak·*si* *pro*·tis ke *ţhef*·te·ris *the*·sis

(lit: which is the-nom difference-nom between first-gen and second-gen class-gen)

questions

asking questions

To ask a yes/no question, just raise the intonation at the end of a sentence. Note that Greek uses a semicolon (;) instead of a question mark.

The bus stop is over there.

Η στάση του λεωφορείου είναι εκεί πέρα.	i *sta*·si tu le·o·fo·*ri*·u *i*·ne e·*ki* *pe*·ra

(lit: the-nom stop-nom the-gen bus-gen is there over)

Is the bus stop over there?

Η στάση του λεωφορείου είναι εκεί πέρα;	i *sta*·si tu le·o·fo·*ri*·u *i*·ne e·*ki* *pe*·ra

(lit: the-nom stop-nom the-gen bus-gen is there over)

The subject and the verb are often reversed in questions (see **word order**). You can also start a question with a question word – the verb comes in the second place, just like in English. The table on the next page lists the main question words.

question words		
How?	Πώς;	pos
How many?	Πόσοι/Πόσες/Πόσα; m/f/n pl	*po*·si/*po*·ses/*po*·sa
How much?	Πόσος/Πόση/Πόσο; m/f/n	*po*·sos/*po*·si/*po*·so
What?	Τι;	ti
When?	Πότε;	*po*·te
Where?	Πού;	pu
Who?	Ποιος/Ποια/Ποιο; m/f/n sg Ποιοι/Ποιες/Ποια; m/f/n pl	pios/pia/pio pii/pies/pia
Which?	Ποιος/Ποια/Ποιο; m/f/n sg Ποιοι/Ποιες/Ποια; m/f/n pl	pios/pia/pio pii/pies/pia
Why?	Γιατί;	yi·a·*ti*

How do you pronounce this?
Πώς προφέρεις αυτό; — pos pro·*fe*·ris af·*to*
(lit: how you-pronounce this-acc)

How much is it?
Πόσο κάνει; — *po*·so *ka*·ni
(lit: how-much makes)

When's the first bus?
Πότε είναι το πρώτο λεωφορείο; — *po*·te *i*·ne to *pro*·to le·o·fo·*ri*·o
(lit: when is the-nom first-nom bus-nom)

Who is that?
Ποιος είναι εκείνος; — pios i·ne e·*ki*·nos
(lit: who-nom is that-nom)

Why can't I board this train?
Γιατί δεν μπορώ να ανεβώ σ'αυτό το τρένο; — yia·ti ţhen bo·ro na a·ne·vo saf·*to* to *tre*·no
(lit: why not can to board to-this-acc the-acc train-acc)

BASICS

requests

giving instructions

A simple and polite way to make a request is to use the verb as found in the table on page 30, in its second-person present form, followed by παρακαλώ pa·ra·ka·*lo* ('please'). Use the informal (singular) form with people you know well, and the polite (plural) form with others.

Would you please open the window?
ανοίγεις το παράθυρο, παρακαλώ; sg inf — a·*ni*·yis to pa·*ra*·thi·ro pa·ra·ka·*lo*
(lit: open the window please)

Would you please open the window?
ανοίγετε το παράθυρο, παρακαλώ; pl pol — a·*ni*·ye·te to pa·*ra*·thi·ro pa·ra·ka·*lo*
(lit: open the window please)

For the negative form, see **negatives**.

verbs

doing things

The dictionary form of all Greek verbs ends in -ω ·o or -ομαι o·me, which is the present tense form of the first person singular (like in 'I eat'). The ending -ω represents 'active' verbs (which show someone actively doing something – πηγαίνω pi·*ye*·no 'go'), while -ομαι is for 'stative' verbs (which show a state or condition, and don't require movement – κάθομαι *ka*·tho·me 'sit'). These endings change according to the subject of the sentence. Sometimes changes in the verb stem (the form of the verb before the ending) occur, but if you use the endings shown on the next page, you'll be understood just fine.

present

Active and stative verbs have different sets of endings.

	active verb eg 'write'		stative verb eg 'think'	
dictionary form	γράφω	*ghra*·fo	σκέφτομαι	*skef*·to·me
I	γράφ**ω**	*ghra*·fo	σκέφτ**ομαι**	*skef*·to·me
you sg inf	γράφ**εις**	*ghra*·fis	σκέφτ**εσαι**	*skef*·te·se
you sg pol	γράφ**ετε**	*ghra*·fe·te	σκέφτ**εστε**	*skef*·tes·te
he/she/it	γράφ**ει**	*ghra*·fi	σκέφτ**εται**	*skef*·te·te
we	γράφ**ουμε**	*ghra*·fu·me	σκεφτ**όμαστε**	skef·*to*·ma·ste
you pl	γράφ**ετε**	*ghra*·fe·te	σκέφτ**εστε**	*skef*·tes·te
they	γράφ**ουν**	*ghra*·fun	σκέφτ**ονται**	*skef*·ton·de

past

The past tense endings for all verbs are provided below. There are some irregularities, however – as the stress in the verb moves back to the third syllable from the end, the prefix ε e· (augment) is added to the verb when there are less than three syllables. Also, the final letter before the ending sometimes changes.

	all verbs eg 'write'	
I	έγραψ**α**	*e*·ghra·psa
you sg inf	έγραψ**ες**	*e*·ghra·pses
you sg pol	γράψ**ατε**	*ghra*·psa·te
he/she/it	έγραψ**ε**	*e*·ghra·pse
we	γράψ**αμε**	*ghra*·psa·me
you pl	γράψ**ατε**	*ghra*·psa·te
they	έγραψ**αν**	*e*·ghra·psan

future

The easiest way to express an action in the future is by using the present tense forms and adding the word θα tha (will) in front of them.

I'll send you a postcard everyday.

Θα σου στέλνω μία κάρτα κάθε μέρα.	tha su *stel*·no mia *kar*·ta *ka*·the *me*·ra

(lit: will you-gen send a-acc postcard-acc every day)

word order

asking questions • making statements • negating

While the sentence order of subject–verb–object is most common in Greek, all other combinations are correct too – the word order is relatively free as Greek uses case (meaning that different word endings express the role of a word in the sentence). You might notice, however, that emphasised words are usually at the beginning of the sentence (see also **negatives** and **questions**).

The cashier didn't give me the correct change.

Ο ταμίας δεν μου έδωσε τα σωστά ρέστα.	o ta·*mi*·as ţhen mu *e*·ţho·se ta so·*sta* *re*·sta

(lit: the-nom cashier-nom not me-gen gave the-acc correct-acc change-acc)

The cashier didn't give me the correct change.

Δεν μου έδωσε τα σωστά ρέστα ο ταμίας.	ţhen mu *e*·ţho·se ta so·*sta* *re*·sta o ta·*mi*·as

(lit: not me-gen gave the-acc correct-acc change-acc the-nom cashier-nom)

Note that the indirect object comes before the direct object.

glossary

active verb	a verb that involves someone actively doing something – 'he **travelled** for many moons'
adjective	a word that describes something – '**ancient** hero'
adverb	a word that explains how an action was done – 'he **heroically** set out to find his father'
article	the words 'a', 'an' and 'the'
case (marking)	word ending that shows the role of the thing or person in the sentence
demonstrative	a word that means 'this' or 'that'
gender	Greek nouns can be masculine, feminine or neuter
imperative	a command – '**prove** to me that you are Odysseus'
noun	a thing, person or idea – 'an odyssey'
number	whether a word is singular or plural – 'journey' or 'journeys'
object (direct)	the thing or person that's directly affected by the action – 'Penelope offered **dinner** to her suitors'
object (indirect)	the person in the sentence that benefits from an action – 'Penelope offered **them** dinner'
personal pronoun	a word that means 'I', 'you', etc
possessive pronoun	a word that means 'mine', 'yours', etc
preposition	a word like 'for' or 'before' in English
stative verb	a verb that doesn't require movement – 'Penelope **missed** her husband very much'
subject	the thing or person that does the action – '**the suitors** took advantage of her hospitality'
tense	marking on the verb that tells you whether the action is in the present, past or future – 'travel**led**'
verb	the word that tells you what action happened – 'Odysseus **disguises** himself as a beggar'
verb stem	the part of a verb which does not change – like 'charm' in 'charmed' and 'charming'

language difficulties
γλωσσικές δυσκολίες

Do you speak (English)?
Μιλάς (Αγγλικά); mi·*las* (ang·gli·*ka*)

Does anyone speak (English)?
Μιλάει κανείς (Αγγλικά); mi·*la*·i ka·*nis* (ang·gli·*ka*)

Do you understand?
Καταλαβαίνεις; ka·ta·la·*ve*·nis

Yes, I understand.
Ναι, καταλαβαίνω. ne ka·ta·la·*ve*·no

No, I don't understand.
Όχι, δεν καταλαβαίνω. *o*·hi ţhen ka·ta·la·*ve*·no

I (don't) understand.
(Δεν) καταλαβαίνω. (ţhen) ka·ta·la·*ve*·no

Pardon?
Συγνώμη; sigh·*no*·mi

I speak (English).
Μιλώ (Αγγλικά). mi·*lo* (ang·gli·*ka*)

I don't speak Greek.
Δεν μιλώ Ελληνικά. ţhen mi·*lo* e·li·ni·*ka*

I speak a little.
Μιλώ λίγο. mi·*lo* *li*·gho

Let's speak Greek.
Ας μιλήσουμε Ελληνικά. as mi·*li*·su·me e·li·ni·*ka*

tongue-tied

If you're after a challenge, try this tongue twister for size.

Ο παπάς ο παχύς έφαγε παχιά φακή.
Γιατί, παπά παχύ, έφαγες παχιά φακή;
o pa·*pas* o pa·*his* *e*·fa·ye pa·*hia* fa·*ki*
yia·*ti* pa·*pa* pa·*hi* *e*·fa·yes pa·*hia* fa·*ki*
(The fat priest ate thick lentil soup.
Why, fat priest, did you eat thick lentil soup?)

I would like to practise Greek.
Θα ήθελα να εξασκήσω τα Ελληνικά μου. — tha *i*·the·la na ek·sa·*ski*·so ta e·li·ni·*ka* mu

What does (*μώλος*) mean?
Τι σημαίνει (μώλος); — ti si·*me*·ni (*mo*·los)

How do you ...?	Πώς ...;	pos ...
pronounce this	προφέρεις αυτό	pro·*fe*·ris af·*to*
write '*Madhuri*'	γράψεις 'Μαδουρή'	*ghrap*·sis ma·ţhu·*ri*

Could you please ...?	Θα μπορούσες παρακαλώ να ...;	tha bo·*ru*·ses pa·ra·ka·*lo* na ...
repeat that	το επαναλάβεις	to e·pa·na·*la*·vis
speak more slowly	μιλάς πιο αργά	mi·*las* pio ar·*gha*
write it down	το γράψεις	to *ghrap*·sis

alphabet soup

Some Greek letters might look like English ones, but they're pronounced quite differently.

upper case	lower case	pronunciation
Β	β	v
Η	η	i
Ρ	ρ	r
Υ	υ	i
Χ	χ	h
Ν	ν	n
Ξ	ξ	ks
Σ	σ/ς	s
Ω	ω	o

See the box on page 14 for the full Greek alphabet.

numbers & amounts
αριθμοί και ποσά

cardinal numbers
απόλυτοι αριθμοί

In Greek, some numbers (one, three, four, and numbers linked to them like 21 and 13) change according to gender – that is, they have different forms when the noun they're associated with is masculine m, feminine f or neuter n. When simply counting, you use the neuter form.

1	ένας/μία/ένα m/f/n	*e*·nas/*mi*·a/*e*·na
2	δύο	*ţhi*·o
3	τρεις/τρία m&f/n	tris/*tri*·a
4	τέσσερις m&f	*te*·se·ris
	τέσσερα n	*te*·se·ra
5	πέντε	*pe*·de
6	έξι	*ek*·si
7	εφτά	ef·*ta*
8	οχτώ	okh·*to*
9	εννέα	e·*ne*·a
10	δέκα	*ţhe*·ka
11	έντεκα	*e*·de·ka
12	δώδεκα	*ţho*·ţhe·ka
13	δεκατρείς m&f	ţhe·ka·*tris*
	δεκατρία n	ţhe·ka·*tri*·a
14	δεκατέσσερις m&f	ţhe·ka·*te*·se·ris
	δεκατέσσερα n	ţhe·ka·*te*·se·ra
15	δεκαπέντε	ţhe·ka·*pe*·de
16	δεκαέξι	ţhe·ka·*ek*·si
17	δεκαεφτά	ţhe·ka·ef·*ta*
18	δεκαοχτώ	ţhe·ka·okh·*to*
19	δεκαεννέα	ţhe·ka·e·*ne*·a
20	είκοσι	*i*·ko·si
21	είκοσι ένας/μία m/f	*i*·ko·si *e*·nas/*mi*·a
	είκοσι ένα n	*i*·ko·si *e*·na

22	είκοσι δύο	*i*·ko·si *ţhi*·o
30	τριάντα	tri·*a*·da
40	σαράντα	sa·*ra*·da
50	πενήντα	pe·*ni*·da
60	εξήντα	ek·*si*·da
70	εβδομήντα	ev·ţho·*mi*·da
80	ογδόντα	ogh·*ţho*·da
90	ενενήντα	e·ne·*ni*·da
100	εκατό	e·ka·*to*
200	διακόσια	ţhia·*ko*·sia
1000	χίλια	*hi*·lia
1,000,000	ένα εκατομμύριο	*e*·na e·ka·to·*mi*·rio

ordinal numbers

τακτικοί αριθμοί

Ordinals agree in gender with the noun they're associated with.

1st	πρώτος/πρώτη **m/f**	*pro*·tos/*pro*·ti
	πρώτο **n**	*pro*·to
2nd	δεύτερος/δεύτερη **m/f**	*ţhef*·te·ros/*ţhef*·te·ri
	δεύτερο **n**	*ţhef*·te·ro
3rd	τρίτος/τρίτη/τρίτο **m/f/n**	*tri*·tos/*tri*·ti/*tri*·to
4th	τέταρτος/τέταρτη **m/f**	*te*·tar·tos/*te*·tar·ti
	τέταρτο **n**	*te*·tar·to
5th	πέμπτος/πέμπτη **m/f**	*pem*·tos/*pem*·ti
	πέμπτο **n**	*pem*·to
6th	έκτος/έκτη/έκτο **m/f/n**	*ek*·tos/*ek*·ti/*ek*·to
7th	έβδομος/έβδομη **m/f**	*ev*·ţho·mos/*ev*·ţho·mi
	έβδομο **n**	*ev*·ţho·mo
8th	όγδοος/όγδοη **m/f**	*ogh*·ţho·os/*ogh*·ţho·i
	όγδοο **n**	*ogh*·ţho·o
9th	ένατος/ένατη/ένατο **m/f/n**	*e*·na·tos/*e*·na·ti/*e*·na·to
10th	δέκατος/δέκατη **m/f**	*ţhe*·ka·tos/*ţhe*·ka·ti
	δέκατο **n**	*ţhe*·ka·to

a quick count

Just as the ordinal numbers have gender in Greek, so too do the abbreviations for '1st', '2nd', '3rd' etc. Masculine ordinals take the abbreviation ος, feminine ordinals take η, and the neuter ones ο. For example '7th' can be written 7ος, 7η, or 7ο depending on gender.

fractions

κλάσματα

a quarter	ένα τέταρτο n	*e*·na *te*·tar·to
a third	ένα τρίτο n	*e*·na *tri*·to
a half	μισό n	mi·*so*
three-quarters	τρία τέταρτα n pl	*tri*·a *te*·tar·ta
all	όλα n pl	*o*·la
none	τίποτε	*ti*·po·te

useful amounts

χρήσιμα ποσά

The words for 'How much?' and 'How many?' take different forms for the gender of the noun they refer to, as shown below.

How much?	Πόσος/Πόση m/f	*po*·sos/*po*·si
	Πόσο; n	*po*·so
How many?	Πόσοι/Πόσες m/f	*po*·si/*po*·ses
	Πόσα; n	*po*·sa
How much water?	Πόσο νερό; n	*po*·so ne·*ro*
How much sugar?	Πόση ζάχαρη; f	*po*·si *za*·kha·ri
How many men?	Πόσοι άντρες; m	*po*·si *a*·dres
How many women?	Πόσες γυναίκες; f	*po*·ses yi·*ne*·kes

I'd like (a) …	Θα ήθελα …	tha *i*·the·la …
Please give me (a) …	Παρακαλώ δώσε μου …	pa·ra·ka·*lo* *ţho*·se mu …
(100) grams	(εκατό) γραμμάρια	(e·ka·*to*) ghra·*ma*·ria
half a dozen	μισή ντουζίνα	mi·*si* du·*zi*·na
dozen	μια ντουζίνα	mia du·*zi*·na
half a kilo	μισό κιλό	mi·*so* ki·*lo*
kilo	ένα κιλό	*e*·na ki·*lo*
bottle	ένα μπουκάλι	*e*·na bu·*ka*·li
jar	ένα βάζο	*e*·na *va*·zo
tin	ένα κουτί	*e*·na ku·*ti*
packet	ένα πακέτο	*e*·na pa·*ke*·to
slice	μια φέτα	mia *fe*·ta
few	λίγα	*li*·gha
less	λιγότερο	li·*gho*·te·ro
(just) a little	(μόνο) λιγάκι	(*mo*·no) li·*gha*·ki
lot	πολύ	po·*li*
many	πολλά	po·*la*
more	πιο πολύ	pio po·*li*
some …	μερικά …	me·ri·*ka* …

To find out how to put these amounts to use, see **self-catering**, page 171.

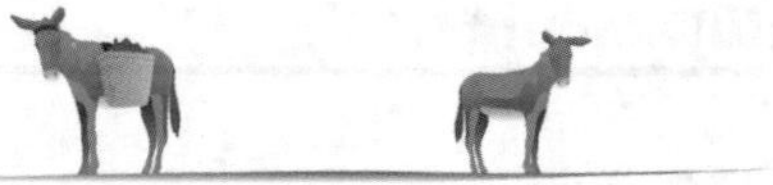

what's in a name?

Although Greeks have moved around their own country and emigrated worldwide, you can sometimes tell from their surnames where they originally come from. People whose name ends in -ακης -a·kis are from Crete, -ατος -a·tos from Cephallonia, -ιδης -i·ţhis from Macedonia, and -πουλος -pu·los from the Peloponnese.

time & dates
ώρα και ημερομηνίες

telling the time
λέγοντας την ώρα

Telling the time in Greek is straightforward. For 'It's … o'clock' simply say είναι *i*·ne (lit: it-is) followed by the number, then η ώρα i *o*·ra (lit: the hour). Note that η ώρα is optional. To give times after the hour say the number of hours, then και ke (lit: and) and the number of minutes. For times before the hour say the number of hours, then παρά pa·*ra* (lit: minus) and the minutes. Instead of 30 or 15 minutes, say μισή mi·*si* (half) for the half hour and τέταρτο *te*·tar·to (quarter).

What time is it?
Τι ώρα είναι; — ti *o*·ra *i*·ne

It's (ten) o'clock.
Είναι (δέκα) η ώρα. — *i*·ne (*ţhe*·ka) i *o*·ra

Five past (ten).
(Δέκα) και πέντε. — (*ţhe*·ka) ke *pe*·de

Quarter past (ten).
(Δέκα) και τέταρτο. — (*ţhe*·ka) ke *te*·tar·to

Half past (ten).
(Δέκα) και μισή. — (*ţhe*·ka) ke mi·*si*

Quarter to (ten).
(Δέκα) παρά τέταρτο. — (*ţhe*·ka) pa·*ra* *te*·tar·to

Twenty to (ten).
(Δέκα) παρά είκοσι. — (*ţhe*·ka) pa·*ra* *i*·ko·si

At what time …?
Τι ώρα …; — ti *o*·ra …

At (ten).
Στις (δέκα). — stis (*ţhe*·ka)

At (7.57pm).
Στις (7.57μ.μ.). — stis (ef·*ta* ke pe·*ni*·da ef·*ta* me·*ta* to me·si·*me*·ri)

short times

The times 'am' and 'pm' are written 'π.μ.' and 'μ.μ.', but you always say the full name – πριν το μεσημέρι prin to me·si·*me*·ri (am) and μετά το μεσημέρι me·*ta* to me·si·*me*·ri (pm).

the calendar

το ημερολόγιο

days

Monday	Δευτέρα	ţhef·*te*·ra
Tuesday	Τρίτη	*tri*·ti
Wednesday	Τετάρτη	te·*tar*·ti
Thursday	Πέμπτη	*pem*·ti
Friday	Παρασκευή	pa·ra·ske·*vi*
Saturday	Σάββατο	*sa*·va·to
Sunday	Κυριακή	ki·ria·*ki*

months

January	Ιανουάριος	i·a·nu·*a*·ri·os
February	Φεβρουάριος	fev·ru·*a*·ri·os
March	Μάρτιος	*mar*·ti·os
April	Απρίλιος	a·*pri*·li·os
May	Μάιος	*ma*·i·os
June	Ιούνιος	i·*u*·ni·os
July	Ιούλιος	i·*u*·li·os
August	Αύγουστος	*av*·ghu·stos
September	Σεπτέμβριος	sep·*tem*·vri·os
October	Οκτώβριος	ok·*tov*·ri·os
November	Νοέμβριος	no·*em*·vri·os
December	Δεκέμβριος	ţhe·*kem*·vri·os

dates

What date is it today?
Τι ημερομηνία είναι σήμερα; ti i·me·ro·mi·*ni*·a *i*·ne *si*·me·ra

It's (18 October).
Είναι (18 Οκτωβρίου). *i*·ne (ţhe·ka·okh·*to* ok·tov·*ri*·u)

BASICS

seasons

spring	άνοιξη f	*a*·nik·si
summer	καλοκαίρι n	ka·lo·*ke*·ri
autumn	φθινόπωρο n	fthi·*no*·po·ro
winter	χειμώνας m	hi·*mo*·nas

present

παρόν

now	τώρα	*to*·ra
today	σήμερα	*si*·me·ra
tonight	το βράδι	to *vra*·ţhi
this week	αυτή την εβδομάδα	af·*ti* tin ev·ţho·*ma*·ţha
this ...	αυτό το ...	af·*to* to ...
morning	πρωί	pro·*i*
afternoon	απόγευμα	a·*po*·yev·ma
month	μήνα	*mi*·na
year	χρόνο	*khro*·no

past

παρελθόν

(three days) ago	(τρεις μέρες) πριν	(tris *me*·res) prin
day before yesterday	προχτές	prokh·*tes*
since (May)	από (το Μάιο)	a·*po* (to *ma*·i·o)
yesterday ...	χτες το ...	khtes to ...
morning	πρωί	pro·*i*
afternoon	απόγευμα	a·*po*·yev·ma
evening	βράδι	*vra*·ţhi

last night/week
την περασμένη νύχτα/εβδομάδα — tin pe·raz·*me*·ni *nikh*·ta/ev·ţho·*ma*·ţha

last month/year
τον περασμένο μήνα/χρόνο — ton pe·raz·*me*·no *mi*·na/*khro*·no

future

μέλλον

tomorrow …	αύριο το …	*av*·ri·o to …
morning	πρωί	pro·*i*
afternoon	απόγευμα	a·*po*·yev·ma
evening	βράδι	*vra*·ţhi
tomorrow	αύριο	*av*·ri·o
day after tomorrow	μεθαύριο	me·*thav*·ri·o
next week	την επόμενη εβδομάδα	tin e·*po*·me·ni ev·ţho·*ma*·ţha
next month	τον επόμενο μήνα	ton e·*po*·me·no *mi*·na
next year	τον επόμενο χρόνο	ton e·*po*·me·no *khro*·no
in (six days)	σε (έξι μέρες)	se (*ek*·si *me*·res)
until (June)	μέχρι (τον Ιούνιο)	*meh*·ri (ton i·*u*·ni·o)

during the day

κατά τη διάρκεια της ημέρας

afternoon	απόγευμα **n**	a·*po*·yev·ma
dawn	αυγή **f**	av·*yi*
day	ημέρα **f**	i·*me*·ra
evening	βράδι **n**	*vra*·ţhi
midday	μεσημέρι **n**	me·si·*me*·ri
midnight	μεσάνυχτα **n pl**	me·*sa*·nikh·ta
morning	πρωί **n**	pro·*i*
night	νύχτα **f**	*nikh*·ta
sunrise	ανατολή του ήλιου **f**	a·na·to·*li* tu *i*·liu
sunset	δύση του ήλιου **f**	*ţhi*·si tu *i*·liu

but the most important time of day …

… is probably the μεσημεριανή ανάπαυση me·si·*me*·ria·*ni* a·*na*·paf·si (siesta). Don't miss out!

money
χρήματα

How much is it?		
Πόσο κάνει;	*po*·so *ka*·ni	
It's (12) euros.		
Κάνει (δώδεκα) ευρώ.	*ka*·ni (ţ*ho*·ţhe·ka) ev·*ro*	
It's free.		
Είναι δωρεάν.	*i*·ne ţho·re·*an*	
Can you write down the price?		
Μπορείς να γράψεις την τιμή;	bo·*ris* na *ghrap*·sis tin ti·*mi*	

Do you accept ...?	Δέχεσαι ...;	ţ*he*·he·se ...
credit cards	πιστωτικές κάρτες	pi·sto·ti·*kes* *kar*·tes
debit cards	χρεωτικές κάρτες	khre·o·ti·*kes* *kar*·tes
travellers cheques	ταξιδιωτικές επιταγές	tak·si·ţhio·ti·*kes* e·pi·ta·*yes*
Where's a/an ...?	Πού είναι ...;	pu *i*·ne ...
automated teller machine	μια αυτόματη μηχανή ανάληψης χρημάτων	mia af·*to*·ma·ti mi·kha·*ni* a·*na*·lip·sis khri·*ma*·ton
foreign exchange office	ένα γραφείο αλλαγής χρημάτων	*e*·na ghra·*fi*·o a·la·*yis* khri·*ma*·ton

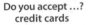

talkin' about money money

The official currency in Greece is the ευρώ ev·*ro* (euro), which is made up of 100 λεπτά lep·*ta* (euro cents). Some vendors are also happy to take foreign currencies.

What's the ...?	Πόσο είναι ...;	*po*·so *i*·ne ...
charge	το κόστος	to *kos*·tos
exchange rate	η τιμή συναλλάγματος	i ti·*mi* si·na·*lagh*·ma·tos
I'd like to ...	Θα ήθελα να ...	tha *i*·the·la na ...
cash a cheque	εξαργυρώσω μια επιταγή	ek·sar·yi·*ro*·so mia e·pi·ta·*yi*
change money	αλλάξω χρήματα	a·*lak*·so *khri*·ma·ta
change a travellers cheque	αλλάξω μια ταξιδιωτική επιταγή	a·*lak*·so mia tak·si·ţhio·ti·*ki* e·pi·ta·*yi*
get a cash advance	κάμω μια ανάληψη σε μετρητά	*ka*·mo mia a·*na*·lip·si se me·tri·*ta*
withdraw money	αποσύρω χρήματα	a·po·*si*·ro *khri*·ma·ta
I'd like ..., please.	Θα ήθελα ..., παρακαλώ.	tha *i*·the·la ... pa·ra·ka·*lo*
my change	τα ρέστα μου	ta *re*·sta mu
a refund	μια επιστροφή χρημάτων	mia e·pi·stro·*fi* khri·*ma*·ton
to return this	να επιστρέψω αυτό	na e·pi·*strep*·so af·*to*

There's a mistake in the bill.
Υπάρχει κάποιο λάθος στο λογαριασμό. — i·*par*·hi *ka*·pio *la*·thos sto lo·gha·riaz·*mo*

Do I need to pay upfront?
Χρειάζεται να πληρώσω από πριν; — khri·*a*·ze·te na pli·*ro*·so a·*po* prin

I don't have that much money.
Δεν έχω τόσα πολλά χρήματα. — ţhen *e*·kho *to*·sa po·*la* *khri*·ma·ta

getting around

κυκλοφορώντας

Which … goes to (Athens)?	Ποιο … πηγαίνει στην (Αθήνα);	pio … pi·*ye*·ni stin (a·*thi*·na)
Is this the … to (Athens)?	Είναι αυτό το … για την (Αθήνα);	*i*·ne af·*to* to … yia tin (a·*thi*·na)
boat	πλοίο	*pli*·o
bus	λεωφορείο	le·o·fo·*ri*·o
ferry	φέρυ	*fe*·ri
plane	αεροπλάνο	a·e·ro·*pla*·no
train	τρένο	*tre*·no

When's the … (bus)?	Πότε είναι το … (λεωφορείο);	*po*·te *i*·ne to … (le·o·fo·*ri*·o)
first	πρώτο	*pro*·to
last	τελευταίο	te·lef·*te*·o
next	επόμενο	e·*po*·me·no

What time does it leave?
Τι ώρα φεύγει; — ti *o*·ra *fev*·yi

What time does it get to (Thessaloniki)?
Τι ώρα φτάνει στη (Θεσσαλονίκη); — ti *o*·ra *fta*·ni sti (the·sa·lo·*ni*·ki)

How long will it be delayed?
Πόση ώρα θα καθυστερήσει; — *po*·si *o*·ra tha ka·thi·ste·*ri*·si

Is this seat free?
Είναι αυτή η θέση ελεύθερη; — *i*·ne af·*ti* i *the*·si e·*lef*·the·ri

That's my seat.
Αυτή η θέση είναι δική μου. — af·*ti* i *the*·si *i*·ne ţhi·*ki* mu

Please tell me when we get to (Thessaloniki).

Παρακαλώ πέστε μου όταν φτάσουμε στη (Θεσσαλονίκη). — pa·ra·ka·*lo* *pe*·ste mu o·tan *fta*·su·me sti (the·sa·lo·*ni*·ki)

How long do we stop here?

Πόση ώρα θα σταματήσουμε εδώ; — *po*·si *o*·ra tha sta·ma·*ti*·su·me e·*ţho*

Are you waiting for more people?

Περιμένεις για περισσότερο κόσμο; — pe·ri·*me*·nis yia pe·ri·*so*·te·ro *koz*·mo

Can you take us around the city, please?

Μπορείς να μας πάρεις γύρω στην πόλη, παρακαλώ; — bo·*ris* na mas *pa*·ris *yi*·ro stin *po*·li pa·ra·ka·*lo*

How many people can ride on this?

Πόσοι άνθρωποι μπορούν να ανεβούν σ'αυτό; — *po*·si *an*·thro·pi bo·*run* na a·ne·*vun* saf·*to*

Can you take me as well?

Μπορείς να πάρεις και εμένα; — bo·*ris* na *pa*·ris ke e·*me*·na

tickets

εισιτήρια

Where do I buy a ticket?

Πού αγοράζω εισιτήριο; — pu a·gho·*ra*·zo i·si·*ti*·ri·o

Do I need to book?

Χρειάζεται να κλείσω θέση; — khri·*a*·ze·te na *kli*·so *the*·si

A bunch of (10) tickets, please.

Μια δέσμη από (δέκα) εισιτήρια, παρακαλώ. — mia *ţhez*·mi a·*po* (*ţhe*·ka) i·si·*ti*·ri·a pa·ra·ka·*lo*

Do you have a timetable (in English)?

Έχεις ένα πρόγραμμα (στα αγγλικά); — *e*·his *e*·na *pro*·ghra·ma (sta ang·gli·*ka*)

Can I get a tourist rail pass?

Μπορώ να έχω ένα τουριστικό πάσο για το τρένο;	bo·*ro* na *e*·kho *e*·na tu·ri·sti·*ko* *pa*·so yia to *tre*·no

A ... ticket to (Patras).	Ένα εισιτήριο ... για την (Πάτρα).	*e*·na i·si·*ti*·ri·o ... yia tin (*pa*·tra)
1st-class	πρώτη θέση	*pro*·ti *the*·si
2nd-class	δεύτερη θέση	*ţhef*·te·ri *the*·si
child's	παιδικό	pe·ţhi·*ko*
deck class (boat)	κατάστρωμα	ka·*ta*·stro·ma
one-way	απλό	a·*plo*
return	με επιστροφή	me e·pi·stro·*fi*
student's	μαθητικό	ma·thi·ti·*ko*
tourist class	τουριστική θέση	tu·ri·sti·*ki* *the*·si

I'd like a/an ... seat.	Θα ήθελα μια θέση ...	tha *i*·the·la mia *the*·si ...
aisle	στο διάδρομο	sto *ţhia*·ţhro·mo
(non)smoking	στους (μη) καπνίζοντες	stus (mi) kap·*ni*·zo·des
window	στο παράθυρο	sto pa·*ra*·thi·ro

listen for ...

Ακυρώστε το εισιτήριο.	a·ki·*ro*·ste to i·si·*ti*·rio	**Punch the ticket.**
ακυρώθηκε	a·ki·*ro*·thi·ke	**cancelled**
απεργία f	a·per·*yi*·a	**strike**
αυτό	af·*to*	**this one**
εκείνο	e·*ki*·no	**that one**
γεμάτο	ye·*ma*·to	**full**
καθυστέρησε	ka·thi·*ste*·ri·se	**delayed**
θυρίδα αγοράς εισιτιρίων f	thi·*ri*·ţha a·gho·*ras* i·si·ti·*ri*·on	**ticket window**
πλατφόρμα f	plat·*for*·ma	**platform**
πρόγραμμα n	*pro*·ghra·ma	**timetable**
ταξιδιωτικός πράκτορας m	tak·si·ţhio·ti·*kos* *prak*·to·ras	**travel agent**

Is there (a) ...?	Υπάρχει ...;	i·*par*·hi ...
air conditioning	έρκοντίσιον	e·kon·*di*·si·on
blanket	κουβέρτα	ku·*ver*·ta
sick bag	σακούλα εμετού	sa·*ku*·la e·me·*tu*
toilet	τουαλέτα	tu·a·*le*·ta

Can I get a sleeping berth?
Μορώ να έχω μια θέση με κρεβάτι; — bo·*ro* na *e*·kho mia *the*·si me kre·*va*·ti

How much is it?
Πόσο κάνει; — *po*·so *ka*·ni

How long does the trip take?
Πόσο διαρκεί το ταξίδι; — *po*·so ţhi·ar·*ki* to tak·*si*·ţhi

Is it a direct route?
Πηγαίνει κατ'ευθείαν; — pi·*ye*·ni ka·tef·*thi*·an

Can I get a stand-by ticket?
Μπορώ να μπω στον κατάλογο αναμονής για εισιτήριο; — bo·*ro* na bo ston ka·*ta*·lo·gho a·na·mo·*nis* yia i·si·*ti*·ri·o

What time should I check in?
Τι ώρα να έρθω στον έλεγχο; — ti *o*·ra na *er*·tho ston *e*·leng·kho

I'd like to ... my ticket, please.	Θα ήθελα να ... το εισιτήριό μου παρακαλώ.	tha *i*·the·la na ... to i·si·*ti*·ri·*o* mu pa·ra·ka·*lo*
cancel	ακυρώσω	a·ki·*ro*·so
change	αλλάξω	a·*lak*·so
confirm	επικυρώσω	e·pi·ki·*ro*·so

it's not roulette

If Athenian locals talk about μονά-ζυγά mo·*na*·zi·*gha* (odds-evens) and δακτύλιος ţhak·*ti*·lios (rings), they refer to traffic restrictions put in place in Athens to help minimise the notorious νέφος *ne*·fos (smog). The system is called 'odd-evens' because certain cars can enter the 'ring' (a restricted zone) on even or odd days of the month. The boundaries of the ţhak·*ti*·lios are marked with yellow hexagonal signs.

luggage

αποσκευές

Where can I find a/the ...?	Πού μπορώ να βρω ...;	pu bo·*ro* na vro ...
baggage claim	το χώρο αποσκευών	to *kho*·ro a·pos·ke·*von*
left-luggage office	φύλαξη αποσκευών	*fi*·lak·si a·pos·ke·*von*
luggage locker	τη φύλαξη αντικειμένων	ti *fi*·lak·si a·di·ki·*me*·non
trolley	ένα καροτσάκι	*e*·na ka·rot·*sa*·ki

My luggage has been ...	Οι αποσκευές μου έχουν ...	i a·pos·ke·*ves* mu *e*·khun ...
damaged	πάθει ζημιά	*pa*·thi zi·*mia*
lost	χαθεί	kha·*thi*
stolen	κλαπεί	kla·*pi*

That's (not) mine.
Αυτό (δεν) είναι δικό μου. af·*to* (ţhen) *i*·ne ţhi·*ko* mu

Can I have some coins/tokens?
Μπορώ να έχω μερικά κέρματα/κουπόνια; bo·*ro* na *e*·kho me·ri·*ka* *ker*·ma·ta/ku·*po*·nia

listen for ...

αποσκευές χειρός f pl	a·pos·ke·*ves* hi·*ros*	carry-on baggage
διαβατήριο n	ţhia·va·*ti*·ri·o	passport
κάρτα επιβίβασης f	*kar*·ta e·pi·*vi*·va·sis	boarding pass
κουπόνι n	ku·*po*·ni	token
μεταβίβαση f	me·ta·*vi*·va·si	transfer
πτήση τσάρτερ f	*pti*·si *tsar*·ter	charter flight
τράνζιτ n	*tran*·zit	transit
υπέρβαρο n	i·*per*·va·ro	excess baggage

plane

αεροπλάνο

Where does flight (10) arrive/depart?
Πού προσγειώνεται/ απογειώνεται η πτήση (δέκα); — pu pros·yi·*o*·ne·te/ a·po·yi·*o*·ne·te i *pti*·si (*ţhe*·ka)

Where's (the) …?	Πού είναι …;	pu *i*·ne …
airport shuttle	το λεωφορείο του αεροδρομίου	to le·o·fo·*ri*·o tu a·e·ro·ţhro·*mi*·u
arrivals hall	η αίθουσα των αφίξεων	i *e*·thu·sa ton a·*fik*·se·on
departures hall	η αίθουσα των ανα χωρήσεων	i *e*·thu·sa ton *a*·na kho·*ri*·se·on
duty-free shops	τα αφορολόγητα	ta a·fo·ro·*lo*·yi·ta
gate (9)	η θύρα (εννέα)	i *thi*·ra (e·*ne*·a)

bus, trolley bus & coach

λεωφορεία, τρόλεϋ και πούλμαν

How often do buses come?
Κάθε πότε έρχονται τα λεωφορεία; — *ka*·the *po*·te *er*·kho·de ta le·o·fo·*ri*·a

Does it stop at (Iraklio)?
Σταματάει στο (Ηράκλειο); — sta·ma·*ta*·i sto (i·*ra*·kli·o)

What's the next stop?
Ποια είναι η επόμενη στάση; — pia *i*·ne i e·*po*·me·ni *sta*·si

I'd like to get off (at Iraklio).
Θα ήθελα να κατεβώ (στο Ηράκλειο). — tha *i*·the·la na ka·te·*vo* (sto i·*ra*·kli·o)

Where's the trolley bus stop?
Πού είναι η στάση του τρόλεϋ; — pu *i*·ne i *sta*·si tu *tro*·le·i

city a	αστικό	a·sti·*ko*
intercity a	υπεραστικό	i·pe·ra·sti·*ko*
local a	τοπικό	to·pi·*ko*

train & metro

τρένο και μετρό

Where's the nearest metro station?
Πού είναι ο πιο κοντινός σταθμός του μετρό; — pu *i*·ne o pio ko·di·*nos* stath·*mos* tu me·*tro*

Which line goes to (the port)?
Ποια γραμμή πηγαίνει (στο λιμάνι); — pia ghra·*mi* pi·*ye*·ni (sto li·*ma*·ni)

What station is this?
Ποιος σταθμός είναι αυτός; — pios stath·*mos* *i*·ne af·*tos*

What's the next station?
Ποιος είναι ο επόμενος σταθμός; — pios *i*·ne o e·*po*·me·nos stath·*mos*

Does it stop at (Kalamata)?
Σταματάει στην (Καλαμάτα); — sta·ma·*ta*·i stin (ka·la·*ma*·ta)

Do I need to change?
Χειάζεται να αλλάξω; — khri·*a*·ze·te na a·*lak*·so

Is it direct/express?
Είναι κατ'ευθείαν/εξπρές; — *i*·ne ka·tef·*thi*·an/eks·*pres*

Which carriage is ...?	Ποια άμαξα είναι (για) ...;	pia *a*·mak·sa *i*·ne (yia) ...
1st class	πρώτη θέση	*pro*·ti *the*·si
for dining	φαγητό	fa·yi·*to*
for (Kalamata)	την (Καλαμάτα)	tin (ka·la·*ma*·ta)

north & south

On Greek maps and road signs, 'N' stands for Νότια *no*·ti·a (south) and 'B' stands for βόρια *vo*·ri·a (north).

boat

βάρκα

Where's the port/port police?

Πού είναι το λιμάνι/ λιμεναρχείο;	pu *i*·ne to li·*ma*·ni/ li·me·nar·*hi*·o

Can I have the ferry timetable?

Μπορώ να έχω το πρόγραμμα του φέρι;	bo·*ro* na *e*·kho to *pro*·ghra·ma tu *fe*·ri

Where does the boat to (Chios) leave from?

Από πού φεύγει το πλοίο για τη (Χίο);	a·*po* pu *fev*·yi to *pli*·o yia ti (*hi*·o)

When is the next boat for (Naxos)?

Πότε είναι το επόμενο πλοίο για τη (Νάξο);	*po*·te *i*·ne to e·*po*·me·no *pli*·o yia ti (*nak*·so)

Does this ferry go to (Rhodos)?

Πηγαίνει αυτό το φέρι στη (Ρόδο);	pi·*ye*·ni af·*to* to *fe*·ri sti (*ro*·ţho)

How many hours is it to (Milos)?
Πόσες ώρες είναι για τη (Μήλο); — *po*·ses *o*·res *i*·ne yia ti (*mi*·lo)

How many stops does the boat make?
Πόσες στάσεις κάνει το πλοίο; — *po*·ses *sta*·sis *ka*·ni to *pli*·o

Where can I get a taxi boat?
Πού μπορώ να νοικιάσω μια βάρκα με βαρκάρη; — pu bo·*ro* na ni·*kia*·so mia *var*·ka me var·*ka*·ri

Where can we hire an uncrewed boat?
Πού μπορώ να νοικιάσω μόνο μια βάρκα; — pu bo·*ro* na ni·*kia*·so *mo*·no mia *var*·ka

I'd like a/an …	Θα ήθελα …	tha *i*·the·la …
cabin for one/two	μια καμπίνα για ένα/δύο	mia ka·*bi*·na yia *e*·na/*ţhi*·o
inside/outside cabin	μια εσωτερική/ εξωτερική καμπίνα	mia e·so·te·ri·*ki*/ ek·so·te·ri·*ki* ka·*bi*·na

What's the sea like today?
Πώς είναι η θάλασσα σήμερα; — pos *i*·ne i *tha*·la·sa *si*·me·ra

Are there life jackets?
Υπάρχουν σωσίβια; — i·*par*·khun so·*si*·vi·a

What island is this?
Ποιο νησί είναι αυτό; — pio ni·*si* *i*·ne af·*to*

What beach is this?
Ποια παραλία είναι αυτή; — pia pa·ra·*li*·a *i*·ne af·*ti*

I feel seasick.
Αισθάνομαι ναυτία. — es·*tha*·no·me naf·*ti*·a

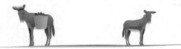

cabin	καμπίνα f	ka·*bi*·na
***caïque* (large fishing boat)**	καΐκι n	ka·*i*·ki
captain	καπετάνιος m	ka·pe·*ta*·nios
car deck	χώρος για αυτοκίνητο στο κατάστρωμα m	*kho*·ros yia af·to·*ki*·ni·to sto ka·*ta*·stro·ma
catamaran	σχεδία καταμαράν f	she·*ţhi*·a ka·ta·ma·*ran*
cruise	κρουαζέρα f	kru·a·*ze*·ra
deck	κατάστρωμα n	ka·*ta*·stro·ma
excursion boat	εκδρομική βάρκα f	ek·ţhro·mi·*ki* *var*·ka
ferry	φέρι n	*fe*·ri
hammock	αιώρα f	e·*o*·ra
hydrofoil	ιπτάμενο δελφίνι n	ip·*ta*·me·no ţhel·*fi*·ni
inter-island boat	πλοίο συγκοινωνίας μεταξύ νησιών n	*pli*·o si·gi·no·*ni*·as me·tak·*si* ni·*sion*
jolly roger	βάρκα πλοίου f	*var*·ka *pli*·u
lifeboat	ναυαγοσωστική λέμβος f	na·va·gho·so·sti·*ki* *lem*·vos
life jacket	σωσίβιο n	so·*si*·vi·o
muster station	χώρος συγκέντρωσης m	*kho*·ros si·*ge*·dro·sis
purser's office	γραφείο λογιστή n	ghra·*fi*·o lo·yi·*sti*
sailing boat	ιστιοφόρο n	i·sti·o·*fo*·ro
small fishing boat	μικρή βάρκα για ψάρεμα f	mi·*kri* *var*·ka yia *psa*·re·ma
yacht	γιωτ n	yiot

taxi

ταξί

I'd like a taxi …	Θα ήθελα ένα ταξί …	tha *i*·the·la *e*·na tak·*si* …
at (9am)	στις (εννέα π.μ.)	stis (e·*ne*·a prin to me·si·*me*·ri)
now	τώρα	*to*·ra
tomorrow	αύριο	*av*·ri·o

Where's the taxi rank?
Πού είναι η στάση για ταξί; — pu *i*·ne i *sta*·si yia tak·*si*

Is this taxi available?
Είναι αυτό το ταξί ελεύθερο; — *i*·ne af·*to* to tak·*si* e·*lef*·the·ro

Please put the meter on.
Παρακαλώ βάλε το ταξίμετρο. — pa·ra·ka·*lo* *va*·le to tak·*si*·me·tro

How much is it (to Petroupoli)?
Πόσο κάνει (για Πετρούπολη); — *po*·so *ka*·ni (yia pe·*tru*·po·li)

Please take me to (this address).
Παρακαλώ πάρε με σε (αυτή τη διεύθυνση). — pa·ra·ka·*lo* *pa*·re me se (af·*ti* ti ţhi·*ef*·thin·si)

How much do you charge for the luggage?
Πόσο χρεώνεις για τις αποσκευές; — *po*·so khre·*o*·nis yia tis a·pos·ke·*ves*

Please …	Παρακλώ …	pa·ra·ka·*lo* …
slow down	πήγαινε πιο σιγά	*pi*·ye·ne pio si·*gha*
stop here	σταμάτα εδώ	sta·*ma*·ta e·*ţho*
wait here	περίμενε εδώ	pe·*ri*·me·ne e·*ţho*

car & motorbike

αυτοκίνητο και μοτοσακό

car & motorbike hire

I'd like to hire a/an …	Θα ήθελα να ενοικιάσω ένα …	tha *i*·the·la na e·ni·ki·*a*·so *e*·na …
4WD	4W ντράιβ	for·ghu·*il dra*·iv
automatic	αυτόματο	af·*to*·ma·to
car	αυτοκίνητο	af·to·*ki*·ni·to
manual	με ταχύτητες	me ta·*hi*·ti·tes
motorbike	μοτοσακό	mo·to·sa·*ko*

with …	με …	me …
air conditioning	έρκοντίσιον	e·kon·*di*·si·on
a driver	οδηγό	o·ţhi·*gho*

How much for daily/weekly hire?

Πόσο νοικάζεται την ημέρα/εβδομάδα; — *po*·so ni·*kia*·ze·te tin i·*me*·ra/ev·ţho·*ma*·ţha

Does that include insurance/mileage?

Αυτό συμπεριλαμβάνει ασφάλεια/χιλιόμετρα; — af·*to* si·be·ri·lam·*va*·ni as·*fa*·li·a/hi·*lio*·me·tra

Can I take the car on a ferry?

Μπορώ να πάρω το αυτοκίνητο στο φέρι; — bo·*ro* na *pa*·ro to af·to·*ki*·ni·to sto *fe*·ri

Do you have a guide to the road rules in English?

Έχετε οδικό κώδικα κυκλοφορίας στα Αγγλικά; — *e*·he·te o·ţhi·*ko* *ko*·ţhi·ka ki·klo·fo·*ri*·as sta ang·gli·*ka*

Do you have a road map?

Έχετε οδικό χάρτη; — *e*·he·te o·ţhi·*ko* *khar*·ti

on the road

What's the speed limit?

Ποιο είναι το όριο ταχύτητας; — pio *i*·ne to *o*·ri·o ta·*hi*·ti·tas

Is this the road to (Lamia)?

Είναι αυτός ο δρόμος για (τη Λαμία); — *i*·ne af·*tos* o *ţhro*·mos yia (ti la·*mi*·a)

Where's a petrol station?

Πού είναι ένα πρατήριο βενζίνας; — *pu* *i*·ne *e*·na pra·*ti*·ri·o ven·*zi*·nas

Fill it up, please.

Γεμίστε το, παρακαλώ. — ye·*mis*·te to pa·ra·ka·*lo*

signs

Απαγορεύεται η είσοδος	a·pa·gho·*re*·ve·te i *i*·so·ţhos	**No Entry**
Διόδια	ţhi·*o*·ţhi·a	**Toll**
Είσοδος	*i*·so·ţhos	**Entrance (Freeway)**
Έξοδος Εθνικής Οδού	*ek*·so·ţhos e·th·ni·*kis* o·*ţhu*	**Exit Freeway**
Προσοχή	pro·so·*hi*	**Drive With Care**
Μονόδρομος	mo·*no*·ţhro·mos	**One-Way**

listen for ...

άδεια οδήγησης f	*a*·ʈhi·a o·*ʈhi*·yi·sis	**drivers licence**
βενζίνα f	ven·*zi*·na	**petrol (gas)**
δωρεάν	ʈho·re·*an*	**free a**
επί τόπου ασφάλεια f	e·*pi to*·pu as·*fa*·li·a	**on-the-spot insurance**
παρκόμετρο n	par·*ko*·me·tro	**parking meter**
Πράσινη κάρτα f	*pra*·si·ni *kar*·ta	**Green Card (international third-party insurance)**
χιλιόμετρα n pl	hi·*lio*·me·tra	**kilometres**

diesel	ντίζελ n	*di*·zel
leaded	μολυβδούχος f	mo·liv·*ʈhu*·khos
LPG	υγραέριο n	igh·ra·*e*·ri·o
premium unleaded	σούπερ αμόλυβδος f	*su*·per a·*mo*·liv·ʈhos
regular	απλή f	ap·*li*
unleaded	αμόλυβδος f	a·*mo*·liv·ʈhos

Can you check the ...?	Μπορείς να κοιτάξεις ...;	bo·*ris* na ki·*tak*·sis ...
oil	το λάδι	to *la*·ʈhi
tyre pressure	την πίεση των τροχών	tin *pi*·e·si ton tro·*khon*
water	το νερό	to ne·*ro*

(How long) Can I park here?
(Πόση ώρα) Μπορώ να παρκάρω εδώ; (*po*·si *o*·ra) bo·*ro* na par·*ka*·ro e·*ʈho*

Do I have to pay?
Πρέπει να πληρώσω; *pre*·pi na pli·*ro*·so

problems

I need a mechanic.
Χρειάζομαι μηχανικό. — khri·*a*·zo·me mi·kha·ni·*ko*

I've had an accident.
Είχα ένα ατύχημα. — *i*·kha *e*·na a·*ti*·hi·ma

The car/motorbike has broken down (at Corinth).
Το αυτοκίνητο/μοτοσακό χάλασε (στην Κόρινθο). — to af·to·*ki*·ni·to/mo·to·sa·*ko* *ha*·la·se (stin *ko*·rin·tho)

The car/motorbike won't start.
Το αυτοκίνητο/μοτοσακό δεν αρχίζει. — to af·to·*ki*·ni·to/mo·to·sa·*ko* ţhen ar·*hi*·zi

I have a flat tyre.
Μ'έπιασε λάστιχο. — *me*·pia·se *la*·sti·kho

I've lost my car keys.
Έχασα τα κλειδιά του αυτοκινήτου μου. — *e*·ha·sa ta kli·*ţhia* tu af·to·ki·*ni*·tu mu

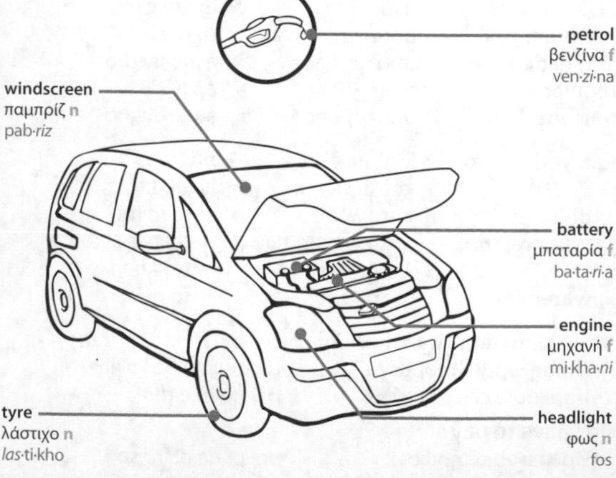

I've locked the keys inside.

Κλείδωσα τα κλειδιά μου στο αυτοκίνητου.	*kli*·ţho·sa ta kli·*ţhia* mu sto af·to·*ki*·ni·to

I've run out of petrol.

Μου τελείωσε η βενζίνα.	mu te·*li*·o·se i ven·*zi*·na

Can you fix it (today)?

Μπορείς να το επισκευάσεις (σήμερα);	bo·*ris* na to e·pis·ke·*va*·sis (*si*·me·ra)

How long will it take?

Πόση ώρα θα κάμει;	*po*·si *o*·ra tha *ka*·mi

bicycle

ποδήλατο

I'd like ...	Θα ήθελα ...	tha *i*·the·la ...
my bicycle repaired	να επισκευάσω το ποδήλατό μου	na e·pis·ke·*va*·so to po·*ţhi*·la·*to* mu
to buy a bicycle	να αγοράσω ένα ποδήλατο	na a·gho·*ra*·so *e*·na po·*ţhi*·la·to
to hire a bicycle	να νοικιάσω ένα ποδήλατο	na ni·*kia*·so *e*·na po·*ţhi*·la·to

I'd like a ... bike.	Θα ήθελα ένα ...	tha *i*·the·la *e*·na ...
mountain	ποδήλατο για βουνό	po·*ţhi*·la·to yia vu·*no*
racing	ποδήλατο κούρσας	po·*ţhi*·la·to *kur*·sas
second-hand	μεταχειρισμένο ποδήλατο	me·ta·hi·riz·*me*·no po·*ţhi*·la·to

How much is it per day?

Πόσο κοστίζει την ημέρα;	*po*·so ko·*sti*·zi tin i·*me*·ra

How much is it per hour?

Πόσο κοστίζει την ώρα;	*po*·so ko·*sti*·zi tin *o*·ra

Do I need a helmet?
Χρειάζομαι κράνος; — khri·*a*·zo·me *kra*·nos

Is there a bicycle-path map?
Υπάρχει χάρτης για δρόμο ποδηλάτου; — i·*par*·hi *khar*·tis yia *ţhro*·mo po·ţhi·*la*·tu

Is this road OK for bicycles?
Είναι αυτός ο δρόμος κατάλληλος για ποδήλατα; — *i*·ne af·*tos* o *ţhro*·mos ka·*ta*·li·los yia po·*ţhi*·la·ta

I have a puncture.
Τρύπησε η ρόδα μου. — *tri*·pi·se i *ro*·ţha mu

gut feelings

Greeks tend to get pretty physical when they talk about their emotions:

I'm not impressed.
Δεν μου γεμίζει το μάτι. — ţhen mu ye·*mi*·zi to *ma*·ti
(lit: It doesn't fill my eye.)

I can't stand him/her.
Δεν τον/την χωνεύω. — ţhen ton/tin tso·ne·*vo*
(lit: I can't digest him/her.)

I've had enough of you.
Μ'έπρηξες. — *me*·prik·ses
(lit: You've made me swollen.)

I regretted it.
Μου βγήκε από τη μύτη. — mu *vyi*·ke a·*po* ti *mi*·ti
(lit: It came out of my nose.)

He/She put me under pressure.
Μου βαλε τα δυο πόδια σ' ένα παπούτσι. — *mu*·va·le ta ţhio *po*·ţhia *se*·na pa·*put*·si
(lit: He/She put both my feet in one shoe.)

PRACTICAL

border crossing

περνώντας τα σύνορα

I'm ...	Είμαι ...	*i*·me ...
in transit	τράνζιτ	*tran*·zit
on business	για δουλειά	yia ţhu·*lia*
on holiday	σε διακοπές	se ţhia·ko·*pes*
I'm here for (three) ...	Είμαι εδώ για (τρεις) ...	*i*·me e·*ţho* yia (tris) ...
days	μέρες	*me*·res
weeks	εβδομάδες	ev·ţho·*ma*·ţhes
months	μήνες	*mi*·nes

I'm going to (Limassol).
Πηγαίνω στη (Λεμεσό). pi·*ye*·no sti (le·me·*so*)

I'm staying at (the Xenia).
Μένω στο (Ξενία) *me*·no sto (kse·*ni*·a)

The children are on this passport.
Τα παιδιά είναι σ'αυτό το βιαβατήριο. ta pe·*ţhia* *i*·ne saf·*to* to ţhia·va·*ti*·ri·o

listen for ...

άδεια f εξαγωγής	*a*·ţhi·a ek·sa·gho·*yis*	**export permit**
βίζα f	*vi*·za	**visa**
διαβατήριο n	ţhia·va·*ti*·ri·o	**passport**
μόνος m	*mo*·nos	**alone**
οικογένεια f	i·ko·*ye*·ni·a	**family**
ομάδα f	o·*ma*·ţha	**group**
ταυτότητα f	taf·*to*·ti·ta	**ID card**

Can you stamp a separate paper instead of the passport?

Μπορείτε να σφραγίσετε ένα χωριστό χαρτί αντί για το διαβατήριο;	bo·*ri*·te na sfra·*yi*·se·te e·na kho·ri·*sto* khar·*ti* a·*di* yia to ţhia·va·*ti*·ri·o

Where can I get a travel permit for (Mt Athos)?

Πού μπορώ να πάρω μια άδεια ταξιδιού για (το Άγιο Όρος);	pu bo·*ro* na *pa*·ro mia *a*·ţhi·a tak·si·*ţhiu* yia (to *a*·yi·o *o*·ros)

at customs

στο τελωνείο

I have nothing to declare.

Δεν έχω τίποτε να δηλώσω.	ţhen *e*·kho *ti*·po·te na ţhi·*lo*·so

I have something to declare.

Έχω κάτι να δηλώσω.	*e*·kho *ka*·ti na ţhi·*lo*·so

Do I have to declare this?

Πρέπει να το δηλώσω αυτό;	*pre*·pi na to ţhi·*lo*·so af·*to*

That's (not) mine.

Αυτό (δεν) είναι δικό μου.	af·*to* (ţhen) *i*·ne ţhi·*ko* mu

I didn't know I had to declare it.

Δεν ήξερα πως έπρεπε να το δηλώσω.	ţhen *ik*·*se*·ra pos *e*·pre·pe na to ţhi·*lo*·so

I have a doctor's certificate for this medication.

Έχω πιστοποιητικό γιατρού για αυτό το φάρμακο.	*e*·kho pis·to·pi·i·ti·*ko* yia·*tru* yia af·*to* to *far*·ma·ko

signs

Αφορολόγητα	a·fo·ro·*lo*·yi·ta	**Duty-Free**
Έλεγχος Διαβατηρίων	*e*·len·ghos ţhia·va·ti·*ri*·on	**Passport Control**
Καραντίνα	ka·ran·*di*·na	**Quarantine**
Τελωνείο	te·lo·*ni*·o	**Customs**
Μετανάστευση	me·ta·*na*·stef·si	**Immigration**

directions
οδηγίες

Where's (the tourist office)?	
Πού είναι (το τουριστικό γραφείο);	pu *i*·ne (to tu·ri·sti·*ko* ghra·*fi*·o)
What's the address?	
Ποια είναι η διεύθυνση;	pia *i*·ne i ţhi·*ef*·thin·si
How far is it?	
Πόσο μακριά είναι;	*po*·so ma·kri·*a* *i*·ne
How do I get there?	
Πώς πηγαίνω εκεί;	pos pi·*ye*·no e·*ki*
What street is this?	
Ποιος δρόμος είναι αυτός;	pios *ţhro*·mos *i*·ne af·*tos*
What village is this?	
Ποιο χωριό είναι αυτό;	pio kho·*rio* *i*·ne af·*to*
Can you show me (on the map)?	
Μπορείς να μου δείξεις (στο χάρτη);	bo·*ris* na mu *ţhik*·sis (sto *khar*·ti)

It's …	Είναι …	*i*·ne …
close	κοντά	ko·*da*
behind …	πίσω …	*pi*·so …
here	εδώ	e·*ţho*
in front of …	μπροστά από …	bros·*ta* a·*po* …
near …	κοντά …	ko·*da* …
next to …	δίπλα από …	*ţhip*·la a·*po* …
on the corner	στη γωνία	sti gho·*ni*·a
opposite …	απέναντι …	a·*pe*·na·di …
straight ahead	κατ'ευθείαν	ka·tef·*thi*·an
there	εκεί	e·*ki*

north	βόρια	*vo*·ri·a
south	νότια	*no*·ti·a
east	ανατολικά	a·na·to·li·*ka*
west	δυτικά	ţhi·ti·*ka*

listen for …

χιλιόμετρα	hi·*lio*·me·tra	**kilometres**
λεπτά	lep·*ta*	**minutes**
μέτρα	*me*·tra	**metres**

avenue	λεωφόρος f	le·o·*fo*·ros
lane	πάροδος f	*pa*·ro·ţhos
street	οδός f	o·*ţhos*
by bus/taxi	με λεωφορείο/ταξί	me le·o·fo·*ri*·o/tak·*si*
on foot	με πόδια	me *po*·ţhia
Turn …	Στρίψε …	*strip*·se …
at the corner	στη γωνία	sti gho·*ni*·a
at the traffic lights	στα φανάρια	sta fa·*na*·ria
left	αριστερά	a·ris·te·*ra*
right	δεξιά	ţhek·si·*a*

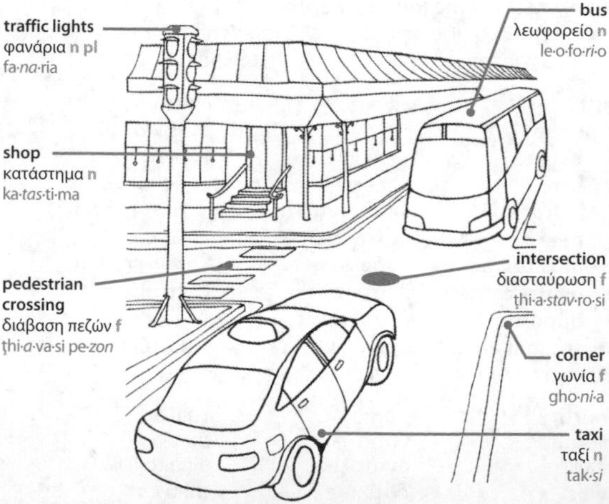

accommodation
κατάλυμα

finding accommodation
βρίσκοντας κατάλυμα

Where's (a) …?	Πού είναι …;	pu *i*·ne …
bed and breakfast	κατάλυμα με πρόγευμα	ka·*ta*·li·ma me *pro*·ghev·ma
camping ground	χώρος για κάμπινγκ	*kho*·ros yia *kam*·ping
guesthouse	ξενώνας	kse·*no*·nas
(3-star) hotel	ξενοδοχείο (τριών αστέρων)	kse·no·ţho·*hi*·o (tri·*on* a·*ste*·ron)
mountain refuge	ορεινό καταφύγιο	o·ri·*no* ka·ta·*fi*·yi·o
pension	πανσιόν	pan·*sion*
room for rent	δωμάτιο για νοίκιασμα	ţho·*ma*·ti·o yia *ni*·kiaz·ma
self-contained apartment	ξεχωριστό διαμέρισμα	kse·kho·ri·*sto* ţhi·a·*me*·riz·ma
some traditional accommodation	παραδοσιακό κατάλυμα	pa·ra·ţho·si·a·*ko* ka·*ta*·li·ma
youth hostel	γιουθ χόστελ	yiuth *kho*·stel

local talk

dive	βουτιά f	vu·*tia*
rat-infested	γεμάτο ποντίκια	ye·*ma*·to po·*di*·kia
top spot	ωραιότατο σημείο n	o·re·*o*·ta·to si·*mi*·o

Can you recommend somewhere ...?	Μπορείτε να συστήσετε κάπου ...;	bo·*ri*·te na si·*sti*·se·te *ka*·pu ...
cheap	φτηνό	fti·*no*
good	καλό	ka·*lo*
nearby	κοντινό	ko·di·*no*
romantic	ρομαντικό	ro·ma·di·*ko*

What's the address?
Ποια είναι η διεύθυνση; — pia *i*·ne i ţhi·*ef*·thin·si

For responses, see **directions**, page 63.

booking ahead & checking in

κλείσιμο θέσης από πριν και εγκατάσταση

I'd like to book a room, please.
Θα ήθελα να κλείσω ένα δωμάτιο, παρακαλώ. — tha *i*·the·la na *kli*·so *e*·na ţho·*ma*·ti·o pa·ra·ka·*lo*

I have a reservation.
Έχω κάμει κάποια κράτηση. — *e*·kho *ka*·mi *ka*·pia *kra*·ti·si

My name's ...
Με λένε ... — me *le*·ne ...

For (three) nights/weeks.
Για (τρεις) νύχτες/εβδομάδες. — yia (tris) *nikh*·tes/ev·ţho·*ma*·ţhes

From (2 July) to (6 July).
Από (τις δύο Ιουλίου) μέχρι (τις έξι Ιουλίου). — a·*po* (tis *ţhi*·o i·u·*li*·u) *me*·khri (tis *ek*·si i·u·*li*·u)

listen for ...

Πόσες νύχτες;	*po*·ses *nikh*·tes	**How many nights?**
διαβατήριο n	ţhia·va·*ti*·ri·o	**passport**
γεμάτο	ye·*ma*·to	**full** a
κλειδί n	kli·*ţhi*	**key**
ρεσεψιόν f	re·sep·*sion*	**reception**

signs

Ελεύθερα δωμάτια	e·*lef*·the·ra ţho·*ma*·ti·a	**Vacancy**
Μπάνιο	*ba*·nio	**Bathroom**
Πλήρες	*pli*·res	**No Vacancy**

Do you have a … room?	Έχετε ένα … δωμάτιο	*e*·he·te *e*·na … ţho·*ma*·ti·o
single	μονό	mo·*no*
double	διπλό	ţhi·*plo*
twin	δίκλινο	*ţhi*·kli·no

How much is it per …?	Πόσο είναι για κάθε …;	*po*·so *i*·ne yia *ka*·the …
night	νύχτα	*nikh*·ta
person	άτομο	*a*·to·mo
week	εβδομάδα	ev·ţho·*ma*·ţha

Can I see it?
Μπορώ να το δω; — bo·*ro* na to ţho

I'll take it.
Θα το πάρω. — tha to *pa*·ro

Do I need to pay upfront?
Χρειάζεται να πληρώσω από πριν; — khri·*a*·ze·te na pli·*ro*·so a·*po* prin

Can I pay by …?	Μπορώ να πληρώσω με …;	bo·*ro* na pli·*ro*·so me …
credit card	πιστωτική κάρτα	pi·sto·ti·*ki* *kar*·ta
travellers cheque	ταξιδιωτική επιταγή	tak·si·ţhio·ti·*ki* e·pi·ta·*yi*

For other methods of payment, see **shopping**, page 77.

requests & queries

παρακλήσεις και ερωτήσεις

When/Where is breakfast served?
Πότε/Πού σερβίρεται το πρόγευμα; — *po*·te/pu ser·*vi*·re·te to *pro*·yev·ma

Please wake me at (seven).
Παρακαλώ ξύπνησέ με στις (εφτά). — pa·ra·ka·*lo* *ksip*·ni·*se* me stis (ef·*ta*)

Do you ... here?	... εδώ;	... e·*ţho*
arrange tours	Κανονίζετε ξεναγήσεις	ka·no·*ni*·ze·te kse·na·*yi*·sis
change money	Αλλάζετε χρήματα	a·*la*·ze·te *khri*·ma·ta

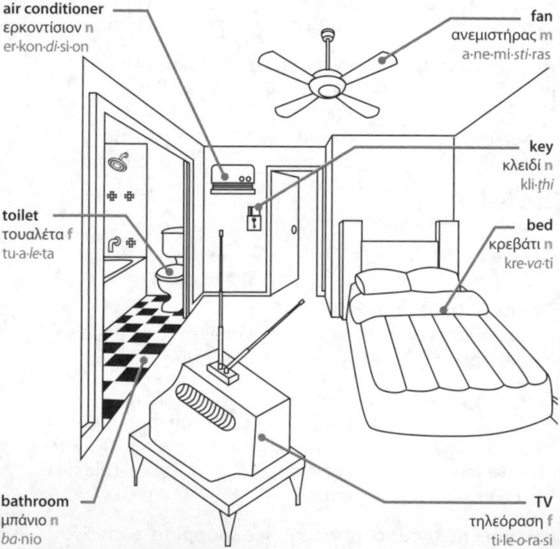

Can I use the …?	Μπορώ να χρησιμοποιήσω …;	bo·*ro* na khri·si·mo·pi·*i*·so …
kitchen	την κουζίνα	tin ku·*zi*·na
laundry	το πλυντήριο	to pli·*di*·ri·o
telephone	το τηλέφωνο	to ti·*le*·fo·no

Do you have a/an …?	Έχετε …;	*e*·he·te …
elevator	ασανσέρ	a·san·*ser*
laundry service	υπηρεσία πλυντηρίου	i·pi·re·*si*·a pli·di·*ri*·u
message board	πίνακα μηνυμάτων	*pi*·na·ka mi·ni·*ma*·ton
safe	χρηματοκιβώτιο	khri·ma·to·ki·*vo*·ti·o
swimming pool	πισίνα	pi·*si*·na

Could I have (a/an) …, please?	Μπορώ να έχω … παρακαλώ;	bo·*ro* na *e*·kho … pa·ra·ka·*lo*
extra blanket	μια κουβέρτα ακόμη	mia ku·*ver*·ta a·*ko*·mi
my key	το κλειδί μου	to kli·*ţhi* mu
mosquito net	μια κουνουπιέρα	mia ku·nu·*pie*·ra
receipt	μια απόδειξη	mia a·*po*·ţhik·si

Is there hot water all day?
Υπάρχει ζεστό νερό όλη την ημέρα; — i·*par*·hi ze·*sto* ne·*ro* *o*·li tin i·*me*·ra

Is there a message for me?
Υπάρχει μήνυμα για μένα; — i·*par*·hi *mi*·ni·ma yia *me*·na

Can I leave a message for someone?
Μπορώ να αφήσω ένα μήνυμα για κάποιον; — bo·*ro* na a·*fi*·so *e*·na *mi*·ni·ma yia *ka*·pion

I'm locked out of my room.
Κλειδώθηκα έξω από το δωμάτιό μου. — kli·*ţho*·thi·ka *ek*·so a·*po* to ţho·*ma*·ti·o mu

complaints

παράπονα

It's too …	Είναι πάρα πολύ …	*i*·ne *pa*·ra po·*li* …
bright	φωτεινό	fo·ti·*no*
cold	κρύο	*kri*·o
dark	σκοτεινό	sko·ti·*no*
expensive	ακριβό	a·kri·*vo*
noisy	θορυβώδες	tho·ri·*vo*·ţhes
small	μικρό	mi·*kro*
The … doesn't work.	… δεν δουλεύει.	… ţhen ţhu·*le*·vi
air conditioner	Το ερκοντίσιον	to er·kon·*di*·si·on
fan	Ο ανεμιστήρας	o a·ne·mi·*sti*·ras
toilet	Η τουαλέτα	i tu·a·*le*·ta

Can I get another (blanket)?
Μπορώ να πάρω μια άλλη (κουβέρτα); — bo·*ro* na *pa*·ro mia *a*·li (ku·*ver*·ta)

This (pillow) isn't clean.
Αυτό (το μαξιλάρι) δεν είναι καθαρό. — af·*to* (to mak·si·*la*·ri) ţhen *i*·ne ka·tha·*ro*

a knock at the door …

Who is it?
Ποιος είναι; — pios *i*·ne

Just a moment.
Μια στιγμή. — mia stigh·*mi*

Come in.
Περάστε. — pe·*ra*·ste

Come back later, please.
Έλα αργότερα, παρακαλώ. — *e*·la ar·*gho*·te·ra pa·ra·ka·*lo*

checking out

αναχώρηση

What time is checkout?
Τι ώρα είναι η αναχώρηση; — ti *o*·ra *i*·ne i a·na·*kho*·ri·si

Can I have a late checkout?
Μπορώ να φύγω αργά; — bo·*ro* na *fi*·gho ar·*gha*

Can you call a taxi for me (for 11 o'clock)?
Μπορείτε να καλέσετε ένα ταξί (για τις έντεκα); — bo·*ri*·te na ka·*le*·se·te *e*·na tak·*si* (yia tis *e*·de·ka)

I'm leaving now.
Φεύγω τώρα. — *fev*·gho *to*·ra

Can I leave my bags here?
Μπορώ να αφήσω τις βαλίτσες μου εδώ; — bo·*ro* na a·*fi*·so tis va·*lit*·ses mu e·*ţho*

There's a mistake in the bill.
Υπάρχει κάποιο λάθος στο λογαριασμό. — i·*par*·hi *ka*·pio *la*·thos sto lo·gha·riaz·*mo*

Could I have my …, please?	Μπορώ να έχω … παρακλώ;	bo·*ro* na *e*·kho … pa·ra·ka·*lo*
deposit	την προκαταβολή μου	tin pro·ka·ta·vo·*li* mu
passport	το διαβατήριό μου	to ţhia·va·*ti*·rio mu
valuables	τα κοσμήματά μου	ta koz·*mi*·ma·*ta* mu

I'll be back …	Θα επιστρέψω …	tha e·pi·*strep*·so …
in (three) days	σε (τρεις) μέρες	se (tris) *me*·res
on (Tuesday)	την (Τρίτη)	tin *tri*·ti

I had a great stay, thank you.
Είχα υπέροχη διαμονή, ευχαριστώ. — *i*·kha i·*pe*·ro·hi ţhi·a·mo·*ni* ef·kha·ri·*sto*

I'll recommend it to my friends.
Θα το συστήσω στους φίλους μου. — tha to si·*sti*·so stus *fi*·lus mu

camping

κάμπινγκ

Do you have (a) …?	Έχετε …	*e*·he·te …
electricity	ηλεκτρισμό	i·lek·triz·*mo*
laundry	πλυντήριο	pli·*di*·ri·o
site	χώρο	*kho*·ro
shower facilities	εγκαταστάσεις για ντουζ	e·ga·ta·*sta*·sis yia duz
tents for hire	τέντες για νοίκιασμα	*te*·des yia *ni*·kiaz·ma

How much is it per …?	Πόσο κοστίζει για κάθε …;	*po*·so ko·*sti*·zi yia *ka*·the …
caravan	τροχόσπιτο	tro·*kho*·spi·to
person	άτομο	*a*·to·mo
tent	τέντα	*te*·da
vehicle	αυτοκίνητο	af·to·*ki*·ni·to

Can I camp here?
Μπορώ να κατασκηνώσω εδώ; — bo·*ro* na ka·ta·ski·*no*·so e·*ţho*

Can I park next to my tent?
Μπορώ να παρκάρω δίπλα στην τέντα μου; — bo·*ro* na par·*ka*·ro *ţhi*·pla stin *te*·da mu

Who do I ask to stay here?
Ποιον ρωτάω για να μείνω εδώ; — pion ro·*ta*·o yia na *mi*·no e·*ţho*

Could I borrow …?
Μπορώ να δανειστώ …; — bo·*ro* na ţha·ni·*sto* …

Is it coin-operated?
Λειτουργεί με κέρματα; — li·tur·*yi* me *ker*·ma·ta

Is the water drinkable?
Είναι το νερό πόσιμο; — *i*·ne to ne·*ro* *po*·si·mo

a chance to be polite

When you're making a request, make it sound more polite by starting your question with μήπως *mi*·pos, the equivalent of the English 'Do you, by any chance, ...?'.

Do you, by any chance, have a room with a view?

Μήπως έχετε ένα δωμάτιο με θέα;	*mi*·pos *e*·hete *e*·na ţho·*ma*·tio me *the*·a

See the **phrasebuilder** for more on requests.

renting

νοικιάζοντας

I'm here about the ... for rent.	Είμαι εδώ για το ... που νοικιάζεται.	*i*·me e·*ţho* yia to ... pu ni·*kia*·ze·te
Do you have a/an ... for rent?	Έχεις ένα ... για νοίκιασμα;	*e*·his *e*·na ... yia *ni*·kiaz·ma
apartment	διαμέρισμα	ţhi·a·*me*·riz·ma
house	σπίτι	*spi*·ti
room	δωμάτιο	ţho·*ma*·ti·o
I'm here about the ... for rent.	Είμαι εδώ για την ... που νοικιάζεται.	*i*·me e·*ţho* yia tin ... pu ni·*kia*·ze·te
Do you have a ... for rent?	Έχεις μια ... για νοίκιασμα;	*e*·his mia ... yia *ni*·kiaz·ma
cabin	καμπίνα	ka·*bi*·na
villa	έπαυλη	*e*·pav·li
furnished	με έπιπλα	me *e*·pi·pla
partly furnished	με λίγα έπιπλα	me *li*·gha *e*·pi·pla
unfurnished	χωρίς έπιπλα	kho·*ris* *e*·pi·pla

staying with locals

διαμονή με τους ντόπιους

Can I stay at your place?

Μπορώ να μείνω στο σπίτι σου;	bo·*ro* na *mi*·no sto *spi*·ti su

Is there anything I can do to help?

Μπορώ να κάνω κάτι για να βοηθήσω;	bo·*ro* na *ka*·no *ka*·ti yia na vo·i·*thi*·so

I have my own …	Έχω το δικό μου …	*e*·kho to ţhi·*ko* mu …
mattress	στρώμα	*stro*·ma
sleeping bag	σλίπινγκ μπαγκ	*sli*·ping bag

Can I …?	Μπορώ να …;	bo·*ro* na …
bring anything for the meal	φέρω κάτι για το φαγητό	*fe*·ro *ka*·ti yia to fa·yi·*to*
do the dishes	πλύνω τα πιάτα	*pli*·no ta *pia*·ta
set/clear the table	στρώσω/μαζέψω το τραπέζι	*stro*·so/ma·*zep*·so to tra·*pe*·zi
take out the rubbish	βγάλω έξω τα σκουπίδια	*vgha*·lo *ek*·so ta sku·*pi*·ţhia

Thanks for your hospitality.

Ευχαριστώ για τη φιλοξενία σας.	ef·kha·ri·*sto* yia ti fi·lok·se·*ni*·a sas

If you're dining with your hosts, see **eating out**, page 157, for additional phrases.

foreign visitors

Punctuality for social engagements is not taken as seriously as you might be used to. An invitation for 9pm means that most people won't show up before 9.30pm. An evening coffee can sometimes extend to dinner, and not end until after midnight.

looking for …

ψάχνοντας για …

Where's …?	Πού είναι …;	pu *i*·ne …
a department store	ένα κατάστημα	*e*·na ka·*ta*·sti·ma
the flea market	το παζάρι	to pa·*za*·ri
the food market	η αγορά τροφίμων	i a·gho·*ra* tro·*fi*·mon
a kiosk	ένα περίπτερο	*e*·na pe·*rip*·te·ro
the street market	η λαϊκή αγορά	i la·i·*ki* a·gho·*ra*
a supermarket	ένα σούπερμάρκετ	*e*·na *su*·per *mar*·ket
a souvenir shop	ένα κατάστημα με σουβενίρ	*e*·na ka·*ta*·sti·ma me su·ve·*nir*

On which day is the street market held?
Ποια μέρα έχει λαϊκή; — pia *me*·ra *e*·hi la·i·*ki*

Where can I buy (a padlock)?
Πού μπορώ να αγοράσω (μια κλειδαριά); — pu bo·*ro* na a·gho·*ra*·so (mia kli·ţha·*ria*)

For phrases on directions, see **directions**, page 63.

listen for …

Μπορώ να σας βοηθήσω; bo·*ro* na sas vo·i·*thi*·so	**Can I help you?**
Τίποτε άλλο; *ti*·po·te *a*·lo	**Anything else?**
Όχι, δεν έχουμε. *o*·hi ţhen *e*·khu·me	**No, we don't have any.**
Να το τυλίξω; na to ti·*lik*·so	**Shall I wrap it?**

making a purchase

αγοράζοντας κάτι

I'm just looking.
Απλά κοιτάζω. — a·*pla* ki·*ta*·zo

I'd like to buy (an adaptor plug).
Θα ήθελα να αγοράσω (ένα μετασχηματιστή). — tha *i*·the·la na a·gho·*ra*·so (*e*·na me·ta·shi·ma·ti·*sti*)

Can I look at it?
Μπορώ να το κοιτάξω; — bo·*ro* na to ki·*tak*·so

Do you have any others?
Έχετε άλλα; — *e*·he·te *a*·la

How much is it?
Πόσο κάνει; — *po*·so *ka*·ni

Can you write down the price?
Μπορείς να γράψεις την τιμή; — bo·*ris* na *ghrap*·sis tin ti·*mi*

Does it have a guarantee?
Έχει εγγύηση; — *e*·hi e·*gi*·i·si

Could I have it wrapped?
Μπορείς να μου το τυλίξεις; — bo·*ris* na mu to ti·*lik*·sis

Could I have a bag/receipt, please?
Μπορώ να έχω μια τσάντα/ απόδειξη, παρακαλώ; — bo·*ro* na *e*·kho mia *tsa*·da/ a·*po*·ţhik·si pa·ra·ka·*lo*

Can I have it sent overseas?
Μπορείς να το στείλεις στο εξωτερικό; — bo·*ris* na to *sti*·lis sto ek·so·te·ri·*ko*

Can you order it for me?
Μπορείς να το παραγγείλεις για μένα; — bo·*ris* na to pa·ra·*gi*·lis yia *me*·na

Can I pick it up later?
Μπορώ να το πραλάβω αργότερα; — bo·*ro* na to pa·ra·*la*·vo ar·*gho*·te·ra

It's faulty.
Είναι ελαττωματικό. — *i*·ne e·la·to·ma·ti·*ko*

local talk

bargain	ευκαιρία f	ef·ke·*ri*·a
rip-off	γδάρσιμο n	*ghţhar*·si·mo
sale	έκπτωση f	*ek*·pto·si
specials	προσφορές f pl	pros·fo·*res*

Do you accept ...?	Δέχεστε ...;	*ţhe*·he·ste ...
credit cards	πιστωτικές κάρτες	pi·sto·ti·*kes* *kar*·tes
debit cards	χρεωτικές κάρτες	khre·o·ti·*kes* *kar*·tes
travellers cheques	ταξιδιωτικές επιταγές	tak·si·ţhio·ti·*kes* e·pi·ta·*yes*
I'd like ..., please.	Θα ήθελα ..., παρακαλώ.	tha *i*·the·la ... pa·ra·ka·*lo*
a refund	επιστροφή χρημάτων	e·pi·stro·*fi* khri·*ma*·ton
my change	τα ρέστα μου	ta *re*·sta mu
to return this	να επιστρέψω αυτό	na e·pi·*strep*·so af·*to*

bargaining

παζάρεμα

That's too expensive.
Είναι πάρα πολύ ακριβό. *i*·ne *pa*·ra po·*li* a·kri·*vo*

I don't have that much money.
Δεν έχω τόσα πολλά χρήματα. ţhen *e*·kho *to*·sa po·*la* *khri*·ma·ta

Do you have something cheaper?
Έχεις κάτι πιο φτηνό; *e*·his *ka*·ti pio fti·*no*

Can you lower the price?

Μπορείς να κατεβάσεις την τιμή;	bo·*ris* na ka·te·*va*·sis tin ti·*mi*

How much for (two)?

Πόσο κάνει για (δύο);	*po*·so *ka*·ni yia (*ţhi*·o)

I'll give you (five euros).

Θα σου δώσω (πέντε ευρώ).	tha su *ţho*·so (*pe*·de ev·*ro*)

books & reading

βιβλία και διάβασμα

Is there an English-language bookshop/section?

Υπάρχει ένα βιβλιοπωλείο/ τμήμα Αγγλικής γλώσσας;	i·*par*·hi *e*·na viv·li·o·po·*li*·o/ *tmi*·ma ang·gli·*kis ghlo*·sas

Can you recommend a book for me?

Μπορείς να μου συστήσεις ένα βιβλίο;	bo·*ris* na mu si·*sti*·sis *e*·na viv·*li*·o

Do you have Lonely Planet guidebooks?

Έχετε βιβλία-οδηγούς του Λόνλι Πλάνετ;	*e*·he·te viv·*li*·a·o·ţhi·*ghus* tu *lon*·li *pla*·net

Do you have ...?	Έχεις ένα ...;	*e*·his *e*·na ...
a book by (Nikos Kazantzakis)	βιβλίο (του Νίκου Καζαντζάκη)	viv·*li*·o (tu *ni*·ku ka·za·*dza*·ki)
an entertainment guide	οδηγό διασκεδάσεων	o·ţhi·*gho* ţhias·ke·*ţha*·se·on

I'd like a ...	Θα ήθελα ...	tha *i*·the·la ...
dictionary	ένα λεξικό	*e*·na lek·si·*ko*
newspaper (in English)	μια εφημερίδα (στα Αγγλικά)	mia e·fi·me·*ri*·ţha (sta ang·gli·*ka*)
notepad	ένα μπλοκ για σημειώσεις	*e*·na blok yia si·mi·*o*·sis

clothes

ρούχα

My size is …	Το νούμερό μου είναι …	to *nu*·me·ro mu *i*·ne …
(40)	(σαράντα)	(sa·*ra*·da)
small	μικρό	mi·*kro*
medium	μεσαίο	me·*se*·o
large	μεγάλο	me·*gha*·lo

Can I try it on?
Μπορώ να το προβάρω; — bo·*ro* na to pro·*va*·ro

It doesn't fit.
Δε μου κάνει. — ţhe mu *ka*·ni

electronic goods

ηλεκτρονικά είδη

Where can I buy duty-free electronic goods?
Πού μπορώ να αγοράσω αφορολόγητα ηλεκτρονικά είδη; — pu bo·*ro* na a·gho·*ra*·so a·fo·ro·*lo*·yi·ta i·lek·tro·ni·*ka* *i*·ţhi

Is this the latest model?
Είναι αυτό το τελευταίο μοντέλο; — *i*·ne af·*to* to te·lef·*te*·o mo·*de*·lo

Is this (240) volts?
Είναι αυτό (240) βολτ; — *i*·ne af·*to* (ţhia·*ko*·sia sa·*ra*·da) volt

I need an adaptor plug.
Χρειάζομαι ένα μετασχηματιστή. — khri·*a*·zo·me *e*·na me·ta·shi·ma·ti·*sti*

boy-words & girl-words

Some phrases in this book are marked with m/f – they refer as a rule to the speaker. Follow the m (masculine) form if you're a 'he' and the f (feminine) form if you're a 'she'.

hairdressing

κομμωτήριο

I'd like (a) ...	Θα ήθελα ένα ...	tha *i*·the·la *e*·na ...
blow wave	στέγνωμα με πιστολάκι	*stegh*·no·ma me pis·to·*la*·ki
colour	βάψιμο	*vap*·si·mo
haircut	κούρεμα	*ku*·re·ma
my beard trimmed	ψαλίδισμα στο μούσι μου	psa·*li*·ţhiz·ma sto *mu*·si mu
shave	ξύρισμα	*ksi*·riz·ma

Don't cut it too short.
Μην τα κόψεις πολύ κοντά. min ta *kop*·sis po·*li* ko·*da*

Please use a new blade.
Παρακαλώ χρησιμοποίησε καινούργιο ξυράφι. pa·ra·ka·*lo* khri·si·mo·*pi*·i·se ke·*nur*·yio ksi·*ra*·fi

Shave it all off!
Ξύρισέ τα όλα. *ksi*·ri·*se* ta *o*·la

I should never have let you near me!
Δεν θα έπρεπε ποτέ να σε αφήσω κοντά μου! ţhen tha *e*·pre·pe po·*te* na se a·*fi*·so ko·*da* mu

barber	κουρέας m	ku·*re*·as
beauty salon	ινστιτούτο αισθητικής n	in·sti·*tu*·to es·thi·ti·*kis*
for both sexes	και για τα δύο φύλα	ke yia ta *ţhi*·o *fi*·la
men's hairdresser	κομμωτής για άντρες m	ko·mo·*tis* yia *a*·dres

women's hairdresser	κομμωτής για γυναίκες m	ko·mo·*tis* yia yi·*ne*·kes

music & DVD

μουσική και DVD

I'm looking for something by (Anna Vissi).
Ψάχνω για κάτι (της Άννας Βίσση). — *psakh*·no yia *ka*·ti (tis *a*·na *vi*·si)

What's his/her best recording?
Ποια είναι η καλύτερη ηχογράφησή του/της; — pia *i*·ne i ka·*li*·te·ri i·kho·*ghra*·fi·*si* tu/tis

Does this work on all DVD players?
Παίζει σε όλα τα DVD; — *pe*·zi se *o*·la ta di·vi·*di*

video & photography

βίντεο και φωτογραφικά

Can you ...?	Μπορείς να ...;	bo·*ris* na ...
develop digital photos	εμφανίσεις ψηφιακές φωτογραφίες	em·fa·*ni*·sis psi·fi·a·*kes* fo·to·ghra·*fi*·es
develop this film	εμφανίσεις αυτό το φιλμ	em·fa·*ni*·sis af·*to* to film
load my film	βάλεις το φιλμ στη μηχανή μου	*va*·lis to film sti mi·kha·*ni* mu
recharge the battery for my digital camera	φορτίσεις την μπαταρία για την ψηφιακή μου μηχανή	for·*ti*·sis tin ba·ta·*ri*·a yia tin psi·fi·a·*ki* mu mi·kha·*ni*
transfer photos from my camera to CD	μεταφέρεις φωτογραφίες από την φωτογραφική μου μηχανή στο CD	me·ta·*fe*·ris fo·to·ghra·*fi*·es a·*po* ti fo·to·ghra·fi·*ki* mu mi·kha·*ni* sto si·*di*

Do you have … for this camera?	Έχεις … για αυτή τη φωτογραφική μηχανή;	e·his … yia af·*ti* ti fo·to·ghra·fi·*ki* mi·kha·*ni*
batteries	μπαταρίες	ba·ta·*ri*·es
memory cards	κάρτες μνήμης	*kar*·tes *mni*·mis

I need a cable to connect my camera to a computer.
Χρειάζομαι ένα καλώδιο για να συνδέσω τη μηχανή μου στο κομπιούτερ. — khri·*a*·zo·me *e*·na ka·*lo*·ţhi·o yia na sin·*ţhe*·so ti mi·kha·*ni* mu sto kom·*piu*·ter

I need a cable to recharge this battery.
Χρειάζομαι ένα καλώδιο για να φορτίσω αυτή τη μπαταρία. — khri·*a*·zo·me *e*·na ka·*lo*·ţhi·o yia na for·*ti*·so af·*ti* ti ba·ta·*ri*·a

Do you have disposable (underwater) cameras?
Έχεις (υποβρύχιες) φωτογραφικές μηχανές μιας χρήσης; — *e*·his (i·pov·*ri*·hi·es) fo·to·ghra·fi·*kes* mi·kha·*nes* mias *khri*·sis

When will it be ready?
Πότε θα είναι έτοιμο; — *po*·te tha *i*·ne *e*·ti·mo

How much is it?
Πόσο κάνει; — *po*·so *ka*·ni

I need a passport photo taken.
Θέλω να βγάλω φωτογραφία για διαβατήριο. — *the*·lo na *vga*·lo fo·to·ghra·*fi*·a yia ţhia·va·*ti*·ri·o

I'm not happy with these photos.
Δεν είμαι ικανοποιημένος/ικανοποιημένη με αυτές τις φωτογραφίες. **m/f** — ţhen *i*·me i·ka·no·pi·i·*me*·nos/ i·ka·no·pi·i·*me*·ni me af·*tes* tis fo·to·ghra·*fi*·es

I don't want to pay the full price.

Δεν θέλω να πληρώσω ολόκληρη την τιμή.	ţhen *the*·lo na pli·*ro*·so o·*lo*·kli·ri tin ti·*mi*

repairs

επισκευές

Can I have my … repaired here?	Μπορώ να επισκευάσω εδώ …;	bo·*ro* na e·pi·ske·*va*·so e·*ţho* …
backpack	το σάκο μου	to *sa*·ko mu
camera	τη φωτογραφική μηχανή μου	ti fo·to·ghra·fi·*ki* mi·kha·*ni* mu
shoes	τα παπούτσια μου	ta pa·*pu*·tsia mu
sunglasses	τα γιαλιά μου του ήλιου	ta yia·*lia* mu tu *i*·liu

When will my … be ready?	Πότε θα είναι έτοιμα τα …;	*po*·te tha *i*·ne e·ti·ma ta …
glasses	γιαλιά μου	yia·*lia* mu
shoes	παπούτσια μου	pa·*put*·sia mu
sunglasses	γιαλιά μου του ήλιου	yia·*lia* mu tu *i*·liu

When will my camera be ready?

Πότε θα είναι έτοιμη η φωτογραφική μηχανή μου;	*po*·te tha *i*·ne *e*·ti·mi i fo·to·ghra·fi·*ki* mi·kha·*ni* mu

When will my backpack be ready?

Πότε θα είναι έτοιμος ο σάκος μου;	*po*·te tha *i*·ne *e*·ti·mos o *sa*·kos mu

souvenirs		
backgammon board	τάβλι n	*tav*·li
baskets	καλάθια n pl	ka·*la*·thia
bouzouki	μπουζούκι n	bu·*zu*·ki
bronzeware	μπρούτζινα n pl	*bru*·dzi·na
carpets	χαλιά n pl	kha·*lia*
ceramics	κεραμικά n pl	ke·ra·mi·*ka*
copperware	χάλκινα n pl	*khal*·ki·na
cushion covers	μαξιλαροθήκες f pl	mak·si·la·ro·*thi*·kes
evil eye (blue eye warding off evil spirits)	φυλαχτό n	fi·lakh·*to*
icons	εικόνες f pl	i·*ko*·nes
lace	δαντέλλα f	ţhan·*te*·la
leather work	δερμάτινα n pl	ţher·*ma*·ti·na
pottery	είδη αγγειοπλαστικής n pl	*i*·ţhi a·gi·o·pla·sti·*kis*
rugs	τάπητες m pl	*ta*·pi·tes
sculptures	γλυπτά n pl	ghlip·*ta*
worry beads	κομπολόγια n pl	ko·bo·*lo*·yia
woven shoulder bag	υφαντή τσάντα ώμου f	i·fa·*di tsa*·da *o*·mu
... jewellery	... κοσμήματα n pl	... koz·*mi*·ma·ta
filigree	φιλιγκράν	fi·li·*gran*
gold	χρυσά	khri·*sa*
silver	ασημένια	a·si·*me*·nia

communications
επικοινωνίες

post office
ταχυδρομείο

I want to send a …	Θέλω να στείλω …	*the*·lo na *sti*·lo …
letter	ένα γράμμα	*e*·na *ghra*·ma
parcel	ένα δέμα	*e*·na *ţhe*·ma
postcard	μια κάρτα	mia *kar*·ta
I want to buy a/an …	Θέλω να αγοράσω ένα …	*the*·lo na a·gho·*ra*·so *e*·na …
envelope	φάκελο	*fa*·ke·lo
stamp	γραμματόσημο	ghra·ma·*to*·si·mo
customs declaration	δήλωση τελωνείου f	*ţhi*·lo·si te·lo·*ni*·u
domestic a	εσωτερικό	e·so·te·ri·*ko*
fragile a	εύθραυστο	*ef*·thraf·sto
international a	διεθνές	ţhi·eth·*nes*
mail	αλληλογραφία f	a·li·lo·ghra·*fi*·a
mailbox	ταχυδρομικό κουτί n	ta·hi·ţhro·mi·*ko* ku·*ti*
postcode	ταχυδρομικός τομέας m	ta·hi·ţhro·mi·*kos* to·*me*·as

snail mail

airmail	αεροπορικώς	a·e·ro·po·ri·*kos*
express mail	εξπρές	eks·*pres*
registered mail	συστημένο	si·sti·*me*·no
sea mail	ατμοπλοϊκώς	at·mo·plo·i·*kos*
surface mail	δια ξηράς	ţhi·*a* ksi·*ras*

Please send it by airmail to (Australia).

Παρακαλώ στείλτε το αεροπορικώς στην (Αυστραλία). — pa·ra·ka·*lo* *stil*·te to a·e·ro·po·ri·*kos* stin (af·stra·*li*·a)

Please send it by surface mail to (New Zealand).

Παρακαλώ στείλτε το δια ξηράς στην (Νέα Ζηλανδία). — pa·ra·ka·*lo* *stil*·te to ţhi·*a* ksi·*ras* stin (*ne*·a zi·nan·*thi*·a)

It contains (souvenirs).

Περιέχει (σουβενίρ). — pe·ri·*e*·hi (su·ve·*nir*)

Where's the poste restante section?

Πού είναι το ποστ ρεστάντ; — pu *i*·ne to post re·*stant*

Is there any mail for me?

Υπάρχουν γράμματα για μένα; — i·*par*·khun *ghra*·ma·ta yia *me*·na

I'd like to collect a parcel.

Θα ήθελα να παραλάβω ένα δέμα. — tha *i*·the·la na pa·ra·*la*·vo *e*·na *ţhe*·ma

Do you have Internet services?

Έχετε υπηρεσία Διαδικτύου; — *e*·he·te i·pi·re·*si*·a ţhi·a·ţhik·*ti*·u

medusa

Medusa, famous for turning mortals to stone, had hair much like the tentacles of a jellyfish. In fact the jellyfish is named after her in Greek (μέδουσα *me*·ţhu·sa), French (*méduse* me·*dooz*) and Spanish (*medusa* me·*doo*·sa), to name just a few languages.

phone

τηλέφωνο

What's your phone number?
Τι αριθμό τηλεφώνου έχεις; — ti a·rith·*mo* ti·le·*fo*·nu *e*·his

Where's the nearest public phone?
Πού είναι το πιο κοντινό δημόσιο τηλέφωνο; — pu *i*·ne to pio ko·di·*no* ţhi·*mo*·si·o ti·*le*·fo·no

Where's the nearest telephone office?
Πού είναι το πιο κοντινό τηλεφωνικό κέντρο; — pu *i*·ne to pio ko·di·*no* ti·le·fo·ni·*ko* *ke*·dro

Do you have a metered phone?
Έχεις τηλέφωνο με μετρητή; — *e*·his ti·*le*·fo·no me me·tri·*ti*

Can I look at a phone book?
Μπορώ να κοιτάξω τον τηλεφωνικό κατάλογο; — bo·*ro* na ki·*tak*·so ton ti·le·fo·ni·*ko* ka·*ta*·lo·gho

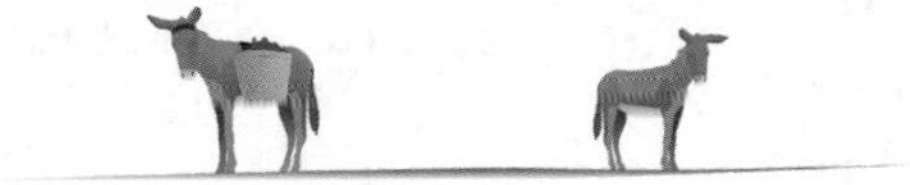

I want to …	Θέλω να …	*the*·lo na …
buy a (2000 unit) phonecard	αγοράσω μια τηλεφωνική κάρτα (2000 μονάδων)	a·gho·*ra*·so mia ti·le·fo·ni·*ki* *kar*·ta (ţhi·*o* hi·*lia*·ţhon mo·*na*·ţhon)
buy a discount card	αγοράσω μια κάρτα με έκπτωση	a·gho·*ra*·so mia *kar*·ta me *ek*·pto·si
call (Singapore)	τηλεφωνήσω (στη Σιγγαπούρη)	ti·le·fo·*ni*·so (sti sing·ga·*pu*·ri)
make a (local) call	κάμω ένα (τοπικό) τηλέφωνο	*ka*·mo *e*·na (to·pi·*ko*) ti·*le*·fo·no
reverse the charges	αντιστρέψω τα έξοδα	a·di·*strep*·so ta *ek*·so·ţha
speak for (three) minutes	μιλήσω για (τρία) λεπτά	mi·*li*·so yia (*tri*·a) lep·*ta*

listen for …

Ποιος μιλάει; pios mi·*la*·i	**Who's calling?**
Σε ποιον θέλετε να μιλήσετε; se pion *the*·le·te na mi·*li*·se·te	**Who do you want to speak to?**
Μια στιγμή. mia stigh·*mi*	**One moment.**
Δεν είναι εδώ. ţhen *i*·ne e·*ţho*	**He's/She's not here.**
Λάθος αριθμός. *la*·thos a·rith·*mos*	**Wrong number.**

How much does … cost?	Πόσο κοστίζει …;	*po*·so ko·*sti*·zi …
a (three)-minute call	ένα τηλεφώνημα (τριών) λεπτών	*e*·na ti·le·*fo*·ni·ma (tri·*on*) lep·*ton*
each extra minute	κάθε έξτρα λεπτό	*ka*·the *eks*·tra lep·*to*

The number is …
Ο αριθμός είναι … — o a·rith·*mos* *i*·ne …

What's the code for (New Zealand)?
Ποιος είναι ο κωδικός αριθμός για (τη Νέα Ζηλανδία); — pios *i*·ne o ko·ţhi·*kos* a·rith·*mos* yia (ti *ne*·a zi·lan·*ţhi*·a)

It's engaged.
Είναι κατειλημμένη. — *i*·ne ka·ti·li·*me*·ni

I've been cut off.
Με διέκοψαν. — me ţhi·*e*·kop·san

The connection's bad.
Η σύνδεση είναι κακή. — i *sin*·ţhe·si *i*·ne ka·*ki*

Hello.
Εμπρός. — e·*bros*

It's …
Είμαι … — *i*·me …

Is … there?
Είναι … εκεί; — *i*·ne … e·*ki*

Can I speak to …?
Μπορώ να μιλήσω με …; — bo·*ro* na mi·*li*·so me …

Can I leave a message?
Μπορώ να αφήσω ένα μήνυμα; — bo·*ro* na a·*fi*·so *e*·na *mi*·ni·ma

Please tell him/her I called.
Παρακαλώ πες του/της ότι τηλεφώνησα. — pa·ra·ka·*lo* pes tu/tis *o*·ti ti·le·*fo*·ni·sa

My number is …
Ο αριθμός μου είναι … — o a·rith·*mos* mu *i*·ne …

I don't have a contact number.
Δεν έχω αριθμό για επικοινωνία. — ţhen *e*·kho a·rith·*mo* yia e·pi·ki·no·*ni*·a

I'll call back later.
Θα τηλεφωνήσω αργότερα. — tha ti·le·fo·*ni*·so ar·*gho*·te·ra

mobile/cell phone

κινητό τηλέφωνο

I'd like a …	Θα ήθελα …	tha *i*·the·la …
charger for my phone	ένα φορτιστή για το τηλέφωνό μου	*e*·na for·ti·*sti* yia to ti·*le*·fo·*no* mu
mobile/cell phone for hire	να νοικιάσω ένα κινητό τηλέφωνο	na ni·*kia*·so *e*·na ki·ni·*to* ti·*le*·fo·no
prepaid mobile/ cell phone	ένα προπληρωμένο κινητό τηλέφωνο	*e*·na pro·pli·ro·*me*·no ki·ni·*to* ti·*le*·fo·no
SIM card for your network	μια κάρτα SIM για το δίκτυό σας	mia *kar*·ta sim yia to *ţhik*·tio sas

What are the rates?
Ποιες είναι οι τιμές; — pies *i*·ne i ti·*mes*

(40c) per (30) seconds.
(40λ) για (30) δευτερόλεπτα. — (sa·*ra*·da lep·*ta*) yia (tri·*a*·da) ţhef·te·*ro*·lep·ta

the internet

το διαδίκτυο

Where's the local Internet cafe?
Πού είναι το τοπικό καφενείο με διαδίκτυο; — pu *i*·ne to to·pi·*ko* ka·fe·*ni*·o me ţhi·a·*ţhik*·ti·o

I'd like to ...	Θα ήθελα να ...	tha *i*·the·la na ...
check my email	ελέγξω την ηλεκτρονική αλληλογραφία μου	e·*leng*·so tin i·lek·tro·ni·*ki* a·li·lo·ghra·*fi*·a mu
get Internet access	έχω πρόσβαση στο Διαδίκτυο	*e*·kho *pros*·va·si sto ţhi·a·*ţhik*·ti·o
use a printer	χρησιμοποιήσω έναν εκτυπωτή	khri·si·mo·pi·*i*·so *e*·nan ek·ti·po·*ti*
use a scanner	χρησιμοποιήσω ένα σκάνερ	khri·si·mo·pi·*i*·so *e*·na *ska*·ner

Do you have ...?	Έχετε ...;	*e*·he·te ...
Macs	Κομπιούτερ Mac	kom·*piu*·ter mak
PCs	Κομπιούτερ PC	kom·*piu*·ter pi si
a Zip drive	Zip drive	zip *dra*·iv

How much per ...?	Πόσο κοστίζει κάθε ...;	*po*·so ko·*sti*·zi *ka*·the ...
hour	ώρα	*o*·ra
page	σελίδα	se·*li*·ţha

How do I log on?
Πώς μπαίνω μέσα; — pos *be*·no *me*·sa

Please change it to the (English)-language setting.
Παρακαλώ άλλαξέ το στην (αγγλική) γλώσσα. — pa·ra·ka·*lo a*·lak·*se* to stin (ang·gli·*ki*) *glo*·sa

Do you have (English) keyboards?
έχεις (Αγγλικό) πληκτρολόγιο; — *e*·his (ang·gli·*ko)* plik·tro·*lo*·yi·o

It's crashed.
κατέρρευσε. — ka·*te*·ref·se

I've finished.
Τελείωσα. — te·*li*·o·sa

PRACTICAL

banking

συνδιαλλαγή με τράπεζα

What time does the bank open?		
Τι ώρα ανοίγει η τράπεζα;		ti *o*·ra a·*ni*·yi i *tra*·pe·za
Where's a/an …?	Πού είναι …;	pu *i*·ne …
automated teller machine	μια αυτόματη μηχανή χρημάτων	mia af·*to*·ma·ti mi·kha·*ni* khri·*ma*·ton
foreign exchange office	ένα γραφείο αλλαγής χρημάτων	*e*·na ghra·*fi*·o a·la·*yis* khri·*ma*·ton
Where can I …?	Πού μπορώ να …;	pu bo·*ro* na …
I'd like to …	Θα ήθελα να …	tha *i*·the·la na …
cash a cheque	εξαργυρώσω μια επιταγή	ek·sar·yi·*ro*·so mia e·pi·ta·*yi*
change money	αλλάξω χρήματα	a·*lak*·so *khri*·ma·ta
change a travellers cheque	αλλάξω μια ταξιδιωτική επιταγή	a·*lak*·so mia tak·si·ţhio·ti·*ki* e·pi·ta·*yi*
get a cash advance	κάμω μια ανάληψη σε μετρητά	*ka*·mo mia a·*na*·lip·si se me·tri·*ta*
withdraw money	αποσύρω χρήματα	a·po·*si*·ro *khri*·ma·ta
What's the …?	Ποια είναι … ;	pia *i*·ne …
exchange rate	η τιμή συναλλάγματος	i ti·*mi* si·na·*lagh*·ma·tos
charge for that	η χρέωση για αυτό	i *khre*·o·si yia af·*to*

Has my money arrived yet?
Έχουν φτάσει τα χρήματά μου; — *e*·khun *fta*·si ta *khri*·ma·*ta* mu

How long will it take to arrive?
Σε πόσο καιρό θα φτάσουν; — se *po*·so ke·*ro* tha *fta*·sun

The automated teller machine took my card.
Η αυτόματη μηχανή χρημάτων κράτησε την κάρτα μου. — i af·*to*·ma·ti mi·kha·*ni* khri·*ma*·ton *kra*·ti·se tin *kar*·ta mu

I've forgotten my PIN.
Ξέχασα τον κωδικό αριθμό μου. — *kse*·ha·sa ton ko·ţhi·*ko* a·rith·*mo* mu

Can I use my credit card to withdraw money?
Μπορώ να χρησιμοποιήσω την πιστωτική μου κάρτα για να αποσύρω χρήματα; — bo·*ro* na khri·si·mo·pi·*i*·so tin pi·sto·ti·*ki* mu *kar*·ta yia na a·po·*si*·ro *khri*·ma·ta

listen for ...

διαβατήριο n	ţhia·va·*ti*·ri·o	**passport**
ταυτότητα f	taf·*to*·ti·ta	**identification**

Δεν μπορούμε να το κάνουμε αυτό.
ţhen bo·*ru*·me na to *ka*·nu·me af·*to* — **We can't do that.**

Τελείωσαν τα χρήματά σας.
te·*li*·o·san ta *khri*·ma·*ta* sas — **You have no funds left.**

Υπάρχει ένα πρόβλημα.
i·*par*·hi *e*·na *prov*·li·ma — **There's a problem.**

Υπογράψτε εδώ.
i·po·*ghrap*·ste e·*ţho* — **Sign here.**

sightseeing
περιήγηση σε αξιοθέατα

I'd like a/an …	Θα ήθελα …	tha *i*·the·la …
audio set	ακουστικά	a·ku·sti·*ka*
catalogue	ένα κατάλογο	*e*·na ka·*ta*·lo·gho
guide	έναν οδηγό	*e*·nan o·ţhi·*gho*
guidebook in (English)	έναν οδηγό στα (Αγγλικά)	*e*·nan o·ţhi·*gho* sta (ang·gli·*ka*)
(local) map	ένα (τοπικό) χάρτη	*e*·na (to·pi·*ko*) *khar*·ti

Do you have information on … sights?	Έχετε πληροφορίες για … χώρους;	*e*·he·te pli·ro·fo·*ri*·es yia … *kho*·rus
ancient	αρχαίους	ar·*he*·us
archaic	αρχαϊκούς	ar·kha·i·*kus*
archeological	αρχαιολογικούς	ar·he·o·lo·yi·*kus*
architectural	αρχιτεκτονικούς	ar·hi·tek·to·ni·*kus*
Byzantine	Βυζαντινούς	vi·za·di·*nus*
classical	κλασσικούς	kla·si·*kus*
cultural	πολιτιστικούς	po·li·ti·sti·*kus*
Hellenistic	Ελληνιστικούς	e·li·ni·sti·*kus*
historical	ιστορικούς	i·sto·ri·*kus*
neoclassical	νεοκλασσικούς	ne·o·kla·si·*kus*
Orthodox	Ορθόδοξους	or·*tho*·dok·sus
Ottoman	Οθωμανικούς	o·tho·ma·ni·*kus*
religious	θρησκευτικούς	thris·kef·ti·*kus*
Roman	Ρωμαϊκούς	ro·ma·i·*kus*

signs

Ανδρών	an·*ţhron*	**Men**
Είσοδος	*i*·so·ţhos	**Entrance**
Έξοδος	*ek*·so·ţhos	**Exit**
Τουαλέτες	tu·a·*le*·tes	**Toilets**
Γυναικών	yi·ne·*kon*	**Women**

I'd like to see (the) …	Θα ήθελα να δω …	tha *i*·the·la na ţho …
Acropolis	την Ακτόπολη	tin ak·*ro*·po·li
amphitheatre	το αμφιθέατρο	to am·fi·*the*·a·tro
Archeological Museum	το Αρχαιολογικό Μουσείο	to ar·he·o·lo·yi·*ko* mu·*si*·o
Byzantine frescoes	Βυζαντινά φρέσκο	vi·za·di·*na* *fres*·ko
labyrinth	τον λαβύρινθο	ton la·*vi*·rin·tho
mosaics	τα μωσαϊκά	ta mo·sa·i·*ka*
Mt Athos monasteries	τα μοναστήρια του Αγίου Όρους	ta mo·na·*sti*·ria tu a·*yi*·u *o*·rus
Mycaenian tombs	Μυκηναϊκούς τάφους	mi·ki·na·i·*kus* *ta*·fus
oracle of Delphi	το μαντείο των Δελφών	to ma·*di*·o ton ţhel·*fon*
palace	το παλάτι	to pa·*la*·ti
ruins	τα ερείπια	ta e·*ri*·pi·a
sculptures	τα γλυπτά	ta ghlip·*ta*
statues	τα αγάλματα	ta a·*ghal*·ma·ta
temple	το ναό	to na·*o*

What's that?
Τι είναι εκείνο; — ti *i*·ne e·*ki*·no

Who made it?
Ποιος το έκαμε; — pios to *e*·ka·me

How old is it?
Πόσο χρονώ είναι; — *po*·so khro·*no* *i*·ne

When was this discovered?
Πότε ανακαλύφτηκε αυτό; — *po*·te a·na·ka·*lif*·ti·ke af·*to*

When were the excavations done?
Πότε έγιναν οι ανασκαφές; — *po*·te *e*·yi·nan i a·nas·ka·*fes*

Could you take a photograph of me?
Μπορείς να μου πάρεις μια φωτογραφία; — bo·*ris* na mu *pa*·ris mia fo·to·ghra·*fi*·a

Can I take a photo (of you)?
Μπορώ να (σου) πάρω μια φωτογραφία; — bo·*ro* na (su) *pa*·ro mia fo·to·ghra·*fi*·a

getting in

είσοδος

What time does it open?
Τι ώρα ανοίγει; — ti *o*·ra a·*ni*·yi

What time does it close?
Τι ώρα κλείνει; — ti *o*·ra *kli*·ni

Is it open every day?
Είναι ανοιχτό κάθε μέρα; — *i*·ne a·nikh·*to* *ka*·the *me*·ra

What's the admission charge?
Πόσο κοστίζει η είσοδος; — *po*·so ko·*sti*·zi i *i*·so·ţhos

Can I go in wearing these clothes?
Μπορώ να μπω με αυτά τα ρούχα; — bo·*ro* na bo me af·*ta* ta *ru*·kha

Is there a discount for …?	Υπάρχει έκπτωση για …;	i·*par*·hi *ek*·pto·si yia …
children	παιδιά	pe·*ţhia*
families	οικογένοιες	i·ko·*ye*·ni·es
groups	γκρουπ	grup
older people	υπερήλικους	i·pe·*ri*·li·kus
pensioners	συνταξιούχους	si·dak·si·*u*·khus
students	σπουδαστές	spu·ţha·*stes*

tours

περιηγήσεις

Can you recommend a tour?
Μπορείς να συστήσεις κάποια περιήγηση; — bo·*ris* na si·*sti*·sis *ka*·pia pe·ri·*i*·yi·si

When's the next tour?
Πότε είναι η επόμενη περιήγηση; — *po*·te *i*·ne i e·*po*·me·ni pe·ri·*i*·yi·si

How long is the tour?
Πόσην ώρα διαρκεί η περιήγηση; — *po*·sin *o*·ra ţhi·ar·*ki* i pe·ri·*i*·yi·si

The guide will pay.
Ο/Η οδηγός θα πληρώσει. m/f — o/i o·ţhi·*ghos* tha pli·*ro*·si

The guide has paid.
Ο/Η οδηγός έχει πληρώσει. m/f — o/i o·ţhi·*ghos* *e*·hi pli·*ro*·si

What time should we be back?
Τι ώρα πρέπει να επιστρέψουμε; — ti *o*·ra *pre*·pi na e·pi·*strep*·su·me

I'm with them.
Είμαι με αυτούς. — *i*·me me af·*tus*

I've lost my group.
Έχασα την ομάδα μου. — *e*·kha·sa tin o·*ma*·ţha mu

business
επιχειρήσεις

doing business

επιχειρησήσεις

I'm attending a …	Παρακολουθώ …	pa·ra·ko·lu·*tho* …
conference	ένα συνέδριο	*e*·na sin·*e*·ţhri·o
course	μια σειρά μαθημάτων	mia si·*ra* ma·thi·*ma*·ton
meeting	μια συνεδρίαση	mia sin·e·*ţhri*·a·si
trade fair	μια εμπορική έκθεση	mia e·bo·ri·*ki* *ek*·the·si

I'm with …	Είμαι με …	*i*·me me …
(Olympiaki)	(την Ολυμπιακή)	(tin o·li·bi·a·*ki*)
my colleague	τον συνάδελφό μου m	ton sin·*a*·ţhel·*fo* mu
	την συναδέλφισσά μου f	tin sin·a·*ţhel*·fi·sa mu
my colleagues	τους συναδέλφους μου	tus sin·a·*ţhel*·fus mu

I'm alone.
Είμαι μόνος/μόνη. m/f — *i*·me *mo*·nos/*mo*·ni

I have an appointment with …
Έχω ένα ραντεβού με … — *e*·kho *e*·na ra·de·*vu* me …

I'm staying at (the Xenia), room (10).
Μένω στο (Ξενία), δωμάτιο (10). — *me*·no sto (kse·*ni*·a) ţho·*ma*·ti·o (*ţhe*·ka)

I'm here for (two) days/weeks.
Είμαι εδώ για (δύο) μέρες/εβδομάδες. — *i*·me e·*ţho* yia (*ţhi*·o) *me*·res/ev·ţho·*ma*·ţhes

Here's my business card.
Ορίστε η κάρτα μου. — o·*ri*·ste i *kar*·ta mu

Can I have your business card?
Μπορώ να έχω την κάρτα σου; — bo·*ro* na *e*·kho tin *kar*·ta su

Here's my …	Ορίστε … μου.	o·*ri*·ste … mu
What's your …?	Ποια είναι η δική σου η …;	pia *i*·ne i ţhi·*ki* su i …
address	διεύθυνση	ţhi·*ef*·thin·si
email address	ηλεκτρονική διεύθυνση	i·lek·tro·ni·*ki* ţhi·*ef*·thin·si
Here's my … number.	Εδώ είναι ο αριθμός … μου.	e·*ţho i*·ne o a·rith·*mos* … mu
What's your … number?	Ποιος είναι ο δικός σου ο αριθμός …;	pios *i*·ne o ţhi·*kos* su o a·rith·*mos* …
fax	του φαξ	tu faks
mobile	του κινητού	tu ki·ni·*tu*
pager	του τηλεειδοποιητή	tu ti·le·i·ţho·pi·i·*ti*
work	της δουλειάς	tis ţhu·*lias*
Where's the …?	Πού είναι …;	pu *i*·ne …
business centre	ο χώρος εργασίας	o *kho*·ros er·gha·*si*·as
conference	το συνέδριο	to sin·*e*·ţhri·o
meeting	η συνεδρίαση	i sin·e·*ţhri*·a·si
I need (a/an) …	Χρειάζομαι …	khri·*a*·zo·me …
computer	ένα κομπιούτερ	*e*·na kom·*piu*·ter
Internet connection	σύνδεση στο διαδύκτιο	*sin*·ţhe·si sto ţhi·a·*ţhik*·ti·o
interpreter	διερμηνέα	ţhi·er·mi·*ne*·a
more business cards	περισσότερες κάρτες	pe·ri·*so*·te·res *kar*·tes
some space to set up	χώρο να τοποθετήσω τα πράγματα	*kho*·ro na to·po·the·*ti*·so ta *ragh*·ma·ta
to send a fax	να στείλω ένα φαξ	na *sti*·lo *e*·na faks

Thank you for your time.
Ευχαριστώ για το χρόνο σου. ef·kha·ri·*sto* yia to *khro*·no su

That went very well.
Πήγε πολύ καλά. *pi*·ye po·*li* ka·*la*

Shall we go for a drink/meal?
Πάμε για ποτό/φαγητό; *pa*·me yia po·*to*/fa·yi·*to*

looking for a job

ψάχνοντας για δουλειά

Where are jobs advertised?
Πού διαφημίζονται οι δουλειές; — pu ţhi·a·fi·*mi*·zo·de i ţhu·*lies*

I'm enquiring about the position advertised.
ζητώ πληροφορίες για τη θέση που διαφημίστηκε. — zi·*to* pli·ro·fo·*ri*·es yia ti *the*·si pu ţhi·a·fi·*mi*·sti·ke

I've had experience.
Έχω πείρα. — *e*·kho *pi*·ra

What's the wage?
Τι μισθό έχει; — ti mi·*stho e*·hi

I'm looking for … work.	Ψάχνω για δουλειά …	*psakh*·no yia ţhu·*lia* …
bar	σε μπαρ	se bar
casual	προσωρινή	pro·so·ri·*ni*
English-teaching	να διδάσκω αγγλικά	na ţhi·*ţha*·sko ang·gli·*ka*
fruit-picking	να μαζεύω φρούτα	na ma·*ze*·vo *fru*·ta
full-time	με πλήρη απασχόληση	me *pli*·ri a·pa·*skho*·li·si
labouring	χειρωνακτική	hi·ro·nak·ti·*ki*
office	γραφείου	ghra·*fi*·u
part-time	μερικής απασχόλησης	me·ri·*kis* a·pa·*skho*·li·sis
waitering	γκαρσόν	gar·*son*

Do I need (a/an)…?	Χειάζομαι …;	khri·*a*·zo·me …
contract	συμβόλαιο	sim·*vo*·le·o
experience	πείρα	*pi*·ra
insurance	ασφάλεια	as·*fa*·li·a
my own transport	δικό μου μεταφορικό μέσο	ţhi·*ko* mu me·ta·fo·ri·*ko me*·so
paperwork	ντοκουμέντα	do·ku·*men*·ta
uniform	στολή	sto·*li*
work permit	άδεια εργασίας	*a*·ţhi·a er·gha·*si*·as

Here is/are my …	Ορίστε …	o·*ri*·ste …
bank account details	ο τραπεζικός μου λογαριασμός	o tra·pi·zi·*kos* mu lo·gha·riaz·*mos*
CV/résumé	το βιογραφικό μου σημείωμα	to vi·o·ghra·fi·*ko* mu si·*mi*·o·ma
residency permit	η άδεια παραμονής μου	i *a*·ţhi·a pa·ra·mo·*nis* mu
visa	η βίζα μου	i *vi*·za mu
work permit	η άδεια εργασίας μου	i *a*·ţhi·a er·gha·*si*·as mu
What time do I …?	Τι ώρα …;	ti *o*·ra …
finish	τελειώνω	te·li·*o*·no
have a break	έχω διάλειμμα	*e*·kho *ţhia*·li·ma
start	αρχίζω	ar·*hi*·*zo*

I can start …	Μπορώ να αρχίσω …	bo·*ro* na ar·*hi*·so …
Can you start …?	Μπορείς να αρχίσεις …;	bo·*ris* na ar·*hi*·sis …
at (eight) o'clock	στις (οχτώ)	stis (okh·*to*)
next week	την επόμενη εβδομάδα	tin e·*po*·me·ni ev·tho·*ma*·ţha
today	σήμερα	*si*·me·ra
tomorrow	αύριο	*av*·ri·o
advertisement	διαφήμιση f	ţhi·a·*fi*·mi·si
contract	συμβόλαιο n	sim·*vo*·le·o
employee	υπάλληλος m&f	i·*pa*·li·los
employer	εργοδότης m εργοδότρια f	er·gho·*ţho*·tis er·gho·*ţho*·tri·a
job	δουλειά f	ţhu·*lia*
work experience	πείρα στη δουλειά f	*pi*·ra sti ţhu·*lia*

senior & disabled travellers
υπερήλικοι και ανάπηροι ταξιδιώτες

I have a disability.
Έχω μια αναπηρία. *e*·kho mia a·na·pi·*ri*·a

I need assistance.
Χρειάζομαι βοήθεια. khri·*a*·zo·me vo·*i*·thi·a

What services do you have for people with a disability?
Τι υπηρεσίες έχετε για άτομα με ειδικές ανάγκες; ti i·pi·re·*si*·es *e*·he·te yia *a*·to·ma me i·ţhi·*kes* a·*na*·ges

Are there disabled toilets?
Υπάρχουν τουαλέτες για άτομα με ειδικές ανάγκες; i·*par*·khun tu·a·*le*·tes yia *a*·to·ma me i·ţhi·*kes* a·*na*·ges

Are there disabled parking spaces?
Υπάρχει πάρκινγκ για άτομα με ειδικές ανάγκες; i·*par*·hi *par*·king yia *a*·to·ma me i·ţhi·*kes* a·*na*·ges

Is there wheelchair access?
Υπάρχει δρόμος για αναπηρικές καρέκλες; i·*par*·hi *ţhro* mos yia a·na·pi·ri·*kes* ka·*re*·kles

How wide is the entrance?
Πόσο πλατιά είναι η είσοδος; *po*·so pla·*tia* *i*·ne i *i*·so·ţhos

Is there somewhere I can sit down?
Υπάρχει κάπου να καθίσω; i·*par*·hi *ka*·pu na ka·*thi*·so

I'm deaf.
Είμαι κουφός. *i*·me ku·*fos*

I have a hearing aid.
Έχω ακουστικά. *e*·kho a·ku·sti·*ka*

Are guide dogs permitted?
Επιτρέπεται στα σκυλιά για τυφλούς; e·pi·*tre*·pe·te sta ski·*lia* yia ti·*flus*

How many steps are there?
Πόσα σκαλοπάτια υπάρχουν; *po*·sa ska·lo·*pa*·tia i·*par*·khun

Is there a lift?
Υπάρχει ασανσέρ; i·*par*·khi a·san·*ser*

Are there rails in the bathroom?

Υπάρχουν στηρίγματα στο μπάνιο;	i·*par*·khun sti·*righ*·ma·ta sto *ba*·nio

Could you call me a disabled taxi?

Μπορείς να καλέσεις ένα ταξί για άτομα με ειδικές ανάγκες;	bo·*ris* na ka·*le*·sis *e*·na tak·*si* yia *a*·to·ma me i·ţhi·*kes* a·*na*·ges

Could you help me cross the street safely?

Μπορείς να με βοηθήσεις να περάσω το δρόμο με ασφάλεια;	bo·*ris* na me vo·i·*thi*·sis na pe·*ra*·so to *ţhro*·mo me as·*fa*·li·a

guide dog	σκυλί για τυφλούς n	ski·*li* yia ti·*flus*
older person	υπερήλικος m	i·pe·*ri*·li·kos
	υπερήλικη f	i·pe·*ri*·li·ki
person with a disability	άτομο με ειδικές ανάγκες n	*a*·to·mo me i·ţhi·*kes* a·*na*·ges
ramp	ράμπα f	*ram*·pa
walking frame	περπατούσα f	per·pa·*tu*·sa
walking stick	μπαστούνι n	ba·*stu*·ni
wheelchair	αναπηρική καρέκλα f	a·na·pi·ri·*ki* ka·*re*·kla

PRACTICAL

travelling with children

ταξιδεύοντας με παιδιά

Is there a ...?	Υπάρχει ...;	i·*par*·hi ...
baby change room	δωμάτιο για άλλαγμα μωρών	ţho·*ma*·ti·o yia *a*·lagh·ma mo·*ron*
child-minding service	υπηρεσία διαφύλαξης παιδιών	i·pi·re·*si*·a ţhi·a·*fi*·lak·sis pe·*ţhion*
children's menu	παιδικό μενού	pe·ţhi·*ko* me·*nu*
child's portion	παιδική μερίδα	pe·ţhi·*ki* me·*ri*·ţha
crèche	βρεφοκομείο	vre·fo·ko·*mi*·o
discount for children	έκπτωση για παιδιά	*ek*·pto·si yia pe·*ţhia*
family ticket	οικογενειακό εισιτήριο	i·ko·ye·ni·a·*ko* i·si·*ti*·ri·o

I need a/an ...	Χρειάζομαι ...	khri·*a*·zo·me ...
baby seat	κάθισμα μωρού	*ka*·thiz·ma mo·*ru*
(English-speaking) babysitter	(αγγλομαθή) μπέημπι σίτερ	(ang·glo·ma·*thi*) *be*·i·bi *si*·ter
booster seat	ανυψωμένο κάθισμα	a·nip·so·*me*·no *ka*·thiz·ma
cot	παιδικό κρεβάτι	pe·ţhi·*ko* kre·*va*·ti
highchair	παιδική καρέκλα	pe·ţhi·*ki* ka·*re*·kla
plastic sheet	πλαστικό σεντόνι	pla·sti·*ko* se·*do*·ni
plastic bag	πλαστική σακούλα	pla·sti·*ki* sa·*ku*·la
potty	γιογιό	yio·*yio*
pram	παιδικό καροτσάκι	pe·ţhi·*ko* ka·rot·*sa*·ki
sick bag	σακούλα εμετού	sa·*ku*·la e·me·*tu*
stroller	καροτσάκι	ka·rot·*sa*·ki

Where's the nearest …?	Πού είναι το πιο κοντινό …;	pu *i*·ne to pio ko·di·*no* …
park	πάρκο	*par*·ko
playground	γήπεδο	*yi*·pe·do
toy shop	κατάστημα παιγνιδιών	ka·*ta*·sti·ma pegh·ni·*ţhion*
Where's the nearest …?	Πού είναι η πιο κοντινή …;	pu *i*·ne i pio ko·di·*ni* …
drinking fountain	βρύση με πόσιμο νερό	*vri*·si me *po*·si·mo ne·*ro*
swimming pool	πισίνα	pi·*si*·na
tap	βρύση	*vri*·si
theme park	παιδική χαρά	pe·ţhi·*ki* kha·*ra*
Do you sell …?	Πουλάτε …;	pu·*la*·te …
baby wipes	πετσέτες για σκούπισμα μωρών	pet·*se*·tes yia *sku*·piz·ma mo·*ron*
painkillers for infants	παυσίπονα για μωρά	paf·*si*·po·na yia mo·*ra*
disposable nappies/diapers	πάνες μιας χρήσης	*pa*·nes mias *khri*·sis
tissues	χαρτομάντηλα	khar·to·*ma*·di·la
Do you hire out …?	Νοικιάζετε …;	ni·*kia*·ze·te …
prams	παιδικά καροτσάκια	pe·ţhi·*ka* ka·rot·*sa*·kia
strollers	καροτσάκια	ka·rot·*sa*·kia

Are there any good places to take children around here?
Υπάρχουν καλά μέρη εδώ κοντά για τα παιδιά;
i·*par*·khun ka·*la* me·ri e·*ţho* ko·*da* yia ta pe·*ţhia*

Is there space for a pram?
Υπάρχει χώρος για το παιδικό καροτσάκι;
i·*par*·hi *kho*·ros yia to pe·ţhi·*ko* ka·rot·*sa*·ki

Are children allowed?
Επιτρέπεται στα παιδιά;
e·pi·*tre*·pe·te sta pe·*ţhia*

Where can I change a nappy?
Πού μπορώ να αλλάξω την πάνα;
pu bo·*ro* na a·*lak*·so tin *pa*·na

Do you mind if I breast-feed here?

Σε πειράζει αν θηλάσω εδώ το μωρό;	se pi·*ra*·zi an thi·*la*·so e·*ţho* to mo·*ro*

Could I have some paper and pencils, please?

Μπορώ να έχω λίγο χαρτί και μολύβια, παρακαλώ.	bo·*ro* na *e*·kho *li*·gho khar·*ti* ke mo·*li*·via pa·ra·ka·*lo*

Is this suitable for (five)-year-old children?

Είναι αυτό κατάλληλο για παιδιά (πέντε) χρονών;	*i*·ne af·*to* ka·*ta*·li·lo yia pe·*ţhia* (*pe*·de) khro·*no*

Do you know a dentist/doctor who is good with children?

Ξέρεις ένα οδοντίατρο/ γιατρό που είναι καλός με τα παιδιά;	*kse*·ris *e*·na o·ţho·*di*·a·tro/ yia·*tro* pu *i*·ne ka·*los* me ta pe·*ţhia*

If your child is sick, see **health**, page 195.

talking with children

μιλώντας με τα παιδιά

What's your name?

Πώς σε λένε;	pos se *le*·ne

How old are you?

Πόσο χρονώ είσαι;	*po*·so khro·*no i*·se

When's your birthday?

Πότε είναι τα γενέθλιά σου;	*po*·te *i*·ne ta ye·*neth*·li·*a* su

Do you go to school/kindergarten?

Πηγαίνεις στο σχολείο/ νηπιαγωγείο;	pi·*ye*·nis sto skho·*li*·o/ ni·pi·a·gho·*yi*·o

What grade are you in?

Σε ποια τάξη είσαι;	se pia *tak*·si *i*·se

Do you like ...?	Σου αρέσει ...;	su a·*re*·si ...
music	η μουσική	i mu·si·*ki*
school	το σχολείο	to skho·*li*·o
your teacher	ο δάσκαλός σου m	o *ţha*·ska·*los* su
	η δασκάλα σου f	i ţha·*ska*·la su

Do you like sport?
Σου αρέσουν τα σπορ; | su a·*re*·sun ta spor

What do you do after school?
Τι κάνεις μετά το σχολείο; | ti *ka*·nis me·*ta* to skho·*li*·o

Do you learn English?
Μαθαίνεις αγγλικά; | ma·*the*·nis ang·gli·*ka*

talking about children

μιλώντας για παιδιά

When's the baby due?
Πότε είναι να γεννηθεί το μωρό; | *po*·te *i*·ne na ye·ni·*thi* to mo·*ro*

What are you going to call the baby?
Πώς θα το ονομάσεις το μωρό; | pos tha to·o·no·*ma*·sis to mo·*ro*

Is this your first child?
Είναι το πρώτο σου παιδί; | *i*·ne to *pro*·to su pe·*ţhi*

How many children do you have?
Πόσα παιδιά έχεις; | *po*·sa pe·*ţhia* *e*·his

What a beautiful child!
Τι όμορφο παιδί! | ti *o*·mor·fo pe·*ţhi*

Is it a boy or a girl?
Είναι αγόρι ή κορίτσι; | *i*·ne a·*gho*·ri i ko·*rit*·si

How old is he/she?
Πόσο χρονώ είναι; | *po*·so khro·*no* *i*·ne

Does he/she go to school?
Πηγαίνει στο σχολείο; | pi·*ye*·ni sto skho·*li*·o

What's his/her name?
Πώς τον/την λένε; | pos ton/tin *le*·ne

Is he/she well-behaved?
Είναι καλό παιδί; | *i*·ne ka·*lo* pe·*ţhi*

He/She has your eyes.
Έχει τα μάτια σου. | *e*·hi ta *ma*·tia su

He/She looks like you.
Σου μοιάζει. | su *mia*·zi

basics

βασικά

Yes.	Ναι.	ne
No.	Όχι.	*o*·hi
Please.	Παρακαλώ.	pa·ra·ka·*lo*
Thank you (very much).	Ευχαριστώ (πολύ).	ef·kha·ri·*sto* (po·*li*)
You're welcome.	Παρακαλώ.	pa·ra·ka·*lo*
Sorry.	Συγνώμη.	si·*ghno*·mi
Excuse me.	Με συγχωρείτε.	me sing·kho·*ri*·te
I beg your pardon?	Ορίστε;/Συγνώμη;	o·*ri*·ste/si·*ghno*·mi
Here you are.	Ορίστε.	o·*ri*·ste

greetings & goodbyes

χαιρετισμοί και αποχαιρετισμοί

Greeks shake hands when greeting each other and saying goodbye. When greeting friends, male or female, they kiss each other on both cheeks.

Hello/Hi.	Γεια σου.	yia su
Good afternoon.	Χαίρετε.	*he*·re·te
Good morning.	Καλή μέρα.	ka·*li me*·ra
Good evening.	Καλή σπέρα.	ka·*li spe*·ra

when in greece ...

Be sure not to turn up empty-handed when you visit a Greek friend's house. It's customary to bring ένα κουτί γλυκά *e*·na ku·*ti* ghli·*ka* (a box of sweets) or μια ανθοδέσμη mia an·tho·*ţhes*·mi (a bunch of flowers).

How are you?
Τι κάνεις; — ti *ka*·nis

So-so.
Έτσι και έτσι. — *et*·si ke *et*·si

Fine. And you?
Καλά. Εσύ; — ka·*la* e·*si*

What's your name?
Πώς σε λένε; — pos se *le*·ne

My name is …
Με λένε … — me *le*·ne …

I'm pleased to meet you.
Χαίρω πολύ. — *he*·ro po·*li*

I'd like to introduce you to … (a man).
Θα ήθελα να σε συστήσω στο … — tha *i*·the·la na se si·*sti*·so sto …

I'd like to introduce you to … (a woman).
Θα ήθελα να σε συστήσω στη … — tha *i*·the·la na se si·*sti*·so sti …

This is my …	Από εδώ …	a·*po* e·ţ*ho* …
child	το παιδί μου	to pe·*ţhi* mu
colleague	ο συνάδελφός μου m	o sin·*a*·ţhel·*fos* mu
	η συναδέλφισσά μου f	i sin·a·*ţhel*·fi·*sa* mu
friend	ο φίλος μου m	o *fi*·los mu
	η φίλη μου f	i *fi*·li mu
husband	ο σύζυγός μου	o *si*·zi·*ghos* mu
partner (intimate)	ο σύντροφός μου m	o *si*·dro·*fos* mu
	η σύντροφός μου f	i *si*·dro·*fos* mu
wife	η σύζυγός μου	i *si*·zi·*ghos* mu

For other family members, see **family**, page 114.

See you later/Goodbye/Bye.
Αντίο. — a·*di*·o

Good night.
Καλή νύχτα. — ka·*li* *nikh*·ta

Bon voyage!
Καλό ταξίδι! — ka·*lo* tak·*si*·ţhi

addressing people

απευθυνόμενος σε ανθρώπους

The Greek language has two forms of the word 'you'. Use the polite form εσείς e·*sis* with adult strangers, elders, or those in a position of authority. In all other cases, you can use the informal form εσύ e·*si*. The polite form is simply the plural form of 'you', and you use it even when addressing one person. In this book we've chosen the appropriate form for the situation that the phrase is used in – it's normally the polite form unless we've marked it otherwise. For phrases where either form might be suitable, we've given both.

Also note that when speaking to older people you know well, their first name comes after Κύριε *ki*·ri·e (Sir), or Κυρία ki·*ri*·a (Madam).

Mr/Sir	Κύριε	*ki*·ri·e
Ms/Mrs	Κα	ki·*ri*·a
Miss	Δις	ţhes·pi·*nis*
Madam	Κυρία	ki·*ri*·a

on friendly terms

People will indicate when you can use the informal form of the word 'you' (εσύ e·*si*). If you want to initiate a more informal conversation with a Greek acquaintance, say:

Please speak to me in the singular.
Μίλα μου στον ενικό. *mi*·la mu ston e·ni·*ko*

And here are a few casual terms to address your Greek pals:

friend	φίλε/φίλη m/f	*fi*·le/*fi*·li
dude	ρε μάγκα	re *ma*·ga
mate (Cyprus only)	κουμπάρε	ku·*ba*·re

making conversation

κάνοντας συζήτηση

How are you going?
Πώς πάμε; — pos *pa*·me

What's happening?
Τι γίνεται; — ti *yi*·ne·te

What's new?
Τι νέα; — ti *ne*·a

What a beautiful day!
Τι όμορφη μέρα! — ti *o*·mor·fi *me*·ra

Nice/Awful weather, isn't it?
Καλός/απαίσιος καιρός, έτσι δεν είναι; — ka·*los*/a·*pe*·si·os ke·*ros* *et*·si ţhen i·*ne*

Where are you going?
Πού πηγαίνεις; — pu pi·*ye*·nis

What are you doing?
Τι κάνεις; — ti *ka*·nis

What's this called?
Πώς το λένε αυτό; — pos to *le*·ne af·*to*

That's (beautiful), isn't it!
Είναι (όμορφο), έτσι δεν είναι! — *i*·ne (*o*·mor·fo) *et*·si ţhen *i*·ne

don't mention the war

Sometimes, discretion is the better part of conversation – these topics are best avoided:

- anything linked to Το Μακεδονικό to ma·ke·ţho·ni·*ko* (the Macedonian issue). A northern region of Greece is called Macedonia, and many Greek patriots object to the Former Yugoslav Republic of Macedonia usurping 'their' name.
- any mention of Το Κυπριακό to kip·ri·a·*ko* (the Cyprus problem). Displaced Greek Cypriots object to the Turkish occupation of Northern Cyprus.

Can I take a photo (of you)?
Μπορώ να (σου) πάρω μια φωτογραφία; — bo·*ro* na (su) *pa*·ro mia fo·to·ghra·*fi*·a

Do you live here?
Μένεις εδώ; — *me*·nis e·*ţho*

Are you here on holiday?
Είσαι εδώ για διακοπές; — *i*·se e·*ţho* yia ţhia·ko·*pes*

I'm here ...	Είμαι εδώ για ...	*i*·me e·*ţho* yia ...
for a holiday	διακοπές	ţhia·ko·*pes*
on business	δουλειά	ţhu·*lia*
to study	σπουδές	spu·*ţhes*

How long are you here for?
Πόσον καιρό θα είσαι εδώ; — *po*·son ke·*ro* tha *i*·se e·*ţho*

I'm here for (four) weeks/days.
Θα είμαι εδώ για (τέσσερις) εβδομάδες/μέρες. — tha *i*·me e·*ţho* yia (*te*·se·ris) ev·tho·*ma*·ţhes/*me*·res

Do you like it here?
Σου αρέσει εδώ; — su a·*re*·si e·*ţho*

I love it here.
Μου αρέσει εδώ. — mu a·*re*·si e·*ţho*

nationalities

εθνικότητες

Where are you from?
Από πού είσαι; — a·*po* pu *i*·se

I'm from ...	Είμαι από ...	*i*·me a·*po* ...
Australia	την Αυστραλία	tin af·stra·*li*·a
Canada	τον Καναδά	ton ka·na·*ţha*
Singapore	τη Σιγγαπούρη	ti si·ga·*pu*·ri

age

ηλικία

How old ...?	Πόσο χρονώ ...;	*po*·so khro·*no* ...
are you	είσαι	*i*·se
is your son	είναι ο γιος σου	*i*·ne o yios su
is your daughter	είναι η κόρη σου	*i*·ne i *ko*·ri su

I'm ... years old.
Είμαι ... χρονώ. — *i*·me ... khro·*no*

He/She is ... years old.
Αυτός/αυτή είναι ... χρονών. — af·*tos*/af·*ti* *i*·ne ... khro·*no*

I'm younger than I look.
Είμαι νεώτερος/νεώτερη από ό,τι φαίνομαι. m/f — *i*·me ne·*o*·te·ros/ne·*o*·te·ri a·*po* *o*·ti *fe*·no·me

For your age, see **numbers & amounts**, page 35.

local talk

Absolutely!	Απολύτως!	a·po·*li*·*tos*
Don't stress!	Μην κάνεις έτσι!	min *ka*·nis *et*·si
Enough!	Αρκετά!	ar·ke·*ta*
Exactly!	Ακριβώς!	a·kri·*vos*
Great!	Απίθανο!	a·*pi*·tha·no
Hey!	Εε!	*e*·e
I don't care.	Δεν με νιάζει.	ţhen me *nia*·zi
I don't give a stuff.	Δεν δίνω δεκάρα.	ţhen *ţhi*·no ţhe·*ka*·ra
It's OK.	Είναι εντάξει.	*i*·ne e·*dak*·si
Just a minute.	Μισό λεπτό.	mi·*so* lep·*to*
Just joking.	Αστειεύομαι.	a·sti·*e*·vo·me
Maybe.	Ίσως.	*i*·sos
No problem.	Δεν υπάρχει πρόβλημα.	ţhen i·*par*·hi *prov*·li·ma
No way!	Αποκλείεται!	a·po·*kli*·e·te
Rubbish!	Σαχλαμάρες!	sakh·la·*ma*·res
Sure.	Σίγουρα.	*si*·ghu·ra
Well now ...	Λοιπόν ...	li·*pon* ...
You're wrong.	Κάνεις λάθος.	*ka*·nis *la*·thos

SOCIAL

the call of the wild ... and the domesticated

Dogs in Greece don't 'woof' – instead, they say ghav. Greek cows, on the other hand, seem to speak English. Here are some animal noises as they sound to Greek ears:

bird	τσίου-τσίου	*tsi*·u *tsi*·u
cat	νιάου	*nia*·ou
chick	κο-κο-κο	ko·ko·*ko*
cow	μου	mu
crow	κρα	kra
dog	γαβ	ghav
hen	κα-κα-κα	ka·ka·*ka*
rooster	κι-κιρίκου	ki·ki·*ri*·ku

occupations & studies

επαγγέλματα και σπουδές

What's your occupation?
Τι δουλειά κάνεις; ti ţhu·*lia ka*·nis

I'm a ...	Είμαι ...	*i*·me ...
businessperson	επιχειρηματίας m&f	e·pi·hi·ri·ma·*ti*·as
journalist	δημοσιογράφος m&f	ţhi·mo·si·o·*ghra*·fos
salesperson	πωλητής m	po·li·*tis*
	πωλήτρια f	po·*li*·tri·a
student	σπουδαστής m	spu·ţha·*stis*
	σπουδάστρια f	spu·*ţha*·stri·a
teacher	δάσκαλος m	*ţha*·ska·los
	δασκάλα f	*ţha*·ska·la
waiter	γκαρσόν	gar·*son*
waitress	γκαρσόνα	gar·*so*·na

I work in ...	Δουλεύω ...	ţhu·*le*·vo ...
administration	στη διοίκηση	sti ţhi·*i*·ki·si
health	στην υγεία	stin i·*yi*·a
sales & marketing	στις πωλήσεις και μάρκετινγκ	stis po·*li*·sis ke *mar*·ke·ting

I'm …	Είμαι …	*i*·me …
retired	συνταξιούχος m/f	si·dak·si·*u*·khos
self-employed	ιδιωτικός/ιδιωτική	i·ţhi·o·ti·*kos*/i·ţhi·o·ti·*ki*
	υπάλληλος m/f	i·*pa*·li·los
unemployed	άνεργος/άνεργη m/f	*an*·er·ghos/*an*·er·yi
What are you studying?	Τι σπουδάζεις;	ti spu·*ţha*·zis
I'm studying …	Σπουδάζω …	spu·*ţha*·zo …
Greek	Ελληνικά	e·li·ni·*ka*
languages	γλώσσες	*ghlo*·ses
science	θετικές επιστήμες	the·ti·*kes* e·pi·*sti*·mes

family

οικογένεια

Are you married? (to a man)
Είσαι παντρεμένος; — *i*·se pa·dre·*me*·nos

Are you married? (to a woman)
Είσαι παντρεμένη; — *i*·se pa·dre·*me*·ni

I live with someone. (with a woman)
Ζω με κάποια. — zo me *ka*·pia

I live with someone. (with a man)
Ζω με κάποιον. — zo me *ka*·pion

I'm …	Είμαι …	i·*me* …
married	παντρεμένος m	pa·dre·*me*·nos
	παντρεμένη f	pa·dre·*me*·ni
separated	χωρισμένος m	kho·riz·*me*·nos
	χωρισμένη f	kho·riz·*me*·ni
single	ανύπαντρος m	a·*ni*·pa·dros
	ανύπαντρη f	a·*ni*·pa·dri

Do you have a/an …?
Έχεις …; — *e*·his …

I (don't) have a/an …
(Δεν) έχω … — (ţhen) *e*·kho …

aunt	θεία f	*thi*·a
brother	αδερφό m	a·ţher·*fo*
brother-in-law	γαμπρό m	gha·*bro*
cousin	ξάδερφο m	*ksa*·ţher·fo
	ξαδέρφη f	ksa·*ţher*·fi
daughter	κόρη f	*ko*·ri
daughter-in-law	νύφη f	*ni*·fi
family	οικογένεια f	i·ko·*ye*·ni·a
father	πατέρα m	pa·*te*·ra
father-in-law	πεθερό m	pe·the·*ro*
granddaughter	εγγονή f	e·go·*ni*
grandfather	παπού m	pa·*pu*
grandmother	γιαγιά f	yia·*yia*
grandson	εγγονό m	e·go·*no*
husband	σύζυγο m	*si*·zi·gho
mother	μητέρα f	mi·*te*·ra
mother-in-law	πεθερά f	pe·the·*ra*
nephew	ανιψιό m	a·nip·*sio*
niece	ανιψιά f	a·nip·*sia*
partner (intimate)	σύντροφο m&f	*si*·dro·fo
sister	αδερφή f	a·ţher·*fi*
sister-in-law	νύφη f	*ni*·fi
son	γιο m	yio
son-in-law	γαμπρό m	gha·*bro*
uncle	θείο m	*thi*·o
wife	σύζυγο f	*si*·zi·gho

farewells

αποχαιρετισμοί

Tomorrow is my last day here.
Αύριο είναι η τελευταία μέρα μου εδώ. — *av*·ri·o *i*·ne i te·lef·*te*·a *me*·ra mu e·*ţho*

It's been great meeting you.
Είναι υπέροχο που σε συνάντησα. — *i*·ne i·*pe*·ro·kho pu se si·*na*·di·sa

If you come to (Scotland) you can stay with me.
Αν έρθεις (στη Σκωτία) μπορείς να μείνεις μαζί μου. — an *er*·this (sti sko·*ti*·a) bo·*ris* na *mi*·nis ma·*zi* mu

Here's my address.
Εδώ είναι η διεύθυνσή μου. — e·ţ*ho* *i*·ne i ţhi·*ef*·thin·*si* mu

What's your address?
Ποια είναι η δική σου διεύθυνση; — pia *i*·ne i ţhi·*ki* su ţhi·*ef*·thin·si

What's your ...?	Ποιο είναι το ... σου;	pio *i*·ne to ... su
Here's my ...	Εδώ είναι το ... μου.	e·*ţho* *i*·ne to ... mu
phone number	τηλέφωνό	ti·*le*·fo·*no*
email address	ημέιλ	i·*me*·il

Keep in touch!
Μη χαθούμε! — mi kha·*thu*·me

We'll talk again soon.
Θα τα πούμε. — tha ta *pu*·me

Farewell.
Γεια χαρά. — yia ha·*ra*

Adieu.
Αντίο. — a·*di*·o

well-wishing

Bless you!	Ο Θεός να σε φυλάει!	o the·*os* na se fi·*la*·i
Bon voyage!	Καλό ταξίδι!	ka·*lo* tak·*si*·ţhi
Congratulations!	Συγχαρητήρια!	sing·kha·ri·*ti*·ri·a
Good luck!	Καλή τύχη!	ka·*li* *ti*·hi
Happy Birthday!	Χαρούμενα γενέθλια!	kha·*ru*·me·na ye·*ne*·thli·a
Have a nice/ good time!	Καλά/Ωραία να περάσεις!	ka·*la*/or·*e*·a na pe·*ra*·sis
Merry Christmas!	Καλά Χριστούγεννα!	ka·*la* khri·*stu*·ye·na

If you're lost for words on a special occasion, just wish people Χρόνια πολλά! *khro*·nia po·*la* (Many years!) – this works for just about any festive occasion.

SOCIAL

common interests

κοινά ενδιαφέροντα

What do you do in your spare time?		
Τι κάνεις τον ελεύθερο χρόνο σου;		ti *ka*·nis ton e·*lef*·the·ro *khro*·no su
Do you like ...?	Σου αρέσει ...;	su a·*re*·si ...
I (don't) like ...	(Δεν) μου αρέσει ...	(ţhen) mu a·*re*·si ...
billiards	το μπιλιάρδο	to bi·*liar*·ţho
chess	το σκάκι	to *ska*·ki
cooking	η μαγειρική	i ma·yi·ri·*ki*
dancing	ο χορός	o kho·*ros*
dominoes	το ντόμινο	to *do*·mi·no
drawing	το σχέδιο	to *she*·ţhi·o
gardening	η κηπουρική	i ki·pu·ri·*ki*
music	η μουσική	i mu·si·*ki*
painting	η ζωγραφική	i zo·ghra·fi·*ki*
reading	το διάβασμα	to *ţhia*·vaz·ma
Do you like ...?	Σου αρέσουν ...;	su a·*re*·sun ...
I (don't) like ...	(Δεν) μου αρέσουν τα ...	(ţhen) mu a·*re*·sun ta ...
films	φιλμ	film
sport	σπορ	spor
Do you like ...?	Σου αρέσει να ...;	su a·*re*·si na ...
shopping	ψωνίζεις	pso·*ni*·zis
travelling	ταξιδεύεις	tak·si·*ţhe*·vis
I (don't) like ...	(Δεν) μου αρέσει να ...	(ţhen) mu a·*re*·si na ...
shopping	ψωνίζω	pso·*ni*·zo
travelling	ταξιδεύω	tak·si·*ţhe*·vo

For sporting activities, see **sport**, page 141.

astrology	αστρολογία f	a·stro·lo·*yi*·a
backgammon	τάβλι n	*tav*·li
***bouzouki* (instrument)**	μπουζούκι n	bu·*zu*·ki
current affairs	επίκαιρα θέματα n pl	e·*pi*·ke·ra *the*·ma·ta
playing cards	χαρτιά n pl	khar·*tia*
politics	πολιτική f	po·li·ti·*ki*
***sirtaki* (Greek dancing)**	συρτάκι n	sir·*ta*·ki

music

μουσική

What music do you like?
Τι μουσική σου αρέσει; — ti mu·si·*ki* su a·*re*·si

Which bands/singers do you like?
Τι μπάντες/τραγουδιστές σου αρέσουν; — ti *ba*·des/tra·ghu·ţhi·*stes* su a·*re*·sun

traditional greek dances

Many traditional dances are specific to certain regions of Greece, while others are popular throughout the country. The most common ones are the Ζεμπέκικο ze·*be*·ki·ko (Zembekiko), the Τσάμικο *tsa*·mi·ko (Tsamiko), Καλαματιανό ka·la·ma·tia·*no* (Kalamatiano) – also called the Συρτό sir·*to* (Sirto) – and the Χασαποσέρβικο ha·sa·po·*ser*·vi·ko (Zorba Dance).

In most of these dances, the participants hold hands to form a semicircle and, moving in repetitive steps, they follow the lead dancer in an anticlockwise direction. The one exception is the Zembekiko, which is danced by individuals – although sometimes called the 'drunken sailor's dance' for its seeming clumsiness, it actually takes great skill to perform.

Other popular dances are the Κότσαρι *kot*·sa·ri (Kotsari), the Κρητικός kri·ti·*kos* (Kritikos) and the Ποντιακός po·di·a·*kos* (Pontiakos).

Do you ...?		
dance	Χορεύεις;	kho·*re*·vis
go to concerts	Πηγαίνεις σε κονσέρτα;	pi·*ye*·nis se kon·*ser*·ta
listen to music	Ακούς μουσική;	a·*kus* mu·si·*ki*
play an instrument	Παίζεις κανένα όργανο;	*pe*·zis ka·*ne*·na *or*·gha·no
sing	Τραγουδάς;	tra·ghu·*ţhas*

blues	μπλουζ **n**	bluz
classical music	κλασσική μουσική **f**	kla·si·*ki* mu·si·*ki*
electronic music	ηλεκτρονική μουσική **f**	i·lek·tro·ni·*ki* mu·si·*ki*
Greek folk music	Ελληνική παραδοσιακή μουσική **f**	e·li·ni·*ki* pa·ra·ţho·si·a·*ki* mu·si·*ki*
jazz	τζαζ **f**	tzaz
pop music	ποπ **f**	pop
rembetika	ρεμπέτικα **n pl**	re·*be*·ti·ka
rock music	μουσική ροκ **f**	mu·si·*ki* rok
traditional music	παραδοσιακή μουσική **f**	pa·ra·ţho·si·a·*ki* mu·si·*ki*

Planning to go to a concert? See **tickets**, page 46, and **going out**, page 127.

cinema & theatre

Σινεμά και θέατρο

I feel like going to a ...	Θέλω να πάω σε ...	*the*·lo na *pa*·o se ...
ballet	μπαλέτο	ba·*le*·to
film	φιλμ	film
play	έργο	*er*·gho

What's showing at the cinema/theatre tonight?

Τι παίζει στο σινεμά/ θέατρο απόψε;	ti *pe*·zi sto si·ne·*ma*/ *the*·a·tro a·*pop*·se

Is it in English/Greek?

Είναι στα Αγγλικά/Ελληνικά;	*i*·ne sta ang·gli·*ka*/e·li·ni·*ka*

Does it have (English) subtitles?

Έχει (Αγγλικούς) υπότιτλους;	*e*·hi (ang·gli·*kus*) i·*po*·tit·lus

Is this seat taken?

Είναι αυτή η θέση πιασμένη;	*i*·ne af·*ti* i *the*·si piaz·*me*·ni

Have you seen …?

Έχεις δει …;	*e*·his ţhi …

Who's in it?

Ποιος παίζει σ' αυτό;	pios *pe*·zi saf·*to*

Did you like the (film)?

Σου άρεσε το (φιλμ);	su *a*·re·se to (film)

I thought it was …	Νομίζω πως ήταν …	no·*ni*·zo pos *i*·tan …
excellent	εξαιρετικό	ek·se·re·ti·*ko*
long	μεγάλο	me·*gha*·lo
OK	εντάξει	e·*dak*·si

I (don't) like …	(Δεν) μου αρέσουν …	(ţhen) mu a·*re*·sun …
action movies	οι ταινίες δράσης	i te·*ni*·es *ţhra*·sis
animated films	τα φιλμ κινουμένων σχεδίων	ta film ki·nu·*me*·non she·*ţhi*·on
comedies	οι κωμωδίες	i ko·mo·*ţhi*·es
documentaries	τα ντοκυμαντέρ	ta do·ki·man·*ter*
drama	τα δραματικά έργα	ta ţhra·ma·ti·*ka* *er*·gha
Greek cinema	τα ελληνικά έργα	ta e·li·ni·*ka* *er*·gha
horror movies	τα έργα τρόμου	ta *er*·gha *tro*·mu
sci-fi	τα έργα επιστημονικής φαντασίας	ta *er*·gha e·pi·sti·mo·ni·*kis* fa·da·*si*·as
short films	τα φιλμ μικρής διάρκειας	ta film mi·*kris* ţhi·*ar*·ki·as
thrillers	τα θρίλερ	ta *thri*·ler
war movies	τα πολεμικά έργα	ta po·le·mi·*ka* *er*·gha

feelings

αισθήματα

Are you …?	Είσαι …;	*i*·se …
I'm (not) …	(Δεν) Είμαι …	(ţhen) *i*·me …
annoyed	ενοχλημένος m	e·no·khli·*me*·nos
	ενοχλημένη f	e·no·khli·*me*·ni
disappointed	απογοητευμένος m	a·po·gho·i·tev·*me*·nos
	απογοητευμένη f	a·po·gho·i·tev·*me*·ni
embarrassed	αμήχανος m	a·*mi*·kha·nos
	αμήχανη f	a·*mi*·kha·ni
happy	ευτυχισμένος m	ef·ti·hiz·*me*·nos
	ευτυχισμένη f	ef·ti·hiz·*me*·ni
hot	ζεστός m	ze·*stos*
	ζεστή f	ze·*sti*
hungry	πεινασμένος m	pi·naz·*me*·nos
	πεινασμένη f	pi·naz·*me*·ni
in a hurry	βιαστικός m	via·sti·*kos*
	βιαστική f	via·sti·*ki*
sad	στενοχωρημένος m	ste·no·kho·ri·*me*·nos
	στενοχωρημένη f	ste·no·kho·ri·*me*·ni
surprised	έκπληκτος m	*ek*·plik·tos
	έκπληκτη f	*ek*·plik·ti
thirsty	διψασμένος m	ţhip·saz·*me*·nos
	διψασμένη f	ţhip·saz·*me*·ni
tired	κουρασμένος m	ku·raz·*me*·nos
	κουρασμένη f	ku·raz·*me*·ni
worried	ανύσυχος m	a·*ni*·si·khos
	ανύσυχη f	a·*ni*·si·hi

I'm (not) cold.	(Δεν) Κρυώνω.	(ţhen) kri·*o*·no

If you're not feeling well, see **health**, page 195.

mixed feelings		
a little	λίγο	*li*·gho
I'm a little sad.	Είμαι λίγο στενοχωρημένος/στενοχωρημένη. m/f	*i*·me *li*·gho ste·no·kho·ri·*me*·nos ste·no·kho·ri·*me*·ni
very	πολύ	po·*li*
I feel very lucky.	Αισθάνομαι πολύ τυχερός/τυχερή. m/f	es·*tha*·no·me po·*li* ti·he·*ros*/ti·he·*ri*
extremely	πάρα πολύ	*pa*·ra po·*li*
I'm extremely sorry.	Λυπάμαι πάρα πολύ.	li·*pa*·me *pa*·ra po·*li*

opinions

γνώμες

Did you like it?
Σου άρεσε; — su *a*·re·se

What do you think of it?
Τι νομίζεις για αυτό; — ti no·*mi*·zis yia af·*to*

I thought it was ...	Νομίζω ήταν ...	no·*mi*·zo *i*·tan ...
It's ...	Είναι ...	*i*·ne ...
awful	απαίσιο	a·*pe*·si·o
beautiful	όμορφο	*o*·mor·fo
boring	πληκτικό	plik·ti·*ko*
great	καταπληκτικό	ka·ta·plik·ti·*ko*
interesting	ενδιαφέρον	en·ʒhia·*fe*·ron
OK	εντάξει	e·*dak*·si
strange	παράξενο	pa·*rak*·se·no
too expensive	πάρα πολύ ακριβό	*pa*·ra po·*li* a·kri·*vo*

politics & social issues

πολιτική και κοινωνικά θέματα

Who do you vote for?	Ποιον ψηφίζεις;	pion psi·*fi*·zis
I support the … party.	Εγώ υποστηρίζω το κόμμα …	e·*gho* i·po·sti·*ri*·zo to *ko*·ma …
I'm a member of the … party.	Είμαι μέλος του κόμματος …	*i*·me *me*·los tu *ko*·ma·tos …
coalition	συνασπισμός	si·nas·piz·*mos*
communist	κομμουνιστικό	ko·mu·ni·sti·*ko*
conservative	συντηρητικό	si·di·ri·ti·*ko*
democratic	δημοκρατικό	ţhi·mo·kra·ti·*ko*
green	οικολογικό	i·ko·lo·yi·*ko*
liberal	φιλελεύθεροι	fil·e·*lef*·the·ri
republican	ρεπουμπλικανικό	re·pu·bli·ka·ni·*ko*
social democratic	κοινωνικό δημοκρατικό	ki·no·ni·*ko* ţhi·mo·kra·ti·*ko*
socialist	σοσιαλιστικο	so·si·a·li·sti·*ko*

Did you hear about …?
Άκουσες για …; — *a*·ku·ses yia …

Do you agree with it?
Συμφωνείς με αυτό …; — sim·fo·*nis* me af·*to* …

I (don't) agree with …
(Δεν) Συμφωνώ με … — (ţhen) sim·fo·*no* me …

How do people feel about …?
Πώς αισθάνονται οι άνθρωποι για …; — pos es·*tha*·no·de i *an*·thro·pi yia …

How can we support …?
Πώς μπορούμε να υποστηρίξουμε …; — pos bo·*ru*·me na i·po·sti·*rik*·su·me …

How can we protest against …?
Πώς μπορούμε να διαμαρτυρηθούμε για …; — pos bo·*ru*·me na ţhi·a·mar·ti·ri·*thu*·me yia …

'no' means 'yes'

Although it may sound like 'no', remember that ναι ne really means 'yes'.

abortion	εκτρώσεις f	ek·*tro*·sis
animal rights	δικαιώματα των ζώων n	ţhi·ke·*o*·ma·ta ton *zo*·on
civil servants	δημοσίους υπαλλήλους m	tus ţhi·mo·*si*·us i·pa·*li*·lus
crime	έγκλημα n	*eng*·li·ma
democracy	δημοκρατία f	ţhi·mo·kra·*ti*·a
diaspora	διασπορά f	ţhi·a·spo·*ra*
discrimination	διακρίσεις f	ţhi·a·*kri*·sis
drugs	ναρκωτικά n	nar·ko·ti·*ka*
the economy	οικονομία f	i·ko·no·*mi*·a
education	εκπαίδευση f	ek·*pe*·ţhef·si
the environment	περιβάλλον n	pe·ri·*va*·lon
equal opportunity	ίσες ευκαιρίες f	*i*·ses ef·ke·*ri*·es
euthanasia	ευθανασία f	ef·tha·na·*si*·a
the European Union	Ευρωπαϊκή Ένωση f	ev·ro·pa·i·*ki* *e*·no·si
gay rights	δικαιώματα των γκέι n	ţhi·ke·*o*·ma·ta ton *ge*·i
globalisation	παγκοσμιοποίηση f	pa·goz·mi·o·*pi*·i·si
human rights	ανθρώπινα δικαιώματα n	an·*thro*·pi·na ţhi·ke·*o*·ma·ta
immigration	μετανάστευση f	me·ta·*na*·stef·si
inequality	ανισότητα f	a·ni·*so*·ti·ta
inflation	πληθωρισμό m	pli·tho·riz·*mo*
the military junta	στρατιωτική χούντα f	stra·ti·o·ti·*ki* *khu*·da
the Macedonian question	Μακεδονικό ζήτημα n	ma·ke·ţho·ni·*ko* *zi*·ti·ma
the monarchy	μοναρχία f	mo·nar·*hi*·a
NATO	NATO n	*na*·to
parliament	κοινοβούλιο n	ki·no·*vu*·li·o

SOCIAL

the partition of Cyprus	διχοτόμηση της Κύπρου **f**	ţhi·kho·*to*·mi·si tis *ki*·pru
party politics	πολιτική του κόμματος **f**	po·li·ti·*ki* tu *ko*·ma·tos
privatisation	ιδιοτικοποίηση **f**	i·ţhi·o·ti·ko·*pi*·i·si
poverty	φτώχεια **f**	*fto*·hia
racism	ρατσισμό **n**	rat·siz·*mo*
refugees	πρόσφυγες **m**	*pros*·*fi*·yes
relations with Turkey	σχέσεις με την Τουρκία **f**	*she*·sis me tin tur·*ki*·a
sexism	σεξισμό **m**	sek·siz·*mo*
social welfare	κοινωνική πρόνοια **f**	ki·no·ni·*ki* *pro*·ni·a
strikes	απεργίες **f**	ap·er·*yi*·es
terrorism	τρομοκρατία **f**	tro·mo·kra·*ti*·a
traffic restrictions	περιορισμό της κυκλοφορίας **m**	pe·ri·o·riz·*mo* tis ki·klo·fo·*ri*·as
unemployment	ανεργία **f**	an·er·*yi*·a
US military bases	στρατιωτικές βάσεις των ΗΠΑ **f**	stra·ti·o·ti·*kes* *va*·sis ton *i*·pa

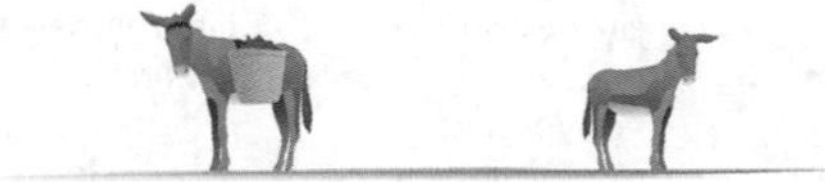

the environment

το περιβάλλον

Is there a … problem here?
Υπάρχει κλάποιο πρόβλημα εδώ με …; — i·*par*·hi *ka*·pio *pro*·vli·ma e·*ţho* me …

What should be done about …?
Τι θα πρέπει να γίνει με …; — ti tha *pre*·pi na *yi*·ni me …

beach cleaning	καθαρισμό των ακτών m	ka·tha·riz·*mo* ton ak·*ton*
conservation	προστασία του περιβάλλοντος f	pro·sta·*si*·a tu pe·ri·*va*·lo·dos
deforestation	αποδάσωση f	a·po·*ţha*·so·si
drought	ανομβρία f	a·nom·*vri*·a
earthquakes	σεισμούς m	siz·*mus*
ecosystem	οικοσύστημα n	i·ko·*si*·sti·ma
endangered species	είδη υπό εξαφάνιση n	*i*·ţhi i·*po* ek·sa·*fa*·ni·si
erosion	διάβρωση f	ţhi·*av*·ro·si
forest fires	φωτιές στα δάση f	fo·*tyes* sta *ţha*·si
genetically modified food	γενετικά μεταλλαγμένο φαγητό n	ye·ne·ti·*ka* me·ta·lagh·*me*·no fa·yi·*to*
hunting	κυνήγι n	ki·*ni*·yi
hydroelectricity	υδροηλεκτρισμό m	i·ţhro·i·lek·triz·*mo*
irrigation	άρδευση f	*ar*·ţhef·si
marine reserves	θαλάσσια διαφύλαξη f	tha·*la*·si·a ţhi·a·*fi*·lak·si
national parks	εθνικά πάρκα n	eth·ni·*ka* *par*·ka
nuclear energy	πυρηνική ενέργεια f	pi·ri·ni·*ki* e·*ner*·yi·a
nuclear testing	πυρηνικές δοκιμές f	pi·ri·ni·*kes* ţho·ki·*mes*
ozone layer	στρώμα του όζοντος n	*stro*·ma tu *o*·zo·dos
pesticides	φυτοφάρμακα n	fi·to·*far*·ma·ka
pollution	μόλυνση f	*mo*·lin·si
recycling program	πρόγραμμα ανκύκλωσης n	*pro*·ghra·ma a·na·*ki*·klo·sis
smog	νέφος n	*ne*·fos
toxic waste	τοξικά απόβλητα n	tok·si·*ka* a·*pov*·li·ta
urban encroachment	αστική εξάπλωση f	a·sti·*ki* ek·*sa*·plo·si
water supply	παροχή ύδατος f	pa·ro·*hi* *i*·ţha·tos

Is this a protected ...?	Είναι αυτό προστατευόμενο ...;	*i*·ne af·*to* pro·sta·te·*vo*·me·no
forest	δάσος	*ţha*·sos
park	πάρκο	*par*·ko
species	είδος	*i*·ţhos

going out

βγαίνουμε έξω

where to go

πού να πάμε

What's there to do in the evenings?
Τι μπορούμε να κάνουμε το βράδι; — ti bo·*ru*·me na *ka*·nu·me to *vra*·ţhi

What's on ...?	Τι γίνεται ...;	ti *yi*·ne·te ...
locally	εδώ γύρω	e·*ţho yi*·ro
this weekend	αυτό το Σαββατοκύριακο	af·*to* to sa·va·to·*ki*·ria·ko
today	σήμερα	*si*·me·ra
tonight	απόψε	a·*pop*·se

Where can I find ...?	Πού μπορώ να βρω ...;	pu bo·*ro* na vro ...
a *bouzouki* place (venue with live Greek music)	ταβέρνα με μπουζούκια	ta·*ver*·na me bu·*zu*·kia
clubs	κλαμπ	klab
gay venues	Χώρους συνάντησης για γκέη	*kho*·rus si·*na*·di·sis yia *ge*·i
an open-air cinema	θερινό κινηματογράφο	the·ri·*no* ki·ni·ma·to·*ghra*·fo
places to eat	εστιατόρια	e·sti·a·*to*·ri·a
pubs	μπυραρίες	bi·ra·*ri*·es

Is there a local ... guide?	Υπάρχει τοπικός οδηγός για ...;	i·*par*·hi to·pi·*kos* o·ţhi·*ghos* yia ...
entertainment	διασκεδάσεις	ţhias·ke·*ţha*·sis
film	φιλμ	film
gay	γκέη	*ge*·i
music	μουσική	mu·si·*ki*

I feel like going to a …	Έχω όρηξη να πάω σε …	e·kho *o*·rek·si na *pa*·o se …
ballet	μπαλέτο	ba·*le*·to
bar	μπαρ	bar
café	καφενείο	ka·fe·*ni*·o
concert	κονσέρτο	kon·*ser*·to
film	φιλμ	film
karaoke bar	καραόκι μπαρ	ka·ra·*o*·ki bar
nightclub	νυχτερινό κέντρο	nikh·te·ri·*no ke*·dro
party	πάρτυ	*par*·ti
performance	θέαμα	the·*a*·ma
play	έργο	*er*·gho
pub	μπυραρία	bi·ra·*ri*·a
***rebetika* club**	κέντρο με ρεμπέτικα	*ke*·dro me re·*be*·ti·ka
restaurant	εστιατόριο	e·sti·a·*to*·ri·o
sports match	αθλητικό παιγνίδι	ath·li·ti·*ko* pegh·*ni*·ţhi

For more on bars and drinks, see **romance**, page 131, and **eating out**, pages 166–170.

invitations

προσκλήσεις

What are you doing …?	Τι κάνεις …;	ti *ka*·nis …
now	τώρα	*to*·ra
this weekend	το Σαββατοκύριακο	to sa·va·to·*ki*·ria·ko
tonight	απόψε	a·*pop*·se

Do you know a good restaurant?
Ξέρεις κανένα καλό εστιατόριο; — *kse*·ris ka·*ne*·na ka·*lo* e·sti·a·*to*·ri·o

My round.
Η σειρά μου. — i si·*ra* mu

We're having a party.
Έχουμε πάρτι. — *e*·khu·me *par*·ti

Would you like to go (for a) ...?	Θα ήθελες να πας ...;	tha *i*·the·les na pas ...
coffee	για καφέ	yia ka·*fe*
dancing	για χορό	yia kho·*ro*
drink	για ποτό	yia po·*to*
meal	για φαγητό	yia fa·yi·*to*
out somewhere	κάπου έξω	*ka*·pu *ek*·so
walk	βόλτα	*vol*·ta

responding to invitations

απαντώντας σε προσκλήσεις

Sure!
Μάλιστα! — *ma*·li·sta

Yes, I'd love to.
Ναι, θα ήθελα πολύ. — ne tha *i*·the·la po·*li*

That's very kind of you.
Πολύ ευγενικό εκ μέρους σου. — po·*li* ev·ye·ni·*ko* ek *me*·rus su

No, I'm afraid I can't.
Όχι, φοβάμαι πως δεν μπορώ. — *o*·hi fo·*va*·me pos ţhen bo·*ro*

What about tomorrow?
Τι θα έλεγες για αύριο; — ti tha *e*·le·yes yia *av*·ri·o

Where shall we go?
Πού θα πάμε; — pu tha *pa*·me

arranging to meet

κανονίζοντας για συνάντηση

What time will we meet?
Τι ώρα θα συναντηθούμε; — ti *o*·ra tha si·na·di·*thu*·me

Where will we meet?
Πού θα συναντηθούμε; — pu tha si·na·di·*thu*·me

Let's meet at …	Ας συναντηθούμε …	as si·na·di·*thu*·me …
(eight) o'clock	στις (οχτώ)	stis (okh·*to*)
the entrance	στην είσοδο	stin *i*·so·ţho

I'll pick you up.
Θα σε πάρω εγώ. — tha se *pa*·ro e·*gho*

Are you ready?
Είσαι έτοιμος/έτοιμη; m/f — *i*·se *e*·ti·mos/*e*·ti·mi

I'm ready.
Είμαι έτοιμος/έτοιμη. m/f — *i*·me *e*·ti·mos/*e*·ti·mi

Where will you be?
Πού θα είσαι; — pu tha *i*·se

If I'm not there by (nine), don't wait for me.
Αν δεν είμαι εκεί μέχρι (τις εννέα), μή με περιμένεις. — an ţhen *i*·me e·*ki* *me*·khri (tis e·*ne*·a) mi me pe·ri·*me*·mis

I'm looking forward to it.
Το περιμένω πώς και πώς. — to pe·ri·*me*·no pos ke pos

OK!	Εντάξει!	e·*dak*·si
I'll see you then.	Θα σε δω τότε.	tha se ţho *to*·te
Sorry I'm late.	Συγνώμη που άργησα.	sigh·*no*·mi pu *ar*·yi·sa

drugs

ναρκωτικά

Do you have a light?
Έχεις φωτιά; — *e*·his fo·*tia*

Do you want to have a smoke?
Θέλεις να καπνίσεις; — *the*·lis na kap·*ni*·sis

I don't take drugs.
Δεν παίρνω ναρκωτικά. — ţhen *per*·no nar·ko·ti·*ka*

I take … occasionally.
Παίρνω … καμιά φορά. — *per*·no … ka·*mia* fo·*ra*

romance
ειδύλλιο

asking someone out

ζητώντας να βγείτε έξω

Where would you like to go (tonight)?
Πού θα ήθελες να πάμε (απόψε); — pu tha *the*·lis na *pa*·me (a·*pop*·se)

Would you like to do something (tomorrow)?
Θα ήθελες να κάνουμε κάτι (αύριο); — tha *i*·the·les na *ka*·nu·me *ka*·ti (*av*·ri·o)

Yes, I'd love to.
Ναι, θα το ήθελα πολύ. — ne tha to *i*·the·la po·*li*

Sorry, I can't.
Συγνώμη, δεν μπορώ. — sigh·*no*·mi ţhen bo·*ro*

pick-up lines

χώροι γνωριμίας

Would you like a drink?
Θα ήθελες ένα ποτό; — tha *i*·the·les *e*·na po·*to*

You look like someone I know. (to a man)
Μοιάζεις με κάποιον που ξέρω. — *mia*·zis me *ka*·pion pu *kse*·ro

You look like someone I know. (to a woman)
Μοιάζεις με κάποια που ξέρω. — *mia*·zis me *ka*·pia pu *kse*·ro

You're a fantastic dancer. (to a man)
Είσαι απίθανος χορευτής. — *i*·se a·*pi*·tha·nos kho·ref·*tis*

You're a fantastic dancer. (to a woman)
Είσαι απίθανη χορεύτρια. — *i*·se a·*pi*·tha·ni kho·*ref*·tria

Can I ...?	Μπορώ να ...;	bo·*ro* na ...
dance with you	χορέψω μαζί σου	kho·*rep*·so ma·*zi* su
sit here	καθίσω εδώ	ka·*thi*·so e·*ţho*
take you home	σε πάρω στο σπίτι	se *pa*·ro sto *spi*·ti

rejections

αρνήσεις

No, thank you.
Όχι, ευχαριστώ. — *o*·hi ef·kha·ri·*sto*

I'd rather not.
Νομίζω όχι. — no·*mi*·zo *o*·hi

I'm here with my boyfriend.
Είμαι εδώ με τον φίλο μου. — *i*·me e·*ţho* me ton *fi*·lo mu

I'm here with my girlfriend.
Είμαι εδώ με την φίλη μου. — *i*·me e·*ţho* me tin *fi*·li mu

Excuse me, I have to go now.
Συγνώμη, πρέπει να πηγαίνω τώρα. — sigh·*no*·mi *pre*·pi na pi·*ye*·no *to*·ra

Leave me alone! (a man)
Άσε με ήσυχο! — *a*·se me *i*·si·kho

Leave me alone! (a woman)
Άσε με ήσυχη! — *a*·se me *i*·si·khi

Piss off!
Άντε από δω, ρε! — *a*·de a·*po* ţho re

local talk

He's a babe.
Είναι κούκλος. — *i*·ne *ku*·klos

She's a babe.
Είναι κούκλα. — *i*·ne *ku*·kla

He's hot.
Είναι θερμός. — *i*·ne ther·*mos*

She's hot.
Είναι θερμή. — *i*·ne ther·*mi*

getting closer

πλησιάζοντας πιο κοντά

I like you very much.
Μου αρέσεις πολύ. — mu a·*re*·sis po·*li*

You're great.
Είσαι θαύμα. — *i*·se *thav*·ma

Can I kiss you?
Μπορώ να σε φιλήσω; — bo·*ro* na se fi·*li*·so

Do you want to come inside for a while?
Θέλεις να έρθεις μέσα, για λίγο; — *the*·lis na *er*·this *me*·sa yia *li*·gho

Do you want a massage?
Θέλεις ένα μασάζ; — *the*·lis *e*·na ma·*saz*

Can I stay over?
Μπορώ να μείνω τη νύχτα; — bo·*ro* na *mi*·no ti *nikh*·ta

sex

σεξ

Kiss me.	Φίλα με.	*fi*·la me
I want you.	Σε θέλω.	se *the*·lo
Touch me here.	Πιάσε με εδώ.	*pia*·se me e·*ţho*
Let's go to bed.	Πάμε στο κρεβάτι.	*pa*·me sto kre·*va*·ti

Do you like this?
Σου αρέσει αυτό; — su a·*re*·si af·*to*

I (don't) like that.
(Δεν) Μου αρέσει αυτό. — (ţhen) mu a·*re*·si af·*to*

I think we should stop now.
Νομίζω πως πρέπει να σταματήσουμε τώρα. — no·*mi*·zo pos *pre*·pi na sta·ma·*ti*·su·me *to*·ra

Do you have a condom?
Έχεις προφυλακτικό; — *e*·his pro·fi·lak·ti·*ko*

Let's use a condom.
Ας χρησιμοποιήσουμε προφυλακτικό. — as khri·si·mo·pi·*i*·su·me pro·fi·lak·ti·*ko*

I won't do it without protection.
Δεν το κάνω χωρίς προφύλαξη. — ţhen to *ka*·no kho·*ris* pro·*fi*·lak·si

It's my first time.
Είναι η πρώτη μου φορά. — *i*·ne i *pro*·ti mu fo·*ra*

It helps to have a sense of humour.
Βοηθάει να έχεις την αίσθηση του χιούμορ. — vo·i·*tha*·i na *e*·his tin *es*·thi·si tu *hiu*·mor

Oh my god!
Ω, θεέ μου! — o the·*e* mu

That's great.
Είναι απίθανο. — *i*·ne a·*pi*·tha·no

Easy tiger! (to a man)
σιγά ρε γόη! — si·*gha* re *gho*·i

Easy tiger! (to a woman)
σιγά ρε γόισσα! — si·*gha* re *gho*·i·sa

That was …	Ήταν …	*i*·tan …
amazing	καταπληπτικό	ka·ta·plik·ti·*ko*
romantic	ρομαντικό	ro·ma·di·*ko*
wild	άγριο	*a*·ghri·o

love

αγάπη

I think we're good together.
Νομίζω ταιριάζουμε. — no·*mi*·zo te·*ria*·zu·me

I love you.
Σ'αγαπώ. — sa·gha·*po*

Will you …?	Θα …;	tha …
go out with me	έρθεις έξω μαζί μου	*er*·this *ek*·so ma·*zi* mu
marry me	με παντρευτείς	me pa·dref·*tis*
meet my parents	συναντήσεις τους γονείς μου	si·na·*di*·sis tus gho·*nis* mu

sweet talk

my baby	μωρό μου	mo·*ro* mu
my darling	μάνα μου	*ma*·na mu
my doll	κουκλί μου	ku·*kli* mu
my hunk	τζουτζούκο μου	tzu·*tzu*·ko mu
my soul	ψυχούλα μου	psi·*hu*·la mu
my treasure	χρυσό μου	khri·*so* mu
sweetheart	καρδούλα μου	kar·*ţhu*·la mu

problems

προβλήματα

Are you seeing someone else? (to a woman)
βλέπεις κάποιον άλλο; — *e*·his *ka*·pion *a*·lon

Are you seeing someone else? (to a man)
βλέπεις κάποια άλλη; — *e*·his ka·pia *a*·li

He/She is just a friend.
Είναι απλά φίλος/φίλη. — *i*·ne a·*pla fi*·los/*fi*·li

You're just using me for sex.
Με θέλεις μόνο για το σεξ. — me *the*·lis *mo*·no yia to seks

I never want to see you again.
Δεν θέλω να σε ξαναδώ. — ţhen *the*·lo na se ksa·na·*ţho*

I don't think it's working out.
Δεν νομίζω ότι δουλεύει. — ţhen no·*mi*·zo *o*·ti ţhu·*le*·vi

We'll work it out.
Θα τα βρούμε. — tha ta *vru*·me

leaving

αναχώρηση

I have to leave (tomorrow).
Πρέπει να φύγω (αύριο). — *pre*·pi na *fi*·gho (*av*·ri·o)

I'll ...	Θα ...	tha ...
keep in touch	βρίσκομαι σε επαφή	*vris*·ko·me se e·pa·*fi*
miss you	μου λείψεις	mu *lip*·sis
visit you	σε επισκεφτώ	se e·pis·kef·*to*

it's a tragedy

The poet Thespis (Θέσπις *thes*·pis) was one of the founders of the theatrical tragedy genre during the 6th century BC. His name survives in the English word 'Thespian', meaning 'dramatic' or 'relating to drama or theatre'.

religion

θρησκεία

What's your religion?
Ποια είναι η θρησκεία σου; — pia *i*·ne i thris·*ki*·a su

I'm not religious.
Δεν είμαι θρήσκος. — ţhen *i*·me *thris*·kos

I'm …	Είμαι …	*i*·me …
agnostic	αγνωστικιστής m	agh·no·sti·ki·*stis*
	αγνωστικίστρια f	agh·no·sti·*ki*·stri·a
Buddhist	Βουδιστής m	vu·ţhi·*stis*
	Βουδίστρια f	vu·*ţhi*·stri·a
Catholic	Καθολικός m	ka·tho·li·*kos*
	Καθολική f	ka·tho·li·*ki*
Christian	Χριστιανός m	khri·stia·*nos*
	Χριστιανή f	khri·stia·*ni*
Hindu	Ινδουιστής m	in·ţhu·i·*stis*
	Ινδουίστρια f	in·ţhu·*i*·stri·a
Jewish	Ιουδαίος m	i·u·*ţhe*·os
	Ιουδαία f	i·u·*ţhe*·a
Muslim	Μουσουλμάνος m	mu·sul·*ma*·nos
	Μουσουλμάνα f	mu·sul·*ma*·na
Orthodox	Ορθόδοξος m	or·*tho*·ţhok·sos
	Ορθόδοξη f	or·*tho*·ţhok·si
I (don't) believe in …	(Δεν) Πιστευω …	(ţhen) pi·*ste*·vo …
astrology	στην αστρολογία	stin a·stro·lo·*yi*·a
fate	στη μοίρα	sti *mi*·ra
God	στο Θεό	sto the·*o*

Can I … here?	Μπορώ να … εδώ;	bo·*ro* na … e·*ţho*
Where can I …?	Πού μπορώ να …;	pu bo·*ro* na …
attend mass	παρακολουθήσω τη λειτουργία	pa·ra·ko·lu·*thi*·so ti li·tur·*yi*·a
attend a service	παρακολουθήσω την ακολουθία	pa·ra·ko·lu·*thi*·so tin a·ko·lu·*thi*·a
pray	προσευχηθώ	pro·sef·hi·*tho*
worship	προσκυνήσω	pros·ki·*ni*·so

cultural differences

πολιτιστικές διαφορές

Is this a local or national custom?
Είναι αυτό τοπικό ή εθνικό έθιμο; — *i*·ne af·*to* to·pi·*ko* i eth·ni·*ko* *e*·thi·mo

I'm not used to this.
Δεν είμαι συνηθισμένος σ'αυτό. — ţhen *i*·me si·ni·thiz·*me*·nos saf·*to*

I'd rather not join in.
Θα προτιμούσα να μη λάβω μέρος. — tha pro·ti·*mu*·sa na mi *la*·vo *me*·ros

I'll try it.
Θα το δοκιμάσω. — tha to ţho·ki·*ma*·so

I didn't mean to do anything wrong.
Δεν ήθελα να κάμω κάτι που δεν έπρεπε. — ţhen *i*·the·la na *ka*·mo *ka*·ti pu ţhen *e*·pre·pe

I didn't mean to say anything wrong.
Δεν ήθελα πω κάτι που δεν έπρεπε. — ţhen *i*·the·la po *ka*·ti pu ţhen *e*·pre·pe

I don't want to offend you.
Δεν θέλω να σε προσβάλω. — ţhen *the*·lo na se proz·*va*·lo

I'm sorry, it's against my …	Συγνώμη, είναι αντίθετο με … μου.	sigh·*no*·mi *i*·ne a·*di*·the·to me … mu
beliefs	την πίστη	tin *pi*·sti
religion	τη θρησκεία	ti thris·*ki*·a

When's the museum open?
Πότε είναι ανοιχτό το μουσείο; *po*·te *i*·ne a·nikh·*to* to mu·*si*·o

When's the gallery open?
Πότε είναι ανοιχτή η πινακοθήκη; *po*·te *i*·ne a·nikh·*ti* i pi·na·ko·*thi*·ki

What kind of art are you interested in?
Τι είδους τέχνη σε ενδιαφέρει; ti *i*·ţhus *tekh*·ni se en·ţhia·*fe*·ri

I'm interested in …
Με ενδιαφέρει … me en·ţhia·*fe*·ri …

What's in the collection?
Τι υπάρχει στη συλλογή; ti i·*par*·hi sti si·lo·*yi*

It's an exhibition of …
Είναι μια έκθεση … *i*·ne mia *ek*·the·si …

Where are the exhibits from (Knossos)?
Πού είναι τα εκθέματα από την (Κνωσσό); pu *i*·ne ta ek·*the*·ma·ta a·*po* tin (kno·*so*)

What style is this?
Τι στυλ είναι αυτό; ti stil *i*·ne af·*to*

Is it an original or a copy?
Είναι αυθεντικό ή αντίγραφο; *i*·ne af·the·di·*ko* i a·*di*·ghra·fo

What do you think of …?
Πώς σου φαίνεται …; pos su *fe*·ne·te …

I like the works of …
Μου αρέσουν τα έργα … mu a·*re*·sun ta *er*·gha

It reminds me of …
Μου θυμίζει … mu thi·*mi*·zi …

Byzantine	Βυζαντινός	vi·za·di·*nos*
classical	κλασσικός	kla·si·*kos*
Hellenistic	Ελληνιστικός	e·li·ni·sti·*kos*
modern	μοντέρνος	mo·*der*·nos
Roman	Ρωμαϊκός	ro·ma·i·*kos*

… civilisation	… πολιτισμός m	… po·li·tiz·*mos*
Cycladic	Κυκλαδικός	ki·kla·ţhi·*kos*
Minoan	Μινωικός	mi·no·i·*kos*
Mycenean	Μυκηναϊκός	mi·ki·ma·i·*kos*
… style	… ρυθμός m	… rith·*mos*
Corinthian	Κορινθιακός	ko·rin·thi·a·*kos*
Doric	Δωρικός	ţho·ri·*kos*
Ionic	Ιωνικός	i·o·ni·*kos*
architecture	αρχιτεκτονική f	ar·hi·tek·to·ni·*ki*
artwork	καλλιτέχνημα n	ka·li·*tekh*·ni·ma
column	κολόνα f	ko·*lo*·na
curator	έφορος μουσείου m	*e*·fo·ros mu·*si*·u
decorative arts	διακοσμητικές τέχνες f pl	ţhi·a·koz·mi·ti·*kes* *tekh*·nes
etching	χαλκογραφία f	khal·ko·ghra·*fi*·a
exhibit	έκθεση f	*ek*·the·si
exhibition hall	αίθουσα έκθεσης f	*e*·thu·sa *ek*·the·sis
fresco	φρέσκο n	*fres*·ko
metalwork	μεταλλικά αντικείμενα n pl	me·ta·li·*ka* a·di·*ki*·me·na
mosaic	μωσαϊκό n	mo·sa·i·*ko*
painter	ζωγράφος m	zo·*ghra*·fos
painting (artwork)	πίνακας m	*pi*·na·kas
painting (the art)	ζωγραφική f	zo·ghra·fi·*ki*
period	περίοδος f	pe·*ri*·o·ţhos
permanent collection	μόνιμη συλλογή f	*mo*·ni·mi si·lo·*yi*
print	αντίγραφο n	a·*di*·ghra·fo
sculptor	γλύπτης m	*ghlip*·tis
sculpture	γλυπτική f	ghlip·ti·*ki*
shield	ασπίδα f	a·*spi*·ţha
spear	δόρυ n	*ţho*·ri
sword	σπαθί n	spa·*thi*
statue	άγαλμα n	*a*·ghal·ma
terracotta pot	αγγείο τερακότα n	a·*gi*·o te·ra·*ko*·ta
tunic	χιτώνας m	hi·*to*·nas
vessel	αγγείο n	a·*gi*·o

sporting interests

αθλητικά ενδιφέροντα

What sport do you follow/play?
Τι σπορ ακολουθείς/παίζεις; — ti spor a·ko·lu·*this*/*pe*·zis

I follow (basketball).
Παρακολουθώ (μπάσκετ). — pa·ra·ko·lu·*tho* (*ba*·sket)

I play (football).
Παίζω (ποδόσφαιρο). — *pe*·zo (po·ţhos·fe·ro)

I do ...	Κάνω ...	*ka*·no ...
athletics	αθλήματα	ath·*li*·ma·ta
hiking	πεζοπορία	pe·zo·po·*ri*·a
sailing	ιστιοπλοΐα	i·sti·o·plo·*i*·a
scuba diving	υπόγειες καταδύσεις	i·*po*·yi·es ka·ta·*ţhi*·sis
sailboarding	γουιντσέρφινγκ	ghu·id·*ser*·fing
water-skiing	θαλάσσιο σκι	tha·*la*·si·o ski

For more sports, see the **dictionary**.

top sport

soccer	ποδόσφαιρο n ευρωπαϊκό	po·*ţhos*·fe·ro ev·ro·pa·i·*ko*
basketball	μπάσκετ n	*bas*·ket
volleyball	βόλεϋ n	*vo*·le·i
gymnastics	κλασσικός αθλητισμός m	kla·si·*kos* ath·li·tiz·*mos*
swimming	κολύμπι n	ko·*lim*·bi

To exercise you brain, try Greece's favourite nonphysical pastime:

backgammon	τάβλι n	*tav*·li

I …	Εγώ …	e·*gho* …
cycle	κάνω ποδήλατο	*ka*·no po·*ţhi*·la·to
run	τρέχω	*tre*·kho
walk	βαδίζω	va·*ţhi*·zo

Do you like (football)?
Σου αρέσει (το ποδόσφαιρο); su a·*re*·si (to po·*ţhos*·fe·ro)

Yes, very much.
Ναι, πάρα πολύ. ne *pa*·ra po·*li*

Not really.
Όχι. *o*·hi

I like watching it.
Μου αρέσει να το κοιτάζω. mu a·*re*·si na to ki·*ta*·zo

What's your favourite team?
Ποια ομάδα υποστηρίζεις; pia o·*ma*·ţha i·po·sti·*ri*·zis

Who's your favourite sportsperson?
Ποιος αθλητής σου αρέσει; pios ath·li·*tis* su a·*re*·si

going to a game

πηγαίνοντας σε ένα παιγνίδι

Would you like to go to a game?
Θα ήθελες να πας σε ένα παιγνίδι; tha *i*·the·les na pas se *e*·na pegh·*ni*·ţhi

Who are you supporting?
Ποιον υποστηρίζεις; pion i·po·sti·*ri*·zis

Who's playing/winning?
Ποιος παίζει/κερδίζει; pios *pe*·zi/ker·*ţhi*·zi

scoring

What's the score?	Ποιο είναι το σκορ;	pio *i*·ne to skor
draw/even	ισοπαλία	i·so·pa·*li*·a
love/zero/nil	μηδέν	mi·*ţhen*
match-point	πόντος για παιγνίδι	*po*·dos yia pegh·*ni*·ţhi

sports talk		
What a …!	Τι …!	ti …
goal	γκολ	gol
hit	χτύπημα	*khti*·pi·ma
kick	κλωτσιά	klot·*sia*
pass	πάσα	*pa*·sa
performance	απόδοση	a·*po*·ţho·si

That was a … game!	Ήταν … παιγνίδι!	*i*·tan … pegh·*ni*·ţhi
bad	άσχημο	*a*·shi·mo
boring	πληκτικό	plik·ti·*ko*
great	υπέροχο	i·*pe*·ro·kho

playing sport

παίζοντας σπορ

Do you want to play?
Θέλεις να παίξεις; — *the*·lis na *pek*·sis

Can I join in?
Να παίξω και εγώ; — na *pek*·so ke e·*gho*

That would be great.
Αυτό θα ήταν υπέροχο. — af·*to* tha *i*·tan i·*pe*·ro·kho

I can't.
Δεν μπορώ. — ţhen bo·*ro*

I have an injury.
Έχω ένα τραύμα. — *e*·kho *e*·na *trav*·ma

Your/My point.
Δικός σου/μου πόντος. — ţhi·*kos* su/mu *po*·dos

Kick it to me!
κλώτσα την σε μένα! — *klot*·sa tin se *me*·na

Pass it to me!
ρίξ'την σε μένα! — *riks*·tin se *me*·na

You're a good player.
Είσαι καλός παίχτης. — *i*·se ka·*los pekh*·tis

Thanks for the game.
Ευχαριστώ για το παιγνίδι. — ef·kha·ri·*sto* yia to pegh·*ni*·ţhi

Where's a good place to ...?	Πού είναι ένα καλό μέρος για να ... κανείς;	pu *i*·ne *e*·na ka·*lo me*·ros yia na ... ka·*nis*
fish	ψαρέψει	psa·*rep*·si
go horse riding	κάμει ιππασία	*ka*·mi i·pa·*si*·a
run	τρέξει	*trek*·si
snorkel	κάμει κατάδυση	*ka*·mi ka·*ta*·ţhi·si
surf	σερφάρει	ser·*fa*·ri

SOCIAL

Where's the nearest ...?	Πού είναι το πιο κοντινό ...;	pu *i*·ne to pio ko·*di*·*no* ...
golf course	γήπεδο του γκολφ	*yi*·pe·ţho tu golf
gym	γυμναστήριο	yim·na·*sti*·ri·o
tennis court	γήπεδο του τένις	*yi*·pe·ţho tu *te*·nis

Where's the nearest swimming pool?
Πού είναι η πιο κοντινή πισίνα; pu *i*·ne i pio ko·di·*ni* pi·*si*·na

Do I have to be a member to attend?
Πρέπει να είμαι μέλος για να πάω; *pre*·pi na *i*·me *me*·los yia na *pa*·o

Is there a women-only session?
Υπάρχει ορισμένη ώρα μόνο για γυναίκες; i·*par*·hi o·riz·*me*·ni *o*·ra *mo*·no yia yi·*ne*·kes

Can I book a lesson?
Μπορώ να κλείσω ένα μάθημα; bo·*ro* na *kli*·so *e*·na *ma*·thi·ma

Where are the changing rooms?
Πού είναι τα αποδυτήρια; pu *i*·ne ta a·po·ţhi·*ti*·ri·a

What's the charge per ...?	Πόσο κοστίζει ...;	*po*·so ko·*sti*·zi ...
day	την ημέρα	tin i·*me*·ra
game	το παιγνίδι	to pegh·*ni*·ţhi
hour	την ώρα	tin *o*·ra
visit	την επίσκεψη	tin e·*pis*·kep·si

Can I hire a ...?	Μπορώ να νοικιάσω ...;	bo·*ro* na ni·*kia*·so ...
ball	μια μπάλα	mia *ba*·la
bicycle	ένα ποδήλατο	*e*·na po·*ţhi*·la·to
court	το γήπεδο	to *yi*·pe·ţho
racquet	μια ρακέτα	mia ra·*ke*·ta

fishing

ψάρεμα

Where are the good spots?
Πού είναι τα καλά μέρη; — pu *i*·ne ta ka·*la* *me*·ri

Do I need a fishing permit?
Χρειάζομαι άδεια για ψάρεμα; — khri·*a*·zo·me *a*·ţhi·a yia *psa*·re·ma

Do you do fishing tours?
Κάνετε εκδρομές για ψάρεμε; — *ka*·ne·te ek·ţhro·*mes* yia *psa*·re·ma

What's the best bait?
Ποιο είναι το καλύτερο δόλωμα; — pio *i*·ne to ka·*li*·te·ro *ţho*·lo·ma

Are they biting?
Τσιμπάει; — tsi·*ba*·i

What kind of fish are you landing?
Τι ψάρι βγάζεις; — ti *psa*·ri *vgha*·zis

How much does it weigh?
Πόσο ζυγίζει; — *po*·so zi·*yi*·zi

bait	δόλωμα **n**	*ţho*·lo·ma
fishing line	πετονιά **f**	pe·to·*nia*
flare	φανάρι **n**	fa·*na*·ri
float	φελλός **f**	fe·*los*
hooks	αγκίστρια **n pl**	a·*gi*·stri·a
lifejacket	σωσίβιο **n**	so·*si*·vi·o
lure	δόλωμα **n**	*ţho*·lo·ma
rod	καλάμι **n**	ka·*la*·mi
sinkers	βαρύδια **n pl**	va·*ri*·ţhia

not biting?

Fishing with dynamite used to be a popular pastime in Greece, but this 'sport' has been outlawed because of its environmental impact. Look out for signs warning Απαγορεύεται η χρήση δυναμίτη (No Dynamite).

horse riding

ιππασία

How much is a (one-)hour ride?
Πόσο κοστίζει η ιππασία (την) ώρα; — *po*·so kos·*ti*·zi i i·pa·*si*·a (tin) *o*·ra

How long is the ride?
πόση ώρα διαρκεί η διαδρομή με το άλογο; — *po*·si *o*·ra ţhi·ar·*ki* i ţhi·a·ţhro·*mi* me to *a*·lo·gho

I'm (not) an experienced rider.
(Δεν) Είμαι πεπειραμένος αναβάτης. — (ţhen) *i*·me pe·pi·ra·me·*nos* a·na·*va*·tis

Can I rent a hat and boots?
Μπορώ να νοικάσω ένα καπέλο και μπότες; — bo·*ro* na ni·*kia*·so *e*·na ka·*pe*·lo ke *bo*·tes

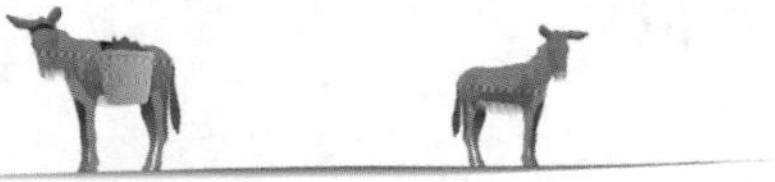

bit	στομίδα f	sto·*mi*·ţha
bridle	χαλινάρι n	kha·li·*na*·ri
canter	τριποδισμός m	tri·po·ţhiz·*mos*
crop	μαστίγιο ιππασίας n	mas·*ti*·yi·o i·pa·*si*·as
gallop	καλπασμός m	kal·paz·*mos*
groom	ιπποκόμος m	i·po·*ko*·mos
horse	άλογο n	*a*·lo·gho
pony	πουλάρι n	pu·*la*·ri
race	κούρσα f	*kur*·sa
reins	γκέμια n pl	*ge*·mia
saddle	σέλλα f	*se*·la
stable	στάβλος m	*stav*·los
stirrup	σκάλα f	*ska*·la
trot	τροχασμός m	tro·khaz·*mos*
walk	βάδισμα n	*va*·ţhiz·ma

soccer/football

ποδόσφαιρο

Who plays for (Iraklis)?
Ποιος παίζει στον (Ηρακλή); pios *pe*·zi ston (i·ra·*kli*)

He's a great (player).
Είναι μεγάλος (παίχτης). *i*·ne me·*gha*·los (*pekh*·tis)

He played brilliantly in the match against (Italy).
Έπαιξε υπέροχα στο ματς εναντίον (της Ιταλίας). *e*·pek·se i·*pe*·ro·kha sto mats e·na·*di*·on (tis i·ta·*li*·as)

Which team is at the top of the league?
Ποια ομάδα είναι στην κορυφή της πρώτης εθνικής; pia o·*ma*·ţha *i*·ne stin ko·ri·*fi* tis *pro*·tis eth·ni·*kis*

What a great/terrible team!
Τι μεγάλη/κουρέλα ομάδα! ti me·*gha*·li/ku·*re*·la o·*ma*·ţha

ball	μπάλα f	*ba*·la
coach	προπονητής m	pro·po·ni·*tis*
corner (kick)	κόρνερ n	*kor*·ner
expulsion	αποβολή n	a·po·vo·*li*
fan	οπαδός m	o·pa·*ţhos*
foul	φάουλ n	*fa*·ul
free kick	φρίκικ n	*fri*·kik
goal (structure)	γκολπόστ n	gol·*post*
goalkeeper	γκολκήπερ m	gol·*ki*·per
manager	μάνατζερ m	*ma*·na·dzer
offside	οφσάιτ n	of·*sa*·it
penalty	πέναλτι n	*pe*·nal·ti
player	παίχτης m	*pekh*·tis
red card	κόκκινη κάρτα f	*ko*·ki·ni *kar*·ta
referee	διαιτητής m	ţhi·e·ti·*tis*
throw in	αναπληρωματικός m	a·na·pli·ro·ma·ti·*kos*
yellow card	κίτρινη κάρτα n	*ki*·tri·ni *kar*·ta

SOCIAL

tennis & table tennis

τένις και πινγκ πονγκ

I'd like to ...	Θα ήθελα να ...	tha *i*·the·la na ...
book a time to play	κλείσω ώρα να παίξω	*kli*·so *o*·ra na *pek*·so
play table tennis	παίξω πινγκ πονγκ	*pek*·so ping pong
play tennis	παίξω τένις	*pek*·so *te*·nis

Can we play at night?
Μπορούμε να παίξουμε τη νύχτα; — bo·*ru*·me na *pek*·su·me ti *nikh*·ta

I need my racquet restrung.
Η ρακέτα μου χρειάζεται επισκευή. — i ra·*ke*·ta mu khri·*a*·ze·te e·pis·ke·*vi*

ace	άσος m	*a*·sos
advantage	πλεονέκτημα n	ple·o·*nek*·ti·ma
bat	ρακέτα f	ra·*ke*·ta
clay	πήλινη σφαίρα f	*pi*·li·ni *sfe*·ra
fault	φάουλ n	*fa*·ul
game, set, match	παιγνίδι, σετ, ματς n	pegh·*ni*·ţhi set mats
grass	γρασίδι n	ghra·*si*·ţhi
hard court	σκληρό γήπεδο n	skli·*ro yi*·pe·ţho
net	δίχτυ n	*ţhikh*·ti
ping-pong ball	μπαλάκι του πιγκ πογκ n	ba·*la*·ki tu ping pong
play doubles v	παίζουμε ζευγάρια	*pe*·zu·me zev·*gha*·ria
racket	ρακέτα f	ra·*ke*·ta
serve v	σερβ	serv
tennis ball	μπαλάκι του τένις n	ba·*la*·ki tu *te*·nis
table-tennis table	τραπέζι του πινγκ πονγκ n	tra·*pe*·zi tu ping pong

water sports

θαλάσσια σπορ

Can I hire (a) …?	Μπορώ να νοικιάσω …;	bo·*ro* na ni·*kia*·so …
boat	μια βάρκα	mia *var*·ka
canoe	ένα κανό	*e*·na ka·*no*
kayak	ένα καγιάκ	*e*·na ka·*yiak*
life jacket	ένα σωσίβιο	*e*·na so·*si*·vi·o
snorkelling gear	μια στολή κατάδυσης	mia sto·*li* ka·*ta*·ţhi·sis
water-skis	θαλάσσια σκι	tha·*la*·si·a ski
wetsuit	αδιάβροχη στολή	a·*ţhiav*·ro·hi sto·*li*

Are there any …?	Υπάρχουν …;	i·*par*·khun …
reefs	ξέρες	*kse*·res
rips	δύνες	*ţhi*·nes
water hazards	θαλάσσιοι κίνδυνοι	tha·*la*·si·i *kin*·ţhi·ni

guide	οδηγός **m&f**	o·ţhi·*ghos*
motorboat	βάρκα με μηχανή **f**	*var*·ka me mi·kha·*ni*
oars	κουπιά **n pl**	ku·*pia*
sailboarding	γουιντσέρφινγκ **n**	ghu·id·*ser*·fing
sailing boat	βάρκα με ιστία **f**	*var*·ka me i·*sti*·a
surfboard	σέρφμπορντ **n**	*serf*·bord
surfing	σέρφινγκ **n**	*ser*·fing
wave	κύμα **n**	*ki*·ma

diving in

During the summer months, ask around for diving classes:

Is there a diving school here?
Υπάρχει σχολή καταδύσεων εδώ; — i·*par*·hi skho·*li* ka·ta·*ţhi*·se·on e·*ţho*

Do you offer diving lessons (in English)?
Προσφέρετε μαθήματα καταδύσεων (στα αγγλικά); — pros·*fe*·re·te ma·*thi*·ma·ta ka·ta·*ţhi*·se·on (sta ang·gli·*ka*)

hiking

πεζοπορία

Where can I …?	Πού μπορώ να …;	pu bo·*ro* na …
buy supplies	αγοράσω προμήθειες	a·gho·*ra*·so pro·*mi*·thi·es
find someone who knows this area	βρω κάποιον που ξέρει αυτή την περιοχή	vro *ka*·pion pu *kse*·ri af·*ti* tin pe·ri·o·*hi*
get a map	πάρω ένα χάρτη	*pa*·ro *e*·na *khar*·ti
hire hiking gear	νοικιάσω εξοπλισμό για πεζοπορία	ni·*kia*·so ek·so·pliz·*mo* yia pe·zo·po·*ri*·a

How …?	Πόσο …;	*po*·so …
high is the climb	ψηλό είναι το ανέβασμα	psi·*lo* *i*·ne to *a*·ne·vaz ma
long is the trail	μακρύ είναι το μονοπάτι	ma·*kri* *i*·ne to mo·no·*pa*·ti

Do we need to take …?	Χρειάζεται να πάρουμε …;	khri·*a*·ze·te na *pa*·ru·me …
bedding	σκεπάσματα	ske·*paz*·*ma*·ta
food	φαγητό	fa·yi·*to*
water	νερό	ne·*ro*

Do we need a guide?
Χρειαζόμαστε οδηγό; — khri·a·*zo*·ma·ste o·ʈhi·*gho*

Are there guided treks?
Υπάρχουν μονοπάτια με σήματα; — i·*par*·khun mo·no·*pa*·tia me *si*·ma·ta

Is there a path to (Profitis Ilias)?
Υπάρχει μονοπάτι για (τον Προφήτη Ηλία); — i·*par*·hi mo·no·*pa*·ti yia (ton pro·*fi*·ti i·*li*·a)

Is it safe?
Είναι ασφαλές; — *i*·ne as·fa·*les*

Is it steep?
Είναι απόκρημνο; — *i*·ne a·*po*·krim·no

Are there any rockfalls?
Πέφτουν πουθενά πέτρες; — *pef*·tun pu·the·*na* *pet*·res

Is there a hut?
Υπάρχει κανένα καλύβι; — i·*par*·hi ka·*ne*·na ka·*li*·vi

When does it get dark?
Πότε σκοτεινιάζει; — *po*·te sko·ti·*nia*·zi

Is the track ...?	Είναι ο δρόμος ...;	*i*·ne o ţhro·*mos* ...
(well-) marked	σημαδεμένος (καλά)	si·ma·ţhe·*me*·nos (ka·*la*)
open	ανοιχτός	a·nikh·*tos*
scenic	γραφικός	ghra·fi·*kos*

Which is the ... route?	Ποια είναι η πιο ... διαδρομή;	pia *i*·ne i pio ... ţhi·a·ţhro·*mi*
easiest	εύκολη	*ef*·ko·li
most interesting	ενδιαφέρουσα	en·ţhia·*fe*·ru·sa
shortest	κοντινή	ko·di·*ni*

Where can I find the ...?	Πού μπορώ να βρω το ...	pu bo·*ro* na vro to ...
camping ground	χώρο του κάμπινγκ	*kho*·ro tu *kam*·ping
nearest village	πιο κοντινό χωριό	pio ko·di·*no* kho·*rio*
showers	ντουζ	duz
toilets	την τουαλέτα	tin tu·a·*le*·ta

Where have you come from?
Από πού ήρθες; — a·*po* pu *ir*·thes

How long did it take?
Πόση ώρα σου πήρε; — *po*·si *o*·ra su *pi*·re

Does this path go to ...?
Πηγαίνει αυτό το μονοπάτι στο ...; — pi·*ye*·ni af·*to* to mo·no·*pa*·ti sto ...

Can I go through here?

Μπορώ να πάω μέσα από εδώ;	bo·*ro* na *pa*·o *me*·sa a·*po* e·*ţho*

Is the water OK to drink?

Είναι εντάξει το νερό για να πιω;	*i*·ne e·*dak*·si to ne·*ro* yia na pio

I'm lost.

Χάθηκα.	*kha*·thi·ka

beach

παραλία

Where's the … beach?	Πού είναι η … παραλία;	pu *i*·ne i … pa·ra·*li*·a
best	καλύτερη	ka·*li*·te·ri
nearest	κοντινότερη	ko·di·*no*·te·ri
public	δημόσια	ţhi·*mo*·si·a

Where's the nudist beach?

Πού είναι η πλαζ γυμνιστών;	pu *i*·ne i plaz yim·ni·*ston*

Do we have to pay?

Πρέπει να πληρώσουμε;	*pre*·pi na pli·*ro*·su·me

What time is high/low tide?

Τι ώρα είναι η παλίρροια/ άμπωτις;	ti *o*·ra *i*·ne i pa·*li*·ri·a/ *a*·bo·tis

Is it safe to dive/swim here?

Είναι ασφαλές να κάμω βουτιές/κολυμπήσω εδώ;	*i*·ne as·fa·*les* na *ka*·mo vu·*ties*/ko·li·*bi*·so e·*ţho*

listen for …

Είναι επικίνδυνο! *i*·ne e·pi·*kin*·ţhi·no	**It's dangerous!**
Πρόσεχε το υπόγειο ρεύμα! pro·*se*·he to i·*po*·yi·o *rev*·ma	**Be careful of the undertow!**

signs		
Απαγορεύεται το κολύμπι	a·pa·gho·*re*·ve·te to ko·*li*·bi	**No Swimming**
Απαγορεύονται οι βουτιές	a·pa·gho·*re*·vo·de i vu·*ties*	**No Diving**

Are there any ...?	Υπάρχουν ...;	i·*par*·khun ...
currents	ρεύματα	*rev*·ma·ta
jelly fish	μέδουσες	*me*·ţhu·ses
rocks	βράχια	*vra*·hia
sea urchins	αχινοί	a·hi·*ni*

How much for a/an ...?	Πόσο για μια ...;	*po*·so yia mia ...
chair	καρέκλα	ka·*re*·kla
hut	καλύβα	ka·*li*·va
umbrella	ομπρέλα	o·*bre*·la

weather

καιρός

What's the weather like?
Πώς είναι ο καιρός; — pos *i*·ne o ke·*ros*

What will the weather be like tomorrow?
Πώς θα είναι ο καιρός αύριο; — pos tha *i*·ne o ke·*ros* *av*·ri·o

It's ...	Είναι ...	*i*·ne ...
cloudy	συννεφιά	si·ne·*fia*
dry	ξηρασία	ksi·ra·*si*·a
fine	καλός καιρός	ka·*los* ke·*ros*
freezing	παγωνιά	pa·gho·*nia*
humid	υγρασία	i·ghra·*si*·a
mild	μαλακός καιρός	ma·la·*kos* ke·*ros*
sunny	λιακάδα	lia·*ka*·ţha

It's …		
raining	Βρέχει.	*vre*·hi
snowing	Χιονίζει.	hio·*ni*·zi
windy	Φυσάει.	fi·*sa*·i
drizzling	Ψιχαλίζει.	psi·kha·*li*·zi
It's …	Κάνει …	*ka*·ni …
cold	κρύο	*kri*·o
hot	πολλή ζέστη	po·*li* *ze*·sti
warm	ζέστη	*ze*·sti
Where can I buy a/an …?	Πού μπορώ να αγοράσω …;	pu bo·*ro* na a·gho·*ra*·so …
rain jacket	ένα αδιάβροχο	*e*·na a·ţhiav·ro·kho
umbrella	μια ομπρέλα	mia o·*bre*·la

weathering the local storms

heatwave	καύσωνας m	*kaf*·so·nas
strong northerly wind	μελτέμι n	mel·*te*·mi
strong cold wind	βαρδάρης m	var·*tha*·ris
thunderstorm	καταιγίδα f	ka·te·*yi*·ţha

flora & fauna

χλωρίδα και πανίδα

What … is that?	Τι … είναι εκείνο;	ti … *i*·ne e·*ki*·no
animal	ζώο	*zo*·o
flower	λουλούδι	lu·*lu*·ţhi
plant	φυτό	fi·*to*
tree	δέντρο	*ţhe*·dro

What's it used for?
Σε τι χρησιμοποιείται; — se ti khri·si·mo·pi·*i*·te

Can you eat the fruit?
Μπορείς να φας τον καρπό; — bo·*ris* na fas ton kar·*po*

Is it …?	Είναι …;	*i*·ne …
common	κοινό	ki·*no*
dangerous	επικίνδυνο	e·pi·*kin*·ţhi·no
endangered	υπό εξαφάνιση	i·*po* ek·sa·*fa*·ni·si
poisonous	δηλητηριώδες	ţhi·li·ti·ri·*o*·ţhes
protected	προστατευόμενο	pro·sta·te·*vo*·me·no

local plants & animals

basil	βασιλικός m	va·si·li·*kos*
carnation	γαρύφαλο n	gha·*ri*·fa·lo
carob	χαρούπι n	kha·*ru*·pi
Dalmatian pelican	Δαλματικός πελεκάνος m	ţhal·ma·ti·*kos* pe·le·*ka*·nos
dolphin	δελφίνι n	ţhel·*fi*·ni
falcon	γεράκι n	ye·*ra*·ki
fig	σύκο n	*si*·ko
iris	κρίνος m	*kri*·nos
lizard	σαύρα f	*sav*·ra
monk seal	φώκια f	*fo*·kia
olive	ελιά f	e·*lia*
orchid	ορχιδέα f	or·hi·*ţhe*·a
pine	πεύκο n	*pef*·ko
rose	τριαντάφυλλο n	tri·a·*da*·fi·lo
sea gull	γλάρος m	*gla*·ros
sea turtle	θαλάσσια χελώνα f	tha·*la*·si·a khe·*lo*·na
snake	φίδι n	*fi*·ţhi
swallow	χελιδόνι n	he·li·*ţho*·ni
wildflowers	αγριολούλουδα n pl	a·ghri·o·*lu*·lu·ţha

SOCIAL

basics

βασικά

breakfast	πρόγευμα n	*pro*·yev·ma
lunch	γεύμα n	*yev*·ma
dinner	δείπνο n	*ţhip*·no
snack	μεζεδάκι n	me·ze·*ţha*·ki
eat v	τρώγω	*tro*·gho
drink v	πίνω	*pi*·no
I'd like …	Θα ήθελα …	tha *i*·the·la …
Please.	Παρακαλώ.	pa·ra·ka·*lo*
Thank you.	Ευχαριστώ.	ef·kha·ri·*sto*
I'm starving!	Πεινώ τρομερά!	pi·*no* tro·me·*ra*
Enjoy your meal.	Καλή όρεξη.	ka·*li* *o*·rek·si

food glorious food

For breakfast, Greeks usually have a hot cup of milk, tea or coffee with φρυγανιά fri·gha·*nia* (dry sweet toast). If eating out, a typical order is a τυρόπιτα ti·*ro*·pi·ta (cheese pie) or σπανακόπιτα spa·na·*ko*·pi·ta (spinach pie).

Lunch, the day's main meal, is an early afternoon affair, usually followed by a απογευματινός ύπνος a·po·yev·ma·ti·*nos* *ip*·nos (siesta). A typical lunch will be a meat dish with rice, pasta or potatoes, or fish with a side salad. Legume dishes such as φακές fa·*kes* (lentil broth) and φασολάδα fa·so·*la*·ţha (bean broth) are especially popular in winter.

Dinner is a light meal eaten between eight and nine o'clock.

Dessert is rarely served. Instead, seasonal fresh fruit finishes off a meal.

finding a place to eat

βρίσκοντας κάπου για φαγητό

Can you recommend a …?	Μπορείς να συστήσεις ένα …;	bo·*ris* na si·*sti*·sis *e*·na …
bar	μπαρ	bar
café	καφεστιατόριο	ka·fe·sti·a·*to*·ri·o
restaurant	ρεστωράν	re·sto·*ran*
Where would you go for (a) …?	Πού θα πήγαινες για …;	pu tha *pi*·ye·nes yia …
celebration	μια γιορτή	mia yior·*ti*
cheap meal	ένα φτηνό γεύμα	*e*·na fti·*no* *yev*·ma
local specialities	τοπικές λιχουδιές	to·pi·*kes* li·khu·*ţhies*
I'd like to reserve a table for …	Θα ήθελα να κρατήσω ένα τραπέζι για …	tha *i*·the·la na kra·*ti*·so *e*·na tra·*pe*·zi yia …
(two) people	(δύο) άτομα	(*ţhi*·o) *a*·to·ma
(eight) o'clock	τις (οχτώ)	stis (okh·*to*)

listen for …

Δεν υπάρχει άδειο τραπέζι. ţhen i·*par*·hi *a*·ţhio tra·*pe*·zi	**We're full.**
Κλείσαμε. *kli*·sa·me	**We're closed.**
Μια στιγμή. mia stigh·*mi*	**One moment.**
Πού θα θέλατε να καθίσετε; pu tha *the*·la·te na ka·*thi*·se·te	**Where would you like to sit?**
Τι μπορώ να σας φέρω; ti bo·*ro* na sas *fe*·ro	**What can I get for you?**
Ορίστε! o·*ri*·ste	**Here you go!**

I'd like (a/the) ..., please.	Θα ήθελα ..., παρακαλώ.	tha *i*·thela ... pa·ra·ka·*lo*
children's menu	ένα μενού για παιδιά	*e*·na me·*nu* yia pe·*ţhia*
drink list	τον κατάλογο με τα ποτά	ton ka·*ta*·lo·gho me ta po·*ta*
half portion	μισή μερίδα	mi·*si* me·*ri*·ţha
menu (in English)	ένα μενού (στα αγγλικά)	*e*·na me·*nu* (sta ang·gli·*ka*)
mixed plate	μια ποικιλία	mia pi·ki·*li*·a
nonsmoking	στους μη καπνίζοντες	stus mi kap·*ni*·zo·des
smoking	στους καπνίζοντες	stus kap·*ni*·zo·des
table for (five)	ένα τραπέζι για (πέντε)	*e*·na tra·*pe*·zi yia (*pe*·de)
table outside	ένα τραπέζι έξω	*e*·na tra·*pe*·zi *ek*·so

Are you still serving food?
Σερβίρετε ακόμη φαγητό; ser·*vi*·re·te a·*ko*·mi fa·ghi·*to*

How long is the wait?
Πόση ώρα θα περιμένουμε; *po*·si *o*·ra tha pe·ri·*me*·nu·me

eateries

Act like a local and order some μερικά παξιμάδια me·ri·*ka* pak·si·*ma*·ţhia (dried bread) for dunking in your coffee or other hot drinks the next time you're at one of these eateries:

καφετηρία f	ka·fe·ti·*ri*·a	cafeteria
καφενείο n	ka·fe·*ni*·o	coffee shop
γλακτοπωλείο n	gha·lak·to·po·*li*·o	dairy shop
φαστφουντάδικο n	fast·fun·*da*·ţhi·ko	fast-food eatery
ουζερί n	u·ze·*ri*	ouzeria
οινοπωλείο n	i·no·po·*li*·o	liquor shop
ταβέρνα f	ta·*ver*·na	taverna

at the restaurant

στο εστιατόριο

What would you recommend?
Τι θα συνιστούσες; — ti tha si·ni·*stu*·ses

What are you serving today?
Τι έχετε σήμερα; — ti *e*·he·te *si*·me·ra

What's that called?
Πώς το λένε αυτό; — pos to *le*·ne af·*to*

What's in that dish?
Τι περιέχει αυτό το φαγητό; — ti pe·ri·*e*·hi af·*to* to fa·ghi·*to*

I'll have that.
Θα πάρω αυτό. — tha *pa*·ro af·*to*

listen for ...

Πώς θα το θέλατε ψημένο;
pos tha to *the*·la·te psi·*me*·no — **How would you like that cooked?**

Σας αρέσει ...;
sas a·*re*·si ... — **Do you like ...?**

Συνιστώ ...
si·ni·*sto* ... — **I suggest the ...**

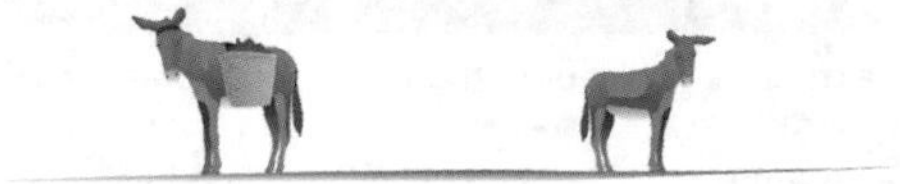

Is it savoury or sweet?
Είναι πικάντικο ή γλυκό; — *i*·ne pi·*ka*·di·ko i ghli·*ko*

I'd like it hot, please.
Θα το ήθελα ζεστό, παρακαλώ. — tha to *i*·the·la ze·*sto* pa·ra·ka·*lo*

Does it take long to prepare?
Θα αργήσει να ετοιμαστεί; — tha ar·*ghi*·si na e·ti·ma·*sti*

Is it self-serve?
Είναι σελφ σέρβις; — *i*·ne self *ser*·vis

Is there a cover charge?
Υπάρχει προσαύξηση τιμής; — i·*par*·hi pro·*saf*·ksi·si ti·*mis*

Is service included in the bill?
Συμπεριλαμβάνεται και η εξυπηρέτηση στο λογαριασμό; — si·be·ri·lam·*va*·ne·te ke i ek·si·pi·*re*·ti·si sto lo·gha·riaz·*mo*

Are these complimentary?
Είναι αυτά δωρεάν; — *i*·ne af·*ta* ţho·re·*an*

How much is that?
Πόσο κάνει αυτό; — *po*·so *ka*·ni af·*to*

I'd like (a/the) …	Θα ήθελα …	tha *i*·the·la …
chicken	το κοτόπουλο	to ko·*to*·pu·lo
local speciality	μια τοπική λιχουδιά	mia to·pi·*ki* li·khu·*ţhia*
meal fit for a king	ένα λουκούλλειο γεύμα	*e*·na lu·*ku*·li·o *yev*·ma
menu	το μενού	to me·*nu*
sandwich	ένα σάντουιτς	*e*·na *sa*·du·its
that dish	εκείνο το φαγητό	e·*ki*·no to fa·yi·*to*

look for …

Ορεκτικά	o·rek·ti·*ka*	Appetisers
Σούπες	*su*·pes	Soups
Προδόρπια	pro·*ţhor*·pi·a	Entrees
Σαλάτες	sa·*la*·tes	Salads
Κύρια φαγητά	*ki*·ri·a fa·yi·*ta*	Main Courses
Ψητά της ώρας	psi·*ta* tis *o*·ras	Freshly Grilled Dishes
Μαγειρεμένα φαγητά	ma·yi·re·*me*·na fa·yi·*ta*	Precooked Dishes
Σαλάτες	sa·*la*·tes	Side Dishes
Μακαρόνια	ma·ka·*ro*·nia	Pasta
Ψάρια	*psa*·ria	Fish
Θαλασσινά	tha·la·si·*na*	Seafood
Επιδόρπια	e·pi·*ţhor*·pi·a	Desserts
Ποτά	po·*ta*	Drinks
Απεριτίφ	a·pe·ri·*tif*	Apéritifs
Αναψυκτικά	a·nap·sik·ti·*ka*	Soft Drinks
Οινοπνευματώδη ποτά	i·nop·nev·ma·*to*·ţhi po·*ta*	Spirits
Μπύρες	*bi*·res	Beers
Σαμπάνια	sam·*pa*·nia	Sparkling Wines
Άσπρο κρασί	*as*·pro kra·*si*	White Wines
Κόκκινο κρασί	*ko*·ki·no kra·*si*	Red Wines
Επιδόρπια κρασιά	e·pi·*ţhor*·pi·a kra·*sia*	Dessert Wines
Ρετσίνα	ret·*si*·na	Retsina
Χωνευτικά	kho·nef·ti·*ka*	Digestifs

street food

If you've got the munchies, try one of these snacks:

κουλούρι n	ku·*lu*·ri	crisp sesame-coated bread rings
γύρος m	*yi*·ros	spit-roast lamb
πασατέμπο n	pa·sa·*tem*·po	pumpkin seeds
σουβλάκι n	suv·*la*·ki	skewered marinated meat
σπανακόπιτα f	spa·na·*ko*·pi·ta	spinach & cheese pie
τυρόπιτα f	ti·*ro*·pi·ta	cheese pie
ψημένα κάστανα n pl	psi·*me*·na *ka*·sta·ma	roasted chestnuts
ψημένο καλαμπόκι n	psi·*me*·no ka·la·*bo*·ki	roasted corn

I'd like it with/ without …	Θα το ήθελα με/ χωρίς …	tha to *i*·the·la me/ kho·*ris* …
cheese	τυρί	ti·*ri*
chilli	πιπεριά	pi·pe·*ria*
chilli sauce	σάλτσα πιπεριάς	*salt*·sa pi·pe·*rias*
garlic	σκόρδο	*skor*·ţho
ketchup	σάλτσα	*salt*·sa
nuts	καρύδια	ka·*ri*·ţhia
oil	λάδι	*la*·ţhi
pepper	πιπέρι	pi·*pe*·ri
salt	αλάτι	a·*la*·ti
tomato sauce	σάλτσα ντομάτας	*salt*·sa do·*ma*·tas
vinegar	ξύδι	*ksi*·ţhi

For additional items, see the **menu decoder**, page 175.
For other specific meal requests, see **vegetarian & special meals**, page 173.

at the table

στο τραπέζι

Please bring (a/the) …	Παρακαλώ φέρε …	pa·ra·ka·*lo* *fe*·re …
bill	το λογαριασμό	to lo·gha·riaz·*mo*
cloth	ένα τραπεζομάντηλο	*e*·na tra·pe·zo·*ma*·di·lo
glass	ένα ποτήρι	*e*·na po·*ti*·ri
serviette	μια πετσέτα	mia pet·*se*·ta
wineglass	ένα ποτήρι κρασιού	*e*·na po·*ti*·ri kra·*siu*

This is …	Αυτό είναι …	af·*to* *i*·ne …
(too) cold	(πολύ) κρύο	(po·*li*) *kri*·o
spicy	πιπεράτο	pi·pe·*ra*·to
superb	καταπληκτικό	ka·ta·plik·ti·*ko*

There's a mistake in the bill.
Υπάρχει κάποιο λάθος στο λογαριασμό. — i·*par*·hi *ka*·pio *la*·thos sto lo·gha·riaz·*mo*

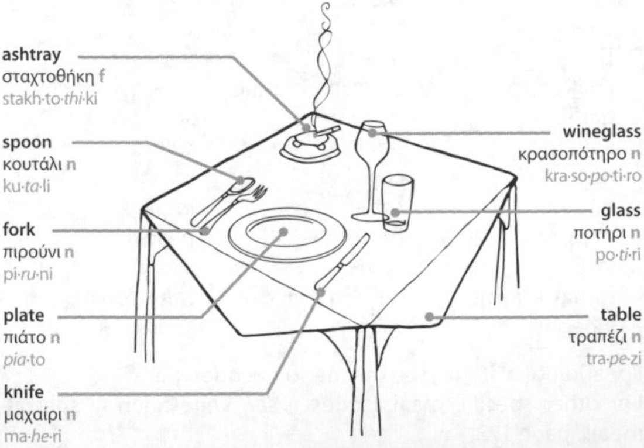

talking food

μιλώντας για φαγητά

I love this dish.	Μου αρέσει πολύ αυτό το φαγητό.	mu a·*re*·si po·*li* af·*to* to fa·yi·*to*
I love the local cuisine.	Μου αρέσει η τοπική κουζίνα.	mu a·*re*·si i to·pi·*ki* ku·*zi*·na
That was delicious!	Ήταν νοστιμότατο!	*i*·tan no·sti·*mo*·ta·to
My compliments to the chef.	Τα συγχαρητήριά μου στο σεφ.	ta sing·kha·ri·*ti*·ri·*a* mu sto sef

methods of preparation

μέθοδος παρασκευής

I'd like it ...	Θα το ήθελα ...	tha to *i*·the·la ...
I don't want it ...	Δεν το θέλω ...	ɖhen to *the*·lo ...
boiled	βρασμένο	vraz·*me*·no
broiled	ψημένο στη σχάρα	psi·*me*·no sti *skha*·ra
deep-fried	τηγανισμένο σε καυτό λίπος	ti·gha·niz·*me*·no se kaf·*to* *li*·pos
fried	τηγανητό	ti·gha·ni·*to*
grilled	στα κάρβουνα	sta *kar*·vu·na
mashed	πουρέ	pu·*re*
reheated	ξαναζεσταμένο	ksa·na·ze·sta·*me*·no
steamed	βρασμένο στον ατμό	vraz·*me*·no ston at·*mo*

how would you like that?

medium	ψημένο κανονικά	psi·*me*·no ka·no·ni·*ka*
rare	μισοψημένο	mi·sop·si·*me*·no
well-done	καλοψημένο	ka·lop·si·*me*·no

nonalcoholic drinks

μη οινοπνευματώδη ποτά

… mineral water	… μεταλλικό νερό n	… me·ta·li·*ko* ne·*ro*
sparkling	γαζόζα	gha·*zo*·za
still	χωρίς ανθρακικό	kho·*ris* an·thra·ki·*ko*
(hot) water	(ζεστό) νερό n	(ze·*sto*) ne·*ro*
bottled water	εμφιαλωμένο νερό n	em·fi·a·lo·*me*·no ne·*ro*
tap water	νερό βρύσης n	ne·*ro vri*·sis
apple juice	χυμός μήλου m	hi·*mos mi*·lu
hot chocolate	ζεστό κακάο n	ze·*sto* ka·*ka*·o
herbal tea	τσάι από βότανα n	*tsa*·i a·*po vo*·ta·na
morello cherry juice	βισινάδα f	vi·si·*na*·ţha
orange juice	χυμός πορτοκάλι m	hi·*mos* por·to·*ka*·li
soft drink	αναψυκτικό n	a·nap·sik·ti·*ko*
(cup of) tea	(ένα φλυτζάνι) τσάι n	(*e*·na fli·*dza*·ni) *tsa*·i
(cup of) coffee	(ένα φλυτζάνι) καφέ m	(*e*·na fli·*dza*·ni) ka·*fe*
with milk	με γάλα	me *gha*·la
with lemon	με λεμόνι	me le·*mo*·ni
sweetened	με ζάχαρη	me *za*·kha·ri
unsweetened	χωρίς ζάχαρη	kho·*ris za*·kha·ri

coffee time

black	χωρίς γάλα	kho·*ris gha*·la
decaffeinated	χωρίς καφεΐνη	kho·*ris* ka·fe·*i*·ni
Greek	ελληνικός	e·li·ni·*kos*
iced	φραπέ	fra·*pe*
instant	στιγμιαίος	stigh·*mi*·e·os
medium	μέτριος	*me*·tri·os
plain (no sugar)	σκέτος	*ske*·tos
strong	δυνατός	ţhi·na·*tos*
sweet	γλυκός	ghli·*kos*
weak	ελαφρύς	e·la·*fris*
white	με γάλα	me *gha*·la

local liquors

κουμανταρία f	ku·ma·da·*ri*·a	traditional Cypriot wine
ζιβανία f	zi·va·*ni*·a	a clear Cypriot apéritif made from grapes
ούζο n	*u*·zo	spirit distilled from grapes with a strong aniseed flavour
ρετσίνα f	ret·*si*·na	pine-resinated wine, served chilled
τσίπουρο n	*tsi*·pu·ro	spirit made from grapes, high in alcohol
τσικουδιά f	tsi·ku·*ţhia*	Crete's version of τσίπουρο

alcoholic drinks

οινοπνευματώδη ποτά

To get drinks at a bar in Greece, you don't have to memorise numerous standard measurements – standard serves are ordered using 'one'. For example: μία μπύρα *mi*·a *bi*·ra (one beer) or ένα ούζο *e*·na *u*·zo (one ouzo). See also **numbers & amounts**, page 35.

beer	μπύρα f	*bi*·ra
brandy	μπράντι n	*bran*·di
champagne	σαμπάνια f	sam·*pa*·nia
cocktail	κοκτέηλ n	kok·*te*·il
a shot of …	ένα … m	*e*·na …
gin	τζιν	dzin
rum	ρούμι	*ru*·mi
whisky	ουίσκι	u·*i*·ski

a shot of …	μία … f	mia …
tequila	τεκίλα	te·*ki*·la
vodka	βότκα	*vot*·ka

a bottle/glass of … wine	ένα μπουκάλι/ ποτήρι … κρασί n	*e*·na bu·*ka*·li/ po·*ti*·ri … kra·*si*
dessert	επιδόρπιο	e·pi·*ţhor*·pi·o
dry	ξηρό	ksi·*ro*
red	κόκκινο	*ko*·ki·no
rosé	ροζέ	ro·*ze*
sparkling	σαμπάνια	sam·*pa*·nia
sweet	γλυκό	ghli·*ko*
white	άσπρο	*a*·spro

a … of beer	ένα … μπύρα n	*e*·na … *bi*·ra
glass	ποτήρι	po·*ti*·ri
pint	μεγάλο ποτήρι	me·*gha*·lo po·*ti*·ri
small bottle	μικρό μπουκάλι	mi·*kro* bu·*ka*·li
large bottle	μεγάλο μπουκάλι	me·*gha*·lo bu·*ka*·li

a … of beer	μια … μπύρα f	mia … *bi*·ra
carafe	καράφα	ka·*ra*·fa
jug	κανάτα	ka·*na*·ta

give it a go

Try more traditional Greek delicacies from these eateries:

αρτοποιείο n	ar·to·pi·*i*·o	bakery
ζαχαροπλαστείο n	za·kha·ro·pla·*sti*·o	patisserie or sweet shop
φαστφουντάδικο n	fast·fu·*da*·ţhi·ko	fast-food eatery
καντίνα f	kan·*ti*·na	canteen or food van
πιτσαρία f	pit·sa·*ri*·a	barbecue-style eatery
σουβλατζίδικο n	suv·lat·*zi*·ţhi·ko	kebab and souvlaki shop
τυροπωλείο n	ti·ro·po·*li*·o	cheese shop
ψαροταβέρνα f	psa·ro·ta·*ver*·na	taverna serving fish
ψησταριά f	psi·sta·*ria*	eatery serving spit-roasted meats

in the bar

στο μπαρ

Excuse me!
Συγνώμη! — sigh·*no*·mi

I'm next.
Είναι η δική μου σειρά. — *i*·ne i ţhi·*ki* mu si·*ra*

I'll have …
Θα πάρω … — tha *pa*·ro …

Same again, please.
Από τα ίδια, παρακαλώ. — a·*po* ta *i*·ţhia pa·ra·ka·*lo*

No ice, thanks.
Όχι πάγο, ευχαριστώ. — *o*·hi *pa*·gho ef·kha·ri·*sto*

I'll buy you a drink.
Θα σε κεράσω εγώ. — tha se ke·*ra*·so e·*gho*

What would you like?
Τι θα ήθελες; — ti tha *i*·the·les

I don't drink alcohol.
Δεν πίνω αλκοόλ. — ţhen *pi*·no al·ko·*ol*

It's my round.
Είναι η σειρά μου. — *i*·ne i si·*ra* mu

How much is that?
Πόσο κάνει αυτό; — *po*·so *ka*·ni af·*to*

Do you serve meals here?
Σερβίρετε φαγητό εδώ; — ser·*vi*·re·te fa·yi·*to* e·*ţho*

listen for …

Τι θα πάρεις;
ti tha *pa*·ris — **What are you having?**

Νομίζω ήπιες αρκετά.
no·*mi*·zo *i*·pies ar·ke·*ta* — **I think you've had enough.**

Τελευταίες παραγγελίες.
te·lef·*te*·es pa·ra·ghe·*li*·es — **Last orders.**

Τα ποτά τα κερνάει το κατάστημα.
ta po·*ta* ta ker·*na*·i to ka·*ta*·sti·ma — **Drinks are on the house.**

drinking up

τα πίνουμε

Cheers!
Εις υγείαν! — is i·*yi*·an

I feel fantastic!
Είμαι στα κέφια μου! — *i*·me sta *ke*·fia mu

I think I've had one too many.
Νομίζω ήπια παραπάνω. — no·*mi*·zo *i*·pia pa·ra·*pa*·no

I'm feeling drunk.
Μέθυσα. — *me*·thi·sa

I feel ill.
Δεν αισθάνομαι καλά. — ţhen es·*tha*·no·me ka·*la*

Where's the toilet?
Πού είναι η τουαλέτα; — pu *i*·ne i tu·a·*le*·ta

I'm tired, I'd better go home.
Είμαι κουρασμένος/κουρασμένη, καλύτερα να πάω σπίτι. m/f — *i*·me ku·raz·*me*·nos/ku·raz·*me*·ni ka·*li*·te·ra na *pa*·o *spi*·ti

Can you call a taxi for me?
Μπορείς να μου καλέσεις ένα ταξί; — bo·*ris* na mu ka·*le*·sis *e*·na tak·*si*

I don't think you should drive.
Νομίζω ότι δεν πρέπει να οδηγήσεις. — no·*mi*·zo *o*·ti ţhen *pre*·pi na o·ţhi·*yi*·sis

pot plant

When you're in Greece, make sure that you don't eat the decoration – βασιλικός va·si·li·*kos* (basil) is favoured as an ornamental plant and is rarely used in cooking.

What's the local speciality?

Ποιες είναι οι τοπικές λιχουδιές;	pies *i*·ne i to·pi·*kes* li·khu·*ţhies*

What's that?

Τι είναι εκείνο;	ti *i*·ne e·*ki*·no

Can I taste it?

Μπορώ να το δοκιμάσω;	bo·*ro* na to ţho·ki·*ma*·so

Can I have a bag, please?

Μπορώ να έχω μια σακούλα, παρακαλώ;	bo·*ro* na *e*·kho mia sa·*ku*·la pa·ra·ka·*lo*

How much is (a kilo of cheese)?

Πόσο κάνει (ένα κιλό τυρί);	*po*·so *ka*·ni (*e*·na ki·*lo* ti·*ri*)

I'd like ...	Θα ήθελα ...	tha *i*·the·la ...
(three) pieces	(τρία) κομμάτια	(*tri*·a) ko·*ma*·tia
(six) slices	(έξι) φέτες	(*ek*·si) *fe*·tes
that one	εκείνο	e·*ki*·no
this one	αυτό	af·*to*

Less.	Πιο λίγο.	pio *li*·gho
A bit more.	Λιγάκι πιο πολύ.	li·*gha*·ki pio po·*li*
Enough.	Αρκετά.	ar·ke·*ta*

For more on quantities, see **numbers & amounts**, page 35.

listen for ...

Δεν υπάρχει άλλο. ţhen i·*par*·hi *a*·lo	**There isn't any.**
Μπορώ να σας βοηθήσω; bo·*ro* na sas vo·i·*thi*·so	**Can I help you?**
Τι θα θέλατε; ti tha *the*·la·te	**What would you like?**
Τίποτε άλλο; *ti*·po·te *a*·lo	**Anything else?**

food stuff

cooked	μαγειρεμένο	ma·yi·re·*me*·no
cured	παστό	pa·*sto*
dried	ξηρό	ksi·*ro*
fresh	φρέσκο	*fre*·sko
frozen	κατεψυγμένο	ka·tep·sigh·*me*·no
grilled	στα κάρβουνα	sta *kar*·vu·na
raw	ωμό	o·*mo*
roasted	ψητό	psi·*to*
savoury	πικάντικο	pi·*ka*·di·ko
smoked	καπνιστό	kap·ni·*sto*
sweet	γλυκό	ghli·*ko*

Do you have …?	Έχετε κάτι …;	*e*·he·te *ka*·ti …
anything cheaper	πιο φτηνό	pio fti·*no*
other kinds	διαφορετικό	ţhia·fo·re·ti·*ko*

Where can I find the … section?	Πού μπορώ να βρω το μέρος με …;	pu bo·*ro* na vro to *me*·ros me …
bread	το ψωμί	to pso·*mi*
dairy	τα γαλακτικά	ta gha·lak·ti·*ka*
fish	τα ψάρια	ta *psa*·ria
frozen goods	τα κατεψυγμένα	ta ka·tep·sigh·*me*·na
fruit and vegetable	τα φρούτα και τα λαχανικά	ta *fru*·ta ke ta la·kha·ni·*ka*
meat	το κρέας	to *kre*·as
poultry	τα πουλερικά	ta pu·le·ri·*ka*
seafood	τα θαλασσινά	ta tha·la·si·*na*

Could I please borrow a …?	Μπορώ παρακαλώ να δανειστώ …;	bo·*ro* pa·ra·ka·*lo* na ţha·ni·*sto* …
I need a …	Χρειάζομαι …	khri·*a*·zo·me …
chopping board	μια σανίδα κοπής	mia sa·*ni*·ţha ko·*pis*
frying pan	ένα τηγάνι	*e*·na ti·*gha*·ni
knife	ένα μαχαίρι	*e*·na ma·*he*·ri
saucepan	μια κατσαρόλα	mia kat·sa·*ro*·la

For more cooking implements, see the **dictionary** (p207).

vegetarian & special meals
φαγητά για χορτοφάγους και ειδικά φαγητά

ordering food
παραγγέλλοντας φαγητό

Do you have … food?	Έχετε φαγητό …;	e·he·te fa·yi·*to* …
halal	χαλάλ	kha·*lal*
kosher	κόσια	*ko*·si·a
Lent	Σαρακοστιανό	sa·ra·ko·stia·*no*
pulse-based	με όσπρια	me *os*·pri·a
vegetarian	για χορτοφάγους	yia khor·to·*fa*·ghus

Is there a … restaurant near here?
Υπάρχει ένα εστιατόριο … εδώ κοντά; — i·*par*·hi *e*·na e·sti·a·*to*·ri·o … e·*ţho* ko·*da*

Is it cooked in/with …?
Είναι μαγειρεμένο σε/με …; — *i*·ne ma·yi·re·*me*·no se/me …

Could you prepare a meal without …?
Μπορείτε να κάνετε φαγητό χωρίς …; — bo·*ri*·te na *ka*·ne·te fa·yi·*to* kho·*ris* …

I don't eat …	Δεν τρώγω …	ţhen *tro*·gho …
butter	βούτυρο	*vu*·ti·ro
eggs	αβγά	av·*gha*
fish	ψάρι	*psa*·ri
fish stock	ζουμί από ψάρι	zu·*mi* a·*po* *psa*·ri
lamb	αρνί	ar·*ni*
(red) meat	(κόκκινο) κρέας	(*ko*·ki·no) *kre*·as
meat stock	ζουμί από κρέας	zu·*mi* a·*po* *kre*·as
oil	λάδι	*la*·ţhi
olives	ελιές	e·*lies*
pork	χοιρινό	hi·ri·*no*
poultry	πουλερικά	pu·le·ri·*ka*

Is this …?	Είναι αυτό …;	*i*·ne af·*to* …
decaffeinated	χωρίς καφεΐνη	kho·*ris* ka·fe·*i*·ni
gluten-free	χωρίς γλουτένη	kho·*ris* ghlu·*te*·ni
low in fat	χαμηλό σε λίπος	kha·mi·*lo* se *li*·pos
low in sugar	χαμηλό σε ζάχαρη	kha·mi·*lo* se *za*·kha·ri
organic	οργανικό	or·gha·ni·*ko*
salt-free	χωρίς αλάτι	kho·*ris* a·*la*·ti

special diets & allergies

ειδική δίαιτα και αλλεργίες

I'm on a special diet.
Κάνω ειδική δίαιτα. *ka*·no i·ţhi·*ki* *ţhi*·e·ta

I'm allergic to …	Είμαι αλλεργικός/ αλλεργική … m/f	*i*·me a·ler·yi·*kos* a·ler·yi·*ki* …
dairy produce	στα γαλακτικά	sta gha·lak·ti·*ka*
eggs	στα αβγά	sta av·*gha*
gluten	στη γλουτένη	sti ghlu·*te*·ni
honey	στο μέλι	sto *me*·li
MSG	στο MSG	sto em si dzi
nuts	στους ξηρούς καρπούς	stus ksi·*rus* kar·*pus*
seafood	στα θαλασσινά	sta tha·la·si·*na*
shellfish	στα οστρακοειδή	sta os·tra·ko·i·*ţhi*

I'm (a) …	Είμαι …	*i*·me …
Buddhist	Βουδιστής m	vu·ţhi·*stis*
	Βουδίστρια f	vu·*ţhi*·stri·a
Hindu	Ινδουιστής m	in·ţhu·i·*stis*
	Ινδουίστρια f	in·ţhu·*i*·stri·a
Jewish	Ιουδαίος m	i·u·*ţhe*·os
	Ιουδαία f	i·u·*ţhe*·a
Muslim	Μουσουλμάνος m	mu·sul·*ma*·nos
	Μουσουλμάνα f	mu·sul·*ma*·na
vegan	βέγκαν m&f	*ve*·gan
vegetarian	χορτοφάγος m&f	khor·to·*fa*·ghos

menu decoder
οδηγός μαγειρικής

This miniguide lists dishes and ingredients used in Greek cuisine. It's designed to help you get the most out of your gastronomic experience by providing you with food terms that you may see on menus. For certain dishes we've marked the region or city where they're most popular.

The **menu decoder** has been ordered according to the Greek alphabet:
Αα Ββ Γγ Δδ Εε Ζζ Ηη Θθ Ιι Κκ Λλ Μμ
Νν Ξξ Οο Ππ Ρρ Σσ/ς Ττ Υυ Φφ Χχ Ψψ Ωω

Α α

αβγολέμονο (n) av·ghu·*le*·mo·no *egg and lemon sauce added to meat, chicken or fish soup and other dishes*
αβγοτάραχο (n) av·gho·*ta*·ra·kho *dried & salted grey mullet roe, coated in beeswax*
αγγινάρες (f) pl au·gi·*na*·res *globe artichokes*
— **αλαπολίτα** a·la·po·*li*·ta *'Constantinople style artichokes' – artichokes, carrots & potatoes in dill-spiked chicken stock*
— **καλογρές** ka·lo·*ghres* *'nuns' – artichoke hearts braised in creamy onion broth (Crete)*
αγγουροντομάτα σαλάτα (f) ang·gu·ro·do·*ma*·ta sa·*la*·ta *cucumber slices, tomato wedges & parsley with oil, lemon juice, salt & pepper*
αγγουροσαλάτα (f) ang·gu·ro·sa·*la*·ta *sliced cucumbers sprinkled with salt & served with oil & vinegar*
άγρια χόρτα (n) pl *a*·ghri·a *khor*·ta *seasonal wild greens*
άγρια σπαράγγια (n) pl *a*·ghri·a spa·*rang*·gi·a *wild asparagus*
άγριες αγγινάρες (f) pl *a*·ghri·es ang·gi·*na*·res *small prickly artichokes, eaten raw with salt & lemon juice*
αμπελοπούλια (n) pl am·be·lo·*pu*·lia *tiny birds preserved in vinegar & wine, eaten whole (Cyprus)*
αμελέτητα (n) pl a·me·*le*·ti·ta *lamb testicles*
αμπελοφάσουλα (n) pl am·be·lo·*fa*·su·la *green beans*
αμπερόριζα (f) am·be·*ro*·ri·za *rose geranium (leaves are used as a flavouring for cakes, pastries & preserved fruits)*
αμύγδαλα (n) pl *migh*·ţha·la *almonds*
αμυγδαλωτά (n) pl a·migh·ţha·lo·*ta* *almond shortbread sprinkled with icing sugar & chopped almonds*
αμυγδαλωτό γλύκισμα (n) a·migh·ţha·lo·*to* *ghli*·kiz·ma *nougat*
αναρή (f) a·na·*ri* *soft ricotta-like cheese from goat's or sheep's milk (Cyprus)*
αρακάς (m) a·ra·*kas* *fresh peas*
— **λαδερός** la·*ţhe*·ros *peas stewed with carrots, garlic bulbs & herbs in oil & paprika (Corfu)*
αρνάκι (n) ar·*na*·ki *milk-lamb (very young lamb)*
— **γεμιστό** ye·mi·*sto* *Easter dish of stuffed roast lamb (Dodecanese Islands)*
αρνί (n) ar·*ni* *lamb*
— **βραστό** vra·*sto* *slow-boiled mutton served with mutton-stock soup (Crete)*
— **γιαχνί** yiakh·*ni* *lamb stewed with tomatoes, onions, carrots & celery*
— **γιουβέτσι με κριθαράκι** yiu·*vet*·si me kri·tha·*ra*·ki *lamb baked with tomatoes & barley-shaped pasta in an earthenware pot*
— **εξοχικό** ek·so·hi·*ko* *'country-style lamb' – baked filo parcels of lamb, potato, feta &* **κεφαλοτύρι**

— **φρικασέ με μαρούλι** fri·ka·*se* me ma·*ru*·li *poached lamb with shredded lettuce, egg & lemon sauce*
— **κεφαλάκι ριγανάτο** ke·fa·*la*·ki ri·gha·*na*·to *lamb's head (generally roasted) complete with tongue, cheek, brains & eyes*
— **κοκκινιστό** ko·ki·ni·*sto* *lamb braised in white wine with onions & bay leaves*
— **οφτό** of·*to* *roast lamb on the spit*
— **στη σούβλα** sti *suv*·la *spit-roast lamb basted with olive oil, lemon juice & garlic – a traditional Easter dish*
— **στο φούρνο** sto *fur*·no *roasted leg or shoulder of lamb*
αρνίσια παϊδάκια ⓝ pl ar·*ni*·sia pa·i·*tha*·kia *marinated & chargrilled lamb cutlets*
αστακός a·sta·*kos* ⓜ *lobster, usually boiled or chargrilled*
αφέλια ⓝ pl a·*fe*·lia *meat braised with potato & mushrooms in red wine*
αχηβάδα ⓕ a·hi·*va*·tha *clam*
αχινοί ⓜ pl a·hi·*ni* *sea urchins*
— **σαλάτα** sa·*la*·ta *sea urchin salad*
— **γεμιστοί** ye·mi·*sti* *sea urchin stuffed with rice, onions & tomatoes*

Β β

βασιλόπιτα ⓕ va·si·*lo*·pi·ta *New Year loaf decorated with almonds – whoever finds the coin in the bread gets good luck*
βατόμουρο ⓝ va·*to*·mu·ro *blackberry • raspberry*
βατραχοπόδαρα τηγανητά ⓝ pl va·tra·kho·*po*·tha·ra ti·gha·ni·*ta* *fried frog's legs (Western Greece)*
βυσσινάδα ⓕ vi·si·*na*·tha *syrup of morello cherries – mixed with cold water for summer-time cordials*
βύσσινο ⓝ *vi*·si·no *morello cherry • sour black cherry*
— **γλυκό** ghli·*ko* *morello cherry preserve*
βλίτο ⓝ *vli*·to *amaranth – its sweet nutty flavour & soft texture make it popular for warm salads*
βοδινό ⓝ vo·thi·*no* *beef*
— **καπαμά** ka·pa·*ma* *beef stewed with tomatoes, red wine, cinnamon & cloves*
— **με λαχανικά** me la·kha·ni·*ka* *beef braised with carrots, potatoes & celery*
βολβοί ⓜ pl vol·*vi* *grape hyacinth bulbs*
— **βραστοί** vra·*sti* *bulbs boiled, dressed with dill vinaigrette & accompanied by* **σκορδαλιά**
βρούβα ⓕ *vru*·va *charlock • field green with sharp peppery taste*

Γ γ

γαϊδουρελιά ⓕ gha·i·thu·re·*lia* *'donkey olive' – named so because of its large size*
γαλακτομπούρεκο ⓝ gha·lak·to·*bu*·re·ko *baked custard-cream filo pie sprinkled with a lemony syrup*
γαλοπούλα ⓕ gha·lo·*pu*·la *turkey*
— **γεμιστή** ye·mi·*sti* *stuffed roast turkey*
γαλύπες ⓕ pl gha·*li*·pes *a sea anemone*
— **τηγανητές** ti·gha·ni·*tes* *lightly battered & fried sea anemone*
γαλυποκεφτέδες ⓜ pl gha·li·po·kef·*te*·thes *sea anemone rissoles*
γαρδούμια ⓝ pl ghar·*thu*·mia *small offal rolls made from strips of lamb's stomach, bound with intestines then roasted*
γαρίδες ⓕ pl gha·*ri*·thes *prawns • shrimps*
— **σαγανάκι** sa·gha·*na*·ki *prawns fried with tomatoes & red wine, topped with feta & baked*
— **τηγανητές** ti·gha·ni·*tes* *fried prawns*
— **βραστές** vra·*stes* *boiled prawns accompanied by* **λαδολέμονο**
— **γιουβετσάκι** yiu·vet·*sa*·ki *prawns with tomatoes, parsley, oregano & feta chunks baked in earthenware pots*
γαριδοσαλάτα ⓕ gha·ri·tho·sa·*la*·ta *prawn salad*
γαύρος ⓜ *ghav*·ros *fresh anchovy*
γεμιστά ⓝ pl ye·mi·*sta* *stuffed vegetables*
γεμιστός ye·mi·*stos* *method of stuffing meat, fish or vegetables prior to cooking*
γιαούρτι ⓝ yia·*ur*·ti *thick, heavy yogurt with a tangy bite, made from sheep's, goat's or cow's milk*
— **αγελάδος** a·ye·*la*·thos *cow's milk yogurt*
— **φρούτων** *fru*·ton *fruit yogurt*
— **με μέλι** me *me*·li *yogurt with honey*
— **πρόβειο** *pro*·vio *sheep's milk yoghurt*

γιαουρτογλού ⓕ yia·ur·to·ghlu *pie cooked with finely sliced grilled meat, topped with a yogurt sauce*
γιαουρτόπιτα ⓕ yia·ur·to·pi·ta *light moist cake made with yogurt, sugar, lemon rind & lots of eggs*
γίδα βραστή ⓕ yi·ţha vra·sti *aromatic dish of boiled goat*
γύρος yi·ros *'to spin' – seasoned lamb packed onto a spit & rotisseried upright, carved for meat platters or served in* **πίτα** *with tomatoes, onions &* **τζατζίκι**
γιορτή ⓕ yior·ti *small pieces of pork & goat boiled with corn, topped with melted butter, cinnamon & pepper (Samos)*
γιουβαρλάκια ⓝ pl yiu·var·la·kia *egg-shaped rissoles of minced beef or lamb simmered in a light stock*
γιουβέτσι ⓝ yiu·vet·si *casserole of meat & seafood with tomatoes & barley pasta*
— **με θαλασσινά** me tha·la·si·na *casserole of seafood, barley pasta, tomatoes & chicken stock (Ionian Islands)*
γιουσλεμέδες ⓜ pl yiuz·le·me·ţhes *golden pies filled with eggs &* **κεφαλοτύρι**, *deep-fried then served with grated cheese (Lesvos)*
γλιστρίδα ⓕ ghli·stri·ţha *purslane – small-leafed plant with lemony flavour & crisp texture used mainly in salads*
— **με καππαρόφυλλα σαλάτα** me ka·pa·ro·fi·la sa·la·ta *purslane leaves, sliced tomatoes, black olives & caper leaves with oil & lemon dressing*
— **με γιαούρτι** me yia·ur·ti *chopped purslane beaten with strained yogurt, garlic, lemon, salt & oil (Crete)*
γλυκά κουταλιού ⓝ pl ghli·ka ku·ta·liu *'spoon sweets' – preserved fruits*
γλυκάνισο ⓝ ghli·ka·ni·so *aniseed*
γλυκά ταψιού ⓝ pl ghli·ka tap·siu *sweets made with filo pastry*
γλύκισμα ⓝ pl ghli·kiz·ma *sweet pastry • cake*
γλυκοκολοκύθα ⓕ ghli·ko·ko·lo·ki·tha *marrow • pumpkin • squash*
γλώσσα ⓕ ghlo·sa *tongue (fish) • generic name for any flat fish*
— **μοσχαρίσια κρασάτη** mo·sha·ri·sia kra·sa·ti *tongue (fish) fried in butter, then poached in white wine*
γουρουνάκι (του γάλακτος) ⓝ ghu·ru·na·ki (tu gha·lak·tos) *piglet • suckling pig*
— **στη σούβλα** sti suv·la *whole suckling pig spit-roasted until tender*
— **γεμιστό με φέτα** ye·mi·sto me fe·ta *suckling pig stuffed with feta & roasted*
γυαλιστερές ⓕ pl yia·li·ste·res *shellfish eaten alive with a squeeze of lemon juice (Dodecanese Islands)*

Δ δ

δάχτυλα ⓝ pl ţhakh·ti·la *'fingers' – deep-fried, nut-filled pastries (Cyprus)*
δίπλες ⓕ pl ţhi·ples *sweet pastry, deep-fried & drizzled with honey & sesame seeds*
— **Δράμας** ţhra·mas *yogurt pie with vine leaves*
δρύλοι αλευρολέμονο ⓜ pl ţhri·li a·lev·ro·le·mo·no *wild greens in lemon*

Ε ε

ελαιόλαδο ⓝ e·le·o·la·ţho *olive oil*
ελαιόπιτες ⓕ pl e·le·o·pi·tes *small olive & leek pies (Cyprus)*
ελαιότη ⓕ e·le·o·ti *bread with a layer of chopped black olives & onions (Cyprus)*
ελαιόψωμο ⓝ e·le·op·so·mo *olive bread*
ελιές ⓕ pl e·lies *olives*
— **Αμφίσσης** am·fi·sis *large blue-black olives with nutty flavour*
— **Αταλάντης** a·ta·lan·dis *big fruity greenish-purple or purple olives*
— **χαμούρες** ha·mu·res *dried newly fallen olives*
— **Ιονίων πράσινες** i·o·ni·on pra·si·nes *mild green olives (Ionian Islands)*
— **Καλαμάτας** ka·la·ma·tas *large black olives with pungent flavour*
— **μαύρες** mav·res *black olives*
— **Ναυπλίου** naf·pli·u *nutty flavoured green olives (Nafplio)*
— **παστές** pa·stes *dried salted olives*
— **πελτέ** pel·te *olive paste*
— **πράσινες** pra·si·nes *green olives*

— **τσακιστές** tsa·ki·*stes* *cracked green olives marinated in oil, lemon & herbs*
— **τουρσί** tur·*si* *pickled olives*
ελίτσες ⓕ pl e·*lit*·ses *tiny sweet black olives*
εντόσθια ⓝ pl en·*do*·sthi·a *offal • innards (usually lamb)*
— **κοκκινιστά** ko·ki·ni·*sta* *chicken giblets in a rich gravy*
— **πουλιών** pu·*lion* *giblets*

Ζ ζ

ζαχαροπούλια ⓝ pl za·kha·ro·*pu*·lia *marzipan sweets (Lesvos)*
ζαχαρωτό με αμύγδαλο ⓝ za·kha·ro·*to* me a·*migh*·ţha·lo *marzipan*
ζαμπόν ⓝ zam·*bon* *ham*
ζαργάνα ⓕ zar·*gha*·na *garfish*
ζύμη ⓕ *zi*·mi *pastry*
— **με γιαούρτι** me yia·*ur*·ti *baked pasta dish consisting of homemade macaroni, strained yogurt & onions (Kos)*

Θ θ

θαλασσινά ⓝ pl tha·la·si·*na* *seafood*
— **του Αιγαίου** tu e·*ye*·u *paella-style rice dish cooked with seafood (Hydra)*
θρούμπες ⓕ pl *thru*·mbes *ripe black olives*
θυμάρι ⓝ thi·*ma*·ri *thyme*

Ι ι

ιμάμ-μπαϊλντί ⓝ i·*mam*·ba·il·*di* *Turkish-inspired dish of eggplant stuffed with eggplant pulp, tomato, garlic, onion, parsley, then baked*

Κ κ

καβούρι ⓝ ka·*vu*·ri *crab*
— **βραστό** vra·*sto* *crab boiled & dressed with* **λαδολέμονο**
καϊμάκι ⓝ to ka·i·*ma*·ki *froth that forms on top of Greek coffee while it brews*
— **πηγμένο** pigh·*me*·no *clotted cream*
κακαβιά ⓕ ka·ka·*via* *saltwater fish soup*
καλαμαράκια ⓝ pl ka·la·ma·*ra*·kia *baby squid*
καλαμάρι ⓝ ka·la·*ma*·ri *squid*
— **γεμιστό** ye·mi·*sto* *squid stuffed with rice & baked in a lemony broth*
— **Λεβριανά** lev·ria·*na* *squid stewed in dry red wine with green olives, tomatoes, onions & parsley*
— **με ρύζι** me *ri*·zi *fried squid with onions simmered with water, crushed tomatoes, rice & cinnamon*
— **τηγανητό** ti·gha·ni·*to* *squid cut in rings or strips, lightly battered & fried*
καλιτσούνια ⓝ pl ka·lit·*su*·nia *small cheese pies*
καπαμάς ⓜ ka·pa·*mas* *method of stewing meat with tomatoes, wine, cinnamon & sometimes red capsicum & cloves*
κάππαρη ⓕ *ka*·pa·ri *capers, usually pickled & eaten as an appetiser*
κάπρος ⓜ *ka*·pros *wild boar*
καραμέλα ⓕ ka·ra·*me*·la *candy • caramel*
καραβίδα ⓕ ka·ra·*vi*·ţha *crayfish*
καρύδια ⓝ pl ka·*ri*·ţhia *walnuts*
— **γεμιστά** ye·mi·*sta* *walnuts & roasted almonds preserved in syrup (Cyprus)*
καρυδόπιτα ⓕ ka·ri·*ţho*·pi·ta *rich moist walnut cake*
κάσιου ⓝ *ka*·siu *cashews*
καταΐφι ⓝ ka·ta·*i*·fi *'angel hair' pastry – syrupy nest-like nut-filled rolls*
κατσικάκι ⓝ kat·si·*ka*·ki *goat • kid*
— **πατούδο** pa·*tu*·ţho *roast kid stuffed with liver, rice, bread-crumbs, feta & raisins or* **κεφαλοτύρι**, *bacon, rice & dill (Cyclades)*
— **ψητό** psi·*to* *roast kid, sometimes served with a spicy red wine sauce*
καφές ⓜ ka·*fes* *coffee*
— **ελληνικός** e·li·ni·*kos* *freshly brewed Greek coffee*
— **γλυκός** ghli·*kos* *sweet coffee*
— **μέτριος** *me*·tri·os *medium-strength coffee with a little sugar*
— **πολλά βαρύς** po·*la* va·*ris* *strong coffee*
— **σκέτος** *ske*·tos *sugarless coffee*
— **βαρύγλυκος** va·*ri*·ghli·kos *strong & sweet coffee*
κεφαλάκι ⓝ ke·fa·*la*·ki *head – usually refers specifically to lamb's head*

κεφτεδάκια ⓝ pl kef·te·*ţha*·kia *miniature meat rissoles served at parties*
κεφαλοτύρι ⓝ ke·fa·lo·*ti*·ri *'head cheese' – known as 'kefalotiri', a hard, pale yellow cheese made from sheep and goat's milk*
κεφτέδες ⓜ pl kef·*te*·ţhes *small tasty rissoles, often made with minced lamb, pork or veal*
— **στη σχάρα** sti *skha*·ra *chargrilled meat rissoles*
κιχώρι ⓝ ki·*kho*·ri *chicory • green leaves*
κιμαδόπιτα ⓕ ki·ma·*ţho*·pi·ta *mincemeat pie*
κιμάς ki·*mas* ⓜ *sauce made from mincemeat, onions & tomatoes served with pasta or rice*
κληματόφυλλο ⓝ kli·ma·*to*·fi·lo *vine leaf*
κοφίσι ⓝ ko·*fi*·si *pie made from boiled & shredded dried fish mixed with onion, garlic, rice & tomatoes (Kefallonia)*
κόκκοι καφέ ⓜ pl *ko*·ki ka·*fe* *coffee beans*
κοκκινέλι ⓝ ko·ki·*ne*·li *red resinated wine*
κόκκινη πιπεριά ⓕ *ko*·ki·ni pi·pe·*ria* *red capsicum (pepper)*
κοκκινιστό ⓝ ko·ki·ni·*sto* *'reddened' – method of simmering meat, chicken or rice with tomatoes*
κόκκινο φασόλι ⓝ *ko*·ki·no fa·*so*·li *red kidney bean*
— **λάχανο** *la*·kha·no *red cabbage*
κοκκινοπίπερο ⓝ ko·ki·no·*pi*·pe·ro *cayenne (spice)*
κόκορας ⓜ *ko*·ko·ras *rooster*
— **κρασάτος** kra·*sa*·tos *lightly floured rooster fried with onions & spices, then cooked in red wine sauce*
κοκορέτσι ⓝ ko·ko·*ret*·si *chopped lamb offal wrapped in lamb's intestines & grilled*
κοκορόζουμο ⓝ ko·ko·ro·zu·mo *lemony rooster broth used as a post-party pick-me-up (Cyclades)*
κολιός ⓜ ko·li·*os* *mackerel*
— **λαδορίγανη** la·ţho·*ri*·gha·ni *mackerel baked with oil, lemon, oregano, garlic & parsley*
— **σε κληματόφυλλα** kli·ma·*to*·fi·la *mackerel in vine leaves*
κολιτσάνοι ⓜ pl ko·lit·*sa*·ni *a sea anemone*
κολοκέτα ⓝ pl ko·lo·*ke*·ta *pastries stuffed with red pumpkin, raisins & cracked wheat (Cyprus)*
κολοκύθα ⓕ ko·lo·*ki*·tha *marrow • pumpkin • squash*
κολοκυθάκια ⓝ pl ko·lo·ki·*tha*·kia *zucchini*
— **με αβγά** me av·*gha* *zucchini & egg omelette*
— **τηγανητά** ti·gha·ni·*ta* *zucchini battered & deep-fried, served with lemon &* **σκορδαλιά**
— **βραστά** vra·*sta* *boiled baby zucchini with oil & lemon dressing*
κολοκύθι ⓝ ko·lo·*ki*·thi *marrow • pumpkin • squash*
κολοκυθόανθοι ⓜ pl ko·lo·ki·*tho*·an·thi *zucchini flowers*
— **τηγανητοί** ti·gha·ni·*ti* *zucchini flowers & cheese fritters (Andros)*
— **γεμιστοί** ye·mi·*sti* *zucchini flower* **ντολμάδες** *stuffed with rice, tomato & parsley & simmered until tender*
κολοκυθοκεφτέδες ko·lo·ki·tho·kef·*te*·ţhes *rissoles of puréed zucchini, parsley, onion, mint & garlic*
κολοκυθόπιτα ⓕ ko·lo·ki·*tho*·pi·ta *zucchini pie*
κόλυβα ⓝ pl *ko*·li·va *wheat mixed with fruit, pomegranate seeds, sugar & nuts – eaten after the death of a family member & on the anniversary of their death*
κομπόστα ⓕ ko·*bo*·sta *compote • stewed fruit*
κονσερβολιά ⓕ kon·ser·vo·*lia* *common type of olive from the central mainland*
κοντοσούβλι ⓝ kon·do·*suv*·li *spit-roast pieces of lamb or pork seasoned with onions, oregano, salt & pepper*
κορωναίικη ⓕ ko·ro·*ne*·i·ki *a smaller, oil-bearing variety of the kalamata olive*
κοτόπιτα ⓕ ko·*to*·pi·ta *chicken filo pastry*
κοτόπουλο ⓝ ko·*to*·pu·lo *chicken*
— **χυλοπίτες** hi·lo·*pi*·tes *whole chicken & noodles simmered in tomato, onion & cinnamon broth until liquid is absorbed*
— **λεμονάτο** le·mo·*na*·to *roast chicken basted with butter & lemon juice*
— **με μπάμιες** me *ba*·mies *chicken & okra braised in tomato & onion gravy*

κοτόσουπα ⓕ ko·*to*·su·pa
soup made from boiled whole chicken
κρασί ⓝ kra·*si* *wine*
— **άσπρο** *a*·spro *white wine*
— **κόκκινο** *ko*·ki·no *red wine*
— **λευκό** lef·*ko* *white wine*
— **ροζέ** ro·*ze* *rosé wine*
κρέας ⓝ *kre*·as *meat*
— **ελαφιού** e·la·*fiu* *venison*
— **στη στάμνα** sti *stam*·na
meat cooked in a pot
— **στο φούρνο με πατάτες** sto *fur*·no me pa·*ta*·tes *roast meat with potatoes*
κρεατικά ⓝ pl kre·a·ti·*ka*
meat dishes, mostly stewed or roasted
κρεατόπιτα ⓕ kre·a·*to*·pi·ta
lamb or veal pie, usually with cinnamon
— **Κεφαλλονίτικη** ke·fa·lo·*ni*·ti·ki
meat pie cooked with onions, eggs, rice, potatoes, tomatoes & spices (Kefallonia)
— **της Κρήτης** tis *kri*·tis
pie of alternating layers of cubed lamb (or goat) & **μυζήθρα** *covered in butter & baked in shortcrust pastry (Crete)*
κρεατόσουπα ⓕ kre·a·*to*·su·pa *nourishing broth made from boiled meat – sometimes thickened with rice &* **αβγολέμονο**
κρεμμυδόπιτα ⓕ kre·mi·*ţho*·pi·ta
pie with a filling of **μυζήθρα**, *grated onion, eggs & dill (Mykonos)*
Κρητική κρεατόπιτα ⓕ
kri·ti·*ki* kre·a·*to*·pi·ta
see **κρεατόπιτα της Κρήτης**
κριθαράκι ⓝ kri·tha·*ra*·ki
tiny spindle-shaped barley pasta used for pasta dishes, soups & casseroles
— **με βούτυρο και τυρί** me *vu*·ti·ro ke ti·*ri* *pasta baked with brown butter, cheese, lemon juice & herbs*
κουκουβάγια ⓕ ku·ku·*va*·yia
see **παξιμάδια σαλάτα**
κουκιά ⓝ pl ku·*kia* *broad beans*
— **ξερά βραστά** kse·*ra* vra·*sta* *broad beans boiled in water & lemon juice & served with oil, dill & onion rings*
— **με αγριαγκινάρες**
me a·ghri·ang·gi·*na*·res
broad beans with artichokes

κουλουκόψωμο ⓝ ku·lu·*kop*·so·mo
see **παξιμάδια με ντομάτες και φέτα**
κουλουράκια ⓝ pl ku·lu·*ra*·kia
cookies • biscuits • buns
— **με πετιμέζι** me pe·ti·*me*·zi
sweet buns made with syrup, cinnamon & spices
κουλούρι ⓝ ku·*lu*·ri *crisp sesame-coated bread rings sold on streets & outside church after Sunday mass • generic name for circular rolls, buns & biscuits*
κουλούρια αστυπαλίτικα ⓝ pl ku·*lu*·ri·a a·sti·pa·*li*·ti·ka *saffron biscuits (Astypalea)*
κουμκουάτ ⓝ kum·ku·*at* *cumquat*
— **λικέρ** li·*ker* *cumquat liqueur (Corfu)*
Κουμμανταρία ⓕ ku·man·da·*ri*·a
heavy dessert wine originally made during the Crusades by the Knights of the Order of St John (Cyprus)
κουνέλι ⓝ ku·*ne*·li *rabbit*
— **κρασάτο** kra·*sa*·to *rabbit casserole with red wine, garlic & bay leaves*
— **με καρύδι** me ka·*ri*·ţhi *marinated rabbit, fried & simmered in white wine infused with coarsely ground walnuts*
— **με γιαούρτι** me yia·*ur*·ti
rabbit marinated in lemon juice & black pepper, then baked with a creamy egg & yogurt sauce
— **στιφάδο** sti·*fa*·ţho *rabbit ragout spiced with cloves, cinnamon & cumin*
κουπέπια ⓝ pl ku·*pe*·pia **ντολμάδες** *made with minced lamb & veal, served hot with* **αβγολέμονο** *sauce (Cyprus)*
κούπες ⓕ pl *ku*·pes *deep-fried pastries of mincemeat, onion & spices (Cyprus)*
κουραμπιέδες ⓜ pl ku·ra·*bie*·ţhes
buttery almond shortbread
κυδώνι ⓝ ki·*ţho*·ni *quince*
— **μπελτές** bel·*tes* *quince jelly*
— **γλυκό** ghli·*ko* *quince preserve flavoured with rose geranium*
— **στο φούρνο** sto *fur*·no *buttered quince baked in a water & sugar solution until liquid has caramelised*
— **γεμιστό** ye·mi·*sto*
large quince stuffed with minced beef, rice, onions, raisins, cloves & nutmeg

κυδωνόπαστο ⓝ ki·ţho·*no*·pa·sto *dark-red quince paste dried until firm, cut in small diamonds & dusted with sugar*

Λλ

λαβράκι ⓝ lav·*ra*·ki *sea bass*
— **στο αλάτι** sto a·*la*·ti *whole sea bass buried in salt & baked – the salt-encrusted skin is slit & the flesh is eaten from the bone with an oil & lemon dressing*

λαγάνα ⓕ la·*gha*·na *bread sprinkled with sesame seeds baked on the first day of Lent*

λαγός ⓜ la·*ghos* *hare*
— **στιφάδο** sti·*fa*·ţho *hare ragout spiced with cumin & cloves, usually marinated in vinegar prior to cooking*

λαγωτό ⓝ la·gho·*to* *hare ragout (Kefallonia)*

λαδόξιδο ⓝ la·ţhok·si·ţho *vinaigrette of oil, vinegar, parsley, salt & pepper*

λαδολέμονο ⓝ la·ţho·*le*·mo·no *thick dressing of oil beaten with lemon juice, salt & pepper*

λάχανα ⓝ pl *la*·kha·na *seasonal wild greens*
— **με λαρδί** me lar·*ţhi* *casserole of seasonal greens & fatty bacon (Mykonos)*

λαχανικά ⓝ pl la·kha·ni·*ka* *vegetables*
— **της θάλασσας** tis *tha*·la·sas *sea vegetables*

λάχανο ⓝ *la*·kha·no *cabbage*
— **κοκκινιστό** ko·ki·ni·*sto* *cabbage stewed with tomatoes, onions, parsley, dill & paprika (Corfu)*
— **με κιμά** me ki·*ma* *cabbage braised with onions, mincemeat & tomatoes, finished with fresh butter (Chios)*

λαχανοσαλάτα ⓕ la·kha·no·sa·*la*·ta *shredded white cabbage sprinkled with oil, lemon juice & salt*

λεμονάτος ⓜ le·mo·*na*·tos *method of cooking with oil & lemon juice*

λιθρίνι ⓝ li·*thri*·ni *sea bream*

λουκάνικα ⓝ pl lu·*ka*·ni·ka *pork sausages seasoned with coriander & orange peel • generic word for sausages & frankfurters*

λουκανόπιτες ⓕ pl lu·ka·*no*·pi·tes *filo-wrapped sausages*

λουκουμάδες ⓜ pl lu·ku·*ma*·ţhes *rosette-shaped, light-as-air doughnuts served hot with honey & cinnamon*

λουκούμι ⓝ lu·*ku*·mi *Turkish delight*

λουκούμια ⓝ pl lu·*ku*·mia *wedding shortbread (Cyprus)*

λούντζα ⓕ *lun*·dza *spicy ham made from cured smoked pork fillet (Cyprus, Cyclades)*
— **με χαλούμι** me kha·*lu*·mi *grilled ham topped with melted* **χαλούμι** *(Cyprus)*

λουβιά ⓝ pl lu·*via* *black-eyed peas*
— **με λάχανα** me *la*·kha·na *warm salad of black-eyed peas & seasonal greens with oil & lemon dressing (Cyprus)*

λουζές ⓜ lu·*zes* *salted fillet of pork stuffed into thick pig's intestine & sun-dried (Mykonos)*

λιαστός ⓜ lia·*stos* *sun-dried*

Μμ

μαγειρίτσα ⓕ ma·yi·*rit*·sa *lamb's offal soup thickened with rice &* **αβγολέμονο**, *eaten to celebrate the end of Lent*

μακαρόνια ⓝ pl ma·ka·*ro*·nia *macaroni • spaghetti*
— **με κιμά** me ki·*ma* *pasta with a sauce of mincemeat, tomatoes, onions & red wine*
— **με σάλτσα** me *sal*·tsa *pasta with tomato, onion & oregano sauce*
— **με βούτυρο και τυρί** me *vu*·ti·ro ke ti·*ri* *pasta with butter sauce & cheese*
— **στο φούρνο** sto *fur*·no *pasta baked in cheese & butter sauce*

μαντί ⓝ man·*di* *small pasta pockets filled with mincemeat, cooked in meat broth seasoned with capsicum & served with a yogurt & garlic sauce (Northern Greece)*

μάραθο ⓝ *ma*·ra·tho *fennel*
— **με ούζο σούπα** me *u*·zo *su*·pa *ouzo & fennel soup*

μαχαλεπί ⓝ ma·kha·le·*pi* *creamy custard pudding in rose-water syrup (Cyprus)*

μαχλέπι ⓝ ma·*khle*·pi *pungent bitter-sweet black cherry pips used for spicing breads & stuffings*

μαρίδα πικάντικη ⓕ ma·*ri*·ţha pi·*kan*·di·ki *whitebait, tomato & mint fritters (Rhodes)*

μαρίδες ⓕ pl ma·*ri*·ţhes *whitebait*
— **λιαστές** lia·*stes* *whitebait seasoned with oregano & strung out to dry then chargrilled & served with oil & lemon juice*

— **τηγανητές** ti·gha·ni·*tes* *whitebait rolled in flour & deep fried until crisp, served with lemon wedges*
μαστίχα ⓕ ma·*sti*·kha *mastic • crystallised resin from the mastic bush, eaten as chewing gum & used as a flavouring (Chios)*
μαυρομάτικα φασόλια ⓝ pl mav·ro·*ma*·ti·ka fa·so·lia *black-eyed peas*
— **με χόρτα** me *khor*·ta *black-eyed peas stewed with greens, onions, tomatoes, parsley, mint & garlic (Crete)*
μεγαρίτικη ⓕ me·gha·*ri*·ti·ki *olives grown in Attica, near Athens, named after the city of Megara*
μελανούρι ⓝ me·la·nu·ri *sea bream*
μεζές ⓜ me·*zes* *snack*
μεζεδάκι ⓝ me·ze·*ţha*·ki *tasty morsels served with ouzo – favourites include olives, salted cucumber slices, feta, salted anchovies, mackerel & mini-meat rissoles*
μέλι ⓝ *me*·li *honey*
— **με ξηρούς καρπούς** me ksi·*rus* kar·*pus* *honey poured over walnuts or almonds*
μελιτζάνες ⓕ pl me·li·*dza*·nes *eggplant*
— **στο φούρνο** sto *fur*·no *sliced eggplant fried with potatoes, & baked with tomatoes, cumin, parsley & feta*
— **τηγανητές** ti·gha·ni·*tes* *see* **κολοκυθάκια τηγανητά**
μελιτζανοσαλάτα ⓕ me·li·dza·no·sa·*la*·ta *smoky purée of grilled mashed eggplant, onion, garlic, oil & lemon*
μελιτίνι ⓝ me·li·*ti*·ni *golden pastry tarts filled with fresh cheese, eggs & sugar, traditionally eaten at Easter*
μελόπιτα ⓕ me·*lo*·pi·ta *cheesecake made with* **μυζήθρα** *& clear honey*
μηλοπιτάκια ⓝ pl mi·lo·pi·*ta*·kia *crescent-shaped apple & walnut pies*
μοσχάρι ⓝ mo·*sha*·ri *veal*
— **κατσαρόλας με αρακά** kat·sa·*ro*·las me a·ra·*ka* *veal stewed with fresh peas in white wine & thyme*
— **κοκκινιστό με μακαρόνια** ko·ki·ni·*sto* me ma·ka·*ro*·nia *veal stewed with tomatoes, served with spaghetti*
— **ψητό** psi·*to* *rolled veal rubbed with lemon juice, pepper & salt, pot-roasted with onion, tomatoes & wine*
— **στιφάδο** sti·*fa*·ţho *veal ragout with garlic, peppercorns & bay leaves*
μουσακάς ⓜ mu·sa·*kas* *thick-sliced eggplant & mincemeat arranged in layers, topped with béchamel & baked*
— **με αγγινάρες** me ang·gi·*na*·res *alternating layers of minced veal & artichoke hearts*
μουσταλευριά ⓕ mu·sta·lev·ri·*a* *dark gelatinous pudding made from boiled grape must, thickened with flour & sprinkled with cinnamon, seeds & nuts*
μούστος ⓜ *mu*·stos *grape must collected from crushed wine grapes*
— **κουλούρα** ku·*lu*·ra *hard, turban-shaped grape must buns*
μπακαλιάρος ⓜ ba·ka·*lia*·ros *dried salt cod soaked for several hours prior to cooking*
μπουρδέτο ⓝ bur·*ţhe*·to *salt cod stew*
— **κροκετάκια** kro·ke·*ta*·kia *deep-fried salt cod mashed with potato & nutmeg*
— **πλακί** pla·*ki* *salt cod simmered with onions, potatoes, celery, carrots & garlic in a tomato-based sauce*
— **τηγανητός** ti·gha·ni·*tos* *salt cod fried in crisp, golden batter, traditionally accompanied with* **σκορδαλιά**
μπακλαβάς ⓜ pl ba·kla·*vas* *nut-filled layers of filo bathed in honey syrup*
μπάμιες ⓕ pl *ba*·mies *okra*
— **λαδερές** la·ţhe·*res* *okra stewed in oil*
— **γιαχνί** yia·*khni* *okra braised with pulped tomatoes & onions*
μπαρμπούνια ⓝ pl bar·*bu*·nia *small, sweet-fleshed red mullet*
— **ψητά στον άνιθο** psi·*ta* ston *a*·ni·tho *red mullet on a bed of dill*
— **στη σκάρα** sti *ska*·ra *red mullet basted with oil & lemon & chargrilled*
— **τηγανητά** ti·gha·ni·*ta* *red mullet rolled in seasoned flour & fried*
μπεκάτσα ⓕ be·*kat*·sa *woodcock*
— **κρασάτη** kra·*sa*·ti *woodcock casserole with dry red wine, tomatoes & spices, served on fried bread*
μπεκρή μεζέ ⓜ be·*kri* me·*ze* *'drunken* **μεζέ**' *– meat cooked in tomato & wine sauce*

μπομπότα ⓕ bo·bo·ta
sweet corn bread studded with raisins, walnuts, cloves & flavoured with cinnamon & orange juice (Zakynthos)
μπισκότα ⓝ pl bi·sko·ta *biscuits • cookies*
μπιζελόσουπα ⓕ bi·ze·lo·su·pa
fragrant pea soup loaded with dill
μπόλια bo·li·a ⓕ
lacy caul of fat encasing lamb's stomach
μπριάμι ⓝ bri·a·mi *casserole of sliced potatoes, zucchini, capsicums, tomatoes & herbs • roast vegetables*
μπριζόλες ⓕ pl bri·zo·les *chops • steak*
μπουγάτσα ⓕ bu·ghat·sa *creamy semolina pudding wrapped in pastry & baked*
μπουρδέτο ⓝ bur·the·to
hot fish casserole spiked with paprika
μπουρεκάκια ⓝ pl bu·re·ka·kia *little filo pies in cigar, cigarette & envelope shapes*
μπουρέκια ⓝ pl bu·re·kia *filo pies shaped into thin long rolls, batons & pinwheels*
— **με ανερί** me a·ne·ri *deep-fried pastry pouches stuffed with cheese (Cyprus)*
μυαλά ⓝ pl mia·la *brains*
— **αρνίσια λαδολέμονο** ar·ni·si·a la·tho·le·mo·no *poached lamb's brains*
— **τηγανητά** ti·gha·ni·ta *fried brains*
μύδια ⓝ pl mi·thia *mussels*
— **κρασάτα** kra·sa·ta
poached mussels in a white wine sauce
— **τηγανητά** ti·gha·ni·ta *mussels shucked, lightly battered, fried in hot oil & served with a garlic yogurt sauce*
— **γεμιστά** ye·mi·sta *mussels stuffed with rice, onions & parsley, slow-simmered in fish stock, tomato purée & white wine*
μυζήθρα ⓕ mi·zi·thra
soft mild ricotta-like cheese made from sheep's or goat's milk (sweet or savoury)
μυζηθρόπιτες ⓕ pl mi·zi·thro·pi·tes *delicate deep-fried pies with* **μυζήθρα** *(Crete)*

Ν ν

νεγκόσκα ⓕ ne·go·ska *variety of red grape*
νεραντζάκι γλυκό ⓝ ne·ran·dza·ki ghli·ko
preserved small bitter green oranges
νεράτη ⓕ ne·ra·ti
variety of cheese pie (Crete)
νουμπουλό ⓝ num·bu·lo
bacon-flavoured sausage (Corfu)
ντολμάδες dol·ma·thes ⓜ pl
dolmades – parcels of rice-wrapped leaves (usually vine leaves) & cooked in water, oil & lemon juice
— **φυλλιανές** fi·lia·nes *Christmas & New Year dish of onion sleeves stuffed with minced veal, pork & rice (Lesvos)*
— **με αυγολέμονο** me av·gho·le·mo·no
dolmades with rice, minced lamb, tomatoes, mint & cumin, served hot with **αλευρολέμονο**
— **με κουκιά** me ku·kia
dolmades with boiled & sliced broad beans & dried ox meat, cooked on a bed of beef bones (Northern Greece)
— **με λαχανόφυλλα** me la·kha·no·fi·la
stuffed cabbage leaves, served hot with **αβγολέμονο**
— **γιαλαντζί** yia·lan·dzi
'fraud' – stuffed meatless dolmades
— **Σμυρναίικα** zmir·ne·i·ka
dolmades stuffed with sautéed onions, rice, eggplant, oregano, dill, garlic & cooked in tomato broth
ντομάτες ⓕ pl do·ma·tes *tomatoes*
— **λιαστές** lia·stes *sun-dried tomatoes*
— **γεμιστές** ye·mi·stes
large tomatoes stuffed with rice, tomato pulp, onion, garlic & herbs
ντοματοκεφτέδες ⓜ pl
do·ma·to·kef·te·thes
deep-fried tomato rissoles
ντοματομπελτές ⓜ do·ma·to·pel·tes
tomato paste
ντοματόσουπα ⓕ do·ma·to·su·pa *soup made with tomatoes & sometimes pasta*
νυχάκι ⓝ ni·kha·ki *kalamata table olive (Messenia & Laconia)*

Ξ ξ

ξεροτήγανα ⓝ pl kse·ro·ti·gha·na *see* **δίπλες**
ξινόχοντρος ⓜ ksi·no·khon·dros *ground wheat cooked in sour milk & dried*
ξινομυζήθρα ⓕ ksi·no·mi·zi·thra
savoury **μυζήθρα**

O o

οινοπνευματώδη ⓝ pl i·nop·nev·ma·*to*·ţhi *alcoholic spirits*
οστρακοειδή ⓝ pl o·stra·ko·i·*ţhi* *shellfish*
ούζο ⓝ *u*·zo *clear spirit distilled from grape seeds, stems & skins with a strong aniseed flavour*
οφτή σαλάτα ⓕ of·*ti* sa·*la*·ta *grilled salad of potatoes, onions &* **σταφιδολιές** *foil-wrapped & chargrilled (Crete)*
οφτό ⓝ of·*to* *sausage made from pig's intestines, rice, walnuts, pistachios, raisins, cinnamon & orange peel (Crete)*
ουρά βοδιού ⓕ u·*ra* vo·*ţhiu* *oxtail*

Π π

παϊδάκια ⓝ pl pa·i·*ţha*·kia *chops • cutlets*
παξιμάδια ⓝ pl pak·si·*ma*·ţhia *hard wheat or barley rusks eaten slightly moistened with water at meal times (both wheat & barley varieties are common)*
— **με ντομάτες και φέτα** me do·*ma*·tes ke *fe*·ta **παξιμάδια** *moistened with water or tomato juice & topped with sliced tomatoes, feta, oregano, oil, salt & pepper – very popular snack or light lunch*
— **σαλάτα** sa·*la*·ta **παξιμάδια** *broken into pieces, moistened with water & sprinkled with diced tomatoes, crumbled feta or oregano, oil, salt & pepper*
παλαμίδα ⓕ pa·la·*mi*·ţha *bonito • tunny fish (a variety of tuna)*
— **ψητή με χόρτα** psi·*ti* me *khor*·ta *marinated bonito steaks*
παλικάρια ⓝ pl pa·li·*ka*·ri·a *mix of legumes & grains boiled & tossed with oil, onions & dill*
πανέ pa·*ne* *crumbed & fried*
παντρεμένοι ⓜ pl pan·dre·*me*·ni *beans with other foods (rice, meat, tomatoes)*
παντζάρι ⓝ pan·*dza*·ri *beetroot*
— **σαλάτα** sa·*la*·ta *boiled thickly sliced beetroot dressed with vinaigrette & served with* **σκορδαλιά**
παντσέττα ⓕ pan·*tse*·ta *pancetta*
— **γεμιστή στο φούρνο** ye·mi·*sti* sto *fur*·no *pig's stomach stuffed with parmesan, garlic, onions & oregano, basted with oil, wine & lemon juice & baked with potatoes (Zakynthos)*
πάπια ⓕ *pa*·pia *duck*
— **με σάλτσα ροδιού** me *sal*·tsa ro·*ţhiu* *fried duck breast served with sauce made from pomegranate seeds, lemon juice, duck stock & walnuts (Northern Greece)*
— **σαλμί** sal·*mi* *whole duck seared in oil, then jointed & cooked in its own juices, wine, orange juice & onions*
πάπρικα ⓕ *pa*·pri·ka *paprika*
παπουτσάκι ⓝ pa·put·*sa*·ki *'little shoe' – stuffed baby eggplant topped with béchamel sauce & baked*
παρμεζάνα ⓕ par·me·*za*·na *parmesan*
πασατέμπος ⓜ pa·sa·*te*·bos *'pass the time' – roasted pumpkin seeds sold as a snack*
πάστα ⓕ *pa*·sta *gateau*
παστέλι ⓝ pa·*ste*·li *sweet honey & sesame seed wafers*
παστιτσάδα ⓕ pa·stit·*sa*·ţha *pot-roasted veal with tomato, red wine, cloves, cinnamon & paprika (Corfu)*
παστίτσιο ⓝ pa·*stit*·si·o *baked layers of buttery macaroni & minced lamb topped with white sauce & grated* **κεφαλοτύρι**
παστός pa·*stos* *salted & dried*
παστουρμάς ⓜ pa·stur·*mas* *spicy dried ox meat*
πατάτες ⓕ pl pa·*ta*·tes *potatoes*
— **γιαχνί** yia·*khni* *potatoes stewed with tomatoes, onions & oregano*
— **κεφτέδες** kef·*te*·ţhes *fried potato, feta & parsley rissoles*
— **λεμονάτες** le·mo·*na*·tes *potatoes roasted with oil, lemon juice, oregano, salt & pepper*
— **πουρέ** pu·*re* *mashed potatoes*
— **στο φούρνο** sto *fur*·no *potatoes baked or roasted with oil, salt & oregano*
— **τηγανητές** ti·gha·ni·*tes* *fried potato slices*
πατατοσαλάτα ⓕ pa·ta·to·sa·*la*·ta *potato salad*
πατατού ⓕ pa·ta·*tu* *baked mashed potato pie (Cyclades)*

FOOD

πατσάς pat·sas ⓜ *tripe • rich-textured & surprisingly delicate-flavoured soup made with the stomach of a young lamb & finished with* **αβγολέμονο**

πατούδα ⓕ pa·tu·ţha *pastries filled with walnuts, almonds & cinnamon, baked, sprinkled with orange flower water & dredged in icing sugar (Crete)*

πεϊνιρλί ⓝ pe·i·nir·li *savoury pastries with a variety of fillings such as mincemeat, feta, ham & egg, & dried ox meat*

πέρδικες ⓕ pl per·ţhi·kes *partridges*

— **με ελιές και σέλινο** me e·lies ke se·li·no *partridges browned in butter & simmered in their own juices with green olives, sliced celery & tomatoes*

πέρκα ⓕ per·ka *sea perch*

πέστροφα ⓕ pe·stro·fa *trout*

πεταλίδες ⓕ pl pe·ta·li·ţhes *limpets*

— **με θαλασσινούς χοχλιούς** me tha·la·si·nus kho·khli·us *limpets & sea snails stewed with ripe tomatoes, onions & black pepper (Lesvos)*

πετιμέζι ⓝ pe·ti·me·zi *syrup made from unfermented grape juice, used to flavour rolls, cakes & sweets – when mixed with cold water makes a refreshing drink*

πιλάφι ⓝ pi·la·fi *pilau – rice & stock cooked to a creamy consistency – served to complement boiled meat or chicken*

— **με ντομάτες** me do·ma·tes *pilau with the addition of tomatoes, meat stock, garlic, parsley, salt & pepper*

— **με γαρίδες** me gha·ri·ţhes *pilau with prawns, onions & oregano*

— **με μύδια** me mi·ţhia *pilau with fresh mussels, onions & white wine*

— **με περδίκια** me per·ţhi·ki·a *pilau with partridge, tomato & cloves (Kefallonia)*

πιπέρι ⓝ pi·pe·ri *black pepper*

πιροσκί ⓝ pi·ro·ski *deep-fried, dough-wrapped sausage roll*

πίτα ⓕ pi·ta *pie – filo is the most common pastry used • flat doughy circular bread seared on grill until golden, mainly used for wrapping* **σουβλάκι** & **γύρος**

πιτσούνια ⓝ pl pit·su·nia *squab • lovebird • any tiny bird used for cooking*

— **κρασάτα** kra·sa·ta *baby squabs doused in red wine, tomato pulp, cinnamon & cloves then braised*

— **με κουκουνάρια** me ku·ku·na·ria *squab ignited with brandy, splashed with retsina & dressed with a garlic cream sauce (Northern Greece)*

— **με κουκιά** me ku·kia *stewed squab & fresh broad beans cooked in chicken stock, white wine, dill, garlic & lots of black pepper*

πλακί pla·ki *method of baking or braising with tomatoes, onion, garlic & parsley*

ποδαράκια ⓝ pl po·ţha·ra·kia *trotters*

— **αρνίσια** ar·ni·si·a *boiled lamb's trotters browned in butter & garlic, roasted, then finished with egg & lemon sauce*

πόρτο ⓝ por·to *port*

πορτοκάλι ⓝ por·to·ka·li *orange*

— **γλυκό** ghli·ko *preserved orange*

ποτό ⓝ po·to *drinks • spirits (on menus)*

πράσα ⓝ pl pra·sa *leeks*

— **αλευρολέμονο** a·lev·ro·le·mo·no *braised leeks in lemony sauce*

— **με δαμάσκηνα** me ţha·ma·ski·na *leeks & prunes sprinkled with cinnamon & nutmeg*

— **με ρύζι** me ri·zi *leeks & celery simmered with rice & crushed tomatoes*

πρασάκια με πατάτες ⓝ pl pra·sa·ki·a me pa·ta·tes *leeks & sliced potatoes cooked in butter, chicken stock, onions, oregano & parsley*

πρασόπιτα ⓕ pra·so·pi·ta *pie made with braised leeks, feta,* **μυζήθρα** *& skim milk (Western Greece)*

Ρ ρ

ραβιόλες ⓕ pl ra·vi·o·les *pasta envelopes stuffed with a mixture of cheese & mint, served with melted butter & grated cheese (Cyprus)*

ραδίκι ⓝ ra·ţhi·ki *chicory • term used for common varieties of* **χόρτα**

— **σαλάτα** sa·la·ta *spring salad of young dandelion leaves splashed with oil & lemon*

ρακί Ⓝ ra·*ki* fiery village spirit made from grapes, like ouzo but without the aniseed taste, high in alcohol
ραφιόλια Ⓝ pl ra·fi·o·li·a sweet half-moon filo pastries stuffed with cheese, eggs, cinnamon, orange rind & ouzo (Cyclades)
ρεβανί Ⓝ re·va·*ni* very sweet semolina sponge, flavoured with vanilla & orange juice & smothered with honey syrup
ρεβίθια Ⓝ pl re·*vi*·thia chickpeas
— **αλευρολέμονο** a·lev·ro·*le*·mo·no chickpeas simmered in a rich lemony broth
— **στο φούρνο** sto *fur*·no casserole of chickpeas, onions, garlic & bay leaves – favourite fasting food during Lent
— **σούπα** *su*·pa chickpea soup
ρεβιθοκεφτέδες Ⓜ pl re·vi·tho·kef·*te*·ţhes rissoles of mashed chickpeas, potatoes, onion, parsley & black pepper
ρέγγα Ⓕ *reng*·ga smoked herrings, eaten plain or grilled with oil & lemon
ρέσσι Ⓝ *re*·si pilau made with burghul & lamb (including the tail) & served at weddings (Cyprus)
ρετσίνα Ⓕ ret·*si*·na retsina – pine-resinated wine, often served chilled
ριγανάτος Ⓜ ri·gha·*na*·tos seasoned with oregano, salt & pepper
ρίγανη Ⓕ *ri*·gha·ni pungent Greek oregano
ριζάδα Ⓕ ri·*za*·ţha thick soup made with rice & shellfish or tiny game birds (Corfu)
ριζόγαλο Ⓝ ri·*zo*·gha·lo vanilla-flavoured rice pudding sprinkled with cinnamon
ρόδι Ⓝ *ro*·ţhi pomegranate – used to flavour sweets, syrups, cakes & salads
ροδόνερο Ⓝ ro·*ţho*·ne·ro fragrant rose-water used to flavour cakes, pies & sweets
ροφός Ⓜ ro·*fos* grouper • blackfish
ρολό από κιμά Ⓝ ro·*lo* a·*po* ki·*ma* baked mincemeat roll with hard-boiled eggs cuddled in the middle
ρύζι Ⓝ *ri*·zi rice

Σ σ

σαλάχι Ⓝ sa·*la*·hi ray fish • skate
— **σαλάτα** sa·*la*·ta boiled ray fish salad dressed with **λαδολέμονο**
σαλιγκάρια Ⓝ pl sa·ling·*ga*·ri·a snails – cooked in the shell & eaten with a fork
— **φρικασέ** fri·ka·*se* large snails sautéed in oil & stewed with zucchini, onions, fresh dill & finished with **αβγολέμονο**
— **με σάλτσα** me *sal*·tsa snails cooked with crushed tomatoes, tomato paste, onions & oregano
— **συμπεθεριό** sim·be·the·*rio* 'in-laws' – snails cooked with sliced eggplant, tomato pulp & **ξινόχοντρος**
— **στα κάρβουνα** sta *kar*·vu·na live snails chargrilled & doused with **λαδολέμονο** & bay leaves (Cyclades)
— **στιφάδο** sti·*fa*·ţho snail ragout with bay leaves (Crete)
σαλμί Ⓝ sal·*mi* method of casseroling game with red wine, vegetables & herbs
σάλτσα Ⓕ *sal*·tsa sauce • generic term for tomato sauce
— **από ζωμό κρέατος** a·*po* zo·*mo* *kre*·a·tos gravy
— **άσπρη** *a*·spri béchamel sauce with egg
— **άσπρη ξινή** *a*·spri ksi·*ni* 'sharp white sauce' – made with butter, flour, meat stock, eggs & lemon
— **αυγολέμονο** av·gho·*le*·mo·no see **αβγολέμονο**
— **ντομάτα** do·*ma*·ta tomato sauce with bay leaves
— **ντομάτα με κιμά** do·*ma*·ta me ki·*ma* tomato & mincemeat sauce
— **μαρινάτα** ma·ri·*na*·ta marinade
— **μουστάρδα** mu·*star*·ţha mustard & garlic beaten with lemon juice
— **ταρτάρ** tar·*tar* tartare sauce
Σάμος *sa*·mos rich golden dessert wine (Samos)
σαρακοστιανά Ⓝ pl sa·ra·ko·sti·a·*na* see **νηστήσιμα**
σαρδέλες Ⓕ pl sar·*ţhe*·les sardines
— **παστές** pa·*stes* salted sardines
— **στο φούρνο** sto *fur*·no sardines baked with oil, lemon, garlic & oregano
σαρμάς Ⓜ sar·*mas* pie-like offal dish (Northern Greece)
σβίγγοι Ⓜ pl *zving*·gi deep-fried fritters served with honey, cinnamon & cognac syrup

σελινόριζα (f) se·li·no·ri·za *celeriac*
— **με αυγολέμονο** me av·gho·le·mo·no *creamy dish of celeriac in chicken stock & finished with egg & lemon sauce*
— **με πράσα** me pra·sa *braised celeriac wedges & leek strips thickened with* **αβγολέμονο**
σέσκουλο (n) se·sku·lo *swiss chard, type of* **χόρτα**
— **με κιμά** me ki·ma *silverbeet sautéed with chopped onion in butter & cooked with minced lamb, rice, dill, lemon juice & salt*
σεσκουλόρυζο (n) se·sku·lo·ri·zo *see* **σπανακόρυζο**
σεφταλιά (f) sef·ta·lia *pork rissoles wrapped in sheep's caul & chargrilled (Cyprus)*
σκαλτσοτσέτα (n) pl skal·tsot·se·ta *paper-thin slices of fillet steak skewered & simmered in oil, water & tomatoes*
σκορδαλιά (f) skor·ţha·lia *thick paste of walnuts, bread, potatoes, olive oil, lemon & garlic*
σκόρδο (n) skor·ţho *garlic*
— **στούμπι** stu·bi *vinegar bottled with a garlic bulb, used for dressing vegetable dishes & salads (Ionian Islands)*
— **τσιγαριστά** tsi·gha·ri·sta *fried whole garlic bulbs • peeled & sliced garlic cloves fried & simmered in white wine, tomato paste, salt & pepper (Ithaca)*
σκουμπρί (n) sku·bri *mackerel*
σνακς (n) pl snaks *snacks*
σοφρίτο (n) so·fri·to *fried veal slices braised in a sauce of crushed garlic, wine vinegar, parsley, mint & brandy (Corfu)*
σοκολάτα (f) so·ko·la·ta *chocolate*
— **γάλα** gha·la *hot chocolate*
σουσάμι (n) su·sa·mi *sesame seed*
σούβλα (f) suv·la *spit-roasted • skewers • method of chargrilling meat or fish*
σουβλάκι (n) suv·la·ki *souvlaki – tender chunks of seasoned or marinated meat (or fish) skewered & chargrilled*
— **με πίτα** me pi·ta *souvlaki with* **πίτα**
σούγλι (n) sugh·li *sun-dried baby bogue fish coated in batter & fried (Cyclades)*
σούπα (f) su·pa *soup*
— **ξιδάτη** ksi·ţha·ti *sour soup of lentils, parsley & vinegar*
— **με τσουκνίδες** me tsuk·ni·ţhes *electric-green soup of stinging nettles & diced potatoes cooked in chicken stock & thickened with milk*
σουπιές (f) pl su·pies *cuttlefish*
— **κρασάτες** kra·sa·tes *cuttlefish cooked in wine*
— **με σάλτσα μελάνης** me sal·tsa me·la·nis *cuttlefish cooked in a rich sauce made from its own black ink & wine (Crete)*
— **με σπανάκι** me spa·na·ki *cuttlefish cooked with spinach, onions, dill & mint*
σουτζουκάκια (n) pl su·dzu·ka·kia *rissoles of minced lamb, veal or pork braised in a very spicy tomato gravy*
σουτζούκι (n) su·dzu·ki *strings of almonds dipped in syrup & sun-dried*
σπάλα (f) spa·la *shoulder of meat*
— **μοσχαρίσια** mos·kha·ri·si·a *silverside*
σπανακόπιτα (f) spa·na·ko·pi·ta *spinach filo pie, often includes feta or* **κεφαλοτύρι**, *eggs & herbs*
σπανακόρυζο (n) spa·na·ko·ri·zo *sautéed spinach, rice, spring onions & dill simmered in water until liquid is absorbed*
σπετζοφάι (n) spe·dzo·fa·i *sliced pork sausages stewed with sweet green peppers, eggplant, tomatoes & oregano*
σπλήνα (f) spli·na *spleen*
— **γεμιστή** ye·mi·sti *calf's spleen stuffed with chopped sautéed liver, onion, garlic & herbs, then roasted*
σπληνάντερο (n) spli·nan·de·ro *spit-roast sausage made from intestine stuffed with sliced spleen & garlic*
σταφίδες (f) pl sta·fi·ţhes *raisins • currants*
σταφιδολιές (f) pl sta·fi·ţho·lies *type of olive sun-dried until wrinkled, lightly salted & packed, or immersed in oil*
σταφιδωτά (n) pl sta·fi·ţho·ta *oval shortbread biscuits with chewy raisin centres*
σταφύλια (n) pl sta·fi·li·a *grapes*
στάκα (f) sta·ka *creamy butter made from fresh goat's or sheep's milk, used to flavour pies, stuffed vegetables & pilau*
— **με αβγά** me av·gha *omelette with* **στάκα** *(Crete)*

στάμνα ⓕ *stam*·na *method of cooking meat & potatoes in a pot sealed with wet clay & baked in charcoal embers*
στιφάδο ⓝ sti·*fa*·ţho
meat, game or seafood ragout
στραγάλια ⓝ pl stra·*gha*·lia
roasted chickpeas for snacking
σύκο ⓝ *si*·ko *fig*
— **αποστολιάτικο** a·po·sto·*lia*·ti·ko
young green fig
— **γλυκό** ghli·*ko* *green fig preserve*
— **στο φούρνο** sto *fur*·no *figs baked in a syrup of honey, vanilla, orange juice & orange flower water*
συκόπιτα ⓕ si·*ko*·pi·ta *fig cake (Corfu)*
συκόψωμο ⓝ si·*kop*·so·mo *heavy aromatic fig cake • dried green figs minced & mixed with ouzo shaped into balls, flattened, dried & wrapped in vine leaves*
συκωταριά ⓕ si·ko·ta·*ria* *innards • offal*
συκώτι ⓝ si·*ko*·ti *liver*
— **κρασάτα** kra·*sa*·ta
chopped liver marinated in red wine
— **λαδορίγανη** la·ţho·*ri*·gha·ni
grilled liver with oil, lemon & oregano
— **μαρινάτα** ma·ri·*na*·ta
thinly sliced livers fried & finished with vinegar, white wine & rosemary
— **με κρεμμυδάκια** me kre·mi·*ţha*·kia
livers fried with spring onions & cloves in a sauce of white wine & tomato juice
σφακιανόπιτες ⓕ pl sfa·ki·a·*no*·pi·tes
cheese pies consisting of balls of cheese wrapped in dough, then fried & served with a dollop of honey
σφουγγάτο ⓝ sfung·*ga*·to *Spanish-style omelette made with more vegetables than eggs, fried or baked (Rhodes)*

Τ τ

ταβάς ⓜ ta·*vas* *casserole of seasoned beef or lamb, fried onions, diced tomatoes, oil, vinegar & cinnamon*
ταλαττούρι ⓝ ta·la·*tu*·ri **τζατζίκι** *flavoured with mint (Cyprus)*
ταραμάς ⓜ ta·ra·*mas* *salted pressed roe of the grey mullet or cod*
ταράξακο ⓝ ta·*rak*·sa·ko *dandelion*
ταχίνι ⓝ ta·*hi*·ni *sesame seed paste*
ταχινόσουπα ⓕ ta·hi·*no*·su·pa
creamy lemony soup made from sesame paste (popular during Lent)
τελεμές ⓜ te·le·*mes*
heavily salted feta-style cheese
τηγανόψωμο ⓝ ti·gha·*nop*·so·mo *fried tomato & spring onion bread (Santorini)*
τίλιο ⓝ *ti*·li·o *infusion of lime leaves*
τζατζίκι ⓝ dza·*dzi*·ki *refreshing purée of grated cucumber, yogurt & garlic*
τσόχος ⓜ *tso*·khos *milk thistle – mild sweet-tasting green used in warm salads, pies & stews • type of* **χόρτα**
της ώρας tis *o*·ras *dishes cooked to order, such as steaks or chops*
τσουρέκι ⓝ tot·su·*re*·ki *braided Easter bread spiced with lemon rind & cherry pips, sprinkled with almonds & crushed* **μαστίχα**
τραχανόσουπα ⓕ tra·kha·*no*·su·pa
thick gruel of granulated pasta cooked in chicken broth with butter, lemon juice
τριαντάφυλλο γλυκό ⓝ
tri·an·*da*·fi·lo ghli·*ko* *delicate soft jam made from dark red rose petals*
τσικουδιά ⓕ tsi·ku·*ţhia* *see* **ρακί**
τσιπούρα ⓕ tsi·*pu*·ra
gilt head bream • snapper
τσίπουρο ⓝ *tsi*·pu·ro *see* **ρακί**
τσίρος ⓜ *tsi*·ros *small dried mackerel*
τσουκνίδες ⓕ pl tsu·*kni*·ţhes *stinging nettles used in salads & soups*
τουρσί ⓝ tur·*si* *pickles • pickled*
τούρτα ⓕ *tur*·ta *cake • gateau • tart*
τυρί ⓝ ti·*ri* *cheese*
— **μπλε** ble *blue cheese*
— **ημίσκληρο** i·*mi*·skli·ro *semi-firm cheese*
— **κατσικίσιο** kat·si·*ki*·si·o *goat's cheese*
— **κρεμώδες** kre·*mo*·ţhes *cream cheese*
— **μαλακή μυζήθρα** ma·la·*ki* mi·zi·thra
cottage cheese
— **μαλακό** ma·la·*ko* *soft cheese*
— **σαγανάκι** sa·gha·*na*·ki
sharp, hard cheese fried until crispy on the outside & soft in the centre, served with a squeeze of lemon juice
— **σκληρό** skli·*ro* *hard cheese*
τυρόπηγμα ⓝ ti·ro·pigh·ma *curd*

τυρόπιτα ⓕ ti·ro·pi·ta *cheese pies, the classic mixture is feta &* **κεφαλοτύρι** *wrapped in flaky filo pastry & baked*
τυροβολιά ⓕ ti·ro·vo·*lia* *cheese variety*

Φ φ

φάβα ⓕ *fa*·va *yellow split pea purée served with raw onion rings*
— **παντρεμένη** pan·dre·*me*·ni *'married' – leftover* **φάβα** *served as a hot dish with the addition of tomatoes & cumin*
φαγρί ⓝ fa·*ghri* *sea bream*
φακές ⓕ pl fa·*kes* *lentils*
— **με μακαρόνια** me ma·ka·*ro*·nia *lentils simmered in water & vinegar with mint, garlic & pearl pasta (Astypalea)*
— **σούπα** *su*·pa *lentil soup*
Φανουρόπιτα ⓕ fa·nu·*ro*·pi·ta *cake spiced with dried fruit, brandy & cinnamon – served on Saint Fanourios Day*
φασκόμηλο ⓝ fa·*sko*·mi·lo *sage*
φασολάδα ⓕ fa·so·*la*·ţha *thick fragrant soup of beans, tomatoes, tomato paste, carrots, celery, garlic & parsley*
φασολάκια ⓝ pl fa·so·*la*·kia *green beans*
— **λαδερά** la·ţhe·*ra* *green beans cooked in oil with tomatoes & onions*
— **σαλάτα** sa·*la*·ta *boiled fresh green beans with* **λαδολέμονο** *or* **λαδόξιδο**
φασόλια ⓝ pl fa·so·li·a *dried beans – usually refers to white haricot/lima beans*
— **μάραθο** *ma*·ra·tho *dried beans browned in oil & onions, simmered with tomato pulp & fennel leaves*
— **σαλάτα** sa·*la*·ta *bean salad*
φέτα ⓕ *fe*·ta *feta – white, crumbly, salty cheese*
— **σχάρας** *skha*·ras *grilled feta*
φέτες ψαριού με ντομάτα και σταφίδες ⓕ pl *fe*·tes psa·*riu* me do·*ma*·ta ke sta·*fi*·ţhes *fish with tomato & currants*
φιλέτο ⓝ fi·*le*·to *fillet • steak*
φιρίκια ⓝ pl fi·*ri*·ki·a *small crisp apples (Northern Greece)*
— **με αμύγδαλα** me a·*migh*·ţha·la *baked* **φιρίκια** *stuffed with almonds*
— **γεμιστά** ye·mi·*sta* **φιρίκια** *stuffed with minced veal, coriander & cumin*
φιστίκια ⓝ pl fi·*sti*·kia *peanuts*
— **Αιγίνης** e·*yi*·nis *pistachios*
φλαούνες ⓕ pl fla·*u*·nes *baked savoury tarts (Cyprus)*
φοινίκια ⓝ pl fi·*ni*·ki·a *honey-dipped shortbread sprinkled with cinnamon & marked with a criss-cross design*
φρικασέ ⓝ fri·ka·*se* *meat or vegetable stew thickened & flavoured with* **αβγολέμονο**
φρουταλιά ⓕ fru·ta·*lia* *omelette-type dish consisting of eggs, potatoes, parsley & sliced smoked pork sausages (Andros)*
φρυγαδέλια ⓝ pl fri·gha·*ţhe*·lia *liver parcels in lamb's caul, fried or skewered & chargrilled (Northern Greece, Thessaly)*
φύλλο ⓝ *fi*·lo *flaky tissue-thin pastry used for pies & sweet pastries*

Χ χ

χαβιάρι ⓝ kha·*via*·ri *caviar*
χαλβάς ⓜ khal·*vas* *rich creamy sweet made from sesame seeds & honey, flavoured with pistachio, chocolate or almonds*
— **σιμιγδαλένιος** si·migh·ţha·*le*·nios *moist cake of semolina & honey, decorated with almonds & cinnamon*
— **της Ρίνας** tis *ri*·nas *baked semolina & almond cake served hot with sugar syrup*
χαλορίνι ⓝ kha·lo·*ri*·ni *pouch-shaped cheese filled with crushed coriander (Cyprus)*
χαλούμι ⓝ kha·*lu*·mi *firm, white, sheep's milk cheese with elastic texture & salty taste (Cyprus)*
χαλουμόπιτες ⓕ pl kha·lu·*mo*·pi·tes *savoury cake made with* **χαλούμι**, *eggs, mint, sultanas &* **μαστίχα** *(Cyprus)*
χαλουμόψωμο ⓝ kha·lu·*mop*·so·mo *bread baked with chunks of* **χαλούμι** *(Cyprus)*
χαμομήλι ⓝ kha·mo·*mi*·li *chamomile*
χαμψιά ⓕ kham·*psia* *fresh anchovy*
χαμψοπίλαφο ⓝ kham·pso·*pi*·la·fo *onion & anchovy pilau seasoned with oregano*
χείλη της χανούμισσας ⓝ pl *hi*·li tis kha·*nu*·mi·sas *'the Turkish lady's lips' – crunchy honey cakes (Rhodes)*
χέλι ⓝ *he*·li *eel*
— **πλακί** pla·*ki* *eel baked with tomatoes, onions, potatoes & herbs (Corfu)*

χοιρινές Ⓕ pl hi·ri·*nes* *pork chops*
— **κρασάτες** kra·*sa*·tes *pork chops simmered in red wine*
— **στη σχάρα** sti *skha*·ra *pork chops chargrilled with salt, pepper & lemon juice*
— **τηγανητές** ti·gha·ni·*tes* *fried pork chops*
χοιρινό Ⓝ hi·ri·*no* *pork*
— **με κυδώνια** me ki·*ţho*·nia *pork & quinces simmered in red wine spiced with orange peel & cinnamon*
— **με πράσα** me *pra*·sa *pork & leek casserole*
— **με σέλινο αυγολέμενο** me *se*·li·no av·gho·*le*·mo·no *pork & celery in egg & lemon sauce*
— **μπούτι ψητό** *bu*·ti psi·*to* *crispy, roast leg of pork*
— **παστό** pa·*sto* *salted pork*
χοιρομέρι Ⓝ hi·ro·*me*·ri *cured leg of ham (Cyprus, Zakynthos)*
χόντρος Ⓜ *khon*·dros *hand-milled wheat used in soups, dolmades, snail dishes & stews (see also* **ξινόχοντρος**)
χόρτα Ⓝ pl *khor*·ta *wild or cultivated greens used in salads, pie fillings, casseroles or boiled & served hot with an oil & lemon dressing*
— **τσιγάρι** tsi·*gha*·ri *lightly fried wild greens*
χορτόπιτα Ⓕ khor·*to*·pi·ta *pies made from seasonal greens*
χορτοσαλάτα Ⓕ khor·to·sa·*la*·ta *warm salad of greens dressed with salt, oil & lemon*
χορτόσουπα Ⓕ khor·*to*·su·pa *vegetable soup*
χουρμάδες Ⓜ pl khur·*ma*·ţhes *dates*
χοχλιοί Ⓜ pl kho·khli·*i* *snails*
— **μπουμπουριστοί** bu·bu·ri·*sti* *'upside-down' – live snails deep-fried & doused with vinegar & rosemary*
χριστόψωμο Ⓝ khri·*stop*·so·mo *sweet Christmas bread baked in the shape of a cross*
χταπόδι Ⓝ khta·*po*·ţhi *octopus*
— **βραστό** vra·*sto* *boiled octopus coated with oil & lemon sauce*
— **κεφτέδες** kef·te·ţhes *rissoles of minced octopus, onion, mint & cheese*
— **κρασάτο** kra·*sa*·to *octopus cooked in red wine sauce*
— **λιαστό** lia·*sto* *sun-dried, chargrilled octopus sprinkled with oil & lemon juice*
— **με μακαρόνι κοφτό** me ma·ka·*ro*·ni kof·*to* *casserole of octopus, tomatoes, macaroni & red wine*
— **στα κάρβουνα** sta *kar*·vu·na *grilled octopus*
— **στιφάδο** sti·*fa*·ţho *octopus ragout*
— **τουρσί** tur·*si* *pickled octopus*
χυλόφτα Ⓝ pl hi·*lof*·ta *macaroni served with hot butter & grated cheese (Crete)*
χωριάτικη σαλάτα Ⓕ kho·ri·*a*·ti·ki sa·*la*·ta *'village salad' – salad of tomatoes, cucumber, olives & feta (known outside Greece as 'Greek salad')*

Ψ ψ

ψάρι Ⓝ *psa*·ri *fish*
— **μαρινάτο** ma·ri·*na*·to *fish fried until golden, served with a piquant sauce of garlic, rosemary & vinegar (also called* **ψάρι σαβόρι**)
— **πλακί** pla·*ki* *whole fish basted with oil, lemon & parsley, baked on a bed of chopped tomatoes & onions*
— **σαβόρι** sa·*vo*·ri *see* **ψάρι μαρινάτο**
— **Σπετσιώτο** spet·si·*o*·to *fish baked with bread crumbs & white wine (Spetses)*
— **στη σχάρα** sti *skha*·ra *chargrilled fish*
— **στο φούρνο λαδορίγανη** sto *fur*·no la·ţho·*ri*·gha·ni *sliced fish & potato wedges baked in a broth of oil, water & lemon juice*
— **τηγανητό** ti·gha·ni·*to* *battered fish*
— **βραστό με λαχανικά** vra·*sto* me la·kha·ni·*ka* *poached fish with vegetables – the broth is often strained, thickened with* **αβγολέμονο**
ψαροκεφτέδες Ⓜ pl psa·ro·kef·*te*·ţhes *fried fish rissoles*
ψαρονέφρι Ⓝ psa·ro·*ne*·fri *pork fillet steak*
ψαρόσουπα Ⓕ psa·*ro*·su·pa *fish soup thickened with rice &* **αβγολέμονο**
ψητός psi·*tos* *an all-purpose term for grilling, baking & barbecueing*
ψωμιά με ανάγλυφες διακοσμήσεις Ⓝ pl pso·*mia* me a·*na*·ghli·fes ţhi·a·koz·*mi*·sis *decorated bread (usually made with doughs of different colours) eaten at festivals, baptisms & weddings*

emergencies

έκτακτη ανάγκη

Help!	Βοήθεια!	vo·*i*·thia
Stop!	Σταμάτα!	sta·*ma*·ta
Go away!	Φύγε!	*fi*·ye
Thief!	Κλέφτης!	*klef*·tis
Fire!	Φωτιά!	fo·*tia*
Watch out!	Πρόσεχε!	*pro*·se·he

Call an ambulance!
Κάλεσε το ασθενοφόρο. — *ka*·le·se to as·the·no·*fo*·ro

Call the doctor!
Κάλεσε ένα γιατρό. — *ka*·le·se *e*·na yia·*tro*

Call the police!
Κάλεσε την αστυνομία. — *ka*·le·se tin a·sti·no·*mi*·a

It's an emergency.
Είναι μια έκτακτη ανάγκη. — *i*·ne mia *ek*·tak·ti a·*na*·gi

There's been an accident.
Έγινε ατύχημα. — *e*·yi·ne a·*ti*·hi·ma

Could you please help?
Μπορείς να βοηθήσεις, παρακαλώ; — bo·*ris* na vo·i·*thi*·sis pa·ra·ka·*lo*

signs

Αστυνομία	a·sti·no·*mi*·a	**Police**
Αστυνομικός Σταθμός	a·sti·no·mi·*kos* stath·*mos*	**Police Station**
Νοσοκομείο	no·so·ko·*mi*·o	**Hospital**
Σταθμός Πρώτων Βοηθειών	stath·*mos pro*·ton vo·i·thi·*on*	**Emergency Department**

Is it safe ...?	Είναι ασφαλές ...;	*i*·ne as·fa·*les* ...
at night	τη νύχτα	ti *nikh*·ta
for gay people	για γκέι	yia *ge*·i
for travellers	για ταξιδιώτες	yia tak·si·*ţhio*·tes
for women	για γυναίκες	yia yi·*ne*·kes
on your own	χωρίς παρέα	kho·*ris* pa·*re*·a

I'm lost.
Έχω χαθεί. — *e*·kho kha·*thi*

Where are the toilets?
Πού είναι η τουαλέτα; — pu *i*·ne i tu·a·*le*·ta

Is that a UN zone?
Είναι αυτή η ζώνη του ΟΗΕ; — *i*·ne af·*ti* i *zo*·ni tu o·i·*e*

Where's the demarcation line?
Πού είναι η διαχωριστική γραμμή; — pu *i*·ne i ţhi·a·kho·ri·sti·*ki* ghra·*mi*

Are there military bases in this region?
Υπάρχουν στρατιωτικές βάσεις σ' αυτή την περιοχή; — i·*par*·khun stra·ti·o·ti·*kes* *va*·sis saf·*ti* tin pe·ri·o·*hi*

police

αστυνομία

Where's the police station?
Πού είναι ο αστυνομικός σταθμός; — pu *i*·ne o a·sti·no·mi·*kos* stath·*mos*

Please telephone the Tourist Police.
Παρακαλώ τηλεφώνα την τουριστική αστυνομία. — pa·ra·ka·*lo* ti·le·*fo*·na tin tu·ri·sti·*ki* a·sti·no·*mi*·a

I want to report an offence.
Θέλω να αναφέρω μια παρανομία. — *the*·lo na a·na·*fe*·ro mia pa·ra·no·*mi*·a

It was him/her.
Ήταν αυτός/αυτή. — *i*·tan af·*tos*/af·*ti*

I have insurance.
Έχω ασφάλεια. — *e*·kho as·*fa*·li·a

I've been …	Με έχουν …	me *e*·khun …
He/She has been …	Τον/Την έχουν …	ton/tin *e*·khun …
assaulted	κακοποιήσει	ka·ko·pi·*i*·si
raped	βιάσει	vi·*a*·si
robbed	ληστέψει	li·*step*·si

the police may say …

Κατηγορείσαι για … ka·ti·gho·*ri*·se yia …	**You're charged with …**
Αυτός κατηγορείται για … af·*ti* ka·ti·gho·*ri*·te yia …	**He's charged with …**
Αυτή κατηγορείται για … af·*ti* ka·ti·gho·*ri*·te yia …	**She's charged with …**

διατάραξη ησυχίας	ţhi·a·*ta*·rak·si i·si·*hi*·as	**disturbing the peace**
εξαγωγή αρχαιοτήτων χωρίς άδεια	ek·sa·gho·*yi* ar·he·o·*ti*·ton kho·*ris* *a*·ţhi·a	**exporting antiquities without a permit**
κακοποίηση	ka·ko·*pi*·i·si	**assault**
κλοπή από κατάστημα	klo·*pi* a·*po* ka·*ta*·sti·ma	**shoplifting**
κλοπή	klo·*pi*	**theft**
μετακίνηση αρχαιοτήτων	me·ta·*ki*·ni·si ar·he·o·*ti*·ton	**removing antiquities**
μη κατοχή βίζας	mi ka·to·*hi* *vi*·zas	**not having a visa**
κατοχή (παράνομων ουσιών)	ka·to·*hi* (pa·*ra*·no·mon u·si·*on*)	**possession (of illegal substances)**
υπέρβαση της βίζας	i·*per*·va·si tis *vi*·zas	**overstaying a visa**
Είναι πρόστιμο για …	*i*·ne *pro*·sti·mo yia …	**It's a … fine.**
πάρκινγκ	*par*·king	**parking**
ταχύτητα	ta·*hi*·ti·ta	**speeding**

I've lost my …	Έχασα … μου.	*e*·kha·sa … mu
My … was/were stolen.	Έκλεψαν … μου.	*e*·klep·san … mu
bags	τις βαλίτσες	tis va·*lit*·se
money	τα χρήματά	ta *khri*·ma·*ta*
passport	το διαβατήριό	to ţhia·va·*ti*·rio

What am I accused of?
Για τι πράγμα κατηγορούμαι;
yia ti *pra*·ghma ka·ti·gho·*ru*·me

I didn't realise I was doing anything wrong.
Δεν κατάλαβα ότι έκαμα κάτι λάθος.
ţhen ka·*ta*·la·va *o*·ti *e*·ka·ma *ka*·ti *la*·thos

I didn't do it.
Δεν το έκαμα.
ţhen to *e*·ka·ma

I'm sorry.
Συγνώμη.
sigh·*no*·mi

Can I pay an on-the-spot fine?
Μπορώ να πληρώσω ένα πρόστιμο επί τόπου;
bo·*ro* na pli·*ro*·so *e*·na *pro*·sti·mo e·*pi* *to*·pu

I want to contact my embassy.
Θέλω να έρθω σε επαφή με την πρεσβεία μου.
the·lo na *er*·tho se e·pa·*fi* me tin prez·*vi*·a mu

Can I make a phone call?
Μπορώ να κάμω ένα τηλεφώνημα;
bo·*ro* na *ka*·mo *e*·na ti·le·*fo*·ni·ma

Can I have a lawyer (who speaks English)?
Μπορώ να έχω ένα δικηγόρο (που να μιλάει αγγλικά);
bo·*ro* na *e*·kho *e*·na ţhi·ki·*gho*·ro (pu na mi·*la*·i ang·gli·*ka*)

This drug is for personal use.
Αυτό το φάρμακο είναι για προσωπική χρήση.
af·*to* to *far*·ma·ko *i*·ne yia pro·so·pi·*ki* *hri*·si

I have a prescription for this drug.
Έχω συνταγή για αυτό το φάρμακο.
e·kho si·da·*yi* yia af·*to* to *far*·ma·ko

I (don't) understand.
(Δεν) καταλαβαίνω.
(ţhen) ka·ta·la·*ve*·no

doctor

γιατρός

Where's the nearest …?	Πού είναι το πιο κοντινό…;	pu *i*·ne to pio ko·di·*no* …
emergency department	πρώτων βοηθειών	*pro*·ton vo·i·thi·*on*
hospital	νοσοκομείο	no·so·ko·*mi*·o
medical centre	ιατρικό κέντρο	i·a·tri·*ko* *ke*·dro
(night) pharmacy	(νυχτερινό) φαρμακείο	(nikh·te·ri·*no*) far·ma·*ki*·o

Where's the nearest …?	Πού είναι ο πιο κοντινός …;	pu *i*·ne o pio ko·di·*nos* …
dentist	οδοντίατρος	o·ţho·di·a·*tros*
doctor	γιατρός	yia·*tros*
optometrist	οφθαλμίατρος	of·thal·*mi*·a·tros

I need a doctor (who speaks English).
Χρειάζομαι ένα γιατρό (που να μιλάει αγγλικά). — khri·*a*·zo·me *e*·na yia·*tro* (pu na mi·*la*·i ang·gli·*ka*)

Could I see a female doctor?
Μπορώ να δω μια γυναίκα γιατρό; — bo·*ro* na ţho mia yi·*ne*·ka yia·*tro*

Could the doctor come here?
Μπορεί ο γιατρός να έρθει εδώ; — bo·*ri* o yia·*tros* na *er*·thi e·*ţho*

Is there an after-hours emergency number?
Υπάρχει τηλεφωνικός αριθμός για επείγουσες ανάγκες τη νύχτα; — i·*par*·hi ti·le·fo·ni·*kos* a·rith·*mos* yia e·*pi*·ghu·ses a·*na*·ges ti *nikh*·ta

I've run out of my medication.
Μου έχουν τελειώσει τα φάρμακά μου. — mu *e*·khun te·li·*o*·si ta *far*·ma·*ka* mu

This is my usual medicine.
Αυτά είναι τα συνηθισμένα μου φάρμακα. — af·*ta* *i*·ne ta si·ni·thiz·*me*·na mu *far*·ma·ka

What's the correct dosage?
Ποια είναι η σωστή δόση; — pia *i*·ne i so·*sti* *ţho*·si

I don't want a blood transfusion.
Δεν θέλω μετάγγιση αίματος. — ţhen *the*·lo me·*ta*·gi·si *e*·ma·tos

Please use a new syringe.
Παρακαλώ χρησιμοποίησε καινούργια σύριγγα. — pa·ra·ka·*lo* khri·si·mo·*pi*·i·se ke·*nur*·yia *si*·ri·ga

I have my own syringe.
Έχω δική μου σύριγγα. — *e*·kho ţhi·*ki* mu *si*·ri·ga

I've been vaccinated against …
Έχω κάμει εμβόλιο για … — *e*·kho *ka*·mi em·*vo*·li·o yia

He/She has been vaccinated against …	Αυτός/Αυτή έχει κάμει εμβόλιο για …	af·*tos*/af·*ti* *e*·khi *ka*·mi em·*vo*·li·o yia …
hepatitis A/B/C	ηπατίτιδα A/B/C	i·pa·*ti*·ti·ţha *e*·i/bi/si
tetanus	τέτανο	*te*·ta·no
typhoid	τύφο	*ti*·fo

I need new …	Χρειάζομα …	khri·*a*·zo·me …
contact lenses	καινούργιους φακούς επαφής	ke·*nur*·yius fa·*kus* e·pa·*fis*
glasses	καινούργια γιαλιά	ke·*nur*·yia yia·*lia*

My prescription is …
Η συνταγή μου είναι … — i si·da·*yi* mu *i*·ne …

How much will it cost?
Πόσο θα κοστίσει; — *po*·so tha ko·*sti*·si

Can I have a receipt for my insurance?
Μπορώ να έχω μια απόδειξη για την ασφάλειά μου; — bo·*ro* na *e*·kho mia a·*po*·ţhik·si yia tin as·*fa*·li·*a* mu

the doctor may say ...

Ποιο είναι το πρόβλημα; pio *i*·ne to *prov*·li·ma	**What's the problem?**
Πού πονάει; pu po·*na*·i	**Where does it hurt?**
Έχετε πυρετό; *e*·he·te pi·re·*to*	**Do you have a temperature?**
Πόσον καιρό είστε έτσι; *po*·son ke·*ro* *i*·ste *et*·si	**How long have you been like this?**
Το είχατε αυτό πριν; to *i*·kha·te af·*po* prin	**Have you had this before?**
Έχετε σεξουαλικές σχέσεις; *e*·he·te sek·su·a·li·*kes* *she*·sis	**Are you sexually active?**
Μήπως είχατε σεξ χωρίς προφύλαξη; *mi*·pos *i*·kha·te seks kho·*ris* pro·*fi*·lak·si	**Have you had unprotected sex?**
Πίνετε;/Καπνίζτε; *pi*·ne·te/ka·*pni*·ze·te	**Do you drink/smoke?**
Παίρνετε ναρκωτικά; *per*·ne·te nar·ko·ti·*ka*	**Do you take drugs?**
Είστε αλλεργικός σε κάτι; *i*·ste a·ler·yi·*kos* se *ka*·ti	**Are you allergic to anything?**
Παίρνετε φάρμακα; *per*·ne·te *far*·ma·ka	**Are you on medication?**
Πόσον καιρό ταξιδεύετε; *po*·son ke·*ro* tak·si·*ţhe*·ve·te	**How long are you travelling for?**
Πρέπει να μπείτε στο νοσοκομείο. *pre*·pi na *bi*·te sto no·so·ko·*mi*·o	**You need to be admitted to hospital.**
Πρέπει να το ελέγξετε όταν επιστρέψετε στη χώρα σας. *pre*·pi na to e·*leng*·kse·te o·tan e·pi·*strep*·se·te sti *kho*·ra sas	**You should have it checked when you go home.**

the doctor may say ...

Πρέπει να επιστρέψετε στη χώρα σας για θεραπεία. *pre*·pi na e·pi·*strep*·se·te sti *kho*·ra sas yia the·ra·*pi*·a	**You should return home for treatment.**
Είστε υποχονδριακός/υποχονδριακή. m/f *i*·ste i·po·khon·ţhri·a·*kos*/ po·khon·ţhri·a·*ki*	**You're a hypochondriac.**

symptoms & conditions

συμπτώματα και καταστάσεις

I'm sick.
Είμαι άρρωστος. — i·*me* *a*·ro·stos

My friend is (very) sick. (about a man)
Ο φίλος μου είναι (πολύ) άρρωστος. — o *fi*·los mu *i*·ne (po·*li*) *a*·ro·stos

My friend is (very) sick. (about a woman)
Η φίλη μου είναι (πολύ) άρρωστη. — i *fi*·li mu *i*·ne (po·*li*) *a*·ro·sti

My child is (very) sick.
Το παιδί μου είναι (πολύ) άρρωστο. — to pe·*ţhi* mu *i*·ne (po·*li*) *a*·ro·sto

He/She is having a/an ...	Αυτός/Αυτή έχει ...	af·*tos*/af·*ti* *e*·hi ...
allergic reaction	αλλεργική αντίδραση	a·ler·yi·*ki* a·*di*·ţhra·si
asthma attack	προσβολή από άσθμα	proz·vo·*li* a·*po* *as*·thma
epileptic fit	επιληπτική κρίση	e·pi·lip·ti·*ki* *kri*·si
heart attack	καρδιακή προσβολή	kar·ţhi·a·*ki* pros·vo·*li*

He/She has been ...	Αυτός/Αυτή ...	af·*tos*/af·*ti* ...
injured	έχει τραυματιστεί	*e*·hi trav·ma·ti·*sti*
vomiting	κάνει εμετό	*ka*·ni e·me·*to*

I've been ...		
injured	Έχω τραυματιστεί.	*e*·kho trav·ma·ti·*sti*
vomiting	Κάνω εμετό.	*ka*·no e·me·*to*

I've been bitten/ stung by a ...	Με έχει δαγκώσει/ τσιμπήσει ...	me *e*·hi ţha·*go*·si/ tsi·*bi*·si ...
bee	μέλισσα	*me*·li·sa
jellyfish	μέδουσα	*me*·ţhu·sa
sea urchin	αχινός	a·hi·*nos*
snake	φίδι	*fi*·ţhi
wasp	σφήκα	*sfi*·ka
weever fish	δράκαινα	*ţhra*·ke·na

I feel ...	Αισθάνομαι ...	es·*tha*·no·me ...
anxious	ανυπόμονος/η m/f	a·ni·*po*·mo·nos/i
better	καλύτερα m&f	ka·*li*·te·ra
depressed	θλιμμένος/η m/f	thli·*me*·nos/i
dizzy	ζαλάδα m&f	za·*la*·ţha
hot and cold	ζέστη και κρύο m&f	*ze*·sti ke *kri*·o
nauseous	ναυτία m&f	naf·*ti*·a
shivery	ρίγος m&f	*ri*·ghos
strange	παράξενα m&f	pa·*rak*·se·na
weak	αδύνατος/η m/f	a·*ţhi*·na·tos/i
worse	χειρότερα m&f	hi·*ro*·te·ra

It hurts here.	
Πονάει εδώ.	po·*na*·i e·*ţho*
I can't sleep.	
Δεν μπορώ να κοιμηθώ.	ţhen bo·*ro* na ki·mi·*tho*
I think it's the medication I'm on.	
Νομίζω είναι τα φάρμακα που παίρνω.	no·*mi*·zo *i*·ne ta *far*·ma·ka pu *per*·no
I'm on medication for ...	
Παίρνω φάρμακα για ...	*per*·no *far*·ma·ka yia ...
He/She is on medication for ...	
Αυτός/αυτή παίρνει φάρμακα για ...	af·*tos*/af·*ti per*·ni *far*·ma·ka yia ...

I have (a/an) …
Έχω … — *e*·kho …

He/She has (a/an) …
Αυτός/αυτή έχει … — af·*tos*/af·*ti* *e*·hi …

I've recently had (a/an) …
Είχα πρόσφατα … — *i*·kha *pros*·fa·ta …

He/She has recently had (a/an) …
Αυτός/αυτή είχε πρόσφατα … — af·*tos*/af·*ti* *i*·he *pros*·fa·ta …

AIDS	Έηντς **n**	*e*·idz
asthma	άσθμα **n**	*as*·thma
burn	έγκαυμα **n**	*e*·gav·ma
cold	κρύωμα **n**	*kri*·o·ma
constipation	δυσκοιλιότητα **f**	ţhis·ki·li·*o*·ti·ta
cough	βήχα **m**	*vi*·kha
dehydration	αφυδάτωση **f**	a·fi·*ţha*·to·si
diabetes	διαβήτη **m**	ţhia·*vi*·ti
diarrhoea	διάρροια **f**	ţhi·*a*·ri·a
encephalitis	εγκεφαλίτιδα **f**	e·ge·fa·*li*·ti·ţha
fever	πυρετό **m**	pi·re·*to*
headache	πονοκέφαλο **m**	po·no·*ke*·fa·lo
heatstroke	ηλιακή συμφόρηση **f**	i·lia·*ki* sim·*fo*·ri·si
indigestion	δυσπεψία **f**	ţhis·pep·*si*·a
(fungal) infection	(μυκητώδη) μόλυνση **f**	(mi·ki·*to*·ţhi) *mo*·lin·si
insect bite	τσίμπημα από έντομο **n**	*tsi*·bi·ma a·*po* *e*·do·mo
Lyme disease	νόσο του lyme **f**	*no*·so tu *la*·im
nausea	ναυτία **f**	naf·*ti*·a
pain	πόνο **m**	*po*·no
rabies	λύσσα **f**	*li*·sa
rash	εξάνθημα **n**	ek·*san*·thi·ma
sea sickness	ναυτία **f**	naf·*ti*·a
sore throat	πονόλαιμο **m**	po·*no*·le·mo
sprain	στραμπούλισμα **n**	stra·*bu*·liz·ma
stomachache	στομαχόπονο **m**	sto·ma·*kho*·po·no
sunburn	ηλιακό έγκαυμα **n**	i·li·a·*ko* *e*·gav·ma
tick typhus	τσιμπούρι τύφου **n**	tsi·*bu*·ri *ti*·fu

women's health

υγεία γυναικών

(I think) I'm pregnant.
(Νομίζω) Είμαι έγγυος. — (no·*mi*·zo) *i*·me *e*·gi·os

I'm on the pill.
Παίρνω το Χάπι. — *per*·no to *kha*·pi

I haven't had my period for (six) weeks.
Δεν έχω περίοδο για (έξι) εβδομάδες. — ţhen *e*·kho pe·*ri*·o·ţho yia (*ek*·si) ev·ţho·*ma*·ţhes

I've noticed a lump here.
Παρατήρησα ένα εξόγκωμα εδώ. — pa·ra·*ti*·ri·sa *e*·na ek·*so*·go·ma e·*ţho*

Do you have something for (period pain)?
Έχετε κάτι για (πόνο για την περίοδο); — *e*·he·te *ka*·ti yia (*po*·no yia tin pe·*ri*·o·ţho)

I have a ...	Έχω ...	*e*·kho ...
urinary tract infection	μόλυνση στον ουρικό σωλήνα	*mo*·lin·si ston u·ri·*ko* so·*li*·na
yeast infection	μυκωτική μόλυνση	mi·ko·ti·*ki* *mo*·lin·si

the doctor may say ...

Χρησιμοποιείτε αντισυλληπτικά;
khri·si·mo·pi·*i*·te a·di·si·lip·ti·*ka* — **Are you using contraception?**

Έχετε περίοδο;
e·he·te pe·*ri*·o·ţho — **Are you menstruating?**

Είστε έγγυος;
i·ste *e*·gi·os — **Are you pregnant?**

Πότε είχατε περίοδο τελευταία;
po·te *i*·kha·te pe·*ri*·o·ţho te·lef·*te*·a — **When did you last have your period?**

Είστε έγγυος.
i·ste *e*·gi·os — **You're pregnant.**

I need (a/the) …	Χρειάζομαι …	khri·*a*·zo·me …
contraception	αντισυλληπτικό	a·di·si·lip·ti·*ko*
morning-after pill	το χάπι του επόμενου πρωινού	to *kha*·pi tu e·*po*·me·nu pro·i·*nu*
pregnancy test	τεστ εγγυμοσύνης	test e·gi·mo·*si*·nis

allergies

αλλεργίες

I have a skin allergy.
Έχω αλλεργία στο δέρμα. *e*·kho a·ler·*yi*·a sto *ţher*·ma

I'm allergic to …	Είμαι αλλεργικός/ αλλεργική … m/f	*i*·me a·ler·yi·*kos* a·ler·yi·*ki*
He's allergic to …	Αυτός είναι αλλεργικός …	af·*tos i*·ne a·ler·yi·*kos* …
She's allergic to …	Αυτή είναι αλλεργική …	af·*ti i*·ne a·ler·yi·*ki* …
antibiotics	στα αντιβιωτικά	sta a·di·vi·o·ti·*ka*
anti-inflammatories	στα αντιφλεγμονώδη	sta a·di·flegh·mo·*no*·ţhi
aspirin	στην ασπιρίνη	stin as·pi·*ri*·ni
bees	στις μέλισσες	stis *me*·li·ses
codeine	στην κωδεΐνη	stin ko·ţhe·*i*·ni
penicillin	στην πενικιλλίνη	stin pe·ni·ki·*li*·ni
pollen	στη γύρη	sti *yi*·ri
sulphur-based drugs	στα φάρμακα με θείο	sta *far*·ma·ka me *thi*·o
wasps	στις σφήκες	stis *sfi*·kes

inhaler	αναπνευστήρας m	a·nap·nef·*sti*·ras
injection	ένεση f	*e*·ne·si
antihistamines	αντιισταμίνες f	a·di·i·sta·*mi*·nes

For food-related allergies, see **vegetarian & special meals**, page 173.

parts of the body

μέρη του σώματος

My … hurts.
Πονάει … | po·*na*·i …

I can't move my …
Δεν μπορώ να κουνήσω … | ţhen bo·*ro* na ku·*ni*·so …

I have a cramp in my …
Έχω κράμπα … | *e*·kho *kra*·ba …

My … is swollen.
Είναι πρησμένο … | *i*·ne priz·*me*·no …

It hurts when you touch it.
Πονάει όταν το αγγίζεις. | po·*ne* *o*·tan to a·*gi*·zis

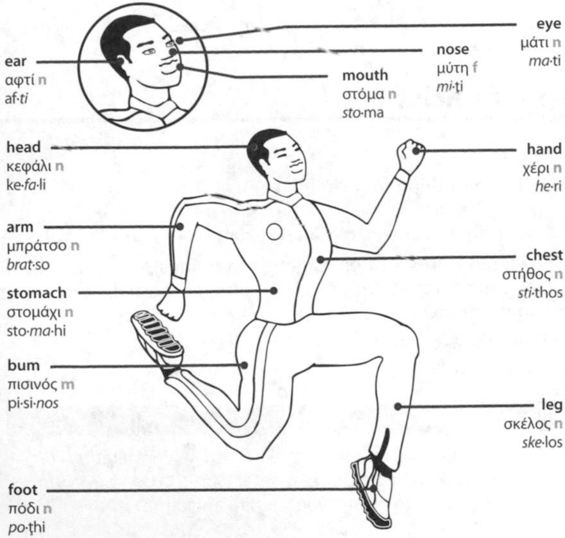

health

alternative treatments

εναλλακτικές θεραπείες

I don't use (Western medicine).

Δεν χρησιμοποιώ (συμβατική ιατρική).	ţhen khri·si·mo·pi·*o* (sim·va·ti·*ki* i·a·tri·*ki*)

I prefer ...	Προτιμώ ...	pro·ti·*mo* ...
Can I see someone who practises ...?	Μπορώ να δω κάποιον που ασκεί ...;	bo·*ro* na ţho *ka*·pion pu a·*ski* ...
acupuncture	βελονισμό	ve·lo·niz·*mo*
naturopathy	φυσική θεραπεία	fi·si·*ki* the·ra·*pi*·a
reflexology	αντανακλαστική	a·da·na·kla·sti·*ki*

pharmacist

φαρμακοποιός

I need something for (a headache).

Χρειάζομαι κάτι για (πονοκέφαλο).	khri·*a*·zo·me *ka*·ti yia (po·no·*ke*·fa·lo)

Do I need a prescription for (antihistamines)?

Χρειάζομαι συνταγή για (αντιισταμίνες);	khri·*a*·zo·me si·da·*yi* yia (a·di·i·sta·*mi*·nes)

I have a prescription.

Έχω συνταγή.	*e*·kho si·da·*yi*

come again?

If you need something repeated in a consultation or conversation, say Ορίστε; o·*ris*·te (Sorry?). Use Συγνώμη sigh·*no*·mi (Sorry) when you need to apologise.

How many times a day?
Πόσες φορές την ημέρα; *po*·ses fo·*res* tin i·*me*·ra

Will it make me drowsy?
Θα με κάμει να νυστάζω; tha me *ka*·mi na ni·*sta*·zo

antiseptic	αντισηπτικό n	a·di·sip·ti·*ko*
condoms	προφυλακτικά n pl	pro·fi·lakh·ti·*ka*
contraceptives	αντισυλληπτικά n pl	a·di·si·lip·ti·*ka*
insect repellent	εντομοαπωθητικό n	e·do·mo·a·po·thi·ti·*ko*
laxative	καθαρτικό n	ka·thar·ti·*ko*
painkillers (for infants)	παυσίπονα (για μωρά) n pl	paf·*si*·po·na (yia mo·*ra*)
rehydration salts	ενυδρωτικά άλατα n pl	en·i·ţhro·ti·*ka* *a*·la·ta
spray for insect bites	σπρέι για τσιμπήματα κουνουπιών n	*spre*·i yia tsi·*bi*·ma·ta ku·nu·*pion*
sunburn lotion	λοσιόν για ηλιακό έγκαυμα n	lo·*sion* yia i·li·a·*ko* *e*·gav·ma
sunscreen	αντιηλιακό n	a·di·i·li·a·*ko*
talcum powder	ταλκ n	talk
thermometer	θερμόμετρο n	ther·*mo*·me·tro
zinc cream	ψευδαργυρούχος αλοιφή f	psev·ţhar·yi·*ru*·khos a·li·*fi*

the pharmacist may say ...

Δυο φορές την ημέρα (με φαγητό).
ţhio fo·*res* tin i·*me*·ra (me fa·yi·*to*) — **Twice a day (with food).**

Το έχετε ξαναπάρει;
to *e*·he·te ksa·na·*pa*·ri — **Have you taken this before?**

Πρέπει να τελειώσετε όλη τη σειρά.
pre·pi na te·li·*o*·se·te *o*·li ti si·*ra* — **You must complete the course.**

dentist

οδοντίατρος

I have a …	Έχω …	e·ho …
broken tooth	ένα σπασμένο δόντι	e·na spaz·*me*·no *ţho*·di
cavity	ένα κούφιο δόντι	e·na *ku*·fio *ţho*·di
toothache	πονόδοντο	po·*no*·ţho·do

I've lost a filling.
Έχασα ένα σφράγισμα. — *e*·kha·sa *e*·na *sfra*·yiz·ma

My dentures are broken.
Οι μασέλες μου έσπασαν. — i ma·*se*·les mu *e*·spa·san

My gums hurt.
Πονούν τα ούλα μου. — po·*nun* ta *u*·la mu

I need an anaesthetic/a filling.
Χρειάζομαι αναισθητικό/σφράγισμα. — khri·*a*·zo·me a·nes·thi·ti·*ko*/*sfra*·yiz·ma

I don't want it extracted.
Δεν θέλω να το βγάλω. — ţhen *the*·lo na to *vgha*·lo

Ouch!
Όου! — *o*·u

the dentist may say …

Ανοίξτε το στόμα πολύ a·*nik*·ste to *sto*·ma po·*li*.	**Open wide.**
Δεν θα πονέσει καθόλου. ţhen tha po·*ne*·si ka·*tho*·lu	**This won't hurt a bit.**
Δαγκώστε αυτό. ţha·*go*·ste af·*to*	**Bite down on this.**
Μην κινείστε. min ki·*ni*·ste	**Don't move.**
Ξεβγάλτε! ksev·*ghal*·te	**Rinse!**
Γυρίστε πίσω, δεν τελείωσα. yi·*ri*·ste *pi*·so ţhen te·*li*·o·sa	**Come back, I haven't finished.**

DICTIONARY > english–greek

Greek nouns in the **dictionary** have their gender indicated by (m) masculine, (f) feminine or (n) neuter. If it's a plural noun you'll also see pl. When a word that could be either a noun or a verb has no gender indicated, it's a verb. Adjectives are given in the masculine form only – see **adjectives & adverbs** in the **phrasebuilder** for more on how to form feminine and neuter adjectives. Both nouns and adjectives are provided in the nominative case only – refer to the **phrasebuilder** for more information on **case**. Note that we've also added the abbreviations a adjective and v verb for added clarity where required.

A

aboard (επάνω στο) κατάστρωμα (e·*pa*·no sto) ka·*tas*·tro·ma
abortion έκτρωση (f) *ek*·tro·si
about περίπου pe·*ri*·pu
above από πάνω a·*po pa*·no
abroad στο εξωτερικό sto ek·so·te·ri·*ko*
accident ατύχημα (n) a·*ti*·hi·ma
accommodation κατάλυμα (n) ka·*ta*·li·ma
account λογαριασμός (m) lo·gha·riaz·*mos*
across απέναντι a·*pe*·na·di
activist ακτιβιστής/ακτιβίστρια (m)/(f) a·kti·vi·*stis*/a·kti·*vi*·stri·a
actor ηθοποιός (m)&(f) i·tho·pi·*os*
acupuncture βελονισμός (m) ve·lo·niz·*mos*
adaptor μετασχηματιστής (m) me·ta·shi·ma·ti·*stis*
addiction εθισμός (m) e·thiz·*mos*
address διεύθυνση (f) ţhi·*ef*·thin·si
administration διοίκηση (f) ţhi·*i*·ki·si
admission (price) τιμή εισόδου (m) ti·*mi* i·*so*·ţhu
admit δέχομαι *ţhe*·kho·me
adult ενήλικος/ενήλικη (m)/(f) e·*ni*·li·kos/e·*ni*·li·ki
advertisement διαφήμιση (f) ţhi·a·*fi*·mi·si
advice συμβουλή (f) sim·vu·*li*
Aegean Αιγαίο (n) e·*ye*·o
aerobics αερόμπικς (n) pl a·e·*ro*·biks
aeroplane αεροπλάνο (n) a·e·ro·*pla*·no
Africa Αφρική (f) a·fri·*ki*
after μετά me·*ta*
(this) afternoon (αυτό το) απόγευμα (n) (af·*to* to) a·*po*·yev·ma
aftershave κολόνια ξυρίσματος (f) ko·*lo*·ni·a ksi·*riz*·ma·tos
again πάλι *pa*·li
age ηλικία (f) i·li·*ki*·a
(three days) ago (τρεις μέρες) πριν (tris *me*·res) prin
agree συμφωνώ sim·fo·*no*
agriculture γεωργία (f) ye·or·*yi*·a
ahead εμπρός e·*bros*
AIDS Έιντς (n) *e*·idz
air αέρας (m) a·*e*·ras
air-conditioned με ερκοντίσιον me er·kon·*di*·si·on
air conditioning έρκοντίσιον (n) er kon·*di*·si·on
airline αερογραμμή (f) a·e·ro·ghra·*mi*
airmail αεροπορικό ταχυδρομείο (n) a·e·ro·po·ri·*ko* ta·hi·ţhro·*mi*·o
airplane αεροπλάνο (n) a·e·ro·*pla*·no
airport αεροδρόμιο (n) a·e·ro·*ţhro*·mi·o
airport tax δασμός αεροδρομίου (m) ţhaz·*mos* a·e·ro·ţhro·*mi*·u
aisle (on plane) διάδρομος (αεροπλάνου) (m) ţhi·*a*·ţhro·mos (a·e·ro·*pla*·nu)
alarm clock ξυπνητήρι (n) ksi·pni·*ti*·ri
Albania Αλβανία (f) al·va·*ni*·a
alcohol αλκοόλ (n) al·ko·*ol*
all όλοι (m) *o*·li
allergy αλλεργία (f) a·ler·*yi*·a
almond αμύγδαλο (n) a·*migh*·ţha·lo
almost σχεδόν she·*ţhon*
alone μόνος *mo*·nos
already ήδη *i*·ţhi
also επίσης e·*pi*·sis

A

english–greek

altar βωμός ⓜ vo·*mos*
altitude ύψος ⓝ *ip*·sos
always πάντα *pa*·da
ambassador πρέσβης/πρέσβειρα ⓜ/ⓕ *prez*·vis/*prez*·vi·ra
ambulance νοσοκομειακό ⓝ no·so·ko·mi·a·*ko*
America Αμερική ⓕ a·me·ri·*ki*
American football Αμερικανικό ποδόσφαιρο ⓝ a·me·ri·ka·ni·*ko* po·*ţhos*·fe·ro
amphitheatre αμφιθέατρο ⓝ am·fi·*the*·a·tro
anaemia αναιμία ⓕ a·ne·*mi*·a
anarchist αναρχικός/αναρχική ⓜ/ⓕ a·nar·hi·*kos*/a·nar·hi·*ki*
ancient a αρχαίος ar·*he*·os
and και ke
angry θυμωμένος thi·mo·*me*·nos
animal ζώο ⓝ *zo*·o
ankle αστράγαλος ⓜ a·*stra*·gha·los
another ένας άλλος *e*·nas *a*·los
answer απάντηση ⓕ a·*pa*·di·si
ant μυρμήγκι ⓝ mir·*mi*·gi
antibiotics αντιβιοτικά ⓝ pl a·di·vi·o·ti·*ka*
antinuclear αντιπυρηνικό ⓝ a·di·pi·ri·ni·*ko*
antique αντίκα ⓕ an·*ti*·ka
antiseptic αντισηπτικό ⓝ a·di·si·lip·ti·*ko*
any καθόλου ka·*tho*·lu
anxious ανυπόμονος/ανυπόμονη ⓜ/ⓕ a·ni·*po*·mo·nos/a·ni·*po*·mo·ni
apartment διαμέρισμα ⓝ ţhi·a·*me*·riz·ma
appendix (body) σκωληκοειδίτης ⓜ sko·li·ko·i·*ţhi*·tis
apple μήλο ⓝ *mi*·lo
appointment ⓝ ραντεβού ra·de·*vu*
apricot βερύκοκο ⓝ ve·*ri*·ko·ko
April Απρίλιος ⓜ a·*pri*·li·os
archaic αρχαϊκός ar·kha·i·*kos*
archaeological αρχαιολογικός ar·he·o·lo·yi·*kos*
architect αρχιτέκτονας ⓜ&ⓕ ar·hi·*tek*·to·nas
architecture αρχιτεκτονική ⓕ ar·hi·tek·to·ni·*ki*
argue συζητώ si·zi·*to*
arm χέρι ⓝ *he*·ri
aromatherapy αρωμοθεραπεία ⓕ a·ro·mo·the·ra·*pi*·a
arrest v συλλαμβάνω si·lam·*va*·no
arrivals αφίξεις ⓕ pl a·*fik*·sis
arrive φτάνω *fta*·no
art τέχνη ⓕ *tekh*·ni
art gallery πινακοθήκη ⓕ pi·na·ko·*thi*·ki
artist καλλιτέχνης/καλλιτέχνιδα ⓜ/ⓕ ka·li·*tekh*·nis/ka·li·*tekh*·ni·ţha
ashtray σταχτοθήκη ⓕ stakh·to·*thi*·ki
Asia Ασία ⓕ a·*si*·a
ask (a question) ρωτάω ro·*ta*·o
ask (for something) ζητάω zi·*ta*·o
asparagus σπαράγγι ⓝ spa·*ra*·gi
aspirin ασπιρίνη ⓕ a·spi·*ri*·ni
asthma άσθμα ⓝ *asth*·ma
astrology αστρολογία ⓕ a·stro·lo·*yi*·a
at σε se
athletics αθλητικά ⓝ pl a·thli·ti·*ka*
atmosphere ατμόσφαιρα ⓕ at·*mos*·fe·ra
aubergine μελιτζάνα ⓕ me·li·*dza*·na
August Αύγουστος ⓜ *av*·ghu·stos
aunt θεία ⓕ *thi*·a
Australia Αυστραλία ⓕ af·stra·*li*·a
Australian Rules Football Αυστραλέζικο ποδόσφαιρο ⓝ af·stra·*le*·zi·ko po·*ţhos*·fe·ro
automated teller machine (ATM) αυτόματη μηχανή χρημάτων ⓕ af·*to*·ma·ti mi·kha·*ni* khri·*ma*·ton
autumn φθινόπωρο ⓝ fthi·*no*·po·ro
avenue λεωφόρος ⓕ le·o·*fo*·ros
avocado αβοκάντο ⓝ a·vo·*ka*·do
awful απαίσιος a·*pe*·si·os

B

B&W (film) μαυρόασπρο (φιλμ) ⓝ mav·*ro*·a·spro (film)
baby μωρό ⓝ mo·*ro*
baby food φαγητό για μωρά ⓝ fa·yi·*to* yia mo·*ra*
baby powder ταλκ ⓝ talk
babysitter μπέιμπι σίτερ ⓕ *be*·i·bi *si*·ter
back (body) πλάτη ⓕ *pla*·ti
back (position) πίσω *pi*·so
backgammon τάβλι ⓝ *tav*·li
backpack σακίδιο ⓝ sa·*ki*·ţhi·o
bacon μπέικον ⓝ *be*·i·kon
bad κακός ka·*kos*
bag σάκος ⓜ *sa*·kos

baggage αποσκευές ⓕ pl a·po·ske·*ves*
baggage allowance
επιτρεπόμενες αποσκευές ⓕ pl
e·pi·tre·*po*·me·nes a·po·ske·*ves*
baggage claim παραλαβή αποσκευών
ⓕ pa·ra·la·*vi* a·po·ske·*von*
bakery φούρνος ⓜ *fur*·nos
balance (account) υπόλοιπο
(λογαριασμού) ⓝ
i·*po*·li·po (lo·gha·riaz·*mu*)
Balcans Βαλκάνια ⓝ pl val·*ka*·ni·a
balcony μπαλκόνι ⓝ bal·*ko*·ni
ball (sport) μπάλα ⓕ *ba*·la
ballet μπαλέτο ⓝ ba·*le*·to
banana μπανάνα ⓕ ba·*na*·na
band (music) μπάντα ⓕ *ba*·da
bandage επίδεσμος ⓜ e·*pi*·ţhez·mos
Band-Aid τσιρότο ⓝ tsi·*ro*·to
bank τράπεζα ⓕ *tra*·pe·za
bank account τραπεζικός λογαριασμός
ⓜ tra·pe·zi·*kos* lo·gha·riaz·*mos*
banknote χαρτονόμισμα ⓝ
khar·to·*no*·miz·ma
baptism βάπτιση ⓕ *vap*·ti·si
bar μπαρ ⓝ bar
barber κουρέας ⓜ ku·*re*·as
bar work δουλειά σε μπαρ ⓕ ţhu·*lia* se bar
baseball μπέηζμπολ ⓝ *be*·iz·bol
basket καλάθι ⓝ ka·*la*·thi
basketball μπάσκετ ⓝ *ba*·sket
bath μπάνιο ⓝ *ba*·nio
bathing suit μαγιό ⓝ ma·*yio*
bathroom μπάνιο ⓝ *ba*·nio
battery μπαταρία ⓕ ba·ta·*ri*·a
be είμαι *i*·me
beach παραλία ⓕ pa·ra·*li*·a
beach volleyball βόλεϋ παραλίας ⓝ
vo·le·i pa·ra·*li*·as
bean φασόλι ⓝ fa·*so*·li
beansprouts φύτρα φασολιών ⓕ
fi·tra fa·so·*lion*
beautiful όμορφος *o*·mor·fos
beauty salon ινστιτούτο αισθητικής ⓝ
in·sti·*tu*·to es·thi·ti·*kis*
because διότι ţhi·o·ti
bed κρεβάτι ⓝ kre·*va*·ti
bedding σκεπάσματα ⓝ pl ske·*paz*·ma·ta
bed linen σεντόνια ⓝ pl se·*do*·nia
bedroom υπνοδωμάτιο ⓝ
ip·no·ţho·*ma*·ti·o
bee μέλισσα ⓕ *me*·li·sa
beef βοδινό ⓝ vo·ţhi·*no*
beer μπύρα ⓕ *bi*·ra
beetroot πατζάρι ⓝ pat·*za*·ri
before πριν prin
beggar ζητιάνος/ζητιάνα ⓜ/ⓕ
zi·*tia*·nos/zi·*tia*·na
behind πίσω *pi*·so
Belgium Βέλγιο ⓝ *vel*·yi·o
below κάτω *ka*·to
beside δίπλα *ţhi*·pla
best a ο καλύτερος o ka·*li*·te·ros
bet στοίχημα ⓝ *sti*·hi·ma
better καλύτερος/καλύτερη ⓜ/ⓕ
ka·*li*·te·ros/ka·*li*·te·ri
between ανάμεσα a·*na*·me·sa
bible Βίβλος ⓕ *viv*·los
bicycle ποδήλατο ⓝ po·*ţhi*·la·to
big μεγάλος me·*gha*·los
bigger μεγαλύτερος me·gha·*li*·te·ros
biggest ο μεγαλύτερος o me·gha·*li*·te·ros
bike ποδήλατο ⓝ po·*ţhi*·la·to
bike chain αλυσίδα ποδηλάτου ⓕ
a·li·*si*·ţha po·ţhi·*la*·tu
bike lock κλειδαριά ποδηλάτου ⓕ
kli·ţha·*ria* po·ţhi·*la*·tu
bike path δρόμος ποδηλάτου ⓜ
ţhro·mos po·thi·*la*·tu
bike shop κατάστημα ποδηλάτου ⓝ
ka·*ta*·sti·ma po·ţhi·*la*·tu
bill (restaurant etc) λογαριασμός ⓜ
lo·gha·riaz·*mos*
billiards μπιλιάρδο ⓝ bi·*liar*·ţho
binoculars κιάλια ⓝ pl *kia*·lia
bird πουλί ⓝ pu·*li*
birthday γενέθλια ⓝ pl ye·*ne*·thli·a
birth certificate πιστοποιητικό
γεννήσεως ⓝ pi·sto·pi·i·ti·*ko* ye·*ni*·se·os
biscuit μπισκότο ⓝ bi·*sko*·to
bite (dog) δαγκωματιά ⓕ ţha·go·ma·*tia*
bite (insect) τσίμπημα ⓝ *tsi*·bi·ma
bitter πικρός pi·*kros*
black a μαύρος *mav*·ros
bladder κύστη ⓕ *ki*·sti
blanket κουβέρτα ⓕ ku·*ver*·ta
blind a τυφλός ti·*flos*
blister φουσκάλα ⓕ fu·*ska*·la
blocked μπλοκαρισμένος blo·ka·riz·*me*·nos
blood αίμα ⓝ *e*·ma
blood group ομάδα αίματος ⓕ
o·*ma*·ţha *e*·ma·tos

blood pressure πίεση αίματος (f) *pi*·e·si *e*·ma·tos
blood test εξέταση αίματος (f) ek·se·ta·si *e*·ma·tos
blue a μπλε ble
board (transport) v ανεβαίνω a·ne·*ve*·no
boarding house πανσιόν (f) pan·*sion*
boarding pass κάρτα επιβίβασης (f) *kar*·ta e·pi·*vi*·va·sis
boat βάρκα (f) *var*·ka
body σώμα (n) *so*·ma
boiled βρασμένος vraz·*me*·nos
bone κόκαλο (n) *ko*·ka·lo
book βιβλίο (n) viv·*li*·o
book (reserve) v κλείνω θέση *kli*·no *the*·si
booked out πλήρες *pli*·res
bookshop βιβλιοπωλείο (n) viv·li·o·po·*li*·o
boot (footwear) μπότα (f) *bo*·ta
boots (footwear) μπότες (f) pl *bo*·tes
border σύνορο (n) *si*·no·ro
bored βαριεστημένος va·ri·e·sti·*me*·nos
boring ανιαρός a·ni·a·*ros*
borrow δανείζομαι ţha·*ni*·zo·me
botanical garden βοτανικός κήπος (m) vo·ta·ni·*kos* *ki*·pos
both και οι δύο ke i *ţhi*·o
bottle μπουκάλι (n) bu·*ka*·li
bottle opener ανοιχτήρι (n) a·nikh·*ti*·ri
bottle shop κάβα (f) *ka*·va
bottom (body) πισινός (m) pi·si·*nos*
bottom (position) κάτω *ka*·to
bouzouki (traditional music) μπουζούκι (n) bu·*zu*·ki
bouzouki place μπουζουκτσίδικο (n) bu·zuk·*tsi*·ţhi·ko
bowl μπωλ (n) bol
box κουτί (n) ku·*ti*
boxer shorts σλιπάκι (n) sli·*pa*·ki
boxing μποξ (n) boks
boy αγόρι (n) a·*gho*·ri
boyfriend φίλος (m) *fi*·los
bra σουτιέν (n) su·ti·*en*
brakes φρένα (n) pl *fre*·na
brandy κονιάκ (n) ko·*niak*
brave γενναίος ye·*ne*·os
bread ψωμί (n) pso·*mi*
bread rolls ψωμάκια (n) pl pso·*ma*·kia
break v σπάω *spa*·o
break down χαλάω ha·*la*·o
breakfast πρόγευμα (n) *pro*·yev·ma
breast (body) στήθος (n) *sti*·thos
breathe αναπνέω a·nap·*ne*·o
bribe v δωροδοκώ ţho·ro·ţho·*ko*
bridge γεφύρι (n) ye·*fi*·ri
briefcase (m) χαρτοφύλακας khar·to·*fi*·la·kas
brilliant λαμπρός la·*bros*
bring φέρνω *fer*·no
broccoli μπρόκολο (n) *bro*·ko·lo
brochure μπροσούρα (f) bro·*su*·ra
broken σπασμένος spaz·*me*·nos
broken down χαλασμένος kha·laz·*me*·nos
bronchitis βροχίτιδα (f) vro·*hi*·ti·ţha
bronze μπρούτζος (m) *bru*·dzos
brother αδερφός (m) a·ţher·*fos*
brown καφέ ka·*fe*
bruise σημάδι από χτύπημα (n) si·*ma*·ţhi a·po *khti*·pi·ma
brush βούρτσα (f) *vur*·tsa
bucket κουβάς (m) ku·*vas*
Buddhist Βουδιστής/Βουδίστρια vu·ţhi·*stis*/vu·*ţhi*·stri·a (m)/(f)
budget προϋπολογισμός (m) pro·i·po·lo·yiz·*mos*
buffet μπουφές (m) bu·*fes*
bug κοριός (m) ko·*rios*
build v χτίζω *khti*·zo
builder χτίστης (m) *khti*·stis
building κτήριο (n) *kti*·ri·o
Bulgaria Βουλγαρία (f) vul·gha·*ri*·a
bumbag πορτοφόλι μέσης (n) por·to·fo·*li* *me*·sis
burn έγκαυμα (n) *e*·gav·ma
burnt καμένος ka·*me*·nos
bus (city) αστικό λεωφορείο (n) a·sti·*ko* le·o·fo·*ri*·o
bus (intercity) υπεραστικό λεωφορείο (n) i·per·as·ti·*ko* le·o·fo·*ri*·o
bus station σταθμός λεωφορείου (m) stath·*mos* le·o·fo·*ri*·u
bus stop σταση λεωφορείου (f) *sta*·si le·o·fo·*ri*·u
business επιχείρηση (f) e·pi·*hi*·ri·si
business class μπιζνες κλασ *biz*·nes klas
businessperson επιχειρηματίας (m)&(f) e·pi·hi·ri·ma·*ti*·as
business trip ταξίδι εργασίας (n) tak·*si*·ţhi er·gha·*si*·as
busker περιοδεύων τραγουδιστής (m) pe·ri·o·*ţhe*·von tra·ghu·ţhi·*stis* περιοδεύουσα τραγουδίστρια (f) pe·ri·o·*ţhe*·vu·sa tra·ghu·*ţhi*·stri·a

busy απασχολημένος a·pa·skho·li·*me*·nos
but αλλά a·*la*
butcher χασάπης ⓜ kha·*sa*·pis
butcher's shop κρεοπωλείο ⓝ kre·o·po·*li*·o
butter βούτυρο ⓝ *vu*·ti·ro
butterfly πεταλούδα ⓕ pe·ta·*lu*·ţha
button κουμπί ⓝ ku·*bi*
buy v αγοράζω a·gho·*ra*·zo
Byzantine Βυζαντινός vi·za·di·*nos*

C

cabin καμπίνα ⓕ ka·*bi*·na
cabbage μάπα ⓕ *ma*·pa
cable car τελεφερίκ ⓝ te·le·fe·*rik*
café καφεστιατόριο ⓝ ka·fe·sti·a·*to*·ri·o
cafeteria καφετηρία ⓕ ka·fe·ti·*ri*·a
cake γλυκό ⓝ ghli·*ko*
cake shop ζαχαροπλαστείο ⓝ za·kha·ro·pla·*sti*·o
calculator αριθμομηχανή ⓕ a·rith·mo·mi·kha·*ni*
calendar ημερολόγιο ⓝ i·me·ro·*lo*·yi·o
call v καλώ ka·*lo*
camera φωτογραφική μηχανή ⓕ fo·to·ghra·fi·*ki* mi·kha·*ni*
camera shop κατάστημα φωτογραφικών ειδών ⓝ ka·*ta*·sti·ma fo·to·ghra·fi·*kon* i·*ţhon*
camp v κατασκηνώνω ka·ta·ski·*no*·no
camping ground χώρος για κάμπινγκ ⓜ *kho*·ros yia *kam*·ping
camping store κατάστημα ειδών κατασκήνωσης ⓝ ka·*ta*·sti·ma i·*ţhon* ka·ta·*ski*·no·sis
campsite χώρος για κάμπινγκ ⓜ *kho*·ros yia *kam*·ping
can (be able) v μπορώ bo·*ro*
can (tin) κουτί ⓝ ku·*ti*
can opener ανοιχτήρι ⓝ a·nikh·*ti*·ri
Canada Καναδάς ⓜ ka·na·*ţhas*
cancel ακυρώνω a·ki·*ro*·no
cancer καρκίνος ⓜ kar·*ki*·nos
candle κερί ⓝ ke·*ri*
candy καραμέλα ⓕ ka·ra·*me*·la
cantaloupe πεπόνι ⓝ pe·*po*·ni
capsicum πιπεριά ⓕ pi·pe·*ria*
car αυτοκίνητο ⓝ af·to·*ki*·ni·to
caravan τροχόσπιτο ⓝ tro·*kho*·spi·to
cardiac arrest καρδιακή προσβολή ⓕ kar·ţhi·a·*ki* proz·vo·*li*
cards (playing) χαρτιά ⓝ pl khar·*tia*
care (for someone) φροντίζω fro·*di*·zo
car hire ενοικίαση αυτοκινήτου ⓕ e·ni·*ki*·a·si af·to·ki·*ni*·tu
carob χαρούπι ⓝ kha·*ru*·pi
car owner's title τίτλος κατόχου αυτοκινήτου ⓜ *tit*·los ka·*to*·khu af·to·ki·*ni*·tu
car park χώρος στάθμευσης αυτικινήτων ⓜ *kho*·ros *stath*·mef·sis af·to·ki·*ni*·tu
carpenter μαραγκός ⓜ ma·ra·*gos*
car registration άδεια κυκλοφορίας αυτοκινήτου ⓕ *a*·ţhia ki·klo·fo·*ri*·as af·to·ki·*ni*·tu
carrot καρότο ⓝ ka·*ro*·to
carry μεταφέρω me·ta·*fe*·ro
carton χαρτοκιβώτιο ⓝ khar·to·ki·*vo*·ti·o
cash μετρητά ⓝ pl me·tri·*ta*
cash (a cheque) v εξαργυρώνω ek·sar·yi·*ro*·no
cash register ταμείο ⓝ ta·*mi*·o
cashew κάσιου ⓝ *ka*·si·u
cashier ταμίας ⓜ&ⓕ ta·*mi*·as
casino καζίνο ⓝ ka·*zi*·no
cassette κασέτα ⓕ ka·*se*·ta
castle κάστρο ⓝ *ka*·stro
casual work ημερομίσθια εργασία ⓕ i·me·ro·*mi*·sthi·a er·gha·*si*·a
cat γάτα ⓕ *gha*·ta
catamaran καταμαράν ⓝ ka·ta·ma·*ran*
cathedral μητρόπολη ⓕ mi·*tro*·po·li
Catholic Καθολικός/Καθολική ⓜ/ⓕ ka·tho·li·*kos*/ka·tho·li·*ki*
cauliflower κουνουπίδι ⓝ ku·nu·*pi*·ţhi
cave σπηλιά ⓕ spi·*lia*
CD σι ντι ⓝ si di
celebration γιορτή ⓕ yior·*ti*
cellphone κινητό ⓝ ki·ni·*to*
cemetery κοιμητήριο ⓝ ki·mi·*ti*·ri·o
cent σεντ ⓝ sent
centimetre εκατοστόμετρο ⓝ e·ka·to·*sto*·me·tro
centre κέντρο ⓝ *ke*·dro
ceramics κεραμικά ⓝ pl ke·ra·mi·*ka*
cereal δημητριακά ⓝ pl ţhi·mi·tri·a·*ka*
certificate πιστοποιητικό ⓝ pi·sto·pi·i·ti·*ko*
chain αλυσίδα ⓕ a·li·*si*·ţha
chair καρέκλα ⓕ ka·*re*·kla
chairlift (skiing) τελεφερίκ ⓝ te·le·fe·*rik*
champagne σαμπάνια ⓕ sam·*pa*·nia

english–greek

championships αγώνες πρωταθλήματος ⓜ pl a·*gho*·nes pro·ta·*thli*·ma·tos
chance πιθανότητα ⓕ pi·tha·*no*·ti·ta
change αλλαγή ⓕ a·la·*yi*
change (coins) ψιλά ⓝ pl psi·*la*
change (from sale) ρέστα ⓝ pl *re*·sta
change (money) v αλλάζω a·*la*·zo
changing room (in shop) δοκιμαστήριο ρούχων ⓝ ţho·ki·ma·*sti*·ri·o *ru*·khon
charming χαριτωμένος kha·ri·to·*me*·nos
charter flight πτήση τσάρτερ ⓕ *pti*·si *tsar*·ter
chat up (somebody) v ψήνω *psi*·no
cheap φτηνός fti·*nos*
cheat απατεώνας/απατεώνισσα ⓜ/ⓕ a·pa·te·*o*·nas/a·pa·te·*o*·ni·sa
check v ελέγχω e·*leng*·kho
check (banking) προσωπική επιταγή ⓕ pro·so·pi·*ki* e·pi·ta·*yi*
check (bill) λογαριασμός ⓜ lo·gha·riaz·*mos*
check-in (desk) ρεσεψιόν ⓕ re·sep·*sion*
checkpoint σημείο ελέγχου ⓝ si·*mi*·o e·*leng*·khu
cheese τυρί ⓝ ti·*ri*
cheese shop τυροπωλείο ⓝ ti·ro·po·*li*·o
chef ⓜ σεφ sef
chemist (shop) φαρμακείο ⓝ far·ma·*ki*·o
chemist (pharmacist) φαρμακοποιός ⓜ&ⓕ far·ma·ko·pi·*os*
cheque προσωπική επιταγή ⓕ pro·so·pi·*ki* e·pi·ta·*yi*
cherry κεράσι ⓝ ke·*ra*·si
chess σκάκι ⓝ *ska*·ki
chessboard σκακιέρα ⓕ ska·*kie*·ra
chest (body) στήθος ⓝ *sti*·thos
chestnut κάστανο ⓝ *ka*·sta·no
chewing gum μαστίχα ⓕ ma·*sti*·kha
chicken κοτόπουλο ⓝ ko·*to*·pu·lo
chicken pox ανεμοβλογιά ⓕ a·ne·mov·lo·*yia*
chickpea στραγάλι ⓝ stra·*gha*·li
child παιδί ⓝ pe·*ţhi*
childminding επιτήρηση παιδιών ⓕ e·pi·*ti*·ri·si pe·*ţhion*
children παιδιά ⓝ pl pe·*ţhia*
child seat παιδικό κάθισμα ⓝ pe·ţhi·*ko* *ka*·thiz·ma
chilli πιπεριά ⓕ pi·pe·*ria*
chilli sauce σάλτσα πιπεριάς ⓕ *sal*·tsa pi·pe·*rias*
chipura τσίπουρο ⓝ *tsi*·pu·ro
chiropractor χειροπράκτωρ ⓜ&ⓕ hi·ro·*prak*·stor
chocolate σοκολάτα ⓕ so·ko·*la*·ta
choose διαλέγω ţhia·*le*·gho
chopping board σανίδα κοπής ⓕ sa·*ni*·ţha ko·*pis*
chopsticks τσοπ στικς ⓝ pl tsop stiks
Christian Χριστιανός/Χριστιανή ⓜ/ⓕ khri·sti·a·*nos*/khri·sti·a·*ni*
Christian name μικρό όνομα ⓝ mi·*kro* *o*·no·ma
Christmas Χριστούγεννα ⓝ pl khri·*stu*·ye·na
Christmas Day ημέρα Χριστουγέννων ⓕ i·*me*·ra khri·stu·*ye*·non
Christmas Eve παραμονή Χριστουγέννων ⓕ pa·ra·mo·*ni* khri·stu·*ye*·non
church εκκλησία ⓕ e·kli·*si*·a
cider κρασί από μήλο ⓝ kra·*si* a·*po* *mi*·lo
cigar πούρο ⓝ *pu*·ro
cigarette τσιγάρο ⓝ tsi·*gha*·ro
cigarette lighter αναπτήρας ⓜ a·nap·*ti*·ras
cinema σινεμά ⓝ si·ne·*ma*
circus τσίρκο ⓝ *tsir*·ko
citizenship ιθαγένεια ⓕ i·tha·*ye*·ni·a
city πόλη ⓕ *po*·li
city centre κέντρο της πόλης ⓝ *ke*·dro tis *po*·lis
civil rights πολιτικά δικαιώματα ⓝ pl po·li·ti·*ka* ţhi·ke·*o*·ma·ta
civil servant δημόσιος υπάλληλος ⓜ&ⓕ ţhi·*mo*·si·os i·*pa*·li·los
class (category) τάξη ⓕ *tak*·si
classical κλασσικός kla·si·*kos*
class system ταξικό σύστημα ⓝ tak·si·*ko* *si*·sti·ma
clean a καθαρός ka·tha·*ros*
clean v καθαρίζω ka·tha·*ri*·zo
cleaning καθάρισμα ⓝ ka·*tha*·riz·ma
client πελάτης/πελάτισσα ⓜ/ⓕ pe·*la*·tis/pe·*la*·ti·sa
cliff γκρεμός ⓜ gre·*mos*
climb v αναρριχούμαι a·na·ri·*khu*·me
cloakroom ιματιοφυλάκιο ⓝ i·ma·ti·o·fi·*la*·ki·o
clock ρολόι ⓝ ro·*lo*·i
close a κοντινός ko·di·*nos*
close v κλείνω *kli*·no
closed κλεισμένος kliz·*me*·nos

clothesline μύλος (για ρούχα) ⓜ *mi*·los (yia *ru*·kha)
clothing ρούχα ⓝ pl *ru*·kha
clothing store κατάστημα ρούχων ⓝ ka·*ta*·sti·ma *ru*·khon
cloud σύννεφο ⓝ *si*·ne·fo
cloudy συννεφιασμένος si·ne·fiaz·*me*·nos
clutch (car) συμπλέκτης ⓜ si·*ble*·ktis
coach (sport) προπονητής/προπονήτρια ⓜ/ⓕ pro·po·ni·*tis*/pro·po·*ni*·tri·a
coalition συνασπισμός ⓜ sin·as·piz·*mos*
coast ακτή ⓕ ak·*ti*
coat παλτό ⓝ pal·*to*
cocaine κοκαΐνη ⓕ ko·ka·*i*·ni
cockroach κοριός ⓜ *ko*·*rios*
cocktail κοκτέηλ ⓝ kok·*te*·il
cocoa κακάο ⓝ ka·*ka*·o
coconut ινδική καρύδα ⓕ in·ţhi·*ki* ka·*ri*·ţha
coffee καφές ⓜ ka·*fes*
coffee shop καφενείο ⓝ ka·fe·*ni*·o
coins κέρματα ⓝ pl *ker*·ma·ta
cold κρύο ⓝ *kri*·o
cold a κρυωμένος kri·o·*me*·nos
colleague συνάδελφος/συναδέλφισσα ⓜ/ⓕ si·*na*·ţhel·fos/si·na·*ţhel*·fi·sa
collect call κλήση με αντιστροφή της επιβάρυνσης ⓕ *kli*·si me a·dis·tro·*fi* tis e·pi·*va*·rin·sis
college κολλέγιο ⓝ ko·*le*·yi·o
colour χρώμα ⓝ *khro*·ma
column κολώνα ⓕ ko·*lo*·na
comb χτένα ⓕ *khte*·na
come έρχομαι *er*·kho·me
comedy κωμωδία ⓕ ko·mo·*ţhi*·a
comfortable άνετος *a*·ne·tos
commission προμήθεια ⓕ pro·*mi*·thi·a
communications (profession) επικοινωνίες ⓕ pl e·pi·ki·no·*ni*·es
communion κοινωνία ⓕ ki·no·*ni*·a
communist κομμουνιστής/κομμουνίστρια ⓜ/ⓕ ko·mu·ni·*stis*/ko·mu·*ni*·stri·a
companion σύντροφος/συντρόφισσα ⓜ/ⓕ *si*·dro·fos/si·*dro*·fi·sa
company (firm) εταιρεία ⓕ e·te·*ri*·a
company (friends) συντροφιά ⓕ si·dro·*fia*
compass πυξίδα ⓕ pik·*si*·ţha
complain παραπονούμαι pa·ra·po·*nu*·me
complaint παράπονο ⓝ pa·*ra*·po·no
complimentary (free) δωρεάν ţho·re·*an*
computer κομπιούτερ ⓝ kom·*piu*·ter
computer game παιγνίδι στο κομπιούτερ ⓝ pegh·*ni*·ţhi sto kom·*piu*·ter
concert κονσέρτο ⓝ kon·*ser*·to
concussion κλονισμός ⓜ klo·niz·*mos*
conditioner (hair) κοντίσιονερ ⓝ kon·*di*·si·o·ner
condom προφυλακτικό ⓝ pro·fi·lak·ti·*ko*
conference (big) συνέδριο ⓝ si·*ne*·ţhri·o
conference (small) σεμινάριο ⓝ se·mi·*na*·ri·o
confession εξομολόγηση ⓕ ek·so·mo·*lo*·ghi·si
confirm (a booking) επικυρώνω e·pi·ki·*ro*·no
conjunctivitis επιπεφυκίτις ⓜ e·pi·pe·fi·*ki*·tis
connection σύνδεσμος ⓜ *sin*·ţhez·mos
conservative a συντηρητικός si·di·ri·ti·*kos*
constipation δυσκοίλια ⓕ ţhis·*ki*·li·a
consulate προξενείο ⓝ prok·se·*ni*·o
contact lenses φακοί επαφής ⓜ pl fa·*ki* e·pa·*fis*
contact lens solution υγρό φακών επαφής ⓝ i·*ghro* fa·*kon* e·pa·*fis*
contraceptives αντισυλληπτικά ⓝ pl a·di·si·lip·ti·*ka*
contract συμβόλαιο ⓝ sim·*vo*·le·o
convenience store σούπερ μάρκετ ⓝ *su*·per *mar*·ket
convent μοναστήρι γυναικών ⓝ mo·na·*sti*·ri yi·ne·*kon*
cook μάγειρας/μαγείρισσα ⓜ/ⓕ *ma*·yi·ras/ma·*yi*·ri·sa
cook v μαγειρεύω ma·yi·*re*·vo
cookie μπισκότο ⓝ bis·*ko*·to
cooking μαγείρεμα ⓝ ma·*yi*·re·ma
cool (temperature) δροσερό ţhro·se·*ro*
copper χαλκός ⓜ khal·*kos*
copy αντίγραφο ⓝ a·*di*·ghra·fo
Corinthian Κορινθιακός ko·rin·thi·a·*kos*
corkscrew ανοιχτήρι ⓝ a·nikh·*ti*·ri
corn καλαμπόκι ⓝ ka·la·*bo*·ki
corner γωνία ⓕ gho·*ni*·a
cornflakes κορν φλέικς ⓝ pl korn *fle*·iks
corrupt διεφθαρμένος ţhi·ef·thar·*me*·nos
cost v κοστίζω ko·*sti*·zo
cotton βαμπάκι ⓝ va·*ba*·ki
cotton balls μπαλάκια από βαμπάκι ⓝ pl ba·*la*·kia a·*po* va·*ba*·ki
cotton buds ξιλάκι με βαμπάκι ⓝ ksi·*la*·ki me va·*ba*·ki

c

english–greek

cough v βήχω *vi*·kho
cough medicine φάρμακο για το βήχα ⓝ *far*·ma·ko yia to *vi*·kha
count v μετράω me·*tra*·o
counter (at bar) πάγκος ⓜ *pa*·gos
country χώρα ⓕ *kho*·ra
countryside εξοχή ⓕ ek·so·*hi*
coupon κουπόνι ⓝ ku·*po*·ni
courgette κολοκυθάκι ⓝ ko·lo·ki·*tha*·ki
court (legal) δικαστήριο ⓝ ţhi·ka·*sti*·ri·o
court (tennis) γήπεδο ⓝ *yi*·pe·ţho
couscous κουσκούς ⓝ kus·*kus*
cover charge προσαύξηση τιμής ⓕ pro·*saf*·ksi·si ti·*mis*
cow γελάδα ⓕ ye·*la*·ţha
cracker (biscuit) γαλέτα ⓕ gha·*le*·ta
craft τέχνη ⓕ *tekh*·ni
crash ⓜ κρότος *kro*·tos
crazy τρελλός tre·*los*
cream κρέμα ⓕ *kre*·ma
crèche παιδικός σταθμός ⓜ pe·ţhi·*kos* stath·*mos*
credit πίστωση ⓕ *pi*·sto·si
credit card πιστωτική κάρτα ⓕ pi·sto·ti·*ki* *kar*·ta
cricket (sport) κρίκετ ⓝ *kri*·ket
crop σοδειά ⓕ so·*ţhia*
cross (religious) σταυρός ⓜ stav·*ros*
crowded γεμάτο (κόσμο) ye·*ma*·to (*koz*·mo)
cruise κρουαζέρα ⓕ kru·a·*ze*·ra
cucumber αγγούρι ⓝ a·*gu*·ri
cup φλυτζάνι ⓝ fli·*dza*·ni
cupboard ντουλάπι ⓝ du·*la*·pi
currency exchange τιμή συναλλάγματος ⓕ ti·*mi* si·na·*lagh*·ma·tos
current (electricity) ρεύμα ⓝ *rev*·ma
current affairs επίκαιρα θέματα ⓝ pl e·*pi*·ke·ra *the*·ma·ta
curry κάρι ⓝ *ka*·ri
cushion cover μαξιλαροθήκη ⓕ mak·si·la·ro·*thi*·ki
custom έθιμο ⓝ *e*·thi·mo
customs τελωνείο ⓝ te·lo·*ni*·o
cut v κόβω *ko*·vo
cutlery μαχαιροπήρουνα ⓝ pl ma·he·ro·*pi*·ru·na
CV βιογραφικό σημείωμα ⓝ vi·o·ghra·fi·*ko* si·*mi*·o·ma
Cycladic Κυκλαδικός ki·kla·ţhi·*kos*
cycle v κάνω ποδηλατο *ka*·no po·*ţhi*·la·to
cycling ποδηλασία ⓕ po·ţhi·la·*si*·a
cyclist ποδηλάτης/ποδηλάτισσα ⓜ/ⓕ po·ţhi·*la*·tis/po·ţhi·*la*·ti·sa
Cypriot (person) Κύπριος/Κύπρια ⓜ/ⓕ *ki*·pri·os/*ki*·pri·a
Cypriot (wine etc) κυπριακός/κυπριακή ⓜ/ⓕ ki·pri·a·*kos*/ki·pri·a·*ki*
Cyprus Κύπρος ⓕ *ki*·pros
cystitis κύστη ⓕ *ki*·sti

D

dad μπαμπάς ⓜ ba·*bas*
daily καθημερινός ka·thi·me·ri·*nos*
dairy shop γαλακτοπωλείο ⓝ gha·lak·to·po·*li*·o
dance v χορεύω kho·*re*·vo
dancing χορός kho·*ros*
dangerous επικίνδυνος e·pi·*kin*·ţhi·nos
dark (night) a σκοτεινός sko·ti·*nos*
dark (colour) a σκούρος *sku*·ros
date (a person) v βγαίνω (με κάποιον) *vye*·no (me *ka*·pion)
date (appointment) ραντεβού ⓝ ra·de·*vu*
date (day) ημερομηνία ⓕ i·me·ro·mi·*ni*·a
date (fruit) χουρμάς ⓜ khur·*mas*
date of birth ημερομηνία γεννήσεως ⓕ i·me·ro·mi·*ni*·a ye·*ni*·se·os
daughter κόρη ⓕ *ko*·ri
dawn αυγή ⓕ av·*yi*
day ημέρα ⓕ i·*me*·ra
day after tomorrow μεθαύριο me·*thav*·ri·o
day before yesterday προχθές prokh·*tes*
dead a νεκρός ne·*kros*
deaf a κουφός ku·*fos*
deal (cards) μοιράζω (χαρτιά) mi·*ra*·zo (khar·*tia*)
December Δεκέμβριος ⓜ de·*kem*·vri·os
decide αποφασίζω a·po·fa·*si*·zo
deck κατάστρωμα ⓝ ka·*ta*·stro·ma
deep βαθύς va·*this*
deforestation αποδάσωση ⓕ a·po·*ţha*·so·si
degrees (temperature) βαθμοί ⓜ pl vath·*mi*

dehydration αφυδάτωση ⓕ a·fi·*ţha*·to·si
delay καθυστέρηση ⓕ ka·thi·*ste*·ri·si
delicatessen ντελικατέσεν ⓝ de·li·ka·*te*·sen
delineation line διαχωριστική γραμμή ⓕ ţhi·a·kho·ri·sti·*ki* ghra·*mi*
deliver παραδίνω pa·ra·*ţhi*·no
democracy δημοκρατία ⓕ ţhi·mo·kra·*ti*·a
demonstration διαδήλωση ⓕ ţhi·a·*ţhi*·lo·si
Denmark Δανία ⓕ ţha·*ni*·a
dental floss οδοντιατρική κλωστή ⓕ o·ţho·di·a·tri·*ki* klo·*sti*
dentist οδοντίατρος ⓜ&ⓕ o·ţho·*di*·a·tros
deodorant αποσμητικό ⓝ a·poz·mi·ti·*ko*
depart (leave) αναχωρώ a·na·kho·*ro*
department store κατάστημα ⓝ ka·*ta*·sti·ma
departure αναχώρηση ⓕ a·na·*kho*·ri·si
departure gate θύρα αναχώρησης ⓕ *thi*·ra a·na·*kho*·ri·sis
deposit (bank) κατάθεση ⓕ ka·*ta*·the·si
deposit (on house etc) προκαταβολή ⓕ pro·ka·ta·vo·*li*
depressed θλιμμένος/θλιμμένη ⓜ/ⓕ thli·*me*·nos/thli·*me*·ni
derailleur εκτροχιασμός ⓜ ek·tro·hi·az·*mos*
descendent απόγονος ⓜ a·*po*·gho·nos
desert έρημος ⓕ *e*·ri·mos
design σχέδιο ⓝ *skhe*·ţhi·o
dessert επιδόρπιο ⓝ e·pi·*ţhor*·pi·o
destination προορισμός ⓜ pro·o·riz·*mos*
details λεπτομέρειες ⓕ pl lep·to·*me*·ri·es
diabetes διαβήτης ⓜ ţhi·a·*vi*·tis
dial tone ήχος κλήσης ⓜ *i*·khos *kli*·sis
diaper πάνα ⓕ *pa*·na
diaphragm διάγραμμα ⓝ ţhi·*a*·ghra·ma
diarrhoea διάρροια ⓕ ţhi·*a*·ri·a
diary ημερολόγιο ⓝ i·me·ro·*lo*·yi·o
diaspora διασπορά ⓕ ţhi·a·spo·*ra*
dice ζάρια ⓝ pl *za*·ria
dictionary λεξικό ⓝ lek·si·*ko*
die v πεθαίνω pe·*the*·no
diet δίαιτα ⓕ *ţhi*·e·ta
different διαφορετικός ţhia·fo·re·ti·*kos*
difficult δύσκολος *ţhi*·sko·los
digital a ψηφιακός psi·fi·a·*kos*
dining car βαγόνι φαγητού ⓝ va·*gho*·ni fa·yi·*tu*
dinner δείπνο ⓝ *ţhip*·no
direct a άμεσος *a*·me·sos
direct-dial κατ' ευθείαν γραμμή ⓕ ka·tef·*thi*·an gra·*mi*
direction κατεύθυνση ⓕ ka·*tef*·thin·si
director διευθυντής/διευθύντρια ⓜ/ⓕ ţhi·ef·thi·*dis*/ţhi·ef·*thi*·dri·a
dirty a βρώμικος *vro*·mi·kos
disabled a ανάπηρος a·*na*·pi·ros
disco ντισκοτέκ ⓕ di·sko·*tek*
discount έκπτωση ⓕ *ek*·pto·si
discrimination διάκριση ⓕ ţhi·*a*·kri·si
disease ασθένεια ⓕ a·*sthe*·ni·a
dish πιάτο ⓝ *pia*·to
disk (CD-ROM) σι ντι ρομ ⓝ si di rom
disk (floppy) δισκέτα ⓕ ţhi·*ske*·ta
diving βουτιά ⓕ vu·*tia*
diving equipment εξαρτήματα βουτηχτή ⓝ pl ek·sar·*ti*·ma·ta vu·tikh·*ti*
divorced a διαζευγμένος/διαζευγμένη ⓜ/ⓕ ţhi·a·zev·*ghme*·nos/ţhi·a·zev·*ghme*·ni
dizzy ζαλισμένος/ζαλισμένη ⓜ/ⓕ za·liz·*me*·nos/za·liz·*me*·ni
do v κάνω *ka*·no
doctor γιατρός ⓜ&ⓕ yia·*tros*
documentary ντοκυμαντέρ ⓝ do·ki·man·*ter*
dog σκυλί ⓝ ski·*li*
dole επίδομα ανεργίας ⓝ e·*pi*·ţho·ma an·er·*yi*·as
doll κούκλα ⓕ *ku*·kla
dollar δολλάριο ⓝ ţho·*la*·ri·o
dolphin δελφίνι ⓝ ţhel·*fi*·ni
dhomatia (room for rent) δωμάτια (για νοίκιασμα) ⓝ pl ţho·*ma*·ti·a (yia *ni*·kiaz·ma)
dominoes ντόμινο ⓝ *do*·mi·no
door πόρτα ⓕ *por*·ta
dope (drugs) ναρκωτικά ⓝ pl nar·ko·ti·*ka*
Doric Δωρικός ţho·ri·*kos*
double a διπλός ţhi·*plos*
double bed διπλό κρεβάτι ⓝ ţhi·*plo* kre·*va*·ti
double room διπλό δωμάτιο ⓝ ţhi·*plo* ţho·*ma*·ti·o
down κάτω *ka*·to
downhill κατηφορικά ka·ti·fo·ri·*ka*
dozen ντουζίνα ⓕ du·*zi*·na
drama δράμα ⓝ *ţhra*·ma
dream όνειρο ⓝ *o*·ni·ro
dress ⓝ φόρεμα ⓝ *fo*·re·ma

dried ξηρός ksi·*ros*
dried fruit ξηρά φρούτα (n) pl ksi·*ra* *fru*·ta
drink ποτό (n) po·*to*
drink v πίνω *pi*·no
drink (alcoholic) ποτό (αλκοολικό) (n) po·*to* (al·ko·o·li·*ko*)
drive v οδηγώ o·ţhi·*gho*
drivers licence άδεια οδήγησης (f) *a*·ţhi·a o·*ţhi*·yi·sis
drizzle ψιχάλα (f) psi·*kha*·la
drug (illegal) ναρκωτικό (n) nar·ko·ti·*ko*
drug addiction εθισμός στα ναρκωτικά (m) e·thiz·*mos* sta nar·ko·ti·*ka*
drug dealer έμπορος ναρκωτικών (m)&(f) *e*·bo·ros nar·ko·ti·*kon*
drug trafficking κυκλοφορία ναρκωτικών (f) ki·klo·fo·*ri*·a nar·ko·ti·*kon*
drug user ναρκομανής (m)&(f) nar·ko·ma·*nis*
drugs (illicit) ναρκωτικά (n) pl nar·ko·ti·*ka*
drum τύμπανο (n) *ti*·ba·no
drunk μεθυσμένος me·thiz·*me*·nos
dry a στεγνός stegh·*nos*
dry v στεγνώνω stegh·*no*·no
duck πάπια (f) *pa*·pia
dummy (pacifier) πιπίλα (f) pi·*pi*·la
DVD Ντι-Βι-Ντί (n) di·vi·*di*

E

each καθένας ka·*the*·nas
ear αφτί (n) af·*ti*
early νωρίς no·*ris*
earn κερδίζω ker·*ţhi*·zo
earplugs ωτοασπίδες (f) pl o·to·a·*spi*·ţhes
earrings σκουλαρίκια (n) pl sku·la·*ri*·kia
Earth Γη (f) yi
earthquake σεισμός (m) siz·*mos*
east ανατολή (f) a·na·to·*li*
Easter Πάσχα (n) *pas*·kha
easy εύκολο *ef*·ko·lo
eat τρώγω *tro*·gho
economy class τουριστική θέση (f) tu·ri·sti·*ki* *the*·si
ecstacy (drug) έκσταση (f) *ek*·sta·si
eczema έκζεμα (n) *ek*·ze·ma
education εκπαίδευση (f) ek·*pe*·ţhef·si
egg αβγό (n) av·*gho*
eggplant μελιτζάνα (f) me·li·*dza*·na
election εκλογή (f) ek·lo·*yi*
electrical store κατάστημα ηλεκτρικών ειδών (n) ka·*ta*·sti·ma i·lek·tri·*kon* i·*ţhon*
electricity ηλεκτρισμός (m) i·lek·triz·*mos*
elevator ασανσέρ (n) a·san·*ser*
email ημέιλ (n) i·*me*·il
embarrassed αμήχανος a·*mi*·kha·nos
embassy πρεσβεία (f) pre·*zvi*·a
embroidery κέντημα (n) *ke*·di·ma
emergency έκτακτη ανάγκη (f) *ek*·tak·ti a·*na*·gi
emotional συναισθηματικός si·ne·sthi·ma·ti·*kos*
employee υπάλληλος (m)&(f) i·*pa*·li·los
employer εργοδότης/εργοδότρια (m)/(f) er·gho·*ţho*·tis/er·gho·*ţho*·tri·a
empty a άδειο *a*·ţhi·o
end τέλος (n) *te*·los
endangered species είδη υπό εξαφάνιση (n) pl *i*·ţhi i·*po* ek·sa·*fa*·ni·si
engaged (to marry) αρραβωνιασμένος/αρραβωνιασμένη (m)/(f) a·ra·vo·niaz·*me*·nos/ a·ra·vo·niaz·*me*·ni
engagement (undertaking) υποχρέωση (f) i·po·*khre*·o·si
engine μηχανή (f) mi·kha·*ni*
engineer μηχανικός (m)&(f) mi·kha·ni·*kos*
engineering μηχανική (f) mi·kha·ni·*ki*
England Αγγλία (f) ang·*gli*·a
English (language) Αγγλικά (n) pl ang·gli·*ka*
enjoy oneself απολαμβάνω a·po·lam·*va*·no
enough αρκετά ar·ke·*ta*
enter μπαίνω *be*·no
entertainment guide οδηγός διασκέδασης (m) o·ţhi·*ghos* ţhia·*ske*·ţha·sis
entry είσοδος (f) *i*·so·ţhos
envelope φάκελος (m) *fa*·ke·los
environment περιβάλλον (n) pe·ri·*va*·lon
epilepsy επιληψία (f) e·pi·lip·*si*·a
erosion διάβρωση (f) ţhi·*av*·ro·si
equal opportunity ίσες ευκαιρίες (f) pl *i*·ses ef·ke·*ri*·es
equality ισότητα (f) i·*so*·ti·ta
equipment εξοπλισμός (m) ek·so·pliz·*mos*
escalator κυλιόμενες σκάλες (f) pl ki·li·*o*·me·nes *ska*·les
estate agency κτηματομεσιτικό γραφείο (n) kti·ma·to·me·si·ti·*ko* ghra·*fi*·o
euro ευρώ (n) ev·*ro*

Europe Ευρώπη ⓕ ev·*ro*·pi
European Union Ευρωπαϊκή Ένωση ⓕ ev·ro·pa·i·*ki* e·no·si
euthanasia ευθανασία ⓕ ef·tha·na·*si*·a
evening βράδι ⓝ *vra*·ţhi
every κάθε *ka*·the
everyone καθένας ⓜ ka·*the*·nas
everything καθετί ⓝ ka·the·*ti*
exactly ακριβώς a·kri·*vos*
example παράδειγμα ⓝ pa·*ra*·ţhigh·ma
excavation ανασκαφή ⓕ a·na·ska·*fi*
excellent εξαιρετικός ek·se·re·ti·*kos*
excess (baggage) υπέρβαρο (φορτίο) ⓝ i·*per*·va·ro (for·*ti*·o)
exchange συνάλλαγμα ⓝ si·*na*·lagh·ma
exchange v ανταλλάσσω a·da·*la*·so
exchange rate τιμή συναλλάγματος ⓕ ti·*mi* si·na·*lagh*·ma·tos
excluded εξαιρούμενος ek·se·*ru*·me·nos
exhaust (car) εξάτμιση ⓕ ek·*sat*·mi·si
exhibition έκθεση ⓕ *ek*·the·si
exhibit έκθεμα ⓝ *ek*·the·ma
exit έξοδος ⓕ *ek*·so·ţhos
expensive ακριβός a·kri·*vos*
experience εμπειρία ⓕ e·bi·*ri*·a
exploitation εκμετάλλευση ⓕ ek·me·*ta*·lef·si
export permit άδεια εξαγωγής ⓕ *a*·ţhi·a ek·sa·gho·*yis*
(by) express mail επείγον (ταχυδρομείο) ⓝ e·*pi*·ghon (ta·hi·ţhro·*mi*·o)
extension (visa) παράταση ⓕ pa·*ra*·ta·si
eye μάτι ⓝ *ma*·ti
eye drops σταγόνες ματιών ⓕ pl sta·*gho*·nes ma·ti·*on*
eyes μάτια ⓝ pl *ma*·tia

F

fabric ύφασμα ⓝ *i*·faz·ma
face πρόσωπο ⓝ *pro*·so·po
face cloth πετσέτα προσώπου ⓕ pet·*se*·ta pro·*so*·pu
factory εργοστάσιο ⓝ er·gho·*sta*·si·o
factory worker εργάτης εργοστασίου ⓜ er·*gha*·tis er·gho·sta·*si*·u εργάτρια εργοστασίου ⓕ er·*gha*·tri·a er·gho·sta·*si*·u
falcon γεράκι ⓝ ye·*ra*·ki
fall (autumn) φθινόπωρο ⓝ fthi·*no*·po·ro
fall (down) πτώση ⓕ *pto*·si
family οικογένεια ⓕ i·ko·*ye*·ni·a
family name επώνυμο ⓝ e·*po*·ni·mo
famous a φημισμένος fi·miz·*me*·nos
fan (machine) ανεμιστήρας ⓜ a·ne·mi·*sti*·ras
fan (of sport) οπαδός ⓜ o·pa·*ţhos*
fanbelt λουρί ⓝ lu·*ri*
far μακριά ma·kri·*a*
fare εισιτήριο ⓝ i·si·*ti*·ri·o
farm φάρμα ⓕ *far*·ma
farmer γεωργός ⓜ&ⓕ ye·or·*ghos*
fashion μόδα ⓕ *mo*·ţha
fast a γρήγορος *ghri*·gho·ros
fat a παχύς pa·*his*
father πατέρας ⓜ pa·*te*·ras
father-in-law πεθερός ⓜ pe·the·*ros*
faucet βρύση ⓕ *vri*·si
fault (someone's) λάθος ⓝ *la*·thos
faulty ελαττωματικός e·la·to·ma·ti·*kos*
fax machine μηχανή φαξ ⓕ mi·kha·*ni* faks
February Φεβρουάριος ⓜ fev·ru·*a*·ri·os
feed v ταΐζω ta·*i*·zo
feel (touch) v αγγίζω a·*gi*·zo
feeling (physical) αφή ⓕ a·*fi*
feelings αισθήματα ⓝ pl es·*thi*·ma·ta
female a θηλυκός thi·li·*kos*
fence φράχτης ⓜ *frakh*·tis
fencing (sport) ξιφομαχία ⓕ ksi·fo·ma·*hi*·a
ferry φέρυ ⓝ *fe*·ri
festival φεστιβάλ ⓝ fe·sti·*val*
fever πυρετός ⓜ pi·re·*tos*
few λίγοι *li*·yi
fiancé αρραβωνιαστικός ⓜ a·ra·vo·nia·sti·*kos*
fiancée αρραβωνιαστικιά ⓕ a·ra·vo·nia·sti·*kia*
fiction μυθοπλασία ⓕ mi·tho·pla·*si*·a
fig σύκο ⓝ *si*·ko
fight πάλη ⓕ *pa*·li
filigree (jewellery) φιλιγκράν ⓝ fi·li·*gran*
fill γεμίζω ye·*mi*·zo
fillet φιλέτο ⓝ fi·*le*·to
film (camera/cinema) φιλμ ⓝ film
film speed ταχύτητα φιλμ ⓕ ta·*hi*·ti·ta film
filtered φιλτραρισμένος fil·tra·riz·*me*·nos
find βρίσκω *vri*·sko
fine (penalty) πρόστιμο ⓝ *pros*·ti·mo
fine (weather) a ωραίος o·*re*·os

finger δάκτυλο ⓝ *ţhak*·ti·lo
finish τελείωμα ⓝ te·*li*·o·ma
finish v τελειώνω te·li·*o*·no
Finland Φιλανδία ⓕ fi·lan·*ţhi*·a
fire φωτιά ⓕ fo·*tia*
firewood καυσόξυλα ⓝ pl kaf·*sok*·si·la
first a πρώτος *pro*·tos
first class πρώτη τάξη ⓕ *pro*·ti *tak*·si
first-aid kit κυτίο πρώτων βοηθειών ⓝ ki·*ti*·o *pro*·ton vo·i·thi·*on*
first name μικρό όνομα ⓝ mi·*kro* *o*·no·ma
fish ψάρι ⓝ *psa*·ri
fishing ψάρεμα ⓝ *psa*·re·ma
fish monger ιχθυοπώλης/ιχθυοπώλισσα ⓜ/ⓕ ikh·thi·o·*po*·lis/ikh·thi·o·*po*·li·sa
fish shop ιχθυοπωλείο ⓝ ikh·thi·o·po·*li*·o
flag σημαία ⓕ si·*me*·a
flannel φανέλλα (ύφασμα) ⓕ fa·*ne*·la (*i*·faz·ma)
flashlight φλας ⓝ flas
flat a επίπεδος e·*pi*·pe·ţhos
flat (apartment) διαμέρισμα ⓝ ţhi·a·*me*·riz·ma
flea ψύλλος ⓜ *psi*·los
fleamarket παζάρι ⓝ pa·*za*·ri
flight πτήση ⓕ *pti*·si
flood πλημμύρα ⓕ pli·*mi*·ra
floor πάτωμα ⓝ *pa*·to·ma
floor (storey) όροφος ⓜ *o*·ro·fos
florist ανθοπώλης/ανθοπώλισσα ⓜ/ⓕ an·tho·*po*·lis/an·tho·*po*·li·sa
flour αλεύρι ⓝ a·*lev*·ri
flower λουλούδι ⓝ lu·*lu*·ţhi
flu γρίππη ⓕ *ghri*·pi
fly πετάω v pe·*ta*·o
foggy ομιχλώδης o·mi·*khlo*·ţhis
folk (art) a λαϊκός la·i·*kos*
follow ακολουθώ a·ko·lu·*tho*
food φαγητό ⓝ fa·yi·*to*
food supplies προμήθειες φαγητού ⓕ pl pro·*mi*·thi·es fa·yi·*tu*
foot πόδι ⓝ *po*·ţhi
football (soccer) ποδόσφαιρο ⓝ po·*ţhos*·fe·ro
footpath πεζοδρόμιο ⓝ pe·zo·*ţhro*·mi·o
foreign ξένος *kse*·nos
forest δάσος ⓝ *ţha*·sos
forever πάντα *pa*·da
forget ξεχνώ ksekh·*no*
forgive συγχωρώ sing·kho·*ro*
fork πιρούνι ⓝ pi·*ru*·ni
fortnight δεκαπενθήμερο ⓝ da·ka·pen·*thi*·me·ro
fortune teller μάντης/μάντισσα ⓜ/ⓕ *ma*·dis/*ma*·di·sa
foul φάουλ ⓝ *fa*·ul
foyer φουαγέ ⓝ fu·a·*ye*
fragile εύθραυστος *ef*·thraf·stos
France Γαλλία ⓕ gha·*li*·a
free (available) διαθέσιμος ţhi·a·*the*·si·mos
free (gratis) δωρεάν ţho·re·*an*
free (not bound) ελεύθερος e·*lef*·the·ros
freeze παγώνω pa·*gho*·no
fresco φρέσκο ⓝ *fre*·sko
fresh φρέσκος *fre*·skos
Friday Παρασκευή ⓕ pa·ra·ske·*vi*
fridge ψυγείο ⓝ psi·*yi*·o
fried τηγανισμένος ti·gha·niz·*me*·nos
friend φίλος/φίλη ⓜ/ⓕ *fi*·los/*fi*·li
from από a·*po*
frost παγωνιά ⓕ pa·gho·*nia*
frozen παγωμένος pa·gho·*me*·nos
fruit φρούτα ⓝ pl *fru*·ta
fruit picking μάζεμα φρούτων ⓝ *ma*·ze·ma *fru*·ton
fry v τηγανίζω ti·gha·*ni*·zo
frying pan τηγάνι ⓝ ti·*gha*·ni
full γεμάτο ye·*ma*·to
full-time πλήρους απασχόλησης *pli*·rus a·pa·*skho*·li·sis
fun a διασκεδαστικό ţhia·ske·ţha·sti·*ko*
funeral κηδεία ⓕ ki·*ţhi*·a
funny αστείος a·*sti*·os
furniture έπιπλα ⓝ pl *e*·pi·pla
future μέλλον ⓝ *me*·lon

G

game (football) ματς ⓝ mats
game (sport) παιγνίδι ⓝ pegh·*ni*·ţhi
garage γκαράζ ⓝ ga·*raz*
garbage σκουπίδια ⓝ pl sku·*pi*·ţhia
garbage can σκουπιδοτενεκές ⓜ sku·pi·ţho·te·ne·*kes*
garden κήπος ⓜ *ki*·pos
gardener κηπουρός ⓜ&ⓕ ki·pu·*ros*
gardening κηπουρική ⓕ ki·pu·ri·*ki*
garlic σκόρδο ⓝ *skor*·ţho
gas (for cooking) πετρογκάζ ⓝ pe·tro·*gaz*
gas (petrol) βενζίνα ⓕ ven·*zi*·na

gas cartridge μπουκάλα γκαζιού ⓕ bu·*ka*·la ga·zi·*u*
gastroenteritis γαστροεντερίτιδα ⓕ gha·stro·e·de·*ri*·ti·ţha
gate (airport etc) θύρα ⓕ *thi*·ra
gauze αραχνοΰφαντος ⓜ a·rakh·no·*i*·fa·dos
gay γκέι *ge*·i
gelatine ζελατίνη ⓕ ze·la·*ti*·ni
Germany Γερμανία ⓕ yer·ma·*ni*·a
get παίρνω *per*·no
get off (transport) κατεβαίνω ka·te·*ve*·no
gift δώρο ⓝ *ţho*·ro
gig παράσταση ⓕ pa·*ra*·sta·si
gin τζιν ⓝ dzin
girl κορίτσι ⓝ ko·*rit*·si
girlfriend φιλενάδα ⓕ fi·le·*na*·ţha
give δίνω *ţhi*·no
given name μικρό όνομα ⓝ mi·*kro* *o*·no·ma
glandular fever αδενώδης πυρετός ⓜ a·ţhe·*no*·ţhis pi·re·*tos*
glass (drinking) ποτήρι ⓝ po·*ti*·ri
glasses (spectacles) γυαλιά ⓝ pl yia·*lia*
glove γάντι ⓝ *ghan*·ti
gloves γάντια ⓝ pl *ghan*·tia
glue κόλα ⓕ *ko*·la
go πηγαίνω pi·*ye*·no
go out βγαίνω *vye*·no
go out with (a male) βγαίνω με κάποιον *vye*·no me *ka*·pi·on
go out with (a female) βγαίνω με κάποια *vye*·no me *ka*·pia
go shopping πάω για ψώνια *pa*·o yia *pso*·nia
goal (score/point) γκολ ⓝ gol
goalkeeper τερματοφύλακας ⓜ&ⓕ ter·ma·to·*fi*·la·kas
goat κατσίκα ⓕ kat·*si*·ka
god (general) θεός ⓜ the·*os*
goddess θεά ⓕ the·*a*
goggles προστατευτικά γιαλιά ⓝ pl pro·sta·tef·ti·*ka* yia·*lia*
goggles (swimming) προστατευτικά γιαλιά για κολύμπι ⓝ pl pro·sta·tef·ti·*ka* yia·*lia* yia ko·*li*·bi
gold χρυσάφι ⓝ khri·*sa*·fi
golf ball μπαλάκι του γκολφ ⓝ ba·*la*·ki tu golf
golf course γήπεδο του γκολφ ⓝ *yi*·pe·ţho tu golf

good καλός ka·*los*
government κυβέρνηση ⓕ ki·*ver*·ni·si
gram γραμμάριο ⓝ ghra·*ma*·ri·o
granddaughter εγγονή ⓕ e·go·*ni*
grandfather παπούς ⓜ pa·*pus*
grandmother γιαγιά ⓕ yia·*yia*
grandson εγγονός ⓜ e·go·*nos*
grapefruit γκρέιπ φρούτ ⓝ *gre*·ip frut
grapes σταφύλια ⓝ pl sta·*fi*·lia
grass γρασίδι ⓝ ghra·*si*·ţhi
grateful ευγνώμων ev·*ghno*·mon
grave τάφος ⓜ *ta*·fos
gray γκρίζος *gri*·zos
great (fantastic) απίθανος a·*pi*·tha·nos
Greece Ελλάδα ⓕ e·*la*·ţha
Greek (language) Ελληνικά ⓝ pl e·li·ni·*ka*
Greek (people) Έλληνες ⓜ pl *e*·li·nes
green πράσινος *pra*·si·nos
greengrocer οπωροπώλης/οπωροπώλισσα ⓜ/ⓕ o·po·ro·*po*·lis/o·po·ro·*po*·li·sa
grey γκρίζος *gri*·zos
grilled ψημένο στη σχάρα psi·*me*·no sti *skha*·ra
grocery οπωροπωλείο ⓝ o·po·ro·po·*li*·o
groundnut φυστίκι ⓝ fi·*sti*·ki
grow μεγαλώνω me·ga·*lo*·no
guaranteed εγγυημένος e·ghi·i·*me*·nos
guess v μαντεύω ma·*de*·vo
guesthouse ξενώνας ⓜ *kse*·no·nas
guide (audio) μαγνητοφωνημένες οδηγίες ⓕ pl magh·ni·to·fo·ni·*me*·nes o·dhi·*yi*·es
guide (person) οδηγός ⓜ&ⓕ o·ţhi·*ghos*
guidebook τουριστικός οδηγός ⓜ tu·ri·sti·*kos* o·ţhi·*ghos*
guide dog σκυλί οδηγός ⓜ ski·*li* o·ţhi·*ghos*
guided tour περιήγηση με οδηγό ⓕ pe·ri·*i*·yi·si me o·ţhi·*gho*
guilty a ένοχος *e*·no·khos
guitar κιθάρα ⓕ ki·*tha*·ra
gum μαστίχα ⓕ ma·*sti*·kha
gun όπλο ⓝ *o*·plo
gym (fitness) γυμναστήριο ⓝ yim·na·*sti*·ri·o
gymnastics γυμναστική ⓕ yim·na·sti·*ki*
gynaecologist γυναικολόγος ⓜ&ⓕ yi·ne·ko·*lo*·ghos
gyros γύρος ⓜ *yi*·ros

H

hair μαλλιά ⓝ pl ma·*lia*
hairbrush βούρτσα μαλλιών ⓕ *vur*·tsa ma·*lion*
haircut κούρεμα ⓝ *ku*·re·ma
hairdresser κομμωτής/κομμώτρια ⓜ/ⓕ ko·mo·*tis*/ko·*mo*·tri·a
halal χαλάλ kha·*lal*
half μισό mi·*so*
hallucination παραίσθηση ⓕ pa·*res*·thi·si
ham ζαμπόν ⓝ za·*bon*
hammer ⓝ σφυρί sfi·*ri*
hammock αιώρα ⓕ e·*o*·ra
hand χέρι ⓝ *he*·ri
handbag τσάντα ⓕ *tsa*·da
handball χάντμπολ ⓝ *khand*·bol
handicrafts εργόχειρα ⓝ pl er·*gho*·hi·ra
handkerchief μαντήλι ⓝ ma·*di*·li
handlebars χειρολαβή ⓕ hi·ro·la·*vi*
handmade a χειροποίητο hi·ro·*pi*·i·to
handsome όμορφος *o*·mor·fos
happy ευτυχισμένος ef·ti·hiz·*me*·nos
harassment παρενόχληση ⓕ pa·re·*no*·khli·si
harbour λιμάνι ⓝ li·*ma*·ni
hard (not soft) σκληρός skli·*ros*
hard-boiled σφιχτός sfikh·*tos*
hardware store κατάστημα σιδερικών ⓝ ka·*ta*·sti·ma si·ţhe·ri·*kon*
hash τουρλού ⓝ tur·*lu*
hat καπέλο ⓝ ka·*pe*·lo
have έχω *e*·kho
have a cold έχω κρύωμα *e*·kho *kri*·o·ma
have fun διασκεδάζω ţhia·ske·*ţha*·zo
hay fever ρινική αλλεργία ⓕ ri·ni·*ki* a·ler·*yi*·a
hazelnut φουντούκι ⓝ fu·*du*·ki
he αυτός ⓜ af·*tos*
head κεφάλι ⓝ ke·*fa*·li
headache πονοκέφαλος ⓜ po·no·*ke*·fa·los
headlights μεγάλα φώτα αυτοκινήτου ⓝ pl me·*gha*·la *fo*·ta af·to·ki·*ni*·tu
health υγεία ⓕ i·*yi*·a
hear ακούω a·*ku*·o
hearing aid ακουστικά ⓝ pl a·ku·sti·*ka*
heart καρδιά ⓕ kar·*ţhia*
heart attack καρδιακή προσβολή ⓕ kar·ţhi·a·*ki* proz·vo·*li*
heart condition καρδιακή κατάσταση ⓕ kar·ţhi·a·*ki* ka·*ta*·sta·si
heat ζέστη ⓕ *ze*·sti
heated ζεσταμένος ze·sta·*me*·nos
heater σόμπα ⓕ *so*·ba
heating θέρμανση ⓕ *ther*·man·si
heatstroke θερμοπληξία ⓕ ther·mo·plik·*si*·a
heatwave καύσωνας ⓜ *kaf*·so·nas
heavy βαρύς va·*ris*
Hellenistic Ελληνιστικός e·li·ni·sti·*kos*
helmet περικεφαλαία ⓕ pe·ri·ke·fa·*le*·a
help βοήθεια ⓕ vo·*i*·thi·a
help v βοηθώ vo·i·*tho*
hepatitis ηπατίτιδα ⓕ i·pa·*ti*·ti·ţha
her (ownership/direct object) της tis
herb βότανο ⓝ *vo*·ta·no
herbalist βοτανολόγος ⓜ&ⓕ vo·ta·no·*lo*·ghos
here εδώ e·*ţho*
heroin ηρωίνη ⓕ i·ro·*i*·ni
herring ρέγκα ⓕ *re*·ga
high ψηλός psi·*los*
highchair καρέκλα για μωρά ⓕ ka·*re*·kla yia mo·*ro*
high school γυμνάσιο ⓝ yim·*na*·si·o
highway δημόσιος δρόμος ⓜ ţhi·*mo*·si·os *ţhro*·mos
hike v πεζοπορώ pe·zo·po·*ro*
hiking πεζοπορία ⓕ pe·zo·po·*ri*·a
hiking boots μπότες πεζοπορίας ⓕ pl *bo*·tes pe·zo·po·*ri*·as
hiking route δρόμος πεζοπορίας ⓜ *ţhro*·mos pe·zo·po·*ri*·as
hill λόφος ⓜ *lo*·fos
Hindu Ινδουιστής/Ινδουίστρια ⓜ/ⓕ in·ţhu·i·*stis*/in·ţhu·*i*·stri·a
hire v ενοικιάζω e·ni·ki·*a*·zo
his (ownership/direct object) του tu
historical ιστορικός i·sto·ri·*kos*
history ιστορία ⓕ i·sto·*ri*·a
hitchhike v ταξιδεύω με ωτοστόπ tak·si·*ţhe*·vo me o·to·*stop*
HIV έιτς άι βι ⓝ *e*·idz *a*·i vi
hockey χόκι ⓝ *kho*·ki
holiday αργεία ⓕ ar·*yi*·a
holidays διακοπές ⓕ pl ţhi·a·ko·*pes*
home σπίτι ⓝ *spi*·ti
homeless άστεγος *a*·ste·ghos
homemaker νοικοκύρης/νοικοκυρά ⓜ/ⓕ ni·ko·*ki*·ris/ni·ko·ki·*ra*

H

DICTIONARY

homeopathy ομοιοπαθητική ⓕ o·mi·o·pa·thi·ti·*ki*
homosexual ομοφυλόφιλος ⓜ o·mo·fi·*lo*·fi·los
honey μέλι ⓝ *me*·li
honeymoon ταξίδι του μέλιτος ⓝ tak·*si*·ţhi tu *me*·li·tos
horoscope ωροσκόπιο ⓝ o·ro·*sko*·pi·o
horse άλογο ⓝ *a*·lo·gho
horse riding ιππασία ⓕ i·pa·*si*·a
hospital νοσοκομείο ⓝ no·so·ko·*mi*·o
hospitality φιλοξενία ⓕ fi·lok·se·*ni*·a
hot ζεστός ze·*stos*
hotel ξενοδοχείο ⓝ kse·no·ţho·*hi*·o
hot water ζεστό νερό ⓜ ze·*sto* ne·*ro*
hour ώρα ⓕ *o*·ra
house σπίτι ⓝ *spi*·ti
housework νοικοκυριό ⓜ ni·ko·ki·*rio*
how πώς pos
how much πόσο *po*·so
hug v αγκαλιάζω a·ga·*lia*·zo
huge πελώριος pe·*lo*·ri·os
humanities ανθρωπιστικές σπουδές ⓕ pl an·thro·pi·sti·*kes* spu·*ţhes*
human resources ανθρώπινο δυναμικό ⓝ an·*thro*·pi·no ţhi·na·mi·*ko*
human rights ανθρώπινα δικαιώματα ⓝ pl an·*thro*·pi·na ţhi·ke·*o*·ma·ta
hundred εκατό e·ka·*to*
hungry (be) v πεινώ pi·*no*
hunting κυνήγι ⓝ ki·*ni*·yi
hurt v πληγώνω pli·*gho*·no
husband σύζυγος ⓜ *si*·zi·ghos
hydrofoil ιπτάμενο φελφίνι ⓝ ip·*ta*·me·no ţhel·*fi*·ni

I

I εγώ e·*gho*
ice πάγος ⓜ *pa*·ghos
ice cream παγωτό ⓝ pa·gho·*to*
ice-cream parlour παγωτατζίδικο ⓝ pagho·ta·*dzi*·ţhi·ko
ice hockey άις χόκεϊ ⓝ *a*·is *kho*·ke·i
icon εικόνα ⓕ i·*ko*·na
identification (ID) ταυτότητα ⓕ taf·*to*·ti·ta
idiot βλάκας ⓜ *vla*·kas
if αν an
ill άρρωστος *a*·ro·stos
immigration μετανάστευση ⓕ ma·ta·*na*·stef·si
important σπουδαίος spu·*ţhe*·os
impossible αδύνατος a·*ţhi*·na·tos
in μέσα *me*·sa
in a hurry βιαστικός via·sti·*kos*
in front of μπροστά bro·*sta*
included συμπεριλαμβανομένου si·be·ri·lam·va·no·*me*·nu
income tax φόρος εισοδήματος ⓜ *fo*·ros i·so·*ţhi*·ma·tos
India Ινδίες ⓕ pl in·*ţhi*·es
indicator δείχτης ⓜ *ţhikh*·tis
indigestion δυσπεψία ⓕ ţhis·pep·*si*·a
indoor εσωτερικός ⓜ e·so·te·ri·*kos*
industry βιομηχανία ⓕ vi·o·mi·kha·*ni*·a
infection μόλυνση ⓕ *mo*·lin·si
inflammation φλεγμονή ⓕ flegh·mo·*ni*
inflation πληθωρισμός ⓜ pli·tho·riz·*mos*
influenza γρίπη ⓕ *ghri*·pi
information πληροφορία ⓕ pli·ro·fo·*ri*·a
ingredient συστατικό ⓝ si·sta·ti·*ko*
inject v κάνω ένεση *ka*·no *e*·ne·si
injection ένεση ⓕ *e*·ne·si
injured πληγωμένος pli·gho·*me*·nos
injury πληγή ⓕ pli·*yi*
inner tube (bicycle) εσωτερική σαμπρέλλα ⓕ e·so·te·ri·*ki* sa·*bre*·la
innocent a αθώος a·*tho*·os
insect έντομο ⓝ *e*·do·mo
inside μέσα *me*·sa
instructor δάσκαλος/δασκάλα ⓜ/ⓕ *ţha*·ska·los/*ţha*·ska·la
insurance ασφάλεια ⓕ as·*fa*·li·a
interest (hobby) ενδιαφέρον ⓝ en·ţhia·*fe*·ron
interesting ενδιαφέρων en·ţhia·*fe*·ron
intermission διάλειμμα ⓝ *ţhia*·li·ma
international διεθνής ţhi·eth·*nis*
Internet διαδίκτυο ⓝ ţhi·a·*ţhik*·ti·o
Internet café καφενείο διαδικτύου ⓝ ka·fe·*ni*·o ţhi·a·ţhik·*ti*·u
interpreter διερμηνέας ⓜ&ⓕ ţhi·er·mi·*ne*·as
interview συνέντευξη ⓕ si·*ne*·def·ksi
invite προσκαλώ pros·ka·*lo*
Ioanian Ιωνικός i·o·ni·*kos*
Ireland Ιρλανδία ⓕ ir·lan·*ţhi*·a
iron (for clothes) σίδερο ⓝ *si*·ţhe·ro
iris (eye) ίρις ⓕ *i*·ris
island νησί ⓝ ni·*si*

Israel Ισραήλ (n) iz·ra·*il*
it αυτό af·*to*
IT πληροφορική (f) pli·ro·fo·ri·*ki*
Italy Ιταλία (f) i·ta·*li*·a
itch φαγούρα (f) fa·*ghu*·ra
itemised αναλυτικός a·na·li·ti·*kos*
itinerary κατάλογος (m) ka·*ta*·lo·ghos
IUD (contraceptive)
ενδομήτριο αντισυλληπτικό (n)
en·ţho·*mi*·tri·o a·di·si·lip·ti·*ko*

J

jacket ζακέτα (f) za·*ke*·ta
jail φυλακή (f) fi·la·*ki*
jam μαρμελάδα (f) mar·me·*la*·ţha
January Ιανουάριος (m) i·a·nu·*a*·ri·os
Japan Ιαπωνία (f) i·a·po·*ni*·a
jar βάζο (n) *va*·zo
jaw σαγόνι (n) sa·*gho*·ni
jealous ζηλιάρης zi·*lia*·ris
jeans τζιν (n) dzin
jeep τζιπ (n) dzip
jellyfish μέδουσα (f) *me*·ţhu·sa
jet lag τζετ λαγκ (n) dzet lag
jewellery κοσμήματα (n) pl koz·*mi*·ma·ta
Jewish Ιουδαϊκός/Ιουδαϊκή (m)/(f)
i·u·ţha·i·*kos*/i·u·ţha·i·*ki*
job δουλειά (f) du·*lia*
jogging τρέξιμο (n) *trek*·si·mo
joke αστείο (n) a·*sti*·o
journalist δημοσιογράφος (m)&(f)
ţhi·mo·si·o·*ghra*·fos
journey ταξίδι (n) tak·si·ţhi
judge δικαστής (m)&(f) ţhi·ka·*stis*
jug κανάτα (f) ka·*na*·ta
juice χυμός (m) hi·*mos*
July Ιούλιος (m) i·*u*·li·os
junta χούντα (f) *khu*·da
jump v πηδώ pi·*ţho*
jumper (sweater) πουλόβερ (n) pu·*lo*·ver
jumper leads καλώδια μπαταρίας (n) pl
ka·*lo*·ţhi·a ba·ta·*ri*·as
June Ιούνιος (m) i·*u*·ni·os

K

kebab shop σουβλατζίδικο (n)
suv·la·*tzi*·ţhi·ko
ketchup σάλτσα (f) *salt*·sa
key κλειδί (n) kli·*ţhi*
keyboard πληκτρολόγιο (n) plik·tro·*lo*·yi·o
kick v κλωτσάω klot·*sa*·o
kidney νεφρό (n) ne·*fro*
kilo κιλό (n) ki·*lo*
kilogram χιλιόγραμμο (n) hi·*lio*·gra·mo
kilometre χιλιόμετρο (n) hi·*lio*·me·tro
kind (nice) καλός ka·*los*
kindergarten νηπιαγωγείο (n)
ni·pi·a·gho·*yi*·o
king βασιλιάς (m) va·si·*lias*
kiosk περίπτερο (n) pe·*rip*·te·ro
kiss φιλί (n) fi·*li*
kiss v φιλώ fi·*lo*
kitchen κουζίνα (f) ku·*zi*·na
kiwifruit ακτινίδιο (n) ak·ti·*ni*·ţhi·o
knee γόνατο (n) *gho*·na·to
knife μαχαίρι (n) ma·*he*·ri
know v ξέρω *kse*·ro
kosher a κόσια *ko*·si·a

L

labourer εργάτης/εργάτρια (m)/(f)
er·*gha*·tis/er·*gha*·tri·a
labyrinth λαβύρινθος (m) la·*vi*·rin·thos
lace δαντέλα (f) ţha·*de*·la
lake λίμνη (f) *li*·mni
lamb αρνί (n) ar·*ni*
land ξηρά (f) ksi·*ra*
landlady νοικοκυρά (f) ni·ko·ki·*ra*
landlord ιδιοκτήτης (m) i·ţhi·ok·*ti*·tis
language γλώσσα (f) *ghlo*·sa
laptop λάπτοπ (n) *lap*·top
large μεγάλος me·*gha*·los
last (previous) προηγούμενος
pro·i·*ghu*·me·nos
last week περασμένη εβδομάδα
pe·raz·*me*·ni ev·ţho·*ma*·ţha
late καθυστερημένος ka·thi·ste·ri·*me*·nos
later αργότερα ar·*gho*·te·ra
laugh v γελάω ye·*la*·o
launderette πλυντήριο (n) pli·*di*·ri·o
laundry (place) πλυντήριο (n) pli·*di*·ri·o
law νόμος (m) *no*·mos
law (study, profession) νομικά (n) no·mi·*ka*
lawyer δικηγόρος (m)&(f) ţhi·ki·*gho*·ros
laxative καθαρτικό (n) ka·thar·ti·*ko*
lazy τεμπέλης te·*be*·lis

leader αρχηγός ⓜ&ⓕ ar·hi·*ghos*
leaf φύλλο ⓝ *fi*·lo
learn μαθαίνω ma·*the*·no
leather δέρμα ⓝ *ther*·ma
lecturer λέκτορας ⓜ&ⓕ *lek*·to·ras
ledge ξέρες ⓕ pl *kse*·res
leek πράσο ⓝ *pra*·so
left (direction) αριστερός ⓜ a·ri·ste·*ros*
left-luggage (office)
(γραφείο) φύλαξη αποσκευών ⓝ
(gra·*fi*·o) *fi*·lak·si a·po·ske·*von*
left-wing αριστερά ⓕ a·ri·ste·*ra*
leg πόδι ⓝ *po*·thi
legal νόμιμος *no*·mi·mos
legislation νομοθεσία ⓕ no·mo·the·*si*·a
legume όσπρια ⓝ pl *os*·pri·a
lemon λεμόνι ⓝ le·*mo*·ni
lemonade λεμονάδα ⓕ le·mo·*na*·tha
lens φακός ⓜ fa·*kos*
Lent Σαρακοστή ⓕ sa·ra·ko·*sti*
lentil φακές ⓕ pl fa·*kes*
lesbian λεσβία ⓕ les·*vi*·a
less λιγότερο li·*gho*·te·ro
letter (mail) γράμμα ⓝ *ghra*·ma
lettuce μαρούλι ⓝ ma·*ru*·li
liar ψεύτης/ψεύτρα ⓜ/ⓕ *psef*·tis/*psef*·tra
library βιβλιοθήκη ⓕ viv·li·o·*thi*·ki
licence άδεια ⓕ *a*·thi·a
license plate number αριθμός
κυκλοφορίας ⓜ a·rith·*mos* ki·klo·fo·*ri*·as
lie (not stand) κείτομαι *ki*·to·me
life ζωή ⓕ zo·*i*
life jacket σωσίβιο ⓝ so·*si*·vi·o
lift (elevator) ασανσέρ ⓝ a·san·*ser*
light φως ⓝ fos
light (colour) a ανοιχτός a·nikh·*tos*
light (weight) a ελαφρύς e·la·*fris*
light bulb λάμπα ⓕ *lam*·pa
light meter μετρητής ρεύματος ⓜ
me·tri·*tis* *rev*·ma·tos
lighter αναπτήρας ⓜ a·nap·*ti*·ras
like v μου αρέσει mu a·*re*·si
lime (fruit) κιτρολέμονο ⓝ ki·tro·*le*·mo·no
linen (material) λινό ⓝ li·*no*
linen (sheets) σεντόνια ⓝ pl se·*do*·nia
lip balm αλοιφή για τα χείλη ⓕ
a·li·*fi* yia ta *hi*·li
lips χείλη ⓝ pl *hi*·li
lipstick κραγιόν ⓝ kra·*yion*
liquor store κάβα ⓕ *ka*·va
listen (to) ακούω a·*ku*·o
little (quantity) λίγο *li*·gho
little (size) μικρός mi·*kros*
live (somewhere) v μένω *me*·no
liver συκώτι ⓝ si·*ko*·ti
lizard σαύρα ⓕ *sav*·ra
local a τοπικός to·pi·*kos*
lock κλειδαριά ⓕ kli·tha·*ria*
lock v κλειδώνω kli·*tho*·no
locked κλειδωμένος kli·tho·*me*·nos
lollies καραμέλες ⓕ pl ka·ra·*me*·les
long a μακρύς ma·*kris*
look v κοιτάζω ki·*ta*·zo
look after προσέχω pro·*se*·kho
look for ψάχνω *psakh*·no
lookout παρατηρητήριο ⓝ pa·ra·ti·ri·*ti*·ri·o
loose a χαλαρός kha·la·*ros*
loose change ψιλά ⓝ pl psi·*la*
lose χάνω *kha*·no
lost a χαμένος kha·*me*·nos
lost property office γραφείο
απωλεσθέντων αντικειμένων ⓝ gra·*fi*·o
a·po·les·*the*·don a·di·ki·*me*·non
(a) lot πολύ po·*li*
lotion λοσιόν ⓝ lo·*sion*
loud δυνατός thi·na·*tos*
love αγάπη ⓕ a·*gha*·pi
love v αγαπώ a·gha·*po*
lover εραστής/ερωμένη ⓜ/ⓕ
e·ra·*stis*/e·ro·*me*·ni
low a χαμηλός kha·mi·*los*
lubricant λιπαντικό ⓝ li·pa·di·*ko*
luck τύχη ⓕ *ti*·hi
lucky a τυχερός ti·he·*ros*
luggage αποσκευές ⓕ pl a·po·ske·*ves*
luggage lockers φύλαξη αποσκευών ⓕ
fi·lak·si a·po·ske·*von*
luggage tag ταμπέλα αποσκευών ⓕ
ta·*be*·la a·po·ske·*von*
lump εξόγκωμα ⓝ ek·so·gho·ma
lunch μεσημεριανό φαγητό ⓝ
me·si·me·ria·*no* fa·yi·*to*
lung πνευμόνι ⓝ pnev·*mo*·ni
luxury πολυτέλεια ⓕ po·li·*te*·li·a

M

Macedonia Μακεδονία ⓕ ma·ke·tho·*ni*·a
machine μηχανή ⓕ mi·kha·*ni*
magazine περιοδικό ⓝ pe·ri·o·thi·*ko*

mail (letters) αλληλογραφία ⓕ a·li·lo·ghra·*fi*·a
mail (postal system) ταχυδρομείο ⓝ ta·hi·ţhro·*mi*·o
mailbox ταχυδρομικό κουτί ⓝ ta·hi·ţhro·mi·*ko* ku·*ti*
main κύριος *ki*·ri·os
main road κύριος δρόμος ⓜ *ki*·ri·os *ţhro*·mos
make v κάνω *ka*·no
make-up καλλυντικά ⓝ pl ka·li·di·*ka*
mammogram μαμογράφημα ⓝ ma·mo·*ghra*·fi·ma
man (male) άντρας ⓜ *a*·dras
manager διευθυντής/διευθύντρια ⓜ/ⓕ ţhi·ef·thi·*dis*/ţhi·ef·*thi*·dri·a
mandarin μανταρίνι ⓝ ma·da·*ri*·ni
mango μάνγκο ⓝ *man*·go
manual work χειρωνακτική εργασία ⓕ hi·ro·nak·ti·*ki* er·gha·*si*·a
many πολλοί po·*li*
map χάρτης ⓜ *khar*·tis
March Μάρτιος ⓜ *mar*·ti·os
margarine μαργαρίνη ⓕ mar·gha·*ri*·ni
marijuana μαριχουάνα ⓕ ma·ri·khu·*a*·na
marine reserve θαλάσσια αποθέματα ⓝ pl tha·*la*·si·a a·po·*the*·ma·ta
marital status γαμήλια κατάσταση ⓕ gha·*mi*·li·a ka·*ta*·sta·si
market αγορά ⓕ a·gho·*ra*
marmalade μαρμελάδα ⓕ mar·me·*la*·ţha
marriage γάμος ⓜ *gha*·mos
married a παντρεμένος/παντρεμένη ⓜ/ⓕ pa·dre·*me*·nos/pa·dre·*me*·ni
marry παντρεύομαι pa·*dre*·vo·me
martial arts πολεμική τέχνη ⓕ po·le·mi·*ki* *tekh*·ni
mass (Catholic) λειτουργία ⓕ li·tur·*yi*·a
massage μασάζ ⓝ ma·*saz*
masseur μασέρ ⓜ ma·*ser*
masseuse μασέζ ⓕ ma·*sez*
mat χαλί ⓝ kha·*li*
match (sports) ματς ⓝ mats
matches (for lighting) σπίρτα ⓝ pl *spir*·ta
mattress στρώμα ⓝ *stro*·ma
May Μάιος ⓜ *ma*·i·os
maybe ίσως *i*·sos
mayonnaise μαγιονέζα ⓕ ma·yi·o·*ne*·za
mayor δήμαρχος ⓜ&ⓕ *ţhi*·mar·khos
me εγώ e·*gho*
meal γεύμα ⓝ *yev*·ma
measles ιλαρά ⓕ i·la·*ra*
meat κρέας ⓝ *kre*·as
mechanic μηχανικός ⓜ mi·kha·ni·*kos*
media μέσα ενημέρωσης ⓝ pl *me*·sa e·ni·*me*·ro·sis
medicine (medication) φάρμακο ⓝ *far*·ma·ko
medicine (study, profession) ιατρική ⓕ i·a·tri·*ki*
meditation αυτοσυγκέντρωση ⓕ af·to·si·*ge*·dro·si
Mediterranean Μεσογειακός ⓜ me·so·yi·a·*kos*
meet v συναντώ si·na·*do*
melon πεπόνι ⓝ pe·*po*·ni
member μέλος ⓝ *me*·los
menstruation περίοδος ⓕ pe·*ri*·o·ţhos
menu μενού ⓝ me·*nu*
message μήνυμα ⓝ *mi*·ni·ma
metal μέταλλο ⓝ *me*·ta·lo
metre μέτρο ⓝ *me*·tro
metro (train) μετρό ⓝ me·*tro*
metro station σταθμός μετρό ⓜ stath·*mos* me·*tro*
microwave (oven) φούρνος μικροκυμάτων ⓜ *fur*·nos mi·kro·ki·*ma*·ton
midday (noon) μεσημέρι ⓝ me·si·*me*·ri
midnight μεσάνυχτα ⓝ pl me·*sa*·nikh·ta
migraine ημικρανία ⓕ i·mi·kra·*ni*·a
mild μαλακός ma·la·*kos*
military a στρατιωτικός stra·ti·o·ti·*kos*
military base στρατιωτική βάση ⓕ stra·ti·o·ti·*ki* *va*·si
military service στρατιωτική θητεία ⓕ stra·ti·o·ti·*ki* thi·*ti*·a
milk γάλα ⓝ *gha*·la
millimetre χιλιοστόμετρο ⓝ hi·li·o·*sto*·me·tro
million εκατομμύριο ⓝ e·ka·to·*mi*·ri·o
mince κιμάς ⓜ ki·*mas*
mineral water μεταλλικό νερό ⓝ me·ta·li·*ko* ne·*ro*
Minoan Μινωικός mi·no·i·*kos*
minute λεπτό ⓝ lep·*to*
mirror καθρέφτης ⓜ ka·*thref*·tis
miscarriage αποβολή ⓕ a·po·vo·*li*
Miss Δις ⓕ ţhe·spi·*nis*
miss (feel absence of) μου λείπει mu *li*·pi

mistake λάθος ⓝ *la*·thos
mix v ανακατώνω a·na·ka·*to*·no
mixed plate ποικιλία ⓕ pi·ki·*li*·a
mobile phone κινητό ⓝ ki·ni·*to*
modem μόντεμ ⓝ *mo*·dem
modern μοντέρνος mo·*der*·nos
moisturiser υγραντική κρέμα ⓕ i·ghra·di·*ki kre*·ma
monarchy μοναρχία ⓕ mo·nar·*hi*·a
monastery μοναστήρι ⓝ mo·na·*sti*·ri
Monday Δευτέρα ⓕ def·*te*·ra
money χρήματα ⓝ pl *khri*·ma·ta
monk καλόγερος ⓜ ka·*lo*·ye·ros
monk seal φώκια ⓕ *fo*·ki·a
month μήνας ⓜ *mi*·nas
monument μνημείο ⓝ mni·*mi*·o
moon φεγγάρι ⓝ fe·*gu*·ri
more περισσότερος pe·ri·*so*·te·ros
morning πρωί ⓝ pro·*i*
morning sickness πρωινή αδιαθεσία ⓕ pro·i·*ni* a·ţhi·a·the·*si*·a
mosaic μωσαϊκό ⓝ mo·sa·i·*ko*
mosque τζαμί ⓝ dza·*mi*
mosquito κουνούπι ⓝ ku·*nu*·pi
mosquito coil φιδάκι για κουνούπια ⓝ fi·*dha*·ki yia ku·*nu*·pia
mosquito net κουνουπιέρα ⓕ ku·nu·pi·*e*·ra
motel μοτέλ ⓝ mo·*tel*
mother μητέρα ⓕ mi·*te*·ra
mother-in-law πεθερά ⓕ pe·the·*ra*
motorbike μηχανάκι ⓝ mi·kha·*na*·ki
motorboat βενζινάκατος ⓕ ven·zi·*na*·ka·tos
motorcycle μοτοσυκλέτα ⓕ mo·to·si·*kle*·ta
motorway (tollway) αυτοκινητόδρομος ⓜ af·to·ki·ni·*to*·ţhro·mos
mountain βουνό ⓝ vu·*no*
mountain bike ποδήλατο για βουνό ⓝ po·*ţhi*·la·to yia vu·*no*
mountain path μονοπάτι ⓝ mo·no·*pa*·ti
mountain range οροσειρά ⓕ o·ro·si·*ra*
mountaineering ορειβασία ⓕ o·ri·va·*si*·a
mouse ποντικός ⓜ po·di·*kos*
mouth στόμα ⓝ *sto*·ma
movie φιλμ ⓝ film
Mr Κος ⓜ *khi*·ri·os
Mrs Κα ⓕ khi·*ri*·a
Ms Δις ţhe·spi·*nis*
mud λάσπη ⓕ *la*·spi
muesli δημητριακά ⓝ pl ţhi·mi·tri·a·*ka*
mum μαμά ⓕ ma·*ma*
mumps μαγουλάδες ⓜ pl ma·ghu·*la*·ţhes
murder δολοφονία ⓕ ţho·lo·fo·*ni*·a
murder v δολοφονώ ţho·lo·fo·*no*
muscle μυς ⓜ mis
museum μουσείο ⓝ mu·*si*·o
mushroom μανιτάρι ⓝ ma·ni·*ta*·ri
music μουσική ⓕ mu·si·*ki*
music shop κατάστημα μουσικών ειδών ⓝ ka·*ta*·sti·ma mu·si·*kon* i·*ţhon*
musician μουσικός ⓜ&ⓕ mu·si·*kos*
Muslim Μουσουλμάνος/Μουσουλμάνα ⓜ/ⓕ mu·sul·*ma*·nos/mu·sul·*ma*·na
mussel μύδι ⓝ *mi*·ţhi
mustard μουστάρδα ⓕ mus·*tar*·ţha
mute a βουβός vu·*vos*
my μου mu
Mycenean Μυκηναϊκός mi·ki·na·i·*kos*
mythological μυθολογικός mi·tho·lo·yi·*kos*

N

nail clippers νυχοκόπτης ⓜ ni·kho·*kop*·tis
name όνομα ⓝ *o*·no·ma
napkin πετσετάκι ⓝ pet·se·*ta*·ki
nappy πάνα ⓕ *pa*·na
nappy rash ερεθισμός από πάνα ⓜ e·re·thiz·*mos* a·*po pa*·na
national park εθνικό πάρκο ⓝ eth·ni·*ko par*·ko
nationality εθνικότητα ⓕ eth·ni·*ko*·ti·ta
NATO ΝΑΤΟ ⓝ *na*·to
nature φύση ⓕ *fi*·si
naturopathy φυσιοθεραπευτική ⓕ fi·si·o·the·ra·pef·ti·*ki*
nausea ναυτία ⓕ naf·*ti*·a
near(by) κοντά ko·*da*
nearest το πιο κοντινό to pio ko·di·*no*
necessary αναγκαίο a·na·*ge*·o
neck λαιμός ⓜ le·*mos*
necklace κολιέ ⓝ ko·li·*e*
nectarine νεκταρίνι ⓝ nek·ta·*ri*·ni
need v χρειάζομαι khri·*a*·zo·me
needle (sewing) βελόνα ⓕ ve·*lo*·na
needle (syringe) σύριγκα ⓕ *si*·ri·ga
negative a αρνητικός ar·ni·ti·*kos*
neither κανένα από τα δύο ka·*ne*·na a·*po* ta *ţhi*·o
net δίκτι ⓝ *ţhik*·ti
Netherlands Ολλανδία ⓕ o·lan·*ţhi*·a

english–greek

N

never ποτέ po·*te*
new νέος *ne*·os
New Year's Day Πρωτοχρονιά ⓕ pro·to·khro·*nia*
New Year's Eve Παραμονή Πρωτοχρονιάς ⓕ pa·ra·mo·*ni* pro·to·khro·*nias*
New Zealand Νέα Ζηλανδία ⓕ *ne*·a zi·lan·*ţhi*·a
news νέα ⓝ pl *ne*·a
newsagency πρακτορείο εφημερίδων ⓝ prak·to·*ri*·o e·fi·me·*ri*·ţhon
newspaper εφημερίδα ⓕ e·fi·me·*ri*·ţha
newsstand περίπτερο ⓝ pe·*rip*·te·ro
next a επόμενος e·*po*·me·nos
next to δίπλα *ţhi*·pla
nice ωραίος o·*re*·os
nickname παρατσούκλι ⓝ pa·rat·*su*·kli
night νύχτα ⓕ *nikh*·ta
night out ξενύχτι ⓝ kse·*nikh*·ti
nightclub νάιτ κλαμπ ⓝ *na*·it klab
no όχι *o*·hi
noisy θορυβώδης tho·ri·*vo*·ţhis
none κανένας ka·*ne*·nas
nonsmoking μη καπνίζοντες mi kap·*ni*·zo·des
noodles λαζάνια ⓝ pl la·*za*·nia
noon μεσημέρι ⓝ me·si·*me*·ri
north βοράς ⓜ vo·*ras*
Norway Νορβηγία ⓕ nor·vi·*yi*·a
nose μύτη ⓕ *mi*·ti
not όχι *o*·hi
notebook σημειωματάριο ⓝ si·mi·o·ma·*ta*·ri·o
nothing τίποτε *ti*·po·te
November Νοέμβριος ⓜ no·*em*·vri·os
now τώρα *to*·ra
nuclear energy πυρηνική ενέργεια ⓕ pi·ri·ni·*ki* e·*ner*·yi·a
nuclear testing πυρηνικές δοκιμές ⓕ pl pi·ri·ni·*kes* ţho·ki·*mes*
nuclear waste πυρηνικά απόβλητα ⓝ pl pi·ri·ni·*ka* a·*pov*·li·ta
number αριθμός ⓜ a·rith·*mos*
numberplate αριθμός κυκλοφορίας ⓜ a·rith·*mos* ki·klo·fo·*ri*·as
nun καλόγρια ⓕ ka·*lo*·ghri·a
nurse νοσοκόμος/νοσοκόμα ⓜ/ⓕ no·so·*ko*·mos/no·so·*ko*·ma
nut καρύδι ⓝ ka·*ri*·ţhi

O

oats βρώμη ⓕ *vro*·mi
ocean ωκεανός ⓜ o·ke·a·*nos*
October Οκτώβριος ⓜ ok·*tov*·ri·os
off (food) μπαγιάτικος ba·*yia*·ti·kos
office γραφείο ⓝ ghra·*fi*·o
often συχνά sikh·*na*
oil (cooking) λάδι ⓝ *la*·ţhi
oil (car) λάδι αυτοκινήτου ⓝ *la*·ţhi af·to·ki·*ni*·tu
old παλιός pa·*lios*
olive ελιά ⓕ e·*lia*
olive oil λάδι ελιάς ⓝ *la*·ţhi e·*lias*
Olympic Games Ολυμπιακοί Αγώνες ⓜ o·li·bi·a·*ki* a·*gho*·nes
omelette ομελέττα ⓕ o·me·*le*·ta
on πάνω *pa*·no
on time στην ώρα stin *o*·ra
once μια φορά mia fo·*ra*
one ένα *e*·na
one-way (ticket) απλό εισιτήριο ⓝ a·*plo* i·si·*ti*·ri·o
onion κρεμύδι ⓝ kre·*mi*·ţhi
only μόνο *mo*·no
open a ανοιχτός a·nikh·*tos*
open v ανοίγω a·*ni*·gho
opening hours ώρες λειτουργίας ⓕ pl *o*·res li·tur·*yi*·as
opera (house) όπερα ⓕ *o*·pe·ra
operation (medical) εγχείρηση ⓕ eng·*hi*·ri·si
operator χειριστής/χειρίστρια ⓜ/ⓕ hi·ri·*stis*/hi·*ri*·stri·a
opinion γνώμη ⓕ *ghno*·mi
opposite απέναντι a·*pe*·na·di
optometrist οφθαλμίατρος ⓜ&ⓕ of·thal·*mi*·a·tros
or ή i
oracle χρησμός ⓜ khriz·*mos*
orange (fruit) πορτοκάλι ⓝ por·to·*ka*·li
orange (colour) a πορτοκαλής por·to·ka·*lis*
orange juice χυμός πορτοκάλι ⓜ hi·*mos* por·to·*ka*·li
orchestra ορχήστρα ⓕ or·*hi*·stra
orchid ορχιδέα ⓕ or·hi·*ţhe*·a
order σειρά ⓕ si·*ra*
order v διατάζω ţhia·*ta*·zo

ordinary συνηθισμένος si·ni·thiz·*me*·nos
orgasm οργασμός ⓜ or·ghaz·*mos*
original αρχικός ar·hi·*kos*
Orthodox Ορθόδοξος/Ορθόδοξη ⓜ/ⓕ or·*tho*·ţhok·sos/or·*tho*·ţhok·si
other άλλος *a*·los
Ottoman a Οθωμανικός o·tho·ma·ni·*kos*
our μας mas
outside έξω *ek*·so
ouzo ούζο ⓝ *u*·zo
ouzeria ουζερί ⓝ u·ze·*ri*
ovarian cyst ωοθητική κύστη ⓕ o·o·thi·ti·*ki* *ki*·sti
ovary ωοθήκη ⓕ o·o·*thi*·ki
oven φούρνος ⓜ *fur*·nos
overcoat πανωφόρι ⓝ pa·no·*fo*·ri
overdose υπερβολική δόση ⓕ i·per·vo·li·*ki* *ţho*·si
overnight ολονυχτίς o·lo·nikh·*tis*
overseas εξωτερικό ek·so·te·ri·*ko*
owe οφείλω o·*fi*·lo
owner κάτοχος ⓜ *ka*·to·khos
oxygen οξυγόνο ⓝ ok·si·*gho*·no
oyster στρείδι ⓝ *stri*·ţhi
ozone layer στρώμα όζοντος ⓝ *stro*·ma *o*·zo·dos

P

pacemaker βηματοδότης ⓜ vi·ma·to·*ţho*·tis
pacifier (dummy) πιπίλα ⓕ pi·*pi*·la
package πακέτο ⓝ pa·*ke*·to
packet πακέτο ⓝ pa·*ke*·to
padlock κλειδαριά ⓕ kli·ţha·*ria*
page σελίδα ⓕ se·*li*·ţha
pain πόνος ⓜ *po*·nos
painful οδυνηρός o·ţhi·ni·*ros*
painkiller παυσίπονο ⓝ paf·*si*·po·no
painter ζωγράφος ⓜ&ⓕ zo·*ghra*·fos
painting (a work) πίνακας ⓜ *pi*·na·kas
painting (the art) ζωγραφική ⓕ zo·ghra·fi·*ki*
pair (couple) ζευγάρι ⓝ zev·*gha*·ri
palace παλάτι ⓝ pa·*la*·ti
pan κατσαρόλα ⓕ kat·sa·*ro*·la
pants (trousers) παντελόνι ⓝ pa·de·*lo*·ni
panty liners πετσετάκι υγείας ⓝ pet·se·*ta*·ki i·*yi*·as
pantyhose καλτσόν ⓝ kal·*tson*
paper χαρτί ⓝ khar·*ti*
papers (documents) πιστοποιητικά ⓝ pl pi·sto·pi·i·ti·*ka*
paperwork προετοιμασία ⓕ εγγράφων pro·e·ti·ma·*si*·a e·*gra*·fon
paprika πάπρικα ⓕ *pa*·pri·ka
pap smear τεστ παπ ⓝ test pap
paraplegic παραπληγικός ⓜ pa·ra·pli·yi·*kos*
parcel δέμα ⓝ *ţhe*·ma
parents γονείς ⓜ pl gho·*nis*
park πάρκο ⓝ *par*·ko
park (a car) παρκάρω par·*ka*·ro
parliament Βουλή ⓕ vu·*li*
part (component) εξάρτημα ⓝ ek·*sar*·ti·ma
part-time μερική απασχόληση me·ri·*ki* a·pas·*kho*·li·si
party (night out) πάρτυ ⓝ *par*·ti
party (politics) κόμμα ⓝ *ko*·ma
pass v περνάω per·*na*·o
passenger επιβάτης/επιβάτισσα ⓜ/ⓕ e·pi·*va*·tis/e·pi·*va*·ti·sa
passionfruit πάσιον φρουτ ⓝ *pa*·si·on frut
passport διαβατήριο ⓝ ţhia·va·*ti*·ri·o
passport number αριθμός διαβατηρίου ⓜ a·rith·*mos* ţhia·va·ti·*ri*·u
past παρελθόν ⓝ pa·rel·*thon*
pasta ζυμαρικά ⓝ pl zi·ma·ri·*ka*
pastry φύλλο ⓝ *fi*·lo
path μονοπάτι ⓝ mo·no·*pa*·ti
patisserie ζαχαροπλαστείο ⓝ za·kha·ro·pla·*sti*·o
pay v πληρώνω pli·*ro*·no
payment πληρωμή ⓕ pli·ro·*mi*
pea αρακάς ⓜ a·ra·*kas*
peace ειρήνη ⓕ i·*ri*·ni
peach ροδάκινο ⓝ ro·*ţha*·ki·no
peak (mountain) κορυφή ⓕ ko·ri·*fi*
peanut φυστίκι ⓝ fi·*sti*·ki
pear αχλάδι ⓝ a·*khla*·ţhi
pedal πετάλι ⓝ pe·*ta*·li
pedestrian πεζός ⓜ pe·*zos*
pelican πελεκάνος ⓜ pe·le·*ka*·nos
pen (ballpoint) στυλό ⓝ sti·*lo*
pencil μολύβι ⓝ mo·*li*·vi
penis πέος ⓝ *pe*·os
penknife σουγιάς ⓜ su·*yias*
pension σύνταξη ⓕ *si*·dak·si

pensioner συνταξιούχος/συνταξιούχα ⓜ/ⓕ si·dak·si·*u*·khos/si·dak·si·*u*·kha
people κόσμος ⓜ *koz*·mos
pepper πιπέρι ⓝ pi·*pe*·ri
pepper (bell) πιπεριέρα ⓕ pi·pe·*rie*·ra
per κάθε *ka*·the
per cent τοις εκατό tis e·ka·*to*
perfect a τέλειος *te*·li·os
performance απόδοση ⓕ a·*po*·ţho·si
perfume άρωμα ⓝ *a*·ro·ma
period pain πόνος περιόδου ⓜ *po*·nos pe·ri·*o*·ţhu
permission άδεια ⓕ *a*·ţhi·a
permit άδεια ⓕ *a*·ţhi·a
person πρόσωπο ⓝ *pro*·so·po
petition συλλογή υπογραφών ⓕ si·lo·*yi* i·po·ghra·*fon*
petrol πετρέλαιο ⓝ pe·*tre*·le·o
petrol station πρατήριο βενζίνας ⓝ pra·*ti*·ri·o ven·*zi*·nas
pharmacist φαρμακοποιός ⓜ&ⓕ far·ma·ko·pi·*os*
pharmacy φαρμακείο ⓝ far·ma·*ki*·o
phone book τηλεφωνικός κατάλογος ⓜ ti·le·fo·ni·*kos* ka·*ta*·lo·ghos
phone box δημόσιο τηλέφωνο ⓝ ţhi·*mo*·si·o ti·*le*·fo·no
phonecard τηλεκάρτα ⓕ ti·le·*kar*·ta
photo φωτογραφία ⓕ fo·to·gra·*fi*·a
photographer φωτογράφος ⓜ&ⓕ fo·to·*ghra*·fos
photography φωτογραφική ⓕ fo·to·ghra·fi·*ki*
phrasebook βιβλίο φράσεων ⓕ viv·*li*·o *fra*·se·on
pickaxe τσεκούρι ⓝ tse·*ku*·ri
pickles τουρσί ⓝ tur·*si*
picnic πίκνικ ⓝ pik·*nik*
pie πίτα ⓕ *pi*·ta
piece κομμάτι ⓝ ko·*ma*·ti
pig γουρούνι ⓝ ghu·*ru*·ni
pill χάπι ⓝ *kha*·pi
the pill το Χάπι ⓝ to *kha*·pi
pillow μαξιλάρι ⓝ mak·si·*la*·ri
pillowcase μαξιλαροθήκη ⓕ mak·si·la·ro·*thi*·ki
pine πεύκο ⓝ *pef*·ko
pineapple ανανάς ⓜ a·na·*nas*
pink ροζ roz
pistachio φυστίκι ⓝ fi·*sti*·ki

place θέση ⓕ *the*·si
place of birth τόπος γεννήσεως ⓜ *to*·pos ye·*ni*·se·os
plane αεροπλάνο ⓝ a·e·ro·*pla*·no
planet πλανήτης ⓜ pla·*ni*·tis
plant φυτό ⓝ fi·*to*
plastic a πλαστικός pla·sti·*kos*
plate πιάτο ⓝ *pia*·to
plateau πλατό ⓝ pla·*to*
platform πλατφόρμα ⓕ plat·*for*·ma
play (theatre) θεατρικό έργο ⓝ the·a·tri·*ko* *er*·gho
play cards v παίζω χαρτιά *pe*·zo khar·*tia*
play guitar v παίζω κιθάρα *pe*·zo ki·*tha*·ra
plug (bath) βούλωμα ⓝ *vu*·lo·ma
plug (electricity) βύσμα ⓝ *viz*·ma
plum δαμάσκηνο ⓝ ţha·*ma*·ski·no
poached ποσέ po·*se*
pocket τσέπη ⓕ *tse*·pi
pocket knife σουγιάς ⓜ su·*yias*
poetry ποίηση ⓕ pi·*i*·si
point σημείο ⓝ si·*mi*·o
point v δείχνω *ţhi*·khno
poisonous δηλητηριώδης ţhi·li·ti·ri·*o*·ţhis
police αστυνομία ⓕ a·sti·no·*mi*·a
police officer (in city) αστυφύλακας/αστυφυλακίνα ⓜ/ⓕ a·sti·*fi*·la·kas/a·sti·fi·la·ki·na
police officer (in country) χωροφύλακας/χωροφυλακίνα ⓜ/ⓕ kho·ro·*fi*·la·kas/kho·ro·fi·la·*ki*·na
police station αστυνομικός σταθμός ⓜ a·sti·no·mi·*kos* stath·*mos*
policy πολιτική ⓕ po·li·ti·*ki*
politician πολιτικός ⓜ&ⓕ po·li·ti·*kos*
politics πολιτικά ⓝ pl po·li·ti·*ka*
pollen γύρη ⓕ *yi*·ri
pollution ρύπανση ⓕ *ri*·pan·si
pool (game) μπιλιάρδο ⓝ bi·*liar*·ţho
pool (swimming) πισίνα ⓕ pi·*si*·na
poor a φτωχός fto·*khos*
popular δημοφιλής ţhi·mo·fi·*lis*
pork χοιρινό ⓝ hi·ri·*no*
pork sausage χοιρινό λουκάνικο ⓝ hi·ri·*no* lu·*ka*·ni·ko
port (sea) λιμάνι ⓝ li·*ma*·ni
positive a θετικός the·ti·*kos*
possible δυνατός ţhi·na·*tos*
post v ταχυδρομώ ta·hi·ţhro·*mo*
postage ταχυδρομικά τέλη ⓝ pl ta·hi·ţhro·mi·*ka* *te*·li

postcard κάρτα ⓕ *kar*·ta
postcode ταχυδρομικός τομέας ⓜ ta·hi·ţhro·mi·*kos* to·*me*·as
post office ταχυδρομείο ⓝ ta·hi·ţhro·*mi*·o
poster πόστερ ⓝ *po*·ster
pot (ceramics) κεραμικό ⓝ ke·ra·mi·*ko*
pot (dope) μαριχουάνα ⓕ ma·ri·khu·*a*·na
potato πατάτα ⓕ pa·*ta*·ta
pottery αγγειοπλαστική ⓕ a·gi·o·pla·sti·*ki*
pound (money) λίρα ⓕ *li*·ra
pound (weight) λίτρα ⓕ *li*·tra
poverty φτώχεια ⓕ *fto*·hia
powder πούδρα ⓕ *pu*·ţhra
power δύναμη ⓕ *ţhi*·na·mi
prawn γαρίδα ⓕ gha·*ri*·ţha
prayer προσευχή ⓕ pro·sef·*hi*
prayer book βιβλίο προσευχών ⓝ viv·*li*·o pro·sef·*khon*
prefer προτιμώ pro·ti·*mo*
pregnancy test kit τεστ εγκυμοσύνης ⓝ test e·gi·mo·*si*·nis
pregnant a έγκυος *e*·gi·os
prehistoric προϊστορικός pro·i·sto·ri·*kos*
premenstrual tension ένταση πριν την περίοδο ⓕ *e*·da·si pri tin pe·*ri*·o·ţho
prepare προετοιμάζω pro·e·ti·*ma*·zo
prescription συνταγή ⓕ si·da·*yi*
present (gift) δώρο ⓝ *ţho*·ro
present (time) παρόν ⓝ pa·*ron*
president πρόεδρος ⓜ&ⓕ *pro*·e·ţhros
pressure πίεση ⓕ *pi*·e·si
pretty όμορφος *o*·mor·fos
price τιμή ⓕ ti·*mi*
priest παπάς ⓜ pa·*pas*
prime minister πρωθυπουργός ⓜ&ⓕ pro·thi·pur·*ghos*
printer (computer) εκτυπωτής ⓜ ek·ti·po·*tis*
prison φυλακή ⓕ fi·la·*ki*
prisoner φυλακισμένος ⓜ fi·la·kiz·*me*·nos
private a ιδιωτικός i·ţhi·o·ti·*kos*
problem πρόβλημα ⓝ *pro*·vli·ma
produce v παράγω pa·*ra*·gho
profit κέρδος ⓝ *ker*·ţhos
program πρόγραμμα ⓝ *pro*·gra·ma
projector προβολέας ⓜ pro·vo·*le*·as
promise v υπόσχομαι i·*pos*·kho·me
prostitute πόρνη ⓕ *por*·ni
protect προστατεύω pro·sta·*te*·vo
protected (species) προστατευόμενα (είδη) ⓝ pl pro·sta·te·*vo*·me·na (*i*·ţhi)
protest διαμαρτυρία ⓕ ţhi·a·mar·ti·*ri*·a
protest v διαμαρτύρομαι ţhi·a·mar·*ti*·ro·me
provisions προμήθειες ⓕ pl pro·*mi*·thi·es
prune (dried fruit) ξηρό δαμάσκηνο ⓝ ksi·*ro* ţha·*ma*·ski·no
pub (bar) μπυραρία ⓕ bi·ra·*ri*·a
public gardens εθνικός κήπος ⓜ eth·ni·*kos* *ki*·pos
public relations δημόσιες σχέσεις ⓕ pl ţhi·*mo*·si·es *she*·sis
public telephone δημόσιο τηλέφωνο ⓝ ţhi·*mo*·si·o ti·*le*·fo·no
public toilet δημόσια αποχωρητήρια ⓝ pl ţhi·*mo*·si·a a·po·kho·ri·*ti*·ria
pulse σφυγμός ⓜ sfigh·*mos*
pull v τραβάω tra·*va*·o
pump τρόμπα ⓕ *tro*·ba
pumpkin κολοκύθι ⓝ ko·lo·*ki*·thi
puncture τρύπα ρόδας ⓕ *tri*·pa *ro*·ţhas
punch (ticket) v ακυρώνω a·ki·*ro*·no
pure a καθαρός ka·tha·*ros*
purple μαβής ma·*vis*
purse πορτοφόλι ⓝ por·to·*fo*·li
push v σπρώχνω *sprokh*·no
put βάζω *va*·zo

Q

quadriplegic παραπληγικός ⓜ pa·ra·pli·yi·*kos*
qualifications προσόντα ⓝ pl pro·*so*·da
quality ποιότητα ⓕ pi·*o*·ti·ta
quarantine καραντίνα ⓕ ka·ra·*di*·na
quarter τέταρτο ⓝ *te*·tar·to
queen βασίλισσα ⓕ va·*si*·li·sa
question ερώτηση ⓕ e·*ro*·ti·si
queue ουρά ⓕ u·*ra*
quick a γρήγορος *ghri*·gho·ros
quiet a ήσυχος *i*·si·khos
quit v παραιτούμαι pa·re·*tu*·me

R

rabies λύσσα ⓕ *li*·sa
rabbit κουνέλι ⓝ ku·*ne*·li
race (sport) ιπποδρομία ⓕ i·po·ţhro·*mi*·a

racetrack ιππόδρομος ⓜ i·*po*·ţhro·mos
racing bike ποδήλατο κούρσας ⓝ po·*ţhi*·la·to *kur*·sas
racism ρατσισμός ⓜ rat·sis·*mos*
racquet ρακέτα ⓕ ra·*ke*·ta
radiator ψυγείο αυτοκινήτου ⓝ psi·*yi*·o af·to·ki·*ni*·tu
radio ράδιο ⓝ *ra*·ţhi·o
radish ραπάνι ⓝ ra·*pa*·ni
railway station σιδηροδρομικός σταθμός ⓜ si·ţhi·ro·ţhro·mi·*kos* stath·*mos*
rain ⓝ βροχή vro·*hi*
raincoat αδιάβροχο ⓝ a·ţhi·*av*·ro·ho
raisin σταφίδα ⓕ sta·*fi*·ţha
rally ράλι ⓝ *ra*·li
rape βιασμός ⓜ vi·az·*mos*
rape v βιάζω vi·*a*·zo
rare (uncommon) σπάνιος *spa*·ni·os
rare (food) μισοψημένο ⓝ mi·so·psi·*me*·no
rash εξάνθημα ⓝ ek·*san*·thi·ma
raspberry βατόμουρο ⓝ va·*to*·mu·ro
rat ποντίκι ⓝ po·*di*·ki
raw ωμός *o*·mos
razor ξυριστική μηχανή ⓕ ksi·ri·sti·*ki* mi·kha·*ni*
razor blade ξυράφι ⓝ ksi·*ra*·fi
read διαβάζω ţhia·*va*·zo
reading διάβασμα ⓝ *ţhia*·vaz·ma
ready έτοιμος *e*·ti·mos
real estate agent κτηματομεσίτης/κτηματομεσίτρια ⓜ/ⓕ kti·ma·to·me·*si*·tis/kti·ma·to·me·*si*·tri·a
realistic ρεαλιστικός re·a·li·sti·*kos*
rear (seat etc) οπίσθιος o·*pi*·sthi·os
reason αιτία ⓕ e·*ti*·a
receipt απόδειξη ⓕ a·*po*·ţhik·si
recently πρόσφατα *pros*·fa·ta
recommend συνιστώ si·ni·*sto*
record v καταγράφω ka·ta·*ghra*·fo
recording καταγραφή ⓕ ka·ta·ghra·*fi*
recyclable ανακυκλώσιμο a·na·ki·*klo*·si·mo
recycle ανακυκλώνω a·na·ki·*klo*·no
red κόκκινο *ko*·ki·no
referee διαιτητής/διαιτήτρια ⓜ/ⓕ ţhi·e·ti·*tis*/ţhi·e·*ti*·tri·a
reference (letter) συστατική επιστολή ⓕ si·sta·ti·*ki* e·pi·sto·*li*
reflexology αντανακλαστική ⓕ a·da·na·kla·sti·*ki*
refrigerator ψυγείο ⓝ psi·*yi*·o
refugee πρόσφυγας ⓜ&ⓕ *pros*·fi·ghas
refund ⓕ επιστροφή χρημάτων e·pi·stro·*fi* khri·*ma*·ton
refuse v αρνούμαι ar·*nu*·me
regional τοπικός to·pi·*kos*
(by) registered mail συστημένο sis·ti·*me*·no
rehydration salts υδρωτικά άλατα ⓝ pl i·ţhro·ti·*ka* *a*·la·ta
relationship σχέση ⓕ *she*·si
relax v χαλαρώνω kha·la·*ro*·no
relic κειμήλιο ⓝ ki·*mi*·li·o
religion θρησκεία ⓕ thri·*ski*·a
religious a θρήσκος *thri*·skos
remote a απόμακρος a·*po*·mak·ros
remote control τηλεκατεύθυνση ⓕ ti·le·ka·*tef*·thin·si
rent v ενοικιάζω e·ni·ki·*a*·zo
repair v επισκευάζω e·pi·ske·*va*·zo
republic δημοκρατία ⓕ ţhi·mo·kra·*ti*·a
reservation (booking) κράτηση ⓕ *kra*·ti·si
residency permit άδεια παραμονής ⓕ *a*·ţhi·a pa·ra·mo·*nis*
rest v ξεκουράζομαι kse·ku·*ra*·zo·me
restaurant εστιατόριο ⓝ e·sti·a·*to*·ri·o
restriction περιορισμός ⓜ pe·ri·o·riz·*mos*
résumé (CV) βιογραφικό σημείωμα ⓝ vi·o·ghra·fi·*ko* si·*mi*·o·ma
retired συνταξιούχος si·dak·si·*u*·khos
retsina (drink) ρετσίνα ⓕ ret·*si*·na
return (come back) v επιστρέφω e·pi·*stre*·fo
return (ticket) εισιτήριο μετ' επιστροφής ⓝ i·si·*ti*·ri·o me·te·pis·tro·*fis*
review αναθεώρηση ⓕ a·na·the·*o*·ri·si
rhythm ρυθμός ⓜ rith·*mos*
rib πλευρό ⓝ plev·*ro*
rice ρύζι ⓝ *ri*·zi
rich (wealthy) πλούσιος *plu*·si·os
ride (horse) ιππασία ⓕ i·pa·*si*·a
ride (horse) v ιππεύω i·*pe*·vo
right (correct) a σωστός so·*stos*
right (direction) δεξιός ţhek·si·*os*
right-wing δεξιά ⓕ ţhek·si·*a*
ring (jewellery) δαχτυλίδι ⓝ ţhakh·ti·*li*·ţhi
ring (phone) v τηλεφωνάω ti·le·fo·*na*·o
rip-off γδάρσιμο ⓝ *gţhar*·si·mo
risk ρίσκο ⓝ *ri*·sko
river ποτάμι ⓝ po·*ta*·mi
road δρόμος ⓜ *ţhro*·mos

road map οδικός χάρτης (m) o·ţhi·*kos* *khar*·tis
roasted ψημένος psi·*me*·nos
rob ληστεύω li·*ste*·vo
rock βράχος (m) *vra*·khos
rock climbing αναρρίχηση (f) a·na·*ri*·hi·si
rock music μουσική ροκ (f) mu·si·*ki* rok
rockfalls κατολίσθηση (f) ka·to·*lis*·thi·si
rock group μπάντα ροκ (f) *ba*·da rok
rockmelon πεπόνι (n) pe·*po*·ni
roll (bread) ψωμάκι (n) pso·*ma*·ki
rollerblading τροχοπέδιλο (n) tro·kho·*pe*·ţhi·lo
Roman Ρωμαϊκός ro·ma·i·*kos*
romantic ρομαντικός ro·ma·di·*kos*
room δωμάτιο (n) ţho·*ma*·ti·o
room number αριθμός δωματίου (n) a·rith·*mos* ţho·ma·*ti*·u
rope σκοινί (n) ski·*ni*
round a στρογγυλός stro·gi·*los*
roundabout κυκλική διασταύρωση (f) ki·kli·*ki* ţhi·a·*stav*·ro·si
route δρόμος (m) *ţhro*·mos
rowing κωπηλασία (f) ko·pi·la·*si*·a
rubbish σκουπίδια (n) pl sku·*pi*·ţhia
rubella ερυθρά (f) e·ri·*thra*
rug χαλί (n) kha·*li*
rugby ράγκμπυ (n) *rag*·bi
ruins ερρίπια (n) pl e·*ri*·pi·a
rule (n) κανόνας ka·*no*·nas
rum ρούμι (n) *ru*·mi
run v τρέχω *tre*·kho
running τρέξιμο (n) *trek*·si·mo
runny nose τρέξιμο μύτης (n) *trek*·si·mo *mi*·tis

S

sad λυπημένος li·pi·*me*·nos
saddle σέλλα (f) *se*·la
safe ασφάλεια (f) as·*fa*·li·a
safe a ασφαλής as·fa·*lis*
safe sex ασφαλές σεξ (n) as·fa·*les* seks
saint άγιος/αγία (m)/(f) *a*·yi·os/a·*yi*·a
sailing ιστίο (n) i·*sti*·o
salad σαλάτα (f) sa·*la*·ta
salami σαλάμι (n) sa·*la*·mi
salary μισθός (m) mis·*thos*
sale πώληση (f) *po*·li·si
sales tax φόρος πώλησης (m) *fo*·ros *po*·li·sis
salmon σολομός (m) so·lo·*mos*
salt αλάτι (n) a·*la*·ti
same ίδιος *i*·ţhi·os
sand άμμος (m) *a*·mos
sandal σαντάλι (n) sa·*da*·li
sanitary napkin πετσετάκι υγείας (n) pet·se·*ta*·ki i·*yi*·as
sardine σαρδέλα (f) sar·*ţhe*·la
Saturday Σάββατο (n) *sa*·va·to
sauce σάλτσα (f) *sal*·tsa
saucepan κατσαρόλα (f) kat·sa·*ro*·la
sauna σάουνα (n) *sa*·u·na
sausage λουκάνικο (n) lu·*ka*·ni·ko
savoury πικάντικος pi·*ka*·di·kos
say v λέγω *le*·gho
scalp κρανίο (n) kra·*ni*·o
scarf κασκόλ (n) ka·*skol*
school σχολείο (n) skho·*li*·o
science επιστήμη (f) e·pi·*sti*·mi
scientist επιστήμονας (m)&(f) e·pi·*sti*·mo·nas
scissors ψαλίδι (n) psa·*li*·ţhi
score v σκοράρω sko·*ra*·ro
scoreboard πίνακας σκορ (m) *pi*·na·kas skor
Scotland Σκωτία (f) sko·*ti*·a
scrambled χτυπητά (αβγά) khti·pi·*ta* (av·*gha*)
sculpture γλυπτική (f) ghlip·ti·*ki*
sea θάλασσα (f) *tha*·la·sa
seafood θαλασσινά (n) pl tha·la·si·*na*
(be) seasick πάσχει από ναυτία *pa*·shi a·*po* naf·*ti*·a
seasickness ναυτία (f) naf·*ti*·a
seaside παραλία (f) pa·ra·*li*·a
season εποχή (f) e·po·*hi*
seat (place) θέση (f) *the*·si
seatbelt ζώνη καθίσματος (f) *zo*·ni ka·*thiz*·ma·tos
sea turtle θαλάσσια χελώνα (f) tha·*la*·si·a he·*lo*·na
sea urchin αχινός (m) a·hi·*nos*
second δευτερόλεπτο (n) ţhef·te·*ro*·lep·to
second a δεύτερος *ţhef*·te·ros
second class δεύτερη τάξη (f) *ţhef*·te·ri *tak*·si
second-hand a μεταχειρισμένος me·ta·hi·riz·*me*·nos
second-hand shop παλαιοπωλείο (n) pa·le·o·po·*li*·o

secretary γραμματέας ⓜ&ⓕ ghra·ma·*te*·as
see βλέπω *vle*·po
self-employed a ιδιωτικός υπάλληλος i·ţhi·o·ti·*kos* i·*pa*·li·los
selfish ατομιστής a·to·mi·*stis*
self-service ⓝ σελφ σέρβις self *ser*·vis
sell v πουλάω pu·*la*·o
seminar σεμινάριο ⓝ se·mi·*na*·ri·o
send στέλνω *stel*·no
sensible συνετός si·ne·*tos*
sensual αισθησιακός e·sthi·si·a·*kos*
separate a χωριστός kho·ri·*stos*
September Σεπτέμβριος ⓜ sep·*tem*·vri·os
serious σοβαρός so·va·*ros*
service υπηρεσία ⓕ i·pi·re·*si*·a
service charge τιμή εξυπηρέτησης ⓕ ti·*mi* ek·si·pi·*re*·ti·sis
service station βενζινάδικο ⓝ ven·zi·*na*·ţhi·ko
serviette πετσέτα φαγητού ⓕ pet·*se*·ta fa·yi·*tu*
several μερικοί me·ri·*ki*
sew v ράβω *ra*·vo
sex (intercourse) σεξ ⓝ seks
sexism σεξισμός ⓜ sek·siz·*mos*
sexy σέξυ *sek*·si
shade σκιά ⓕ ski·*a*
shadow σκιά ⓕ ski·*a*
shampoo σαμπουάν ⓝ sam·pu·*an*
shape σχήμα ⓝ *shi*·ma
share (with) μοιράζομαι mi·*ra*·zo·me
shave v ξυρίζω ksi·*ri*·zo
shaving cream κρέμα ξυρίσματος ⓕ *kre*·ma ksi·*riz*·ma·tos
she αυτή af·*ti*
sheep πρόβατο ⓝ *pro*·va·to
sheet (bed) σεντόνι ⓝ se·*do*·ni
shelf ράφι ⓝ *ra*·fi
shiatsu σιάτσου ⓜ si·*at*·su
shield ασπίδα ⓕ as·*pi*·ţha
shingles (illness) έρπης ⓜ *er*·pis
ship πλοίο ⓝ *pli*·o
shirt πουκάμισο ⓝ pu·*ka*·mi·so
shoe παπούτσι ⓝ pa·put·*si*
shoes παπούτσια ⓝ pl pa·*put*·si·a
shoe shop υποδηματοποιείο ⓝ i·po·ţhi·ma·to·pi·*i*·o
shoot v πυροβολώ pi·ro·vo·*lo*
shop μαγαζί ⓝ ma·gha·*zi*
shop v ψωνίζω pso·*ni*·zo
shopping ψώνια ⓝ pl *pso*·nia
shopping centre αγορά ⓕ a·gho·*ra*
short (height) κοντός ko·*dos*
shortage έλλειψη ⓕ *e*·lip·si
shorts σορτς ⓝ sorts
shoulder ώμος ⓜ *o*·mos
shout v φωνάζω fo·*na*·zo
show επίδειξη ⓕ e·*pi*·ţhik·si
show v δείχνω *ţhikh*·no
shower ντουζ ⓝ duz
shrine βωμός ⓜ vo·*mos*
shut a κλειστός kli·*stos*
shy a ντροπαλός dro·pa·*los*
sick a άρρωστος *a*·ro·stos
side πλευρά ⓕ plev·*ra*
siesta μεσημεριανή ανάπαυση ⓕ me·si·me·ria·*ni* a·*na*·paf·si
sign πινακίδα ⓕ pi·na·*ki*·ţha
signature υπογραφή ⓕ i·po·ghra·*fi*
silk μετάξι ⓝ me·*tak*·si
silver ασήμι ⓝ a·*si*·mi
similar παρόμοιος pa·*ro*·mi·os
simple απλός a·*plos*
since (May) από (το Μάη) a·*po* (to *ma*·i)
sing v τραγουδώ tra·ghu·*ţho*
Singapore Σιγγαπούρη ⓕ sing·ga·*pu*·ri
singer τραγουδιστής/τραγουδίστρια ⓜ/ⓕ tra·ghu·ţhi·*stis*/tra·ghu·*ţhi*·stri·a
single (person) a εργένης/εργένισσα ⓜ/ⓕ er·*ye*·nis/er·*ye*·ni·sa
single room μονό δωμάτιο ⓝ mo·*no* ţho·*ma*·tio
singlet φανελλάκι ⓝ fa·ne·*la*·ki
sister αδερφή ⓕ a·ţher·*fi*
sit κάθομαι *ka*·tho·me
size μέγεθος ⓝ *me*·ye·thos
skate v παγοδρομώ pa·gho·ţhro·*mo*
skateboarding πατίνι ⓝ pa·*ti*·ni
ski v κάνω σκι *ka*·no ski
skiing σκι ⓝ ski
skim milk άπαχο γάλα ⓝ *a*·pa·kho *gha*·la
skin δέρμα ⓝ *ţher*·ma
skirt φούστα ⓕ *fu*·sta
skull κρανίο ⓝ kra·*ni*·o
sky ουρανός ⓜ u·ra·*nos*
sleep v κοιμάμαι ki·*ma*·me
sleeping bag σλίπινγκ μπαγκ ⓝ *sli*·ping bag
sleeping berth κρεββατάκι ⓝ kre·va·*ta*·ki

sleeping car βαγκόν λι ⓝ va·*gon* li
sleeping pills υπνωτικά χάπια ⓝ pl ip·no·ti·*ka* *kha*·pia
sleepy νυσταγμένος nis·tagh·*me*·nos
slice φέτα ⓕ *fe*·ta
slide (film) σλάιντ ⓝ *sla*·id
slow a αργός ar·*ghos*
slowly αργά ar·*gha*
small μικρός mi·*kros*
smaller μικρότερος mi·*kro*·te·ros
smallest ο μικρότερος o mi·*kro*·te·ros
smell μυρουδιά ⓕ mi·ru·*ţhia*
smile v χαμογελώ kha·mo·ye·*lo*
smog νέφος ⓝ *ne*·fos
smoke v καπνίζω kap·*ni*·zo
snack μικρό γεύμα ⓝ mi·*kro* *ghev*·ma
snail σαλιγκάρι ⓝ sa·li·*ga*·ri
snake φίδι ⓝ *fi*·dhi
snorkelling υπόγεια κατάδυση ⓕ i·*po*·yi·a ka·*ta*·ţhi·si
snow χιόνι ⓝ *hio*·ni
snowboarding σκι με χιονοσανίδα ⓝ ski me hio·no·sa·*ni*·ţha
snow pea αρακάς ⓜ a·ra·*kas*
soap σαπούνι ⓝ sa·*pu*·ni
soap opera αισθηματικό σίριαλ ⓝ es·thi·ma·ti·*ko* *si*·ri·al
soccer ποδόσφαιρο ⓝ po·*ţhos*·fe·ro
social welfare κοινωνική πρόνοια ⓕ ki·no·ni·*ki* *pro*·ni·a
socialist σοσιαλιστής/σοσιαλίστρια ⓜ/ⓕ so·si·a·li·*stis*/so·si·a·*li*·stri·a
sock κάλτσα ⓕ *kal*·tsa
socks κάλτσες ⓕ pl *kal*·tses
soft drink αναψυκτικό ⓝ a·nap·sik·ti·*ko*
soft-boiled μελάτο ⓝ me·*la*·to
soldier στρατιώτης ⓜ stra·ti·*o*·tis
some μερικοί me·ri·*ki*
someone κάποιος *ka*·pi·os
something κάτι *ka*·ti
sometimes μερικές φορές me·ri·*kes* fo·*res*
son γιος ⓜ yios
song τραγούδι ⓝ tra·*ghu*·ţhi
soon σύντομα *si*·do·ma
sore a πονεμένος po·ne·*me*·nos
soup σούπα ⓕ *su*·pa
sour cream ξινή κρέμα ⓕ ksi·*ni* *kre*·ma
south νότος ⓜ *no*·tos
souvenir σουβενίρ ⓝ su·ve·*nir*
souvenir shop κατάστημα για σουβενίρ ⓝ ka·*ta*·sti·ma yia su·ve·*nir*
souvlaki σουβλάκι ⓝ suv·*la*·ki
soy milk γάλα σόγια ⓝ *gha*·la *so*·yi·a
soy sauce σάλτσα ⓕ σόγια *sal*·tsa *so*·yi·a
space διάστημα ⓝ ţhi·*a*·sti·ma
Spain Ισπανία ⓕ i·spa·*ni*·a
sparkling wine σαμπάνια ⓕ sam·*pa*·ni·a
speak μιλάω mi·*la*·o
special a ειδικός i·ţhi·*kos*
spear καμάκι ⓝ ka·*ma*·ki
specialist σπεσιαλίστας/σπεσιαλίστρια ⓜ/ⓕ spe·si·a·*li*·stas/spe·si·a·*li*·stri·a
speed (velocity) ταχύτητα ⓕ ta·*hi*·ti·ta
speed limit όριο ταχύτητας ⓝ *o*·ri·o ta·*hi*·ti·tas
speedometer ταχύμετρο ⓝ ta·*hi*·me·tro
spider αράχνη ⓕ a·*rakh*·ni
spinach σπανάκι ⓝ spa·*na*·ki
spoiled (food) χαλασμένος kha·laz·*me*·nos
spoke ακτίνα τροχού ⓕ ak·*ti*·na tro·*khu*
spoon κουτάλι ⓝ ku·*ta*·li
sport σπορ ⓝ spor
sportsman σπορτσμαν ⓜ *sports*·man
sportswoman σπορτσγούμαν ⓕ sports·*ghu*·man
sports store κατάστημα των σπορ ⓝ ka·*ta*·sti·ma ton spor
sprain στραμπούλισμα ⓝ stra·*bu*·liz·ma
spring (coil) ελατήριο ⓝ e·la·*ti*·ri·o
spring (season) άνοιξη ⓕ *a*·nik·si
square (town) πλατεία ⓕ pla·*ti*·a
spray σπρέι ⓝ *spre*·i
stadium στάδιο ⓝ *sta*·ţhi·o
stairway σκάλα ⓕ *ska*·la
stale μπαγιάτικος ba·*yia*·ti·kos
stamp γραμματόσημο ⓝ ghra·ma·*to*·si·mo
stand-by ticket εισιτήριο σταντ μπάι ⓝ i·si·*ti*·ri·o stand *ba*·i
star (sky) αστέρι ⓝ a·*ste*·ri
start αρχή ⓕ ar·*hi*
start v αρχίζω ar·*hi*·zo
station σταθμός ⓜ stath·mos
stationer's χαρτοπωλείο ⓝ khar·to·po·*li*·o
statue άγαλμα ⓝ *a*·ghal·ma
stay μένω *me*·no
steak (beef) μπριζόλα ⓕ bri·*zo*·la
steal κλέβω *kle*·vo
steep απόκρημνος a·*po*·krim·nos
step βήμα ⓝ *vi*·ma
stereo στέρεο ⓝ *ste*·re·o
still water νερό χωρίς ανθρακικό ⓝ ne·*ro* kho·*ris* an·thra·ki·*ko*

S

english–greek

sting v τσιμπάω tsi·*ba*·o
stock (food) ζουμί ⓝ zu·*mi*
stockings καλτσόν ⓝ kal·*tson*
stolen κλεμμένο kle·*me*·no
stomach στομάχι ⓝ sto·*ma*·hi
stomachache στομαχόπονος ⓜ sto·ma·*kho*·po·nos
stone πέτρα ⓕ *pe*·tra
stoned (drugged) μαστουρωμένος ma·stu·ro·*me*·nos
stop (bus etc) στάση ⓕ *sta*·si
stop (cease) v σταματάω sta·ma·*ta*·o
stop (prevent) v εμποδίζω e·bo·*ţhi*·zo
storm καταιγίδα ⓕ ka·te·*yi*·ţha
story ιστορία ⓕ i·sto·*ri*·a
stove ηλεκτρική κουζίνα ⓕ i·lek·tri·*ki* ku·*zi*·na
straight ίσιος *i*·si·os
strange παράξενος pa·*rak*·se·nos
stranger (person) ξένος/ξένη ⓜ/ⓕ *kse*·nos/*kse*·ni
strawberry φράουλα ⓕ *fra*·u·la
stream ατμός ⓜ at·*mos*
street οδός ⓕ o·*ţhos*
street market λαϊκή ⓕ la·i·*ki*
strike απεργία ⓕ a·per·*yi*·a
string κλωστή ⓕ klo·*sti*
stroke (health) εγκεφαλικό ⓝ e·ge·fa·li·*ko*
stroller καροτσάκι ⓝ ka·rot·*sa*·ki
strong δυνατός ţhi·na·*tos*
stubborn ισχυρογνώμων is·hi·rog·*no*·mon
student σπουδαστής/σπουδάστρια ⓜ/ⓕ spu·ţha·*stis*/spu·*ţha*·stri·a
studio στούντιο ⓝ *stu*·di·o
stupid χαζός kha·*zos*
style στυλ ⓝ stil
subtitles υπότιτλοι ⓜ pl i·*po*·ti·tli
suburb προάστειο ⓝ pro·*a*·sti·o
subway a υπόγειος i·*po*·yi·os
subway (train) υπόγειος σιδηρόδρομος ⓜ i·*po*·yi·os si·ţhi·*ro*·ţhro·mos
sugar ζάχαρη ⓕ *za*·kha·ri
suitcase βαλίτσα ⓕ va·*lit*·sa
sultana σταφίδα ⓕ sta·*fi*·ţha
summer καλοκαίρι ⓝ ka·lo·*ke*·ri
sun ήλιος ⓜ *i*·li·os
sunblock αντιηλιακό ⓝ a·di·i·li·a·*ko*
sunburn ηλιακό έγκαυμα ⓝ i·li·a·*ko* *e*·gav·ma
Sunday Κυριακή ⓕ ki·ria·*ki*
sunglasses γυαλιά ηλίου ⓝ pl yia·*lia* i·*li*·u
sunny ηλιόλουστος i·li·*o*·lu·stos
sunrise ανατολή ⓕ a·na·to·*li*
sunset δύση ⓕ *ţhi*·si
sunstroke ηλιοπληξία ⓕ i·li·o·plik·*si*·a
supermarket σουπερμάρκετ ⓝ su·per·*mar*·ket
superstition πρόληψη ⓕ *pro*·lip·si
supporter (politics, sport) οπαδός ⓜ&ⓕ o·pa·*ţhos*
surf σερφ ⓝ serf
surface mail (land) δια ξηράς ţhi·a ksi·*ras*
surface mail (sea) ατμοπλοϊκώς at·mo·plo·i·*kos*
surfboard σέρφμπορντ ⓝ *serf*·bord
surfing σέρφινγκ ⓝ *ser*·fing
surname επώνυμο ⓝ e·*po*·ni·mo
surprise έκληξη ⓕ *ek*·plik·si
sweater ζακέτα ⓕ za·*ke*·ta
Sweden Σουηδία ⓕ su·i·*ţhi*·a
sweet a γλυκός ghli·*kos*
sweets γλυκά ⓝ pl ghli·*ka*
swelling πρήξιμο ⓝ *prik*·si·mo
swim v κολυμπώ ko·li·*bo*
swimming (sport) κολύμπι ⓝ ko·*li*·bi
swimming pool πισίνα ⓕ pi·*si*·na
swimsuit μαγιό ⓝ ma·*yio*
Switzerland Ελβετία ⓕ el·ve·*ti*·a
sword σπαθί ⓝ spa·*thi*
synagogue συναγωγή ⓕ si·na·gho·*yi*
synthetic a συνθετικός sin·the·ti·*kos*
syringe σύριγκα ⓕ *si*·ri·ga

T

table τραπέζι ⓝ tra·*pe*·zi
tablecloth τραπεζομάντηλο ⓝ tra·pe·zo·*ma*·di·lo
table tennis πινγκ πονγκ ⓝ ping pong
tail ουρά ⓕ u·*ra*
tailor ράφτης/ράφτρα ⓜ/ⓕ *raf*·tis/*raf*·tra
take παίρνω *per*·no
take a photo βγάζω φωτογραφία *vga*·zo fo·to·gra·*fi*·a
talk v μιλάω mi·*la*·o
tall ψηλός psi·*los*
tampon ταμπόν ⓝ ta·*bon*
tanning lotion λοσιόν για μαύρισμα ⓝ lo·*sion* yia *mav*·riz·ma

tap βρύση (f) *vri*·si
tap water νερό βρύσης (n) ne·*ro* *vri*·sis
tasty νόστιμος *no*·sti·mos
taverna ταβέρνα (f) ta·*ver*·na
tax φόρος (m) *fo*·ros
taxi ταξί (n) tak·*si*
taxi stand στάση ταξί (f) *sta*·si tak·*si*
tea τσάι (n) *tsa*·i
teacher δάσκαλος/δασκάλα (m)/(f)
ţha·ska·los/ţha·*ska*·la
team ομάδα (f) o·*ma*·ţha
teaspoon κουτάλι τσαγιού (n)
ku·*ta*·li tsa·*yiu*
technique τεχνική (f) tekh·ni·*ki*
teeth δόντια (n) *ţho*·dia
telegram τηλεγράφημα (n) ti·le·*ghra*·fi·ma
telephone τηλέφωνο (n) ti·*le*·fo·no
telephone v τηλεφωνώ ti·le·fo·*no*
telephone box δημόσιο τηλέφωνο (n)
ţhi·*mo*·si·o ti·*le*·fo·no
telephone centre τηλεφωνικό κέντρο (n)
ti·le·fo·ni·*ko* *ke*·dro
telescope τηλεσκόπιο (n) ti·le·*sko*·pi·o
television τηλεόραση (f) ti·le·*o*·ra·si
tell λέγω *le*·gho
temperature (fever) πυρετός (m) pi·re·*tos*
temperature (weather) θερμοκρασία (f)
ther·mo·kra·*si*·a
temple (church) ναός (m) na·*os*
tennis τένις (n) *te*·nis
tennis court γήπεδο του τένις (n)
yi·pe·ţho tu *te*·nis
tent τέντα (f) *te*·da
tent peg πάσαλος τέντας (m)
pa·sa·los *te*·das
terracotta pot αγγείο τερακότα (n)
a·*gi*·o te·ra·*ko*·ta
terrible τρομερός tro·me·*ros*
test τεστ (n) test
thank ευχαριστώ ef·kha·ri·*sto*
that (one) εκείνο e·*ki*·no
theatre θέατρο (n) *the*·a·tro
their τους tus
there εκεί e·*ki*
they αυτοί af·*ti*
thick πυκνός pik·*nos*
thief κλέφτης (m) *klef*·tis
thin λεπτός lep·*tos*
think νομίζω no·*mi*·zo
third τρίτος *tri*·tos
thirsty διψασμένος ţhip·saz·*me*·nos
this (one) αυτός (m) af·*tos*
thread κλωστή (f) klo·*sti*
throat λαιμός (m) le·*mos*
thrush (health) μυκητώδης στοματίτις (m)
mi·ki·*to*·ţhis sto·ma·*ti*·tis
thunderstorm καταιγίδα (f) ka·te·*yi*·ţha
Thursday Πέμπτη (f) *pem*·ti
tick τσιμπούρι (n) tsi·*bu*·ri
ticket εισιτήριο (n) i·si·*ti*·ri·o
ticket collector εισπράκτορας (m)&(f)
is·*prak*·to·ras
ticket machine μηχανή εισιτηρίων (f)
mi·kha·*ni* i·si·ti·*ri*·on
ticket office γραφείο εισιτηρίων (n)
ghra·*fi*·o i·si·ti·*ri*·on
tide παλίρροια (f) pa·*li*·ri·a
tight σφιχτός sfikh·*tos*
time ώρα (f) *o*·ra
time difference διαφορά ώρας (f)
ţhia·fo·*ra* *o*·ras
timetable πρόγραμμα (n) *pro* ghra·ma
tin (can) κουτί (n) ku·*ti*
tin opener ανοιχτήρι (n) a·nikh·*ti*·ri
tiny μικροσκοπικός mi·kro·sko·pi·*kos*
tip (gratuity) φιλοδώρημα (n)
fi·lo·*ţho*·ri·ma
tire λάστιχο (n) *la*·sti·kho
tired κουρασμένος ku·raz·*me*·nos
tissues χαρτομάντηλα (n) pl
khar·to·*ma*·di·la
to σε se
toast τοστ (n) tost
toaster τοστιέρα (f) to·sti·*e*·ra
tobacco καπνός (m) kap·*nos*
tobacconist
καπνοπώλης/καπνοπώλισσα (m)/(f)
ka·pno·*po*·lis/ka·pno·*po*·li·sa
today σήμερα *si*·me·ra
toe δάχτυλο ποδιού (n) *ţhakh*·ti·lo po·*ţhiu*
tofu τόφου (n) *to*·fu
together μαζί ma·*zi*
toilet τουαλέτα (f) tu·a·*le*·ta
toilet paper χαρτί υγείαςη (n) khar·*ti* i·*yi*·as
tomato ντομάτα (f) do·*ma*·ta
tomato sauce σάλτσα (f) *sal*·tsa
tomb μνήμα (n) *mni*·ma
tomorrow αύριο *av*·ri·o
tomorrow afternoon αύριο το απόγευμα
av·ri·o to a·*po*·yev·ma

T

english–greek

tomorrow evening αύριο το βράδι *av*·ri·o to *vra*·ţhi
tomorrow morning αύριο το πρωί *av*·ri·o to pro·*i*
tonight απόψε a·*pop*·se
too (excess) πάρα πολύ *pa*·ra po·*li*
tooth δόντι ⓝ *ţho*·di
toothache πονόδοντος ⓜ po·*no*·ţho·dos
toothbrush οδοντόβουρτσα ⓕ o·ţho·*do*·vur·tsa
toothpaste οδοντόπαστα ⓕ o·ţho·*do*·pa·sta
toothpick οδοντογλυφίδα ⓕ o·ţho·do·ghli·*fi*·ţha
torch (flashlight) φακός ⓜ fa·*kos*
touch v αγγίζω a·*gi*·zo
tour περιήγηση ⓕ pe·ri·*i*·yi·si
tourist τουρίστας/τουρίστρια ⓜ/ⓕ tu·*ri*·stas/tu·*ri*·stri·a
tourist office τουριστικό γραφείο ⓝ tu·ri·sti·*ko* ghra·*fi*·o
towards προς pros
towel πετσέτα ⓕ pet·*se*·ta
tower πύργος ⓜ *pir*·ghos
toxic waste τοξικά απόβλητα ⓝ pl tok·si·*ka* a·*pov*·li·ta
toy shop κατάστημα παιγνιδιών ⓝ ka·*ta*·sti·ma pegh·ni·*ţhion*
track (path) μονοπάτι ⓝ mo·no·*pa*·ti
track (sport) στίβος ⓜ *sti*·vos
trade εμπόριο ⓝ e·*bo*·ri·o
tradesperson έμπορος ⓜ&ⓕ *e*·bo·ros
traffic κυκλοφορία ⓕ ki·klo·fo·*ri*·a
traffic light φανάρι ⓝ fa·*na*·ri
trail μονοπάτι ⓝ mo·no·*pa*·ti
train τρένο ⓝ *tre*·no
train station σταθμός τρένου ⓜ stath·*mos tre*·nu
tram τραμ ⓝ tram
transit lounge αίθουσα τράνζιτ ⓕ *e*·thu·sa *tran*·zit
translate μεταφράζω me·ta·*fra*·zo
transport μεταφορά ⓕ me·ta·fo·*ra*
travel v ταξιδεύω tak·si·*ţhe*·vo
travel agency ταξιδιωτικό γραφείο ⓝ tak·si·ţhi·o·ti·*ko* ghra·*fi*·o
travel sickness ναυτία ⓕ naf·*ti*·a
travellers cheque ταξιδιωτική επιταγή ⓕ tak·si·ţhi·o·ti·*ki* e·pi·ta·*yi*
tree δέντρο ⓝ *ţhe*·dro
trip (journey) ταξίδι ⓝ tak·*si*·ţhi
trolley καροτσάκι ⓝ ka·rot·*sa*·ki
trolley bus τρόλεϋ ⓝ *tro*·le·i
trousers παντελόνι ⓝ pa·de·*lo*·ni
truck φορτηγό ⓝ for·ti·*gho*
trust v εμπιστεύομαι e·bi·*ste*·vo·me
try (attempt) προσπαθώ pros·pa·*tho*
T-shirt μπλουζάκι ⓝ blu·*za*·ki
tube (tyre) σαμπρέλα ⓕ sa·*bre*·la
Tuesday Τρίτη ⓕ *tri*·ti
tumour όγκος ⓜ *o*·gos
tuna τόνος ⓜ *to*·nos
tune σκοπός ⓜ sko·*pos*
tunic χιτώνας ⓜ hi·*to*·nas
Turkey Τουρκία ⓕ tur·*ki*·a
turkey γάλοπούλα ⓕ gha·lo·*pu*·la
Turkish (language) Τουρκικά tur·ki·*ka*
Turkish (people) Τούρκοι ⓜ pl *tur*·ki
turn v γυρίζω yi·*ri*·zo
TV τηλεόραση ⓕ ti·le·*o*·ra·si
tweezers τσιμπιδάκι ⓝ tsi·bi·*ţha*·ki
twice δυο φορές ţhio fo·*res*
twin beds δίκλινο δωμάτιο ⓝ *ţhi*·kli·no ţho·*ma*·ti·o
twins δίδυμα ⓝ pl *ţhi*·ţhi·ma
two δύο *ţhi*·o
type τύπος ⓜ *ti*·pos
typhus τύφος ⓜ *ti*·fos
typical τυπικός ti·pi·*kos*
tyre λάστιχο ⓝ *la*·sti·kho

U

ultrasound υπερηχητικό κύμα ⓝ i·pe·ri·hi·ti·*ko ki*·ma
umbrella ομπρέλα ⓕ o·*bre*·la
uncomfortable άβολος *a*·vo·los
understand καταλαβαίνω ka·ta·la·*ve*·no
underwear εσώρουχα ⓝ pl e·*so*·ru·kha
unemployed a άνεργος/άνεργη ⓜ/ⓕ *a*·ner·ghos/*a*·ner·yi
unfair άδικος *a*·ţhi·kos
uniform στολή ⓕ sto·*li*
universe υφήλιος ⓕ i·*fi*·li·os
university πανεπιστήμιο ⓝ pa·ne·pi·*sti*·mi·o
unleaded (petrol) αμόλυβδος ⓕ a·*mo*·liv·ţhos
unsafe ανασφαλής a·nas·fa·*lis*

until μέχρι *me*·khri
unusual ασυνήθιστος a·si·*ni*·thi·stos
UN zone ζώνη των Ηνωμένων Εθνών ⓕ
zo·ni ton i·no·*me*·non e·*thnon*
up πάνω *pa*·no
uphill ανηφορικά a·ni·fo·ri·*ka*
urgent επείγον e·*pi*·ghon
urinary infection ουρική μόλυνση ⓕ
u·ri·*ki mo*·lin·si
USA ΗΠΑ ⓕ *i*·pa
useful χρήσιμος *khri*·si·mos

V

vacancy κενή θέση ⓕ ke·*ni the*·si
vacant ελεύθερος e·*lef*·the·ros
vacation διακοπές ⓕ pl ţhia·ko·*pes*
vaccination εμβόλιο ⓝ em·*vo*·li·o
vagina κόλπος γυναίκας ⓜ
kol·pos yi·*ne*·kas
validate επικυρώνω e·pi·ki·*ro*·no
valley κοιλάδα ⓕ ki·*la*·ţha
valuable πολύτιμος po·*li*·ti·mos
value (price) αξία ⓕ ak·*si*·a
van φορτηγάκι ⓝ for·ti·*gha*·ki
VAT (Value Added Tax) Φ.Π.Α. ⓜ fpa
veal μοσχάρι ⓝ mos·*kha*·ri
vegan βέγκαν ⓜ&ⓕ *ve*·gan
vegetable λαχανικά ⓝ pl la·kha·ni·*ka*
vegetarian a χορτοφάγος ⓜ&ⓕ
khor·to·*fa*·ghos
vein φλέβα ⓕ *fle*·va
venereal disease αφροδισιακό νόσημα
ⓝ a·fro·ţhi·si·a·*ko no*·si·ma
venue χώρος ⓜ *kho*·ros
very πολύς po·*lis*
vessel σκάφος ⓝ *ska*·fos
video recorder βίντεο ρεκόρντερ ⓝ
vi·de·o re·*kor*·der
video tape βιντεοταινία ⓕ vi·de·o·te·*ni*·a
view θέα ⓕ *the*·a
village χωριό ⓝ kho·*rio*
vine κλήμα ⓝ *kli*·ma
vinegar ξύδι ⓝ *ksi*·ţhi
vineyard αμπέλι ⓝ a·*be*·li
virus ιός ⓜ i·*os*
visa βίζα ⓕ *vi*·za
visit επίσκεψη ⓕ e·*pi*·skep·si
visit v επισκέπτομαι e·pi·*ske*·pto·me
vitamins βιταμίνες ⓕ pl vi·ta·*mi*·nes
vodka βότκα ⓕ *vot*·ka
voice φωνή ⓕ fo·*ni*
volleyball ⓝ βόλεϊ *vo*·le·i
vote v ψηφίζω psi·*fi*·zo

W

wage μισθός ⓜ mis·*thos*
wait (for) περιμένω pe·ri·*me*·no
waiter γκαρσόν ⓝ gar·*son*
waiting room αίθουσα αναμονής ⓕ
e·thu·sa a·na·mo·*nis*
waitress σερβιτόρα ⓕ ser·vi·*to*·ra
wake (someone) up ξυπνάω ksip·*na*·o
walk v περπατάω per·pa·*ta*·o
wall (outer) τείχος ⓝ *ti*·khos
wallet πορτοφόλι ⓝ por·to·*fo*·li
want θέλω *the*·lo
war πόλεμος ⓜ *po*·le·mos
wardrobe ντουλάπα ⓕ du·*la*·pa
warm a ζεστός ze·*stos*
warn ζεσταίνω ze·*ste*·no
wash (oneself) v πλένομαι *ple*·no·me
wash (something) v πλένω *ple*·no
wash cloth (flannel) σφουγγάρι ⓝ sfu·*ga*·ri
washing machine πλυντήριο ⓝ pli·*di*·ri·o
wasp σφήκα ⓕ *sfi*·ka
watch v κοιτάζω ki·*ta*·zo
watch ρολόι ⓝ ro·*lo*·i
water νερό ⓝ ne·*ro*
water bottle μπουκάλι νερού ⓝ
bu·*ka*·li ne·*ru*
water bottle (hot) θερμοφόρα ⓕ
ther·mo·*fo*·ra
waterfall καταράχτης ⓜ ka·ta·*rakh*·tis
watermelon καρπούζι ⓝ kar·*pu*·zi
waterproof a αδιάβροχος
a·ţhi·*av*·ro·khos
waterskiing θαλάσσιο σκι ⓝ tha·*la*·si·o ski
wave κύμα ⓝ *ki*·ma
way δρόμος ⓜ *ţhro*·mos
we εμείς e·*mis*
weak a αδύνατος a·*ţhi*·na·tos
wealthy πλούσιος ⓜ *plu*·si·os
wear v φοράω fo·*ra*·o
weather καιρός ⓜ ke·*ros*
weaving υφαντό ⓝ i·fa·*do*
wedding γάμος ⓜ *gha*·mos

wedding cake γαμήλια τούρτα ⓕ gha·*mi*·li·a *tur*·ta
wedding present γαμήλιο δώρο ⓝ gha·*mi*·li·o *ţho*·ro
Wednesday Τετάρτη ⓕ te·*tar*·ti
week εβδομάδα ⓕ ev·ţho·*ma*·ţha
weekend Σαββατοκύριακο ⓝ sa·va·to·*ki*·ria·ko
weigh ζυγίζω zi·*yi*·zo
weight βάρος ⓝ *va*·ros
weights βάρη ⓝ pl *va*·ri
welcome v καλωσορίζω ka·lo·so·*ri*·zo
welfare πρόνοια ⓕ *pro*·ni·a
well (health) καλά ka·*la*
west δύση ⓕ *ţhi*·si
wet a βρεγμένος vregh·*me*·nos
what τι ti
wheel τροχός ⓜ tro·*khos*
wheelchair αναπηρική καρέκλα ⓕ a·na·pi·ri·*ki* ka·*re*·kla
when όταν *o*·tan
where πού pu
which ποιος pios
whisky ουίσκυ ⓝ u·*i*·ski
white άσπρος *as*·pros
who ποιος pios
wholemeal bread ψωμί ολικής αλέσεως ⓝ pso·*mi* o·li·*kis* a·*le*·se·os
why γιατί yia·*ti*
wide πλατύς pla·*tis*
wife σύζυγος ⓕ *si*·zi·ghos
wildflowers αγριολούλουδα ⓝ pl a·ghri·o·*lu*·lu·ţha
win v κερδίζω ker·*ţhi*·zo
wind άνεμος ⓜ *a*·ne·mos
window παράθυρο ⓝ pa·*ra*·thi·ro
windscreen παμπρίζ ⓝ pa·*briz*
windsurfing γουιντσέρφινγκ ⓝ ghu·id·*ser*·fing
wine κρασί ⓝ kra·*si*
wings φτερούγες ⓕ pl fte·ru·*ghes*
winner νικητής ⓜ ni·ki·*tis*
winter χειμώνας ⓜ hi·*mo*·nas
wire καλώδιο ⓝ ka·*lo*·ţhi·o
wish v εύχομαι *ef*·kho·me
with με me
within (an hour) εντός e·*dos*
without χωρίς kho·*ris*
wok γουώκ ⓝ ghu·*ok*
woman γυναίκα ⓕ yi·*ne*·ka
wonderful θαυμάσιος thav·*ma*·si·os
wood δάσος ⓝ *ţha*·sos
wool μαλλί ⓝ ma·*li*
word λέξη ⓕ *lek*·si
work δουλειά ⓕ ţhu·*lia*
work v δουλεύω ţhu·*le*·vo
work experience πείρα εργασίας ⓕ *pi*·ra er·gha·*si*·as
workout εξάσκηση ⓕ ek·*sa*·ski·si
work permit άδεια εργασίας ⓕ *a*·ţhi·a er·gha·*si*·as
workshop εργαστήρι ⓝ er·gha·*sti*·ri
world κόσμος ⓜ *koz*·mos
World Cup Παγκόσμιο Κύπελο ⓝ pa·*goz*·mi·o *ki*·pe·lo
worm σκουλίκι ⓝ sku·*li*·ki
worried ανήσυχος a·*ni*·si·khos
worship v λατρεύω la·*tre*·vo
wrist καρπός ⓜ kar·*pos*
write γράφω *ghra*·fo
writer συγγραφέας ⓜ&ⓕ si·gra·*fe*·as
wrong a λανθασμένος lan·thaz·*me*·nos

Y

year χρόνος ⓜ *khro*·nos
(this) year (αυτό το) χρόνο (af·*to* to) *khro*·no
yellow a κίτρινος *ki*·tri·nos
yes ναι ne
yesterday χτες khtes
(not) yet (όχι) ακόμη (*o*·hi) a·*ko*·mi
yoga γιόγκα ⓕ *yiog*·ka
yogurt γιαούρτι ⓝ yia·*ur*·ti
you sg inf εσύ e·*si*
you sg pol & pl inf&pol εσείς e·*sis*
young νέος *ne*·os
your sg pol & pl inf&pol σας sas
your sg inf σου su
youth hostel γιουθ χόστελ ⓝ yuth *kho*·stel

Z

zip/zipper φερμουάρ ⓝ fer·mu·*ar*
zodiac ζωδιακός ⓜ zo·ţhi·a·*kos*
zoo ζωολογικός κήπος ⓜ zo·o·lo·yi·*kos* *ki*·pos
zucchini κολοκυθάκι ⓝ ko·lo·ki·*tha*·ki

Greek nouns in the **dictionary** have their gender indicated by ⓜ masculine, ⓕ feminine or ⓝ neuter. If it's a plural noun you'll also see pl. When a word that could be either a noun or a verb has no gender indicated, it's a verb. Adjectives are given in the masculine form only – see **adjectives & adverbs** in the **phrasebuilder** for more on how to form feminine and neuter adjectives. Both nouns and adjectives are provided in the nominative case only – refer to the **phrasebuilder** for more information on **case**. You'll also find the English words marked as a adjective and v verb, sg singular, pl plural, inf informal, and pol polite where necessary.

The **greek–english dictionary** has been ordered according to the Greek alphabet:

Α α	Β β	Γ γ	Δ δ	Ε ε	Ζ ζ	Η η	Θ θ	Ι ι	Κ κ	Λ λ	Μ μ
Ν ν	Ξ ξ	Ο ο	Π π	Ρ ρ	Σ σ/ς	Τ τ	Υ υ	Φ φ	Χ χ	Ψ ψ	Ω ω

Α α

άβολος a·vo·los *uncomfortable*
αγάπη a·gha·pi ⓕ *love*
αγαπώ a·gha·po *love* ⓥ
Αγγλία ⓕ ang·gli·a *England*
Αγγλικά ⓝ pl ang·gli·ka *English (language)*
αγορά ⓕ a·gho·ra *market • shopping centre*
αγοράζω a·gho·ra·zo *buy* ⓥ
αγόρι ⓝ a·gho·ri *boy*
άδειο a·ţhi·o *empty* a
αδερφή ⓕ a·ţher·fi *sister*
αδερφός ⓜ a·ţher·fos *brother*
αδιάβροχο a·ţhi·av·ro·ho ⓝ *raincoat*
αδύνατος a·ţhi·na·tos *impossible* a
αερογραμμή ⓕ a·e·ro·ghra·mi *airline*
αεροδρόμιο a·e·ro·ţhro·mi·o ⓝ *airport*
αεροπλάνο a·e·ro·pla·no ⓝ *airplane*
αίθουσα αναμονής
e·thu·sa a·na·mo·nis ⓕ *waiting room*
αίθουσα τράνζιτ ⓕ e·thu·sa tran·zit
transit lounge
αίμα e·ma ⓝ *blood*
ακριβός a·kri·vos *expensive*
ακριβώς a·kri·vos *exactly*
ακυρώνω a·ki·ro·no *cancel*
αλλαγή a·la·yi ⓕ *change*
αλλεργία a·ler·yi·a ⓕ *allergy*
αλληλογραφία a·li·lo·ghra·fi·a ⓕ *mail*
άλλος a·los *other*
άμεσος a·me·sos *direct* a
αναπηρική καρέκλα
a·na·pi·ri·ki ka·re·kla ⓕ *wheelchair*
ανάπηρος a·na·pi·ros *disabled* a
αναπτήρας ⓜ a·nap·ti·ras *cigarette lighter*
ανατολή ⓕ a·na·to·li *east • sunrise*
αναχώρηση ⓕ a·na·kho·ri·si *departure*
αναχωρώ a·na·kho·ro *depart* ⓥ *• leave* ⓥ
ανεβαίνω a·ne·ve·no *board (transport)* ⓥ
ανεμιστήρας ⓜ a·ne·mi·sti·ras
fan (machine)
άνετος a·ne·tos *comfortable*
ανθοπώλης ⓜ an·tho·po·lis *florist*
ανθοπώλισσα ⓕ an·tho·po·li·sa *florist*
ανιαρός a·ni·a·ros *boring*
άνοιξη ⓕ a·nik·si *spring (season)*
ανοιχτήρι ⓝ a·nikh·ti·ri *bottle opener •*
can opener • corkscrew
ανοιχτός a·nikh·tos *light (colour) • open* a
ανταλλάσσω a·da·la·so *exchange* ⓥ
αντιβιοτικά ⓝ pl a·di·vi·o·ti·ka *antibiotics*
αντίγραφο ⓝ a·di·ghra·fo *copy*
αντιηλιακό ⓝ a·di·i·li·a·ko *sunblock*
αντισηπτικό ⓝ a·di·si·lip·ti·ko *antiseptic*
άντρας ⓜ a·dras *man*
απαίσιος a·pe·si·os *awful*
απασχολημένος a·pa·skho·li·me·nos *busy*
απεργία ⓕ a·per·yi·a *strike*
απίθανος a·pi·tha·nos *fantastic • great*
απλό εισιτήριο ⓝ a·plo i·si·ti·ri·o
one-way (ticket)
απόγευμα ⓝ a·po·yev·ma *afternoon*
απόδειξη ⓕ a·po·ţhik·si *receipt*
αποσκευές ⓕ pl a·po·ske·ves *baggage*
αποσμητικό ⓝ a·poz·mi·ti·ko *deodorant*
απόψε a·pop·se *tonight*

αργά ar·gha *slowly*
αργότερα ar·gho·te·ra *later*
αριθμομηχανή (f) a·rith·mo·mi·kha·ni *calculator*
αριθμός (m) a·rith·mos *number*
αριθμός διαβατηρίου (n) a·rith·mos ţhia·va·ti·ri·u *passport number*
αριθμός δωματίου (n) a·rith·mos ţho·ma·ti·u *room number*
αριθμός κυκλοφορίας αυτοκινήτου (f) a·rith·mos ki·klo·fo·ri·as af·to·ki·ni·tu *car registration*
αριθμός οδήγησης (f) a·rith·mos o·ţhi·yi·sis *drivers licence*
αριστερός a·ri·ste·ros *left (direction)* (a)
αρκετά ar·ke·ta *enough*
αρραβωνιασμένη (f) a·ra·vo·niaz·me·ni *engaged (to marry)*
αρραβωνιασμένος (m) a·ra·vo·niaz·me·nos *engaged (to marry)*
αρραβωνιαστικιά (f) a·ra·vo·nia·sti·kia *fiancée*
αρραβωνιαστικός (m) a·ra·vo·nia·sti·kos *fiancé*
άρρωστος a·ro·stos *ill • sick*
αρχιτέκτονας (m)&(f) ar·hi·tek·to·nas *architect*
αρχιτεκτονική (f) ar·hi·tek·to·ni·ki *architecture*
άρωμα (n) a·ro·ma *perfume*
ασανσέρ (n) a·san·ser *elevator • lift*
ασήμι (n) a·si·mi *silver*
άσπρος as·pros *white*
αστείος a·sti·os *funny*
αστικό λεωφορείο (n) a·sti·ko le·o·fo·ri·o *bus*
αστράγαλος (m) a·stra·gha·los *ankle*
αστυνομία (f) a·sti·no·mi·a *police*
αστυνομικός σταθμός (m) a·sti·no·mi·kos stath·mos *police station*
αστυφύλακας (m) a·sti·fi·la·kas *police officer*
αστυφυλακίνα (f) a·sti·fi·la·ki·na *police officer*
ασφάλεια (f) as·fa·li·a *insurance*
ασφαλές σεξ (n) as·fa·les seks *safe sex*
ατύχημα (n) a·ti·hi·ma *accident*
αυγή (f) av·yi *dawn*
αύριο av·ri·o *tomorrow*
αυτοκίνητο (n) af·to·ki·ni·to *car*
αυτοκινητόδρομος (m) af·to·ki·ni·to·ţhro·mos *motorway • tollway*
αυτόματη μηχανή χρημάτων (f) af·to·ma·ti mi·kha·ni khri·ma·ton *ATM*
αυτός (m) af·tos *he • this (one)*
αφή (f) a·fi *feeling (physical)*
αφίξεις (f) pl a·fik·sis *arrivals*
αφτί (n) af·ti *ear*

Β β

βαγκόν λι (n) va·gon li *sleeping car*
βαγόνι φαγητού (n) va·gho·ni fa·yi·tu *dining car*
βαλίτσα (f) va·lit·sa *suitcase*
βαμπάκι (n) va·ba·ki *cotton*
βάρκα (f) var·ka *boat*
βαρύς va·ris *heavy*
βγάζω φωτογραφία vga·zo fo·to·gra·fi·a *take a photo*
βγαίνω vye·no *go out*
βελόνα (f) ve·lo·na *needle (sewing)*
βενζίνα (f) ven·zi·na *gas • petrol*
βενζινάδικο (n) ven·zi·na·ţhi·ko *service station*
βήχω vi·kho *cough* (v)
βιαστικός via·sti·kos *in a hurry*
βιβλίο viv·li·o *book* (n)
βιβλιοθήκη (f) viv·li·o·thi·ki *library*
βιβλιοπωλείο (n) viv·li·o·po·li·o *bookshop*
βιβλίο φράσεων (f) viv·li·o fra·se·on *phrasebook*
βίζα (f) vi·za *visa*
βιντεοταινία (f) vi·de·o·te·ni·a *video tape*
βοήθεια (f) vo·i·thi·a *help*
βοηθώ vo·i·tho *help* (v)
βοράς (m) vo·ras *north*
βούλωμα (n) vu·lo·ma *plug (bath)*
βουνό (n) vu·no *mountain*
βούρτσα (f) vur·tsa *brush*
βράδι (n) vra·ţhi *evening*
βροχή (n) vro·hi *rain*
βρύση (f) vri·si *faucet • tap*
βρώμικος (a) vro·mi·kos *dirty*
βύσμα (n) viz·ma *plug (electricity)*

Γ γ

γάλα (n) gha·la *milk*
γαστροεντερίτιδα (f) gha·stro·e·de·ri·ti·ţha *gastroenteritis*
γεμάτο ye·ma·to *full*
γενέθλια (n) pl ye·ne·thli·a *birthday*
Γερμανία (f) yer·ma·ni·a *Germany*
γεύμα (n) yev·ma *meal*
γεφύρι (n) ye·fi·ri *bridge*

Γη ⓕ yi *Earth*
γήπεδο ⓝ *yi*·pe·ţho *court (tennis)*
  — του γκολφ ⓝ tu golf *golf course*
  — του τένις ⓝ tu *te*·nis *tennis court*
γιαγιά ⓕ yia·*yia* *grandmother*
γιαλιά ⓝ pl yia·*lia* *glasses • spectacles*
γιαλιά ηλίου ⓝ pl yia·*lia* i·*li*·u *sunglasses*
γιατί yia·*ti* *why*
γιατρός ⓜ&ⓕ yia·*tros* *doctor*
γιος ⓜ yios *son*
γιουθ χόστελ ⓝ yuth *kho*·stel *youth hostel*
γκαρσόν ⓝ gar·*son* *waiter*
γκέι *ge*·i *gay* a
γκρίζος *gri*·zos *gray • grey* a
γλυκός ghli·*kos* *sweet* a
γλυπτική ⓕ ghlip·ti·*ki* *sculpture*
γλώσσα ⓕ *ghlo*·sa *language*
γόνατο ⓝ *gho*·na·to *knee*
γονείς ⓜ pl gho·*nis* *parents*
γράμμα ⓝ *ghra*·ma *letter (mail)*
γραμμάριο ⓝ ghra·*ma*·ri·o *gram*
γραμματόσημο ⓝ ghra·ma·*to*·si·mo *stamp*
γραφείο απολεσθέντων αντικειμένων ⓝ ghra·*fi*·o a·po·le·*sthe*·don a·di·ki·*me*·non *left-luggage office*
γραφείο εισιτηρίων ghra·*fi*·o i·si·ti·*ri*·on ⓝ *ticket office*
γράφω *ghra*·fo *write*
γρήγορος a *ghri*·gho·ros *fast*
γρίπη ⓕ *ghri*·pi *influenza • flu*
γυμναστήριο ⓝ yi·mna·*sti*·ri·o *gym (place)*
γυναίκα ⓕ yi·*ne*·ka *woman*

Δ δ

δάκτυλο ⓝ *ţhak*·ti·lo *finger*
δασμός αεροδρομίου ⓜ ţhaz·*mos* a·e·ro·ţhro·*mi*·u *airport tax*
δάσος ⓝ *ţha*·sos *forest • wood*
δαχτυλίδι ⓝ ţhakh·ti·*li*·ţhi *ring (on finger)*
δείπνο ⓝ *ţhip*·no *dinner*
δείχνω *ţhi*·khno *point* ⓥ • *show* ⓥ
δεκαπενθήμερο ⓝ ţha·ka·pen·*thi*·me·ro *fortnight*
δέμα ⓝ *ţhe*·ma *parcel*
δεξιός ţhek·si·*os* *right (direction)* a
δέρμα ⓝ *ţher*·ma *leather • skin*
δεύτερη τάξη ⓕ *ţhef*·te·ri *tak*·si *second class*
δημόσια αποχωρητήρια ⓝ pl ţhi·*mo*·si·a a·po·kho·ri·*ti*·ria *public toilet*
δημόσιο τηλέφωνο ⓝ ţhi·*mo*·si·o ti·*le*·fo·no *phone box • public telephone*
δημοσιογράφος ⓜ&ⓕ ţhi·mo·si·o·*ghra*·fos *journalist*
δημόσιος δρόμος ⓜ ţhi·*mo*·si·os *ţhro*·mos *highway*
δια ξηράς ţhi·a ksi·*ras* *surface mail*
διαβατήριο ⓝ ţhia·va·*ti*·ri·o *passport*
διαδίκτυο ⓝ ţhi·a·*ţhik*·ti·o *Internet*
διάδρομος ⓜ ţhi·*a*·ţhro·mos *aisle*
διαζευγμένη ⓕ ţhi·a·zev·*ghme*·ni *divorced* a
διαζευγμένος ⓜ ţhi·a·zev·*ghme*·nos *divorced* a
διαθέσιμος ţhi·a·*the*·si·mos *free (available)*
διακοπές ⓕ pl ţhia·ko·*pes* *vacation*
διάλειμμα ⓝ *ţhia*·li·ma *intermission*
διαμέρισμα ⓝ ţhi·a·*me*·riz·ma *apartment*
διάρροια ⓕ ţhi·*a*·ri·a *diarrhoea*
διαφορά ώρας ⓕ ţhia·fo·*ra* *o*·ras *time difference*
διαφορετικός ţhia·fo·re·ti·*kos* *different*
διαχωριστική γραμμή ⓕ ţhi·a·kho·ri·sti·*ki* ghra·*mi* *delineation line*
διερμηνέας ⓜ&ⓕ ţhi·er·mi·*ne*·as *interpreter*
διεύθυνση ⓕ ţhi·*ef*·thin·si *address*
δικηγόρος ⓜ&ⓕ ţhi·ki·*gho*·ros *lawyer*
δίκλινο δωμάτιο ⓝ *ţhi*·kli·no ţho·*ma*·ti·o *twin beds*
δίπλα *ţhi*·pla *beside • next to*
διπλό δωμάτιο ⓝ ţhi·*plo* ţho·*ma*·ti·o *double room*
διπλό κρεβάτι ⓝ ţhi·*plo* kre·*va*·ti *double bed*
Δις ⓕ ţhe·spi·*nis* *Ms • Miss*
δισκέτα ⓕ ţhi·*ske*·ta *disk (floppy)*
διψασμένος ţhip·saz·*me*·nos *thirsty*
δοκιμάζω ţho·ki·*ma*·zo *try* ⓥ
δοκιμαστήριο ρούχων ⓝ ţho·ki·ma·*sti*·ri·o *ru*·khon *changing room (in shop)*
δολλάριο ⓝ ţho·*la*·ri·o *dollar*
δουλειά ⓕ ţhu·*lia* *job • work*
δρόμος ⓜ *ţhro*·mos *road • route • way*
δροσερό ţhro·se·*ro* *cool (temperature)*
δυνατός ţhi·na·*tos* *loud • strong • possible*
δύο *ţhi*·o *two*
δύση ⓕ *ţhi*·si *sunset • west*
δυσπεψία ⓕ ţhis·pep·*si*·a *indigestion*
δωμάτιο ⓝ ţho·*ma*·ti·o *room*
δωρεάν ţho·re·*an* *complimentary • free*
δώρο ⓝ *ţho*·ro *gift • present*

Ε ε

εβδομάδα ⓕ ev·ţho·ma·ţha *week*
εγγονή ⓕ e·go·ni *granddaughter*
εγγονός ⓜ e·go·nos *grandson*
εγγυημένος e·ghi·i·me·nos *guaranteed*
έγκαυμα ⓝ e·gav·ma *burn*
έγκυος e·gi·os *pregnant*
εγώ e·gho *me*
εδώ e·ţho *here*
έθιμο ⓝ e·thi·mo *custom*
εισιτήριο ⓝ i·si·ti·ri·o *fare* • *ticket*
— **μετ' επιστροφής** ⓝ me·te·pi·stro·fis *return ticket*
— **σταντ μπάι** ⓝ stand ba·i *stand-by ticket*
είσοδος ⓕ i·so·ţhos *entry*
εκατοστόμετρο ⓝ e·ka·to·sto·me·tro *centimetre*
εκεί e·ki *there*
εκείνο e·ki·no *that (one)*
έκθεμα ⓝ ek·the·ma *exhibit*
έκθεση ⓕ ek·the·si *exhibition*
εκκλησία ⓕ e·kli·si·a *church*
έκπτωση ⓕ ek·pto·si *discount*
έκτακτη ανάγκη ⓕ ek·tak·ti a·na·gi *emergency*
εκτυπωτής ⓜ ek·ti·po·tis *printer (computer)*
ελαττωματικός e·la·to·ma·ti·kos *faulty*
ελαφρύ γεύμα ⓝ e·laf·ri ghev·ma *snack*
ελαφρύς e·la·fris *light (weight)*
ελεύθερος e·lef·the·ros *vacant*
Ελλάδα ⓕ e·la·ţha *Greece*
Έλληνες ⓜ pl e·li·nes *Greek (people)*
Ελληνικά ⓝ pl e·li·ni·ka *Greek (language)*
εμβόλιο ⓝ em·vo·li·o *vaccination*
ένα e·na *one*
ένας άλλος e·nas a·los *another*
ένεση ⓕ e·ne·si *injection*
ενοικιάζω e·ni·ki·a·zo *hire* ⓥ • *rent* ⓥ
ενοικίαση αυτοκινήτου ⓕ e·ni·ki·a·si af·to·ki·ni·tu *car hire*
εξαργυρώνω ⓥ ek·sar·yi·ro·no *cash a cheque*
έξοδος ⓕ ek·so·ţhos *exit*
εξοχή ⓕ ek·so·hi *countryside*
εξπρές eks·pres *express mail* a
έξω ek·so *outside*
εξωτερικό ek·so·te·ri·ko *overseas*
επάνω e·pa·no *aboard*
επείγον e·pi·ghon *urgent*
— **ταχυδρομείο** ⓝ ta·hi·ţhro·mi·o *by express mail*
επιβάτης ⓜ e·pi·va·tis *passenger*
επιβάτισσα ⓕ e·pi·va·ti·sa *passenger*
επίδειξη ⓕ e·pi·ţhik·si *show*
επίδεσμος ⓜ e·pi·ţhez·mos *bandage*
επιδόρπιο ⓝ e·pi·ţhor·pi·o *dessert*
επικίνδυνος e·pi·kin·ţhi·nos *dangerous*
επικυρώνω e·pi·ki·ro·no *confirm (booking)* • *validate*
έπιπλα ⓝ pl e·pi·pla *furniture*
επισκευάζω e·pi·ske·va·zo *repair* ⓥ
επιστήμη ⓕ e·pi·sti·mi *science*
επιστήμονας ⓜ&ⓕ e·pi·sti·mo·nas *scientist*
επιστρέφω e·pi·stre·fo *come back* • *return* ⓥ
επιστροφή χρημάτων ⓕ e·pi·stro·fi khri·ma·ton *refund*
επιτήρηση παιδιών ⓕ e·pi·ti·ri·si pe·ţhion *childminding*
επιτρεπόμενες αποσκευές ⓕ pl e·pi·tre·po·me·nes a·po·ske·ves *baggage allowance*
επιχείρηση ⓕ e·pi·hi·ri·si *business*
επόμενος e·po·me·nos *next* a
εποχή ⓕ e·po·hi *season*
επώνυμο ⓝ e·po·ni·mo *surname*
εργόχειρα ⓝ pl er·gho·hi·ra *handicrafts*
ερείπια ⓝ pl e·ri·pi·a *ruins*
εσείς e·sis *you* sg pol & pl
εστιατόριο ⓝ e·sti·a·to·ri·o *restaurant*
εσύ e·si *you* sg inf
εσώρουχα ⓝ pl e·so·ru·kha *underwear*
εταιρεία ⓕ e·te·ri·a *company (firm)*
ευγνώμων ev·ghno·mon *grateful*
εύθραυστος ef·thraf·stos *fragile*
ευτυχισμένος ef·ti·hiz·me·nos *happy*
εφημερίδα ⓕ e·fi·me·ri·ţha *newspaper*
έχω e·kho *have*

Ζ ζ

ζακέτα ⓕ za·ke·ta *jacket* • *sweater*
ζαχαροπλαστείο ⓝ za·kha·ro·pla·sti·o *cake shop*
ζεστός ze·stos *hot* • *warm* a
ζωγραφική ⓕ zo·ghra·fi·ki *painting (the art)*
ζωγράφος ⓜ&ⓕ zo·ghra·fos *painter*
ζώνη καθίσματος ⓕ zo·ni ka·thiz·ma·tos *seatbelt*
ζωολογικός κήπος ⓜ zo·o·lo·yi·kos ki·pos *zoo*

Η η

ηθοποιός ⓜ&ⓕ i·tho·pi·os *actor*
ηλεκτρισμός ⓜ i·lek·triz·mos *electricity*
ηλιακό έγκαυμα ⓝ i·li·a·ko e·gav·ma *sunburn*
ήλιος ⓜ i·li·os *sun*
ημέρα ⓕ i·me·ra *day*
ημερολόγιο ⓝ i·me·ro·lo·yi·o *diary*
ημερομηνία ⓕ i·me·ro·mi·ni·a *date (day)*
— **γεννήσεως** ⓕ ye·ni·se·os *date of birth*
ΗΠΑ ⓕ i·pa *USA*
ήσυχος i·si·khos *quiet* a
ήχος κλήσης ⓜ i·khos kli·sis *dial tone*

Θ θ

θάλασσα ⓕ tha·la·sa *sea*
θέα ⓕ the·a *view*
θεά ⓕ the·a *goddess*
θεατρικό έργο ⓝ the·a·tri·ko er·gho *play (theatre)*
θέατρο ⓝ the·a·tro *theatre*
θεία ⓕ thi·a *aunt*
θερμοκρασία ⓕ ther·mo·kra·si·a *temperature (weather)*
θερμοπληξία ⓕ ther·mo·plik·si·a *heatstroke*
θερμοφόρα ⓕ ther·mo·fo·ra *(hot) water bottle*
θηλυκός a thi·li·kos *female*
θορυβώδης tho·ri·vo·ţhis *noisy*
Φ.Π.Α. ⓜ fpa *VAT (Value Added Tax)*

Ι ι

ιατρική ⓕ i·a·tri·ki *medicine (job, study)*
ιδιωτικός i·ţhi·o·ti·kos *private* a
ιματιοφυλάκιο ⓝ i·ma·ti·o·fi·la·ki·o *cloakroom*
ινστιτούτο αισθητικής ⓝ in·sti·tu·to es·thi·ti·kis *beauty salon*
ιππασία ⓕ i·pa·si·a *horse riding* • *ride*
ιχθυοπωλείο ⓝ ikh·thi·o·po·li·o *fish shop*

Κ κ

Κα ⓕ khi·ri·a *Mrs*
καθαρίζω ka·tha·ri·zo *clean* ⓥ
καθάρισμα ⓝ ka·tha·riz·ma *cleaning*
καθαρός ka·tha·ros *clean* a
καθαρτικό ⓝ ka·thar·ti·ko *laxative*
κάθε ka·the *every* • *per*
καθένας ka·the·nas *each* • *everyone*
καθετί ⓝ ka·the·ti *everything*
καθημερινός ka·thi·me·ri·nos *daily*
καθρέφτης ⓜ ka·thref·tis *mirror*
καθυστερημένος ka·thi·ste·ri·me·nos *late*
καθυστέρηση ka·thi·ste·ri·si *delay* ⓥ
και ke *and*
και οι δύο ke i ţhi·o *both*
κακός ka·kos *bad*
καλλιτέχνης ⓜ ka·li·tekh·nis *artist*
καλλιτέχνιδα ⓕ ka·li·tekh·ni·ţha *artist*
καλλυντικά ⓝ pl ka·li·di·ka *make-up*
καλοκαίρι ⓝ ka·lo·ke·ri *summer*
καλός ka·los *good* a • *kind* a
κάλτσες ⓕ kal·tses *socks*
καλύτερος ka·li·te·ros *better*
καλώ ka·lo *call* ⓥ
Καναδάς ⓜ ka·na·ţhas *Canada*
καπέλο ⓝ ka·pe·lo *hat*
καπνίζω kap·ni·zo *smoke* ⓥ
καρδιά ⓕ kar·ţhia *heart*
καρδιακή κατάσταση ⓕ kar·dhi·a·ki ka·ta·sta·si *heart condition*
καρέκλα ⓕ ka·re·kla *chair*
καροτσάκι ⓝ ka·rot·sa·ki *stroller* • *trolley*
κάρτα ⓕ kar·ta *postcard*
— **επιβίβασης** ⓕ e·pi·vi·va·sis *boarding pass*
— **τηλεφώνου** ⓕ ti·le·fo·nu *phonecard*
κασέτα ⓕ ka·se·ta *cassette*
κασκόλ ⓝ ka·skol *scarf*
κάστρο ⓝ ka·stro *castle*
κατ' ευθείαν γραμμή ⓕ ka·tef·thi·an gra·mi *direct-dial*
κατάθεση ⓕ ka·ta·the·si *deposit (bank)*
κατάλογος ⓜ ka·ta·lo·ghos *itinerary*
κατάλυμα ⓝ ka·ta·li·ma *accommodation*
κατάστημα ⓝ ka·ta·sti·ma *department store*
— **για σουβενίρ** ⓝ yia su·ve·nir *souvenir shop*
— **ηλεκτρικών ειδών** ⓝ i·lek·tri·kon i·ţhon *electrical store*
— **μουσικών ειδών** ⓝ mu·si·kon i·ţhon *music shop*
— **ρούχων** ⓝ ruk·hon *clothing store*
— **των σπορ** ⓝ ton spor *sports shop*
κατεβαίνω ka·te·ve·no *get off (train, etc)*
κατεύθυνση ⓕ ka·tef·thin·si *direction*

καύσωνας ⓜ *kaf*·so·nas *heatwave*
καφέ ka·*fe* *brown* a
καφενείο ⓝ ka·fe·*ni*·o *coffee shop*
— **διαδικτύου** ⓝ ţhi·a·ţhik·*ti*·u *Internet café*
καφές ⓜ ka·*fes* *coffee*
καφεστιατόριο ⓕ ka·fe·sti·a·*to*·ri·o *café*
κενή θέση ⓕ ke·*ni* *the*·si *vacancy*
κέντημα ⓝ *ke*·di·ma *embroidery*
κέντρο ⓝ *ke*·dro *centre*
κέντρο της πόλης ⓝ *ke*·dro tis *po*·lis *city centre*
κέρματα ⓝ pl *ker*·ma·ta *coins*
κεφάλι ⓝ ke·*fa*·li *head*
κήπος ⓜ *ki*·pos *garden*
κινητό ⓝ ki·ni·*to* *mobile phone*
κίτρινος *ki*·tri·nos *yellow* a
κλειδί ⓝ kli·*ţhi* *key*
κλειδωμένος kli·ţho·*me*·nos *locked*
κλειδώνω kli·*ţho*·no *lock* ⓥ
κλείνω *kli*·no *close* ⓥ
— **θέση** *the*·si *book* ⓥ
κλεισμένος kliz·*me*·nos *closed*
κλειστός kli·*stos* *shut*
κλεμμένο kle·*me*·no *stolen*
κλήση με αντιστροφή της επιβάρυνσης ⓕ *kli*·si me a·dis·tro·*fi* tis e·pi·*va*·rin·sis *collect call*
κλονισμός ⓜ klo·niz·*mos* *concussion*
κόβω *ko*·vo *cut* ⓥ
κοιμάμαι ki·*ma*·me *sleep* ⓥ
κοιμητήριο ⓝ ki·mi·*ti*·ri·o *cemetery*
κόκκινο *ko*·ki·no *red*
κολιέ ⓝ ko·li·*e* *necklace*
κολυμπώ ko·li·*bo* *swim* ⓥ
κολώνα ⓕ ko·*lo*·na *column*
κολόνια ξυρίσματος ⓕ ko·*lo*·ni·a ksi·*riz*·ma·tos *aftershave*
κομμωτής ⓜ ko·mo·*tis* *hairdresser*
κομμώτρια ⓕ ko·*mo*·tri·a *hairdresser*
κοντά ko·*da* *near* • *nearby*
κοντινός ko·di·*nos* *close* a
κοντός ko·*dos* *short (height)*
κόρη ⓕ *ko*·ri *daughter*
κορίτσι ⓝ ko·*rit*·si *girl*
Κος ⓜ *khi*·ri·os *Mr*
κοσμήματα ⓝ pl koz·*mi*·ma·ta *jewellery*
κοστίζω ko·*sti*·zo *cost* ⓥ
κοτόπουλο ⓝ ko·*to*·pu·lo *chicken*
κουβέρτα ⓕ ku·*ver*·ta *blanket*
κουζίνα ⓕ ku·*zi*·na *kitchen*
κουμπί ⓝ ku·*bi* *button*
κουρασμένος ku·raz·*me*·nos *tired*
κούρεμα ⓝ *ku*·re·ma *haircut*
κουτάλι ⓝ ku·*ta*·li *spoon*
— **τσαγιού** ⓝ tsa·*yiu* *teaspoon*
κουτί ⓝ ku·*ti* *box* • *can* • *tin*
κραγιόν ⓝ pl kra·*yion* *lipstick*
κρασί ⓝ kra·*si* *wine*
κράτηση ⓕ *kra*·ti·si *booking* • *reservation*
κρέας ⓝ *kre*·as *meat*
κρεβάτι ⓝ kre·*va*·ti *bed*
κρέμα ⓕ *kre*·ma *cream*
— **ξυρίσματος** ⓕ ksi·*riz*·ma·tos *shaving cream*
κρεοπωλείο ⓝ kre·o·po·*li*·o *butcher's shop*
κρυωμένος kri·o·*me*·nos *cold* a
κτηματομεσιτικό γραφείο ⓝ kti·ma·to·me·si·ti·*ko* ghra·*fi*·o *estate agency*
κτήριο ⓝ *kti*·ri·o *building*
κυλιόμενες σκάλες ⓕ pl ki·li·*o*·me·nes *ska*·les *escalator*
κυτίο πρώτων βοηθειών ⓝ ki·*ti*·o *pro*·ton vo·i·thi·*on* *first-aid kit*

Λ λ

λάδι ⓝ *la*·ţhi *oil*
— **αυτοκινήτου** ⓝ af·to·ki·*ni*·tu *oil (car)*
λαϊκή ⓕ la·i·*ki* *street market*
λαιμός ⓜ le·*mos* *throat*
λάστιχο ⓝ *la*·sti·kho *tire* • *tyre*
λαχανικά ⓝ pl la·kha·ni·*ka* *vegetable*
λαιμός ⓜ le·*mos* *neck*
λεξικό ⓝ lek·si·*ko* *dictionary*
λεπτό ⓝ lep·*to* *minute*
λεσβία ⓕ lez·*vi*·a *lesbian*
λιγότερο li·*gho*·te·ro *less*
λίμνη ⓕ *lim*·ni *lake*
λινό ⓝ li·*no* *linen (material)*
λιπαντικό ⓝ li·pa·di·*ko* *lubricant*
λίρα ⓕ *li*·ra *pound (money)*
λίτρα ⓕ *lit*·ra *pound (weight)*
λογαριασμός ⓜ lo·gha·riaz·*mos* *account* • *bill* • *check*
λοσιόν ⓝ lo·*sion* *lotion*
— **για μαύρισμα** ⓝ yia *mav*·riz·ma *tanning lotion*

Μ μ

μαβής ma·*vis* *purple*
μαγαζί ⓝ ma·gha·*zi* *shop*
μάγειρας ⓜ *ma*·yi·ras *cook*

DICTIONARY Λ

μαγείρισσα ⓕ ma·*yi*·ri·sa *cook*
μαγειρεύω ma·yi·*re*·vo *cook* ⓥ
μαγιό ⓝ ma·*yio* *swimsuit*
μαζί ma·*zi* *together*
μαθαίνω ma·*the*·no *learn*
μακριά ma·kri·*a* *far*
μακρύς ma·*kris* *long* a
μαντήλι ⓝ ma·*di*·li *handkerchief*
μαξιλάρι ⓝ mak·si·*la*·ri *pillow*
μαξιλαροθήκη ⓕ mak·si·la·ro·*thi*·ki *pillowcase*
μας mas *our*
μάτι ⓝ *ma*·ti *eye*
μάτια ⓝ pl *ma*·tia *eyes*
ματς ⓝ mats *game • match*
μαυρόασπρο (φιλμ) ⓝ mav·*ro*·a·spro (film) *B&W (film)*
μαύρος *mav*·ros *black*
μαχαίρι ⓝ ma·*he*·ri *knife*
μαχαιροπήρουνα ⓝ pl ma·he·ro·*pi*·ru·na *cutlery*
με ερκοντίσιον me er kon·*di*·si·on *air-conditioned*
μεγάλα φώτα αυτοκινήτου ⓝ pl me·*gha*·la *fo*·ta af·to·ki·*ni*·tu *headlights*
μεγάλος me·*gha*·los *big • large*
μεγαλύτερος me·gha·*li*·te·ros *bigger*
μέγεθος ⓝ *me*·ye·thos *size (general)*
μεθαύριο me·*thav*·ri·o *day after tomorrow*
μεθυσμένος me·thiz·*me*·nos *drunk*
μενού ⓝ me·*nu* *menu*
μέσα *me*·sa *in • inside*
μεσάνυχτα ⓝ pl me·*sa*·nikh·ta *midnight*
μεσημέρι ⓝ me·si·*me*·ri *midday • noon*
μεσημεριανό φαγητό ⓝ me·si·me·ria·*no* fa·yi·*to* *lunch*
μετά me·*ta* *after*
μεταλλικό νερό ⓝ me·ta·li·*ko* ne·*ro* *mineral water*
μετάξι ⓝ me·*tak*·si *silk*
μετασχηματιστής ⓜ me·ta·shi·ma·ti·*stis* *adaptor*
μεταφράζω me·ta·*fra*·zo *translate*
μετρητά ⓝ pl me·tri·*ta* *cash*
μέχρι *me*·khri *until*
μη καπνίζοντες mi kap·*ni*·zo·des *nonsmoking*
μήνας ⓜ *mi*·nas *month*
μήνυμα ⓝ *mi*·ni·ma *message*
μητέρα ⓕ mi·*te*·ra *mother*
μητρόπολη ⓕ mi·*tro*·po·li *cathedral*

μηχανή ⓕ mi·kha·*ni* *engine • machine*
— **εισιτηρίων** ⓕ i·si·ti·*ri*·on *ticket machine*
— **φαξ** faks *fax machine*
μηχανική ⓕ mi·kha·ni·*ki* *engineering*
μηχανικός ⓜ&ⓕ mi·kha·ni·*kos* *engineer • mechanic*
μικρό όνομα ⓝ mi·*kro* o·no·ma *first name*
μικρότερος mi·*kro*·te·ros *smaller*
μιλάω mi·*la*·o *speak • talk* ⓥ
μισό mi·*so* *half*
μόδα ⓕ *mo*·ţha *fashion*
μοιράζομαι mi·*ra*·zo·me *share with*
μολύβι ⓝ mo·*li*·vi *pencil*
μόλυνση ⓕ *mo*·lin·si *infection*
μονό δωμάτιο ⓝ mo·*no* ţho·*ma*·tio *single room*
μονοπάτι ⓝ mo·no·*pa*·ti *path • track • trail*
μόνος *mo*·nos *alone*
μου mu *my • to me*
μου αρέσει mu a·*re*·si *like* ⓥ
μπαγιάτικος ba·*yia*·ti·kos *off (spoiled) • stale*
μπαίνω *be*·no *enter*
μπαλάκια από βαμπάκι ⓝ pl ba·*la*·kia a·*po* va·*ba*·ki *cotton balls*
μπάνιο ⓝ *ba*·nio *bath • bathroom*
μπάντα ⓕ *ba*·da *band (music)*
μπαρ ⓝ bar *bar*
μπαταρία ⓕ ba·ta·*ri*·a *battery*
μπέιμπι σίτερ ⓕ *be*·i·bi *si*·ter *babysitter*
μπιζνες κλασ *biz*·nes klas *business class*
μπλε ble *blue* a
μπλοκαρισμένος blo·ka·riz·*me*·nos *blocked*
μπλουζάκι ⓝ blu·*za*·ki *T-shirt*
μπότα ⓕ *bo*·ta *boot (footwear)*
μπουκάλι ⓝ bu·*ka*·li *bottle*
μπουφές ⓜ bu·*fes* *buffet*
μπροσούρα ⓕ bro·*su*·ra *brochure*
μπύρα ⓕ *bi*·ra *beer*
μπυραρία ⓕ bi·ra·*ri*·a *bar • pub*
μπωλ ⓝ bol *bowl*
μυρουδιά ⓕ mi·ru·*ţhia* *smell*
μύτη ⓕ *mi*·ti *nose*
μωρό ⓝ mo·*ro* *baby*

Νν

ναι ne *yes*
ναρκωτικά ⓝ pl nar·ko·ti·*ka* *illegal drugs*
ναυτία ⓕ naf·*ti*·a *nausea • seasickness • travel sickness*

N

greek–english

νέα ⓝ pl *ne*·a *news*
Νέα Ζηλανδία ⓕ *ne*·a zi·lan·*ţhi*·a *New Zealand*
νέος *ne*·os *new • young*
νερό ⓝ ne·*ro water*
νοικοκυρά ⓕ ni·ko·ki·*ra housewife*
νοικοκύρης ⓜ ni·ko·*ki*·ris *head of the house*
νησί ⓝ ni·*si island*
νομικά ⓜ no·mi·*ka law (study, profession)*
νοσοκόμος ⓜ no·so·*ko*·mos *nurse*
νοσοκόμα ⓕ no·so·*ko*·ma *nurse*
νοσοκομειακό ⓝ no·so·ko·mi·a·*ko ambulance*
νοσοκομείο ⓝ no·so·ko·*mi*·o *hospital*
νόστιμος *no*·sti·mos *tasty*
νότος ⓜ *no*·tos *south*
ντελικατέσεν ⓝ de·li·ka·*te*·sen *delicatessen*
ντους ⓝ duz *shower*
νύχτα ⓕ *nikh*·ta *night*
νωρίς no·*ris early*

Ξ ξ

ξενοδοχείο ⓝ kse·no·ţho·*hi*·o *hotel*
ξένη ⓕ *kse*·ni *foreign* a • *stranger* ⓝ
ξένος ⓜ *kse*·nos *foreign* a • *stranger* ⓝ
ξενώνας ⓜ *kse*·no·nas *guesthouse*
ξυπνάω ksip·*na*·o *wake • wake (someone) up*
ξυπνητήρι ⓝ ksip·ni·*ti*·ri *alarm clock*
ξυράφι ⓝ ksi·*ra*·fi *razor blade*
ξυρίζω ksi·*ri*·zo *shave* ⓥ
ξυριστική μηχανή ⓕ ksi·ri·sti·*ki* mi·kha·*ni razor*

Ο ο

ο καλύτερος o ka·*li*·te·ros *best* a
ο μεγαλύτερος o me·gha·*li*·te·ros *biggest*
ο μικρότερος o mi·*kro*·te·ros *smallest*
οδηγός ⓜ&ⓕ o·ţhi·*ghos driver • guide (person)*
— **διασκέδασης** ⓜ ţhia·*ske*·ţha·sis *entertainment guide*
οδηγώ o·ţhi·*gho drive* ⓥ
οδοντιατρική κλωστή ⓕ o·ţho·di·a·tri·*ki* klo·*sti dental floss*
οδοντίατρος ⓜ&ⓕ o·ţho·*di*·a·tros *dentist*
οδοντόβουρτσα ⓕ o·ţho·*do*·vur·tsa *toothbrush*
οδοντόπαστα ⓕ o·ţho·*do*·pa·sta *toothpaste*
οδός ⓕ o·*ţhos street*
οδυνηρός o·ţhi·ni·*ros painful*
Οθωμανικός o·tho·ma·ni·*kos Ottoman* a
οικογένεια ⓕ i·ko·*ye*·ni·a *family*
Ολλανδία ⓕ o·lan·*ţhi*·a *Netherlands*
όλοι *o*·li *all*
ολονυχτίς o·lo·nikh·*tis overnight*
ομάδα αίματος ⓕ o·*ma*·ţha *e*·ma·tos *blood group*
όμορφος *o*·mor·fos *beautiful • handsome*
ομοφυλόφιλος ⓜ o·mo·fi·*lo*·fi·los *homosexual*
όνομα ⓝ *o*·no·ma *name*
οπίσθιος o·*pi*·sthi·os *rear (seat etc)*
οπωροπωλείο ⓝ o·po·ro·po·*li*·o *grocery*
όριο ταχύτητας ⓝ *o*·ri·o ta·*hi*·ti·tas *speed limit*
όροφος ⓜ *o*·ro·fos *floor (storey)*
όταν *o*·tan *when*
όχι *o*·hi *no • not*

Π π

πάγος ⓜ *pa*·ghos *ice*
παγωμένος pa·gho·*me*·nos *frozen*
παγωτό ⓝ pa·gho·*to ice cream*
παζάρι ⓝ pa·*za*·ri *fleamarket*
παιδί ⓝ pe·*ţhi child*
παιδιά ⓝ pl pe·*ţhia children*
παιδικό κάθισμα ⓝ pe·ţhi·*ko ka*·thiz·ma *child seat*
παιδικός σταθμός ⓜ pe·ţhi·*kos* stath·*mos crèche*
παλάτι ⓝ pa·*la*·ti *palace*
πάλι *pa*·li *again*
παλιός pa·*lios old* a
παλτό ⓝ pal·*to coat*
πάνα ⓕ *pa*·na *diaper • nappy*
πανεπιστήμιο ⓝ pa·ne·pi·*sti*·mi·o *university*
παντελόνι ⓝ pa·de·*lo*·ni *pants • trousers*
παντρεμένη ⓕ pa·dre·*me*·ni *married*
παντρεμένος ⓜ pa·dre·*me*·nos *married*
πάνω *pa*·no *on • up*
παππούς ⓜ pa·*pus grandfather*
παπούτσι ⓝ pa·*put*·si *shoe*
πάρα πολύ *pa*·ra po·*li too (expensive etc)*
παραδίνω pa·ra·*ţhi*·no *deliver*
παράθυρο ⓝ pa·*ra*·thi·ro *window*
παραλαβή αποσκευών ⓕ pa·ra·la·*vi* a·po·ske·*von baggage claim*
παραλία ⓕ pa·ra·*li*·a *beach • seaside*
Παραμονή Πρωτοχρονιάς ⓕ pa·ra·mo·*ni* pro·to·khro·*nias New Year's Eve*

παράπονο ⓝ pa·ra·po·no *complaint*
παράσταση ⓕ pa·ra·sta·si *gig*
παρκάρω par·ka·ro *park a car*
Πάσχα ⓝ pas·kha *Easter*
πατέρας ⓜ pa·te·ras *father*
παυσίπονο ⓝ paf·si·po·no *painkiller*
παχύς ⓐ pa·his *fat*
πάω για ψώνια pa·o yia pso·nia *go shopping*
πεζοδρόμιο ⓝ pe·zo·ţhro·mi·o *footpath*
πεζοπορία ⓕ pe·zo·po·ri·a *hiking*
πεζοπορώ pe·zo·po·ro *hike* ⓥ
πεθερά ⓕ pe·the·ra *mother-in-law*
πεθερός ⓜ pe·the·ros *father-in-law*
πεινώ pi·no *(be) hungry* ⓥ
πελάτης ⓜ pe·la·tis *client*
πελάτισσα ⓕ pe·la·ti·sa *client*
πέος ⓝ pe·os *penis*
περιήγηση ⓕ pe·ri·i·yi·si *tour*
— **με οδηγό** ⓕ me o·ţhi·gho *guided tour*
περιμένω pe·ri·me·no *wait* ⓥ
περίπτερο ⓝ pe·rip·te·ro *kiosk*
περισσότερος pe·ri·so·te·ros *more*
περπατάω per·pa·ta·o *walk* ⓥ
πετάω pe·ta·o *fly* ⓥ
πετρέλαιο ⓝ pe·tre·le·o *petrol*
πετρογκάζ ⓝ pe·tro·gaz *gas (for cooking)*
πετσέτα ⓕ pet·se·ta *towel*
πετσετάκι ⓝ pet·se·ta·ki *napkin*
— **υγείας** i·yi·as ⓝ *panty liners • sanitary napkins*
πηγαίνω pi·ye·no *go*
πιάτο ⓝ pia·to *dish • plate*
πικρός pi·kros *bitter* ⓐ
πίνακας ⓜ pi·na·kas *painting (a work)*
πινακοθήκη ⓕ pi·na·ko·thi·ki *art gallery*
πίνω pi·no *drink* ⓥ
πιπίλα ⓕ pi·pi·la *dummy • pacifier*
πιρούνι ⓝ pi·ru·ni *fork*
πισίνα ⓕ pi·si·na *swimming pool*
πίστωση ⓕ pi·sto·si *credit*
πιστωτική κάρτα ⓕ pi·sto·ti·ki kar·ta *credit card*
πλατεία ⓕ pla·ti·a *square (town)*
πλάτη ⓕ pla·ti *back (body)*
πλατφόρμα ⓕ plat·for·ma *platform*
πλένω ple·no *wash* ⓥ
πληγή ⓕ pli·yi *injury*
πληγωμένος pli·gho·me·nos *injured* ⓐ
πληροφορία ⓕ pli·ro·fo·ri·a *information*
πληροφορική ⓕ pli·ro·fo·ri·ki *IT*
πληρωμή ⓕ pli·ro·mi *payment*
πλυντήριο ⓝ pli·di·ri·o *launderette • laundry • washing machine*

ποδήλατο ⓝ po·ţhi·la·to *bicycle • bike*
πόδι ⓝ po·ţhi *foot • leg*
ποδόσφαιρο ⓝ po·ţhos·fe·ro *football*
ποιος pios *which • who*
πόλη ⓕ po·li *city*
πολυτέλεια ⓕ po·li·te·li·a *luxury*
πολύτιμος po·li·ti·mos *valuable*
πονόδοντος ⓜ po·no·ţho·dos *toothache*
πονοκέφαλος ⓜ po·no·ke·fa·los *headache*
πόνος ⓜ po·nos *pain*
πόρνη ⓕ por·ni *prostitute*
πορτοκαλής por·to·ka·lis *orange (colour)*
πορτοφόλι ⓝ por·to·fo·li *purse*
ποτάμι ⓝ po·ta·mi *river*
ποτήρι ⓝ po·ti·ri *drinking glass*
ποτό ⓝ po·to *drink*
πού pu *where*
πουκάμισο ⓝ pu·ka·mi·so *shirt*
πουλόβερ ⓝ pu·lo·ver *jumper • sweater*
πούρο ⓝ pu·ro *cigar*
πρακτορείο εφημερίδων ⓝ prak·to·ri·o e·fi·me·ri·ţhon *newsagency*
πράσινος pra·si·nos *green*
πρατήριο βενζίνας ⓝ pra·ti·ri·o ven·zi·nas *petrol station*
πρεσβεία ⓕ prez·vi·a *embassy*
πριν prin *before*
πρόγευμα ⓝ pro·yev·ma *breakfast*
πρόγραμμα ⓝ pro·ghra·ma *timetable*
προετοιμασία εγγράφων ⓕ pro·e·ti·ma·si·a e·gra·fon *paperwork*
προηγούμενος pro·i·ghu·me·nos *last • previous*
προκαταβολή ⓕ pro·ka·ta·vo·li *deposit (on house etc)*
προμήθεια ⓕ pro·mi·thi·a *commission*
προμήθειες φαγητού ⓕ pl pro·mi·thi·es fa·yi·tu *food supplies*
προξενείο ⓝ prok·se·ni·o *consulate*
προορισμός ⓜ pro·o·riz·mos *destination*
προσαύξηση τιμής ⓕ pro·saf·ksi·si ti·mis *cover charge*
πρόστιμο ⓝ pros·ti·mo *fine (penalty)*
προσωπική επιταγή ⓕ pro·so·pi·ki e·pi·ta·yi *check (banking) • cheque*
πρόσωπο ⓝ pro·so·po *face • person*
προϋπολογισμός ⓜ pro·i·po·lo·yiz·mos *budget*
προφυλακτικό ⓝ pro·fi·lak·ti·ko *condom*
προχθές prokh·tes *day before yesterday*
πρωί ⓝ pro·i *morning*
πρώτη τάξη ⓕ pro·ti tak·si *first class*
Πρωτοχρονιά ⓕ pro·to·khro·nia *New Year's Day*

πτήση ⓕ *pti*·si *flight*
πυρετός ⓜ pi·re·*tos* *fever*

Ρ ρ

ράδιο ⓝ *ra*·ţhi·o *radio*
ραντεβού ⓝ ra·de·*vu* *appointment • date*
ράφτης ⓜ *raf*·tis *tailor*
ράφτρα ⓕ *raf*·tra *tailor*
ρεσεψιόν ⓕ re·sep·*sion* *check-in (desk)*
ρέστα ⓝ pl *re*·sta *change (money)*
ρεύμα ⓝ *rev*·ma *current (electricity)*
ρινική αλλεργία ⓕ ri·ni·*ki* a·ler·*yi*·a *hay fever*
ροζ roz *pink*
ρούχα ⓝ pl *ru*·kha *clothing*

Σ σ

Σαββατοκύριακο ⓝ sa·va·to·*ki*·ria·ko *weekend*
σακίδιο ⓝ sa·*ki*·ţhi·o *backpack*
σάκος ⓜ *sa*·kos *bag*
σαμπάνια ⓕ sam·*pa*·nia *champagne*
σαπούνι ⓝ sa·*pu*·ni *soap*
σε se *at • to*
σεισμός ⓜ siz·*mos* *earthquake*
σελφ σέρβις ⓝ self *ser*·vis *self-service*
σεμινάριο ⓝ se·mi·*na*·ri·o *conference (small) • seminar*
σεντόνι ⓝ se·*do*·ni *sheet (bed)*
σεντόνια ⓝ pl se·*do*·nia *bed linen*
σερβιτόρα ⓕ ser·vi·*to*·ra *waitress*
σεξ ⓝ seks *sex*
σεφ ⓜ sef *chef • cook*
σημειωματάριο ⓝ si·mi·o·ma·*ta*·ri·o *notebook*
σήμερα *si*·me·ra *today*
σι ντι ⓝ si di *CD*
σι ντι ρομ ⓝ si di rom *disk (CD-ROM)*
σίδερο ⓝ *si*·ţhe·ro *iron (for clothes)*
σιδηροδρομικός σταθμός ⓜ si·ţhi·ro·ţhro·mi·*kos* stath·*mos* *railway station*
σκάλα ⓕ *ska*·la *stairway*
σκιά ⓕ ski·*a* *shade*
σκληρός skli·*ros* *hard (not soft)*
σκοτεινός sko·ti·*nos* *dark* a
σκουλαρίκια ⓝ pl sku·la·*ri*·kia *earrings*
σκουπιδοτενεκές ⓜ sku·pi·ţho·te·ne·*kes* *garbage can*
σκούρος *sku*·ros *dark (colour)* a
σκυλί ⓝ ski·*li* *dog*
Σκωτία ⓕ sko·*ti*·a *Scotland*
σλάιντ ⓝ *sla*·id *slide (film)*
σοκολάτα ⓕ so·ko·*la*·ta *chocolate*
σορτς ⓝ sorts *shorts*
σουβενίρ ⓝ su·ve·*nir* *souvenir*
σουγιάς ⓜ su·*yias* *penknife*
σουτιέν ⓝ su·ti·*en* *bra*
σπασμένος spaz·*me*·nos *broken*
σπίρτα ⓝ pl *spir*·ta *matches (for lighting)*
σπίτι ⓝ *spi*·ti *home*
σπουδαίος spu·*ţhe*·os *important*
σπουδαστής ⓜ spu·ţha·*stis* *student*
σπουδάστρια ⓕ spu·*ţha*·stri·a *student*
σπρέι ⓝ *spre*·i *spray*
σταθμός ⓜ stath·*mos* *station*
σταθμός λεωφορείου ⓜ stath·*mos* le·o·fo·*ri*·u *bus station*
σταθμός μετρό ⓝ stath·*mos* me·*tro* *metro station*
σταθμός τρένου ⓜ stath·*mos* *tre*·nu *train station*
στάση ⓕ *sta*·si *stop (bus, tram, etc)*
— **λεωφορείου** ⓕ le·o·fo·*ri*·u *bus stop*
— **ταξί** ⓕ tak·*si* *taxi stand*
σταχτοθήκη ⓕ stakh·to·*thi*·ki *ashtray*
στεγνός stegh·*nos* *dry* a
στήθος ⓝ *sti*·thos *chest (body)*
στην ώρα stin *o*·ra *on time*
στόμα ⓝ *sto*·ma *mouth*
στομάχι ⓝ sto·*ma*·hi *stomach*
στομαχόπονος ⓜ sto·ma·*kho*·po·nos *stomachache*
στραμπούλισμα ⓝ stra·*bu*·liz·ma *sprain*
στρώμα ⓝ *stro*·ma *mattress*
στυλό ⓝ sti·*lo* *pen (ballpoint)*
σύζυγος ⓜ&ⓕ *si*·zi·ghos *husband • wife*
συμπεριλαμβανομένου si·be·ri·lam·va·no·*me*·nu *included*
συνάδελφος ⓜ si·*na*·ţhel·fos *colleague*
συναδέλφισσα ⓕ si·na·*ţhel*·fi·sa *colleague*
συνάλλαγμα ⓝ si·*na*·lagh·ma *exchange*
σύνδεσμος ⓜ *sin*·ţhez·mos *connection*
συνέδριο ⓝ si·*ne*·ţhri·o *conference (big)*
συνεισφέρω si·nis·*fe*·ro *contribute*
συνιστώ si·ni·*sto* *recommend*
σύνορο ⓝ *si*·no·ro *border*
συνταγή ⓕ si·da·*yi* *prescription*
σύνταξη ⓕ *si*·dak·si *pension*
συνταξιούχα ⓕ si·dak·si·*u*·kha *pensioner*
συνταξιούχος ⓜ si·dak·si·*u*·khos *pensioner*
σύντομα *si*·do·ma *soon*
συντροφιά ⓕ *si*·dro·fia *company (friends)*

σύντροφος (m) si·dro·fos companion
συντρόφισσα (f) si·dro·fi·sa companion
συστημένο sis·ti·me·no by registered mail
σωσίβιο (n) so·si·vi·o life jacket

Τ τ

ταμείο (n) ta·mi·o cash register
ταμίας (m)&(f) ta·mi·as cashier
ταμπόν (n) ta·bon tampon
ταξίδι (n) tak·si·ţhi journey • trip
  — εργασίας (n) er·gha·si·as business trip
  — του μέλιτος (n) tu me·li·tos honeymoon
ταξίδι με ωτοστόπ tak·si·ţhi me o·to·stop hitchhike (v)
ταξιδιωτική επιταγή (f) tak·si·ţhi·o·ti·ki e·pi·ta·yi travellers cheque
ταξιδιωτικό γραφείο (n) tak·si·ţhi·o·ti·ko ghra·fi·o travel agency
ταυτότητα (f) taf·to·ti·ta identification • identification card
ταχυδρομείο (n) ta·hi·ţhro·mi·o mail • post office
ταχυδρομικό κουτί (n) ta·hi·ţhro·mi·ko ku·ti mailbox
ταχυδρομικός τομέας (m) ta·hi·ţhro·mi·kos to·me·as postcode
ταχυδρομώ ta·hi·ţhro·mo post (v)
ταχύτητα φιλμ (f) ta·hi·ti·ta film film speed
τελεφερίκ (n) te·le·fe·rik chairlift (skiing)
τέλος (n) te·los end
τελωνείο (n) te·lo·ni·o customs
τένις (n) te·nis tennis
τέχνη (f) tekh·ni craft • art
τηγάνι (n) ti·gha·ni frying pan
τηγανίζω ti·gha·ni·zo fry (v)
τηλεγράφημα (n) ti·le·ghra·fi·ma telegram
τηλεκατεύθυνση (f) ti·le·ka·tef·thin·si remote control
τηλεόραση (f) ti·le·o·ra·si television • TV
τηλεφωνικός κατάλογος (m) ti·le·fo·ni·kos ka·ta·lo·ghos phone book
τηλέφωνο (n) ti·le·fo·no telephone
τηλεφωνώ ti·le·fo·no telephone (v)
της tis her (ownership/direct object)
τιμή (f) ti·mi price
  — εισόδου (m) i·so·ţhu admission (price)
  — εξυπηρέτησης (f) ek·si·pi·re·ti·sis service charge
  — συναλλάγματος (f) si·na·lagh·ma·tos currency exchange • exchange rate
τίποτε ti·po·te nothing
τίτλος κατόχου αυτοκινήτου (m) tit·los ka·to·khu af·to·ki·ni·tu car owner's title
το πιο κοντινό to pio ko·di·no nearest
τοπικός to·pi·kos local (a)
τοστ (n) tost toast
τοστιέρα (f) to·stie·ra toaster
του tu his (ownership/direct object)
τουαλέτα (f) tu·a·le·ta toilet
τουριστική θέση (f) tu·ri·sti·ki the·si economy class
τουριστικό γραφείο (n) tu·ri·sti·ko ghra·fi·o tourist office
τουριστικός οδηγός (m) tu·ri·sti·kos o·ţhi·ghos guidebook
τράπεζα (f) tra·pe·za bank
τραπεζικός λογαριασμός (m) tra·pe·zi·kos lo·gha·riaz·mos bank account
τρένο (n) tre·no train
τρόλεϋ (n) tro·le·i trolley bus
τρώγω tro·gho eat (v)
τσάντα (f) tsa·da handbag
τσιγάρο (n) tsi·gha·ro cigarette
τσιμπιδάκι (n) tsi·bi·ţha·ki tweezers
τσίρκο (n) tsir·ko circus
τσιρότο (n) tsi·ro·to Band-Aid
τυρί (n) ti·ri cheese
τώρα to·ra now

Υ υ

υπεραστικό λεωφορείο (n) i·pe·ra·sti·ko le·o·fo·ri·o intercity bus
υπέρβαρο φορτίο (n) i·per·va·ro for·ti·o excess baggage
υπηρεσία (f) i·pi·re·si·a service
υπνοδωμάτιο (n) ip·no·ţho·ma·ti·o bedroom
υπόγειος i·po·yi·os subway (a)
  — σιδηρόδρομος (m) si·ţhi·ro·ţhro·mos subway train
υποδηματοποιείο (n) i·po·ţhi·ma·to·pi·i·o shoe shop
υπότιτλοι (m) pl i·po·ti·tli subtitles
υποχρέωση (f) i·po·khre·o·si engagement • obligation

Φ φ

φαγητό (n) fa·yi·to food
  — για μωρά (n) yia mo·ra baby food
φαγούρα (f) fa·ghu·ra itch

φάκελος Ⓜ *fa*·ke·los *envelope*
φακοί επαφής Ⓜ pl fa·*ki* e·pa·*fis* *contact lenses*
φακός Ⓝ fa·*kos* *lens • flashlight • torch*
φαρμακείο Ⓝ far·ma·*ki*·o *pharmacy*
φάρμακο Ⓝ *far*·ma·ko *medicine*
— **για το βήχα** Ⓝ yia to *vi*·kha *cough medicine*
φαρμακοποιός Ⓜ&Ⓕ far·ma·ko·pi·*os* *pharmacist*
φερμουάρ Ⓝ fer·mu·*ar* *zip • zipper*
φέρυ Ⓝ *fe*·ri *ferry*
φέτα Ⓕ *fe*·ta *slice*
φθινόπωρο Ⓝ fthi·*no*·po·ro *autumn • fall*
φιλενάδα Ⓕ fi·le·*na*·ţha *girlfriend*
φίλη Ⓕ *fi*·li *friend*
φιλμ Ⓝ film *film • movie*
φιλοδώρημα Ⓝ fi·lo·*ţho*·ri·ma *gratuity • tip*
φίλος Ⓜ *fi*·los *boyfriend • friend*
φλας Ⓝ flas *flashlight*
φλυτζάνι Ⓝ fli·*dza*·ni *cup*
φόρεμα Ⓝ *fo*·re·ma *dress*
φούρνος Ⓜ *fur*·nos *bakery • oven*
— **μικροκυμάτων** Ⓜ mi·kro·ki·*ma*·ton *microwave oven*
φουσκάλα Ⓕ fu·*ska*·la *blister*
φούστα Ⓕ *fu*·sta *skirt*
φρένα Ⓝ pl *fre*·na *brakes*
φρέσκος *fre*·skos *fresh*
φρούτα Ⓝ pl *fru*·ta *fruit*
φτηνός fti·*nos* *cheap* a
φύλαξη αποσκευών Ⓕ *fi*·lak·si a·po·ske·*von* *luggage lockers*
φως Ⓝ fos *light*
φωτογραφία Ⓕ fo·to·gra·*fi*·a *photo*
φωτογραφική Ⓕ fo·to·ghra·fi·*ki* *photography*
φωτογραφική μηχανή Ⓕ fo·to·ghra·fi·*ki* mi·kha·*ni* *camera*
φωτογράφος Ⓜ&Ⓕ fo·to·*ghra*·fos *photographer*

Χ χ

χαλασμένος kha·laz·*me*·nos *broken down • out of order • spoiled (food)*
χαλκός Ⓜ khal·*kos* *copper*
χαμένος kha·*me*·nos *lost* a
χάπι Ⓝ *kha*·pi *pill*
χάρτης Ⓜ *khar*·tis *map (of country/town)*
χαρτί Ⓝ khar·*ti* *paper*
— **υγείας** Ⓝ i·*yi*·as *toilet paper*
χαρτομάντηλα Ⓝ pl khar·to·*ma*·di·la *tissues*
χαρτονόμισμα Ⓝ khar·to·*no*·miz·ma *banknote*
χαρτοπωλείο Ⓝ khar·to·po·*li*·o *stationer's shop*
χαρτοφύλακας Ⓜ khar·to·*fi*·la·kas *briefcase*
χειμώνας Ⓜ hi·*mo*·nas *winter*
χειροποίητο hi·ro·*pi*·i·to *handmade* a
χέρι Ⓝ *he*·ri *arm • hand*
χιλιόγραμμο Ⓝ hi·*lio*·gra·mo *kilogram*
χιλιόμετρο Ⓝ hi·*lio*·me·tro *kilometre*
χιόνι Ⓝ *hio*·ni *snow*
χορεύω kho·*re*·vo *dance* Ⓥ
χορός Ⓜ kho·*ros* *dancing*
χορτοφάγος Ⓜ&Ⓕ khor·to·*fa*·ghos *vegetarian* a
χρήματα Ⓝ pl *khri*·ma·ta *money*
Χριστούγεννα Ⓝ pl khri·*stu*·ye·na *Christmas*
χρόνος Ⓜ *khro*·nos *year*
χρυσάφι Ⓝ khri·*sa*·fi *gold*
χρώμα Ⓝ *khro*·ma *colour*
χτένα Ⓕ *khte*·na *comb*
χτες khtes *yesterday*
χωρίς kho·*ris* *without*
χώρος Ⓜ *kho*·ros *venue • place*
— **για κάμπινγκ** Ⓜ yia *kam*·ping *camping ground • campsite*
χωροφύλακας Ⓜ kho·ro·*fi*·la·kas *police officer*
χωροφυλακίνα Ⓕ kho·ro·fi·la·*ki*·na *police officer*

Ψ ψ

ψαλίδι Ⓝ psa·*li*·ţhi *scissors*
ψάρεμα Ⓝ *psa*·re·ma *fishing*
ψηφιακός psi·fi·a·*kos* *digital* a
ψηλός psi·*los* *high • tall*
ψιλά Ⓝ pl psi·*la* *change (money)*
ψιχάλα Ⓕ psi·*kha*·la *drizzle*
ψυγείο Ⓝ psi·*yi*·o *fridge • refrigerator*
ψωμί Ⓝ pso·*mi* *bread*
ψωνίζω pso·*ni*·zo *shop* Ⓥ

Ω ω

ώμος Ⓜ *o*·mos *shoulder*
ώρα Ⓕ *o*·ra *hour • time*
ώρες λειτουργίας Ⓕ pl *o*·res li·tur·*yi*·as *opening hours*

A

B

C

D

E

F

INDEX

G

H

I

J

K

L

M

N

O

P

Q

R

S

T

U

V

W

Y

KEY PATTERNS

When's (the next bus)?	Πότε είναι (το επόμενο λεωφορείο);	*po*·te *i*·ne (to e·*po*·me·no le·o·fo·*ri*·o)
Where's (the station)?	Πού είναι (ο σταθμός);	pu *i*·ne (o stath·*mos*)
How much is it (per night)?	Πόσο είναι (για κάθε νύχτα);	*po*·so *i*·ne (yia *ka*·the *nikh*·ta)
I'm looking for (Ampfilohos).	Ψάχνω για (το Αμφίλοχος).	*psakh*·no yia (to am·*fi*·lo·khos)
Do you have (a local map)?	Έχετε οδικό (τοπικό χάρτη);	*e*·he·te o·thi·*ko* (to·pi·*ko* *khar*·ti)
Is there a (lift)?	Υπάρχει (ασανσέρ);	i·*par*·hi (a·san·*ser*)
Can I (try it on)?	Μπορώ να (το προβάρω);	bo·*ro* na (to pro·*va*·ro)
Do I need (to book)?	Χρειάζεται (να κλείσω θέση);	khri·*a*·ze·te (na *kli*·so *the*·si)
I have (a reservation).	Έχω (κλείσει δωμάτιο).	*e*·kho (*kli*·si tho·*ma*·ti·o)
I need (assistance).	Χρειάζομαι (βοήθεια).	khri·*a*·zo·me (vo·*i*·thi·a)
I'd like (to hire a car).	Θα ήθελα (να ενοικιάσω ένα αυτοκίνητο).	tha *i*·the·la (na e·ni·ki·*a*·so e·na af·to·*ki*·ni·to)
Could you (please help)?	Μπορείς να (βοηθήσεις, παρακαλώ);	bo·*ris* na (vo·i·*thi*·sis pa·ra·ka·*lo*)